Bus

*Handbook*

*September 1997*

*British Bus Publishing*

# The Yorkshire Bus Handbook

The Yorkshire Bus Handbook is part of the Bus Handbook series that details the fleets of stage carriage and express coach operators. Where space allows other significant operators in the areas covered are also included. These handbooks are published by *British Bus Publishing* and cover Scotland, Wales and England north of London. The current list is shown at the end of the book. These provide comprehensive coverage of all the principal operators' fleets in the British Isles.

Quality photographs for inclusion in the series are welcome, for which a fee is payable. The publishers unfortunately cannot accept responsibility for any loss and request you show your name on each picture or slide. Details of changes to fleet information are also welcome.

More information on the Bus Handbook series is available from:

British Bus Publishing,
The Vyne,
16 St Margaret's Drive
Wellington
Telford,
Shropshire  TF1 3PH

Series Editor: Bill Potter

Principal Editors for *The Yorkshire Bus Handbook*: Steve Sanderson

Acknowledgements:
We are grateful to David Donati, Keith Grimes, the PSV Circle and the operating companies for their assistance in the compilation of this book.
To keep the fleets up to date we recommend *Buses*, published monthly by Ian Allan and the news-sheets of the PSV Circle provide more in-depth information.

The cover photograph is by Lee Whitehead, the rear cover pictures by Tony Wilson
Contents correct to August 1997

ISBN 1 897990 37 5
Published by *British Bus Publishing*
The Vyne, 16 St Margarets Drive, Wellington,
Telford, Shropshire, TF1 3PH
Fax/Orderline - 01952 255669

# CONTENTS

# ABBOTTS of LEEMING

DC & CG Abbott, Aumans House, Leeming, North Yorkshire  DL7 9RZ

**Depots** : Sussex Street, Bedale; Penny Pot Camp, Harrogate, The Garage, Leeming & Mantons Cold Store, Flaxby, Northallerton.

| | | | | | |
|---|---|---|---|---|---|
| LBZ5108 | Leyland Leopard PSU3B/4R | Plaxton Elite III Express | C53F | 1973 | Ex Mayne, Manchester, 1994 |
| LBZ6303 | Leyland Leopard PSU3B/4R | Plaxton Elite III Express | C53F | 1973 | Ex Mayne, Manchester, 1994 |
| LBZ7810 | Leyland Leopard PSU3B/4R | Plaxton Elite III Express | C53F | 1974 | Ex Mayne, Manchester, 1994 |
| LBZ5107 | Leyland Leopard PSU3E/4R | Plaxton Elite Express III | C53F | 1974 | Ex Mayne, Manchester, 1994 |
| IAZ2326 | Leyland Leopard PSU3B/4R | Plaxton Elite Express III | C53F | 1974 | Ex Trent (Barton), 1995 |
| ONN290M | Leyland Leopard PSU3B/4R | Plaxton Elite Express III | C53F | 1974 | Ex Trent (Barton), 1995 |
| LAZ4376 | Leyland Leopard PSU3B/4R | Plaxton Elite Express III | C53F | 1974 | Ex Trent (Barton), 1995 |
| GVN914N | Bedford YRT | Duple Dominant | C53F | 1975 | |
| GNG716N | Bristol VRT/SL2/6LX | Eastern Coach Works | H43/31F | 1975 | Ex K-Line, Huddersfield, 1994 |
| KHN85P | Bedford YRT | Plaxton Supreme III | C53F | 1975 | Ex Dobson, Bedale, 1984 |
| MAZ6771 | Leyland Leopard PSU3C/4R | Plaxton Supreme Express III | C53F | 1975 | Ex Trent (Barton), 1995 |
| MAZ6770 | Leyland Leopard PSU3C/4R | Plaxton Supreme Express III | C53F | 1976 | Ex Trent (Barton), 1995 |
| ONN572P | Leyland Atlantean AN68/1R | Eastern Coachworks | H43/31F | 1976 | Ex Trent (Barton), 1995 |
| ORB575P | Leyland Atlantean AN68/1R | Eastern Coachworks | H43/31F | 1976 | Ex Trent (Barton), 1995 |
| MNU629P | Leyland Atlantean AN68A/1R | East Lancashire | H47/31D | 1976 | Ex K-Line, Huddersfield, 1994 |
| OWW906P | Bristol VRT/SL3/6LXB | Eastern Coach Works | H43/31F | 1976 | Ex K-Line, Huddersfield, 1994 |
| MRB804P | Bristol VRT/SL3/6LX | Eastern Coach Works | H43/34F | 1976 | Ex K-Line, Huddersfield, 1994 |
| PVO815R | Bristol VRT/SL3/501 | Eastern Coach Works | H43/31F | 1976 | Ex K-Line, Huddersfield, 1994 |
| OFP88R | Bedford YMT | Plaxton Supreme III Express | C53F | 1976 | Ex Gibson, Barlestone, 1981 |
| ONR90R | Bedford YMT | Duple Dominant | C53F | 1976 | Ex Dobson, Bedale, 1984 |
| REF141R | Bedford YMT | Plaxton Supreme III | C53F | 1977 | |

**New to Abbotts in 1984. 774FUO is a Plaxton Paramount 3500-bodied Volvo B10M. It is seen passing Harrogate railway station. In complying with regulations, a yellow school sign is displayed in the front windscreen to indicate that schoolchildren are being carried.** *Lee Whitehead*

For school contract operations, Abbotts have acquired a number of Leyland Atlanteans from a variety of sources. LAZ2431 was formerly to be found in Greater Manchester but is now carries the Abbotts double-deck livery of cream and maroon. In common with second hand Leopards in the fleet, it has received a Northern Ireland LBZ registration mark. *Lee Whitehead*

| | | | | | |
|---|---|---|---|---|---|
| PBZ3657 | Leyland Atlantean AN68A/1R | Northern Counties | H43/32F | 1977 | Ex Greater Manchester, 1996 |
| PBZ8301 | Leyland Atlantean AN68A/1R | Northern Counties | H43/32F | 1977 | Ex Greater Manchester, 1996 |
| LAZ2430 | Leyland Atlantean AN68A/1R | Northern Counties | H43/32F | 1978 | Ex Greater Manchester, 1996 |
| LAZ2431 | Leyland Atlantean AN68A/1R | Park Royal | H43/32F | 1978 | Ex Greater Manchester, 1996 |
| HUI4483 | Leyland Atlantean AN68A/1R | Park Royal | H43/32F | 1978 | Ex Greater Manchester, 1996 |
| PBZ3658 | Leyland Atlantean AN68A/1R | Park Royal | H43/32F | 1978 | Ex Greater Manchester, 1996 |
| XBU13S | Leyland Fleetline FE30AGR | Northern Counties | H43/32F | 1978 | Ex Greater Manchester, 1996 |
| PBZ3656 | Leyland Fleetline FE30AGR | Northern Counties | H43/32F | 1978 | Ex Greater Manchester, 1996 |
| UDT180S | Leyland Atlantean AN68A/1R | East Lancashire | H45/31F | 1978 | Ex Border, Burnley, 1994 |
| UET677S | Leyland Atlantean AN68A/1R | Alexander AL | H45/29D | 1978 | Ex K-Line, Huddersfield, 1994 |
| XVO129S | Leyland Leopard PSU3E/4R | Plaxton Supreme Express III | C49F | 1978 | Ex Trent (Barton), 1995 |
| ACA188S | Bedford YMT | Duple Dominant II | C53F | 1977 | Ex Hanmer, Wrexham, 1978 |
| TUT660S | Bedford YMT | Duple Dominant II | C53F | 1977 | Ex Dobson, Bedale, 1984 |
| YUM517S | Bristol VRT/SL3/6LXB | Eastern Coach Works | H43/31F | 1977 | Ex K-Line, Huddersfield, 1994 |
| ARB133T | Leyland Leopard PSU3E/4R | Plaxton Supreme Express III | C49F | 1978 | Ex Trent, 1995 |
| BRC135T | Leyland Leopard PSU3E/4R | Plaxton Supreme Express III | C49F | 1979 | Ex Trent (Barton), 1995 |
| BRC136T | Leyland Leopard PSU3E/4R | Plaxton Supreme Express III | C49F | 1979 | Ex Trent (Barton), 1995 |
| BRC139T | Leyland Leopard PSU3E/4R | Plaxton Supreme Express III | C49F | 1979 | Ex Trent, 1995 |
| BDC881T | Bedford YMT | Plaxton Supreme IV | C53F | 1979 | |
| LAZ4377 | Leyland Atlantean AN68A/1R | Park Royal | H43/32F | 1979 | Ex Greater Manchester, 1996 |
| FVR261V | Leyland Atlantean AN68A/1R | Park Royal | H43/32F | 1979 | Ex Castle, Speke, 1997 |
| FVR277V | Leyland Atlantean AN68A/1R | Park Royal | H43/32F | 1979 | Ex Castle, Speke, 1997 |
| FTO535V | Leyland Leopard PSU3E/4R | Plaxton Supreme Express IV | C53F | 1979 | Ex Trent (Barton), 1995 |
| MNC514W | Leyland Atlantean AN68A/1R | Park Royal | H43/32F | 1980 | Ex Stagecoach, Manchester, 1997 |
| LHN433W | Bedford YNT | Plaxton Supreme IV | C53F | 1981 | |
| TPY802X | Bedford YNT | Plaxton Supreme V | C53F | 1982 | |
| AWK516Y | Bedford YNT | Duple Dominant IV | C53F | 1982 | Ex Ardenvale, Knowle, 1984 |
| ANH660Y | Bedford YNT | Duple Dominant IV | C53F | 1983 | Ex Dobson, Bedale, 1984 |
| BVN371Y | Bedford YNT | Plaxton Paramount 3200 | C53F | 1983 | |
| CAJ168Y | Bedford YNT | Plaxton Paramount 3200 | C53F | 1983 | |
| 774FUO | Volvo B10M-61 | Plaxton Paramount 3500 | C53FT | 1984 | |
| D902NUS | Freight Rover Sherpa | Scott | C16F | 1986 | |
| LAZ6889 | Aüwaerter Neoplan N122/3 | Aüwaerter Skyliner | CH57/20CT | 1986 | Ex Zebra, Trimdon Grange, 1988 |

*The Yorkshire Bus Handbook*

GNG716N is one of four Bristol VRs used by Abbotts of Leeming for school contract work for North Yorkshire authorities. Abbotts' double deck fleet includes Fleetlines, Atlanteans and Bristol VRs.
*Donald Akrigg*

| | | | | | |
|---|---|---|---|---|---|
| D38GAJ | Scania K112CRB | Van Hool Alizée | C53F | 1987 | |
| D39GAJ | Scania K112CRB | Van Hool Alizée | C53F | 1987 | |
| D40GAJ | Scania K112CRB | Van Hool Alizée | C53F | 1987 | |
| D41GAJ | Scania K112CRB | Van Hool Alizée | C53F | 1987 | |
| D905FHN | Leyland Royal Tiger RTC | Leyland Doyen | C49FT | 1987 | |
| E532LAJ | Scania K112CRB | Van Hool Alizée | C49FT | 1987 | |
| E268NAJ | Scania K112CRB | Van Hool Alizée | C49FT | 1988 | |
| E905NVN | Scania K112CRB | Van Hool Alizée | C49FT | 1988 | |
| E906NVN | Scania K112CRB | Van Hool Alizée | C49FT | 1988 | |
| E97LWP | DAF SB2305DHTD585 | Duple 320 | C57F | 1988 | Ex Hackett, Stretton, 1993 |
| F26ARN | DAF SB2305DHTD585 | Duple 340 | C59F | 1989 | Ex Jackson, Blackpool, 1994 |
| F432VUY | DAF SB2305DHTD585 | Duple 340 | C53FT | 1989 | Ex Hardings, Redditch, 1994 |
| G997HKW | Scania K93CRB | Duple 320 | C55F | 1990 | Ex K-Line, Kirkburton, 1993 |
| G155NJX | MCW MetroRider MF154/1 | MCW | C26F | 1990 | Ex Pride of the Road, Huddersfield, 1995 |
| H126YGG | Mercedes-Benz 609D | Rapier | B26F | 1991 | Ex van, 1995 |
| J685THN | DAF SB2305DHS585 | Duple 320 | C57F | 1991 | |
| J686THN | DAF SB2305DHS585 | Duple 320 | C57F | 1991 | |
| J238VVN | Scania K113TRB | Van Hool Alizée | C52FT | 1992 | |
| J239VVN | Scania K113TRB | Van Hool Alizée | C52FT | 1992 | |
| J240VVN | Scania K113TRB | Van Hool Alizée | C51FT | 1992 | |

**Previous Registrations:**

| | | | | | |
|---|---|---|---|---|---|
| 774FUO | A717JDC | LAZ4377 | BNC951T | MAZ6770 | MNU474P |
| HUI4483 | UNA839S | LAZ6889 | D324MWG | MAZ6771 | MNU465P |
| IAZ2326 | ONN273M | LBZ5107 | PNN767M | PBZ3656 | ANA39T |
| LAZ2430 | UNA762S | LBZ5108 | RVO671L | PBZ3657 | RJA724R |
| LAZ2431 | UNA828S | LBZ6303 | RVO664L | PBZ3658 | UNA866S |
| LAZ4376 | ONN291M | LBZ7810 | ONN275M | PBZ8301 | UNA782S |

**Livery:** White, blue and red (coaches); cream and maroon (buses).

# AMBERMILE - K-LINE - TAYLORS

K-Line Travel Ltd, Unit 14, Station Yard, Station Road, Honley
West Yorkshire, HD7 2LJ
Headlight Bus Company Ltd, 45 Pilley Green, Tankersley, Barnsley,
South Yorkshire, S75 3AB

**Depots** : Station Road, Honlley,Whitehall Road Industrial Estate, Leeds and Barnsley.

**Note** - The operations under this heading share a common livery and may or may not be connected. The vehicles are listed in a single series as uses are occasionally interchanged between companies. The company was unwilling to confirm authenticity of the fleet details.

| | | | | | |
|---|---|---|---|---|---|
| LWN709L | Leyland National 1151/1R | | B52F | 1973 | Ex West Midlands Travel, 1997 |
| NTC610M | Leyland National 1151/1R/0401 | | B49F | 1973 | Ex ARM Construction, Chorley, 1996 |

| | | | | | |
|---|---|---|---|---|---|
| | Leyland National 11351/1R(DAF) | | B50F | 1974 | Ex West Midlands Travel, 1995-96 |
| ROK473M | TOE481N | TOE507N | | TOE509N | TOE520N |
| ROK475M | TOE483N | | | | |

| | | | | | |
|---|---|---|---|---|---|
| | Leyland National 11351/1R | | B50F | 1974 | Ex West Midlands Travel, 1996 |
| TOE477N | TOE478N | TOE501N | | TOE506N | TOE517N |

| | | | | | |
|---|---|---|---|---|---|
| GEU359N | Leyland National 11351/2R | | B44D | 1975 | Ex West Midlands Travel, 1997 |
| JBN950N | Leyland National 11351/1R | | B52F | 1975 | Ex Dennis's, Ashton-under-Lyne, 1995 |
| GUP900N | Bristol LH6L | Eastern Coach Works | B43F | 1975 | Ex Travel West Midlands, 1997 |
| GUP917N | Bristol LH6L | Eastern Coach Works | B43F | 1975 | Ex Travel West Midlands, 1997 |
| LGR650P | Bristol LH6L | Eastern Coach Works | B43F | 1975 | Ex Travel West Midlands, 1997 |
| MMB968P | Leyland National 11351/1R/SC | | DP48F | 1975 | Ex Pride of the Road, Huddersfield, 1995 |
| JOX510P | Leyland National 11351/1R | | B49F | 1976 | Ex West Midlands Travel, 1997 |
| JOX513P | Leyland National 11351/1R | | B49F | 1976 | Ex West Midlands Travel, 1995 |
| JOX514P | Leyland National 11351/1R | | B49F | 1976 | Ex West Midlands Travel, 1997 |
| PEV702R | Leyland National 11351/1R | | B49F | 1976 | Ex West Midlands Travel, 1997 |
| PJT255R | Leyland National 10351A/1R | | B41F | 1976 | Ex Pride of the Road, Huddersfield, 1994 |
| UHG753R | Leyland National 11351/1R | | B49F | 1976 | Ex West Midlands Travel, 1997 |
| NOE545R | Leyland National 11351/1R | | B49F | 1976 | Ex West Midlands Travel, 1996 |
| NOE608R | Leyland National 11351/1R | | B49F | 1976 | Ex West Midlands Travel, 1995 |
| OOX804R | Leyland National 11351/1R(DAF) | | B50F | 1977 | Ex West Midlands Travel, 1996 |
| OOX814R | Leyland National 11351/1R(DAF) | | B50F | 1977 | Ex West Midlands Travel, 1996 |
| OOX815R | Leyland National 11351/1R(DAF) | | B50F | 1977 | Ex West Midlands Travel, 1995 |
| CGR894S | Bristol LH6L | Eastern Coach Works | B43F | 1977 | Ex Travel West Midlands, 1997 |
| UPB319S | Leyland National 10351/1R | | B41F | 1977 | Ex West Midlands Travel, 1996 |

A recent addition to the K-Line group fleet is Dennis Dart P895PWW. This bus carries the Plaxton Pointer body which is now only available on the standard Dart chassis. All Pointer bodies on SLF Darts will now be the Ogle re-styled version which is to be called Pointer 2.
*Richard Godfrey*

7

| Reg | Model | Body | Seating | Year | Notes |
|---|---|---|---|---|---|
| TOF711S | Leyland National 11351/1R | | B49F | 1978 | Ex West Midlands Travel, 1997 |
| YKO624S | Leyland National 11351/1R | | B49F | 1978 | Ex Chalkwell, Sittingbourne, 1996 |
| TVP839S | Leyland National 11351/1R(DAF) | | B50F | 1978 | Ex West Midlands Travel, 1996 |
| TVP840S | Leyland National 11351/1R(DAF) | | B50F | 1978 | Ex West Midlands Travel, 1996 |
| TVP842S | Leyland National 11351/1R(DAF) | | B50F | 1978 | Ex West Midlands Travel, 1996 |
| TVP846S | Leyland National 11351/1R(DAF) | | B50F | 1978 | Ex West Midlands Travel, 1996 |
| EGB85T | Leyland National 11351A/1R | | B52F | 1978 | Ex Pride of the Road, Huddersfield, 1995 |
| OLS806T | Leyland National 10351B/1R | | B44F | 1978 | Ex Busways, 1995 |
| AHH202T | Leyland National 10351B/1R | | B44F | 1978 | Ex MTL, Manchester, 1995 |
| AHH203T | Leyland National 10351B/1R | | B44F | 1978 | Ex MTL, Manchester, 1995 |
| AHH205T | Leyland National 10351B/1R | | B44F | 1978 | Ex MTL, Manchester, 1995 |
| HMA566T | Leyland National 10351B/1R | | B44F | 1978 | Ex Midland, 1995 |
| WOC721T | Leyland National 11351/1R | | B50F | 1978 | Ex West Midlands Travel, 1997 |
| XOV757T | Leyland National 11351/1R | | B49F | 1979 | Ex West Midlands Travel, 1997 |
| AOL16T | Leyland National 11351/1R(DAF) | | B50F | 1979 | Ex West Midlands Travel, 1995 |
| SBR525V | Leyland Leopard PSU5C/4R | Plaxton Supreme IV | C53F | 1978 | Ex Travel West Midlands, 1997 |
| FWA476V | Leyland National 2 NL106L11/1R | | B44F | 1980 | Ex Citibus, Middleton, 1995 |
| DOC28V | Leyland National 2 NL116L11/1R | | B50F | 1980 | Ex West Midlands Travel, 1996 |
| DOC29V | Leyland National 2 NL116L11/1R | | B50F | 1980 | Ex West Midlands Travel, 1996 |
| DOC41V | Leyland National 2 NL116L11/1R | | B50F | 1980 | Ex West Midlands Travel, 1996 |
| DOC52V | Leyland National 2 NL106L11/1R | | B40F | 1980 | Ex West Midlands Travel, 1996 |
| LRB211W | Leyland National 2 NL116L11/1R | | DP48F | 1981 | Ex Independent, Horsforth, 1995 |
| UWY81X | Leyland Leopard PSU3F/4R | Duple Dominant IV | C49F | 1981 | Ex South Lancs, St Helens, 1997 |
| J23GCX | DAF SB220LC550 | Optare Delta | B49F | 1991 | Ex Dennis's, Ashton-under-Lyne, 1996 |
| H512YCX | DAF SB220LC550 | Optare Delta | DP48F | 1991 | |
| K123TCP | DAF SB220LC550 | Ikarus CitiBus | B48F | 1992 | Ex Stuart's Dukinfield, 1997 |
| K124TCP | DAF SB220LC550 | Ikarus CitiBus | B48F | 1992 | Ex Stuart's Dukinfield, 1997 |
| L512EHD | DAF SB220LC550 | Ikarus CitiBus | B48F | 1993 | |

| | DAF SB220LT550 | Ikarus CitiBus | B49F | 1994 | |
|---|---|---|---|---|---|
| M811RCP | M813RCP | M815RCP | M817RCP | M819RCP |
| M812RCP | M814RCP | M816RCP | M818RCP | |

| P895PWW | Dennis Dart | Plaxton Pointer | B39F | 1997 | |
|---|---|---|---|---|---|

**Previous Registrations:**                                    JBN950N     MAN16D

**Fleets:** Jowitt's, K-Line, Taylors, and Pride of the Road.

**Livery:** White and blue.

*Opposite, top:* **K-Line's expansion of services throughout South and West Yorkshire has been achieved, in recent years, with the acquisition of large numbers of Leyland Nationals formerly with West Midlands Travel. Displaying small K-Line fleetnames is DOC28V, a mark 2 National which joined the fleet in 1996.** *Tony Wilson*

*Opposite, bottom:* **The K-Line group has latterly expanded to incorporate several companies. These separate operations use a common white and blue livery where, in some cases, the fleetname is red. M815RCP is an Ikarus-bodied DAF used on the Taylors of Morley operations and is seen in Boar Lane, Leeds.** *Tony Wilson*

**The Leyland National is utilised by the K-Line group on all its operations. UHG753R was once part of the Ribble fleet but came to Yorkshire from the West Midlands. It is seen on a Headlight Bus Company service from Barnsley to Meadowhall.**
*Tony Wilson*

# ANDREWS - SHEFFIELD OMNIBUS

Andrews (Sheffield) Ltd, Upper Sheffield Road, Barnsley, South Yorkshire, S70 4PP

Part of the Yorkshire Traction Group
**Depot** : Green Lane, Ecclesfield, Sheffield

| | | | | | | | |
|---|---|---|---|---|---|---|---|
| 1500 | E412EPE | Renault-Dodge S56 | | Northern Counties | B20F | 1987 | Ex Yorkshire Terrier, 1996 |
| 1502 | D677SEM | Renault-Dodge S56 | | Northern Counties | B22F | 1986 | Ex Barnsley & District, 1996 |

| *1601-1605* | | Leyland Olympian ON2R56C16Z4 | Alexander RH | | H43/31F | 1993 | |
|---|---|---|---|---|---|---|---|
| **1601** | L601NOS | **1602** | L602NOS | **1603** | L603NOS | **1604** L604NOS | **1605** L605NOS |

| | | | | | | | |
|---|---|---|---|---|---|---|---|
| 1701 | OKW515R | Leyland Fleetline FE30AGR | MCW | H46/25D | 1978 | Ex Yellow Bus, Stoke Mandeville, 1989 |
| 1702 | NOC594R | Leyland Fleetline FE30AGR | Park Royal | H43/33F | 1976 | Ex West Midlands Travel, 1992 |
| 1713 | SDA697S | Leyland Fleetline FE30AGR | MCW | H43/33F | 1978 | Ex West Midlands Travel, 1991 |
| 1714 | SDA749S | Leyland Fleetline FE30AGR | East Lancashire | H43/33F | 1977 | Ex Kettle Products, Kinglassie, 1992 |
| 1715 | SDA762S | Leyland Fleetline FE30AGR | MCW | H43/33F | 1978 | Ex West Midlands Travel, 1991 |
| 1716 | SDA797S | Leyland Fleetline FE30AGR | MCW | H43/33F | 1978 | Ex West Midlands Travel, 1991 |
| 1717 | TVP868S | Leyland Fleetline FE30AGR | MCW | H43/33F | 1978 | Ex West Midlands Travel, 1990 |
| 1718 | DWH684W | Leyland Fleetline FE30AGR | Northern Counties | H43/32F | 1980 | Ex GM Buses, 1991 |
| 1725 | MOM577P | Leyland Fleetline FE30AGR | Park Royal | H43/33F | 1975 | Ex Barnsley & District, 1996 |
| 1727 | SDA733S | Leyland Fleetline FE30AGR | MCW | H43/33F | 1978 | Ex Barnsley & District, 1996 |
| 1730 | KJW307W | MCW Metrobus DR102/22 | MCW | H43/30F | 1981 | Ex Yorkshire Traction, 1997 |
| 1731 | KJW304W | MCW Metrobus DR102/22 | MCW | H43/30F | 1981 | Ex Yorkshire Traction, 1997 |
| 1732 | GOG154W | MCW Metrobus DR102/18 | MCW | H43/30F | 1980 | Ex Yorkshire Traction, 1997 |
| 1801 | SKG913S | Leyland National 11351A/1R | | B49F | 1978 | Ex South Riding, 1995 |
| 1802 | EFN163L | Leyland National 1151/1R/2402 | | B49F | 1973 | Ex South Riding, 1995 |
| 1803 | YWG462T | Leyland National 11351A/1R | | B52F | 1978 | Ex South Riding, 1995 |
| 1804 | JJG884P | Leyland National 11351/1R | | B49F | 1976 | Ex South Riding, 1995 |
| 1805 | MLG960P | Leyland National 11351/1R/SC | | B52F | 1975 | Ex South Riding, 1995 |
| 1806 | YWG463T | Leyland National 11351A/1R | | B52F | 1978 | Ex Yorkshire Traction, 1994 |
| 1807 | YWG467T | Leyland National 11351A/1R | | B52F | 1978 | Ex Yorkshire Traction, 1993 |
| 1808 | DET474V | Leyland National 11351A/1R | | B52F | 1979 | Ex Yorkshire Traction, 1993 |
| 1809 | DET476V | Leyland National 11351A/1R | | B52F | 1979 | Ex Yorkshire Traction, 1994 |
| 1810 | DET475V | Leyland National 11351A/1R | | B52F | 1979 | Ex Yorkshire Traction, 1993 |
| 1811 | CPT636S | Leyland National 11351A/1R | | B49F | 1978 | Ex Yorkshire Traction, 1994 |
| 1812 | SWE444S | Leyland National 11351A/1R | | B52F | 1977 | Ex South Riding, 1995 |
| 1813 | SWE446S | Leyland National 11351A/1R | | B52F | 1977 | Ex South Riding, 1995 |
| 1814 | SKG922S | Leyland National 11351A/1R | | B49F | 1978 | Ex South Riding, 1995 |
| 1815 | SKG926S | Leyland National 11351A/1R | | B49F | 1978 | Ex South Riding, 1995 |
| 1816 | PTF729L | Leyland National 1151/2R/0401 | | B52F | 1972 | Ex South Riding, 1995 |
| 1818 | JBR688T | Leyland National 11351A/1R | | B49F | 1978 | Ex South Riding, 1995 |
| 1819 | GOL433N | Leyland National 11351/1R | | B49F | 1977 | Ex South Riding, 1995 |
| 1820 | MTJ796S | Leyland National 11351A/1R | | B49F | 1977 | Ex Yorkshire Terrier, 1996 |
| 1821 | GUG128N | Leyland National 11351/1R | | B52F | 1975 | Ex Yorkshire Terrier, 1995 |
| 1822 | HHA119L | Leyland National 1151/1R/2501 | | B51F | 1973 | Ex Yorkshire Terrier, 1996 |
| 1823 | OAO563M | Leyland National 1151/1R/0401 | | B49F | 1973 | Ex Yorkshire Terrier, 1996 |
| 1824 | SWE440S | Leyland National 11351A/1R | | B52F | 1977 | Ex Barnsley & District, 1996 |
| 2010 | EDT210V | Leyland National 2 NL116L11/1R | | B52F | 1980 | Ex Yorkshire Traction, 1996 |
| 2011 | EDT211V | Leyland National 2 NL116L11/1R | | B52F | 1980 | Ex Yorkshire Traction, 1996 |
| 2016 | EDT216V | Leyland National 2 NL116L11/1R | | B52F | 1980 | Ex Yorkshire Traction, 1996 |
| 2018 | DMS18V | Leyland National 2 NL116L11/1R | | B52F | 1980 | Ex West Riding, 1993 |
| 2023 | DMS23V | Leyland National 2 NL116L11/1R | | B49F | 1980 | Ex West Riding, 1993 |
| 2025 | DMS25V | Leyland National 2 NL116L11/1R | | B49F | 1980 | Ex West Riding, 1993 |
| 2031 | KWA31W | Leyland National 2 NL116L11/1R | | B52F | 1981 | Ex West Riding, 1993 |

*Opposite, top:* **As well as purchasing the five prototype B6 saloons from Cumberland, Sheffield Omnibus purchased two demonstrators and eight new examples of the type, all of which have Alexander Dash bodies. Now carrying the combined Andrews-Sheffield Omnibus blue and cream livery is 2201, M201EUS seen at Hemingfield.** *Lee Whitehead*
*Opposite, bottom:* **Leyland Nationals from various sources form the majority of the Andrews-Sheffield Omnibus fleet. Number 1803, YWG462T, was originally in the Yorkshire Traction fleet but was transferred to South Riding when that company was acquired by the Yorkshire Traction group. In 1995, South Riding was absorbed into Yorkshire Terrier and Andrews-Sheffield Omnibus, hence the presence of this vehicle in the fleet.** *Lee Whitehead*

*The Yorkshire Bus Handbook*

The Leyland Fleetline was once the standard double decker in the Andrews fleet but the type is now being phased out with replacements that have come in the form of Olympians and Metrobuses. Alexander-bodied Leyland Olympian 1605, L605NOS, was part of the Sheffield Omnibus fleet before the operations were combined. *Tony Wilson*

The Leyland Atlantean is a durable chassis and some operators have sought to extend the lives of this type by re-bodying. Sheffield Omnibus had two examples lengthened and re-bodied as single deckers before the company was taken over by Yorkshire Traction. Of these 2501, IIL2501, is one of the pair of East Lancashire Sprint-bodied vehicles which continue in service in Sheffield in the Andrews fleet. *Tony Wilson*

AJC Coaches now trade as Angloblue. In 1996 operations were exchanged with Yorkshire Rider resulting in the Angloblue bus services passing to Yorkshire Rider and the Gold Rider coach operations joining AJC. H346JFX is a former Dorset Travel Services Volvo B10M seen carrying the Angloblue blue and gold livery in Chesterfield when operating a National Express duplicate service. *Tony Wilson*

| 2082-2087 | | Leyland National 2 NL116L11/1R | | B49F | | 1980-81 | Ex United Counties, 1993 | |
|---|---|---|---|---|---|---|---|---|
| 2082 | NRP582V | 2083 | NRP583V | 2084 | NRP584V | 2085 | SVV585W | 2087 | SVV587W |

| 2088 | UWY67X | Leyland National 2 NL116AL11/1R | | B52F | 1981 | Ex Harrogate & District, 1997 |
|---|---|---|---|---|---|---|
| 2089 | SWX536W | Leyland National 2 NL116AL11/1R | | B52F | 1981 | Ex Harrogate & District, 1997 |
| 2090 | PEX618W | Leyland National 2 NL116AL11/1R | | B49F | 1980 | Ex MK Metro, 1997 |

| 2201-2208 | | Volvo B6-9.9m | | Alexander Dash | | B40F | 1995 | |
|---|---|---|---|---|---|---|---|---|
| 2201 | M201EUS | 2203 | M203EUS | 2205 | M205EUS | 2207 | M207EUS | 2208 | M208EUS |
| 2202 | M202EUS | 2204 | M204EUS | 2206 | M206EUS | | | | |

| 2263 | L163AVC | Volvo B6-9.9m | Alexander Dash | B40F | 1994 | Ex Volvo Demonstrator, 1995 |
|---|---|---|---|---|---|---|

| 2201-2208 | | Volvo B6R | | Alexander Dash | | B40F | 1992 | Ex Cumberland, 1994 | |
|---|---|---|---|---|---|---|---|---|---|
| 2270 | K270ERM | 2271 | K271ERM | 2272 | K272ERM | 2273 | K273ERM | 2274 | J704BRM |

| 2278 | L478TDU | Volvo B6-9.9m | Alexander Dash | B40F | 1993 | Ex Volvo Demonstrator, 1994 |
|---|---|---|---|---|---|---|
| 2335 | K235MAP | Volvo B10M-55 | Alexander PS | B51F | 1992 | |
| 2336 | K236MAP | Volvo B10M-55 | Alexander PS | B51F | 1992 | |
| 2337 | K237MAP | Volvo B10M-55 | Alexander PS | B51F | 1992 | |
| 2501 | IIL2501 | Leyland Atlantean AN68A/1R | East Lancs Sprint(1992) | B47F | 1976 | Ex Hyndburn, 1991 |
| 2505 | XRF26S | Leyland Atlantean AN68A/1R | East Lancs Sprint(1993) | B47F | 1978 | Ex Liverline, 1991 |

**Previous Registrations:**
IIL2501     LJA245P

**Livery:** Blue and cream

# ANGLOBLUE

AJC Fallas of Leeds Ltd, 245 Elland Road, Leeds, West Yorkshire, LS11 8TU

**Depots** : Elland Road, Leeds and Haigh Park Road, Stourton

| NIB4906 | Volvo B10M-61 | Jonckheere Jubilee P50 | C53F | 1986 | Ex Yorkshire Rider, 1996 |
|---|---|---|---|---|---|
| NIB4905 | Volvo B10M-61 | Jonckheere Jubilee P50 | C48FT | 1987 | Ex Yorkshire Rider, 1996 |
| NIB4908 | Volvo B10M-61 | Jonckheere Jubilee P50 | C48FT | 1987 | Ex Yorkshire Rider, 1996 |
| GSU388 | Volvo B10M-61 | Jonckheere Jubilee P50 | C51FT | 1987 | Ex Yorkshire Rider, 1996 |
| NIL2997 | Volvo B10M-60 | Jonckheere Deauville P599 | C48FT | 1989 | Ex Yorkshire Rider, 1996 |
| H346JFX | Volvo B10M-60 | Plaxton Expressliner | C46FT | 1990 | Ex Dorset Travel, 1995 |
| H347JFX | Volvo B10M-60 | Plaxton Expressliner | C46FT | 1990 | Ex Dorset Travel, 1995 |
| H348JFX | Volvo B10M-60 | Plaxton Expressliner | C46FT | 1990 | Ex Dorset Travel, 1995 |
| K524RJX | DAF SB3000DKVF601 | Van Hool Alizée | C51FT | 1993 | Ex Hallmark, Luton, 1995 |
| K526RJX | DAF SB3000DKVF601 | Van Hool Alizée | C51FT | 1993 | Ex Hallmark, Luton, 1995 |
| K531RJX | DAF SB3000DKVF601 | Van Hool Alizée | C51FT | 1993 | Ex Fishwick, Leyland, 1994 |

**Previous Registrations:**

| GSU388 | E405RWR | NIB4906 | C402EWU | NIL2997 | F418EWR, 23PTA |
|---|---|---|---|---|---|
| NIB4905 | D403LUA | NIB4908 | D404LUA | | |

**Livery:** Blue and gold

# ASTON EXPRESS

Daybird Roadline Ltd, Unit 10, Bailey Drive, Killamarsh, Sheffield,
South Yorkshire, S31 8JF

| | | | | | |
|---|---|---|---|---|---|
| LUA324V | Leyland National 2 NL106L11/1R | | B41F | 1980 | Ex Delta, Kirkby in Ashfield, 1997 |
| YSX928W | Leyland National 2 NL106L11/1R | | B44F | 1980 | Ex Fife Scottish, 1997 |
| C808FMC | Leyland Tiger TRCTL11/3RZ | Plaxton Paramount 3200 II | C53F | 1986 | Ex Chambers, Bures, 1995 |
| E129KYW | MCW MetroRider MF150/96 | MCW | B25F | 1987 | Ex Delta, Kirkby in Ashfield, 1996 |
| E643KYW | MCW MetroRider MF158/1 | MCW | B30F | 1988 | Ex Stagecoach (A1 Service), 1997 |
| E874NJD | MCW MetroRider MF150/96 | MCW | B25F | 1988 | Ex Delta, Kirkby in Ashfield, 1996 |
| E840HAP | MCW MetroRider MF158/3 | MCW | DP33F | 1988 | Ex Stagecoach South, 1996 |
| F120YVP | MCW MetroRider MF158/016 | MCW | B28F | 1988 | Ex Stagecoach (A1 Service), 1997 |
| F437CJK | MCW MetroRider MF154/11 | MCW | B31F | 1988 | Ex Stagecoach South, 1996 |
| F438CJK | MCW MetroRider MF154/11 | MCW | B31F | 1988 | Ex Stagecoach South, 1996 |
| F562HPP | MCW MetroRider MF158/9 | MCW | B33F | 1988 | Ex Tillingbourne, 1996 |
| F563HPP | MCW MetroRider MF158/9 | MCW | B33F | 1988 | Ex Stagecoach South, 1996 |
| G88KUB | Mercedes-Benz 811D | Optare StarRider | B26F | 1989 | Ex Metroline, 1996 |
| G92KUB | Mercedes-Benz 811D | Optare StarRider | B26F | 1989 | Ex Metroline, 1996 |
| J281CUL | Leyland-DAF 400 | Leyland-DAF | M16 | 1992 | Ex Poppitt, Marehay, 1996 |

**Livery:** White and blue

**Previous Registrations:**

| | | | |
|---|---|---|---|
| E840HAP | E518YWF, 418DCD | F438CJK | F817CWJ, 417DCD |
| F437CJK | F816CWJ, 416DCD | | |

**Aston Express has been managed by staff associated with the former Delta of Mansfield operations,
hence the number of former Delta vehicles in the fleet. Optare MetroRiders and Mercedes-Benz
midibuses now form the majority of the stock. E643KYW is a MetroRider and came to Aston Express
from Stagecoach Western's A1 operation, having been new to East London.** *Tony Wilson*

# B-LINE

B-Line Travel Ltd, 8 Cross Lane, Royston, Barnsley, South Yorkshire, S71 4AT

**Depot:** 4 Square Garage, Hoyle Mill Road, Kinsley, Pontefract.

| | | | | | |
|---|---|---|---|---|---|
| B265AMG | Mercedes-Benz L608D | Reeve Burgess | C19F | 1984 | Ex Globe, Barnsley, 1997 |
| D140RAK | Renault-Dodge S56 | Reeve Burgess | B25F | 1987 | Ex Globe, Barnsley, 1997 |
| D912PRJ | Freight Rover Sherpa | Made to Measure | M16 | 1987 | Ex Cygnet, Darton, 1996 |
| D44OKH | Iveco Daily 49-10 | Robin Hood City Nippy | B19F | 1987 | Ex East Yorkshire, 1997 |
| E558XRH | Volkswagen LT55 | Optare CityPacer | B25F | 1987 | Ex East Yorkshire, 1997 |

**Previous Registrations:**
E558XRH      E906LVE, OJI7078

**Livery:** Blue and white

**B-Line Travel is a newcomer to the Yorkshire bus scene. Service 244 is operated from Newstead to South Elmsall and on that route at Hemsworth is seen B265AMG, a Reeve Burgess conversion of a Mercedes-Benz L608D van which has been purchased from Globe of Barnsley. Globe have ceased bus operation since our last edition.** *Tony Wilson*

# BARNSLEY & DISTRICT

The Barnsley & District Traction Co Ltd, Upper Sheffield Road, Barnsley, S70 4PP

Part of the Yorkshire Traction Group
**Depot:** Wakefield Road, Barnsley

| | | | | | | |
|---|---|---|---|---|---|---|
| 105 | NFN78M | Leyland National 1151/1R/2402 | | B52F | 1974 | Ex Jowitt, Tankersley, 1990 |
| 109 | SWE437S | Leyland National 11351A/1R | | B52F | 1977 | Ex Yorkshire Traction, 1991 |
| 110 | SWE438S | Leyland National 11351A/1R | | B52F | 1977 | Ex Yorkshire Traction, 1991 |
| 112 | SWE445S | Leyland National 11351A/1R | | B52F | 1977 | Ex Yorkshire Traction, 1991 |
| 113 | YWG460T | Leyland National 11351A/1R | | B52F | 1978 | Ex Yorkshire Traction, 1991 |
| 114 | YWG461T | Leyland National 11351A/1R | | B52F | 1978 | Ex Yorkshire Traction, 1991 |
| 115 | YWG464T | Leyland National 11351A/1R | | B52F | 1978 | Ex Yorkshire Traction, 1991 |
| 116 | DET471V | Leyland National 11351A/1R | | B52F | 1979 | Ex Yorkshire Traction, 1991 |
| 117 | XAK458T | Leyland National 11351A/1R | | B52F | 1978 | Ex Yorkshire Traction, 1994 |
| 118 | PTT87R | Leyland National 11351A/1R | | B52F | 1977 | Ex Globe, Barnsley, 1995 |
| 119 | GOL405N | Leyland National 11351/1R | | B49F | 1975 | Ex South Riding, 1995 |
| 120 | NWG418R | Leyland National 11351A/1R | | B52F | 1976 | Ex Andrews-Sheffield Omnibus, 1996 |
| 122 | WDR675M | Leyland National 1151/2R/0202 | | B49F | 1974 | Ex Globe, Barnsley, 1995 |
| 124 | DET473V | Leyland National 11351A/1R | | B52F | 1979 | Ex Yorkshire Traction, 1993 |
| 125 | VPT599R | Leyland National 11351A/1R | | B49F | 1977 | Ex Yorkshire Traction, 1994 |
| 127 | VPT598R | Leyland National 11351A/1R | | B49F | 1977 | Ex Yorkshire Traction, 1994 |
| 128 | SEO209M | Leyland National 1151/1R/SC | | B52F | 1974 | Ex Globe, Barnsley, 1995 |
| 129 | THX166S | Leyland National 10351A/2R | | B39D | 1978 | Ex Globe, Barnsley, 1995 |
| 130 | A137EPA | Leyland Tiger TRCTL11/2R | Plaxton Paramount 3200 E | C53F | 1984 | Ex Sheffield Omnibus, 1995 |
| 131 | A128EPA | Leyland Tiger TRCTL11/2R | Plaxton Paramount 3200 E | C53F | 1984 | Ex Sheffield Omnibus, 1995 |
| 132 | JBN947N | Leyland National 11351/1R | | B52F | 1975 | Ex Globe, Barnsley, 1995 |
| 133 | AYJ90T | Leyland National 11351A/1R | | B52F | 1979 | Ex Globe, Barnsley, 1995 |
| 134 | N929CKW | Volvo B6-9.5m | Alexander Dash | B40F | 1995 | |
| 135 | N930CKW | Volvo B6-9.5m | Alexander Dash | B40F | 1995 | |
| 136 | N931CKW | Volvo B6-9.5m | Alexander Dash | B40F | 1995 | |
| 137 | M630NAC | Volvo B6-9.5m | East Lancashire EL2000 | B40F | 1995 | Ex Volvo Demonstrator, 1995 |
| 140 | G681KNW | Mercedes-Benz 811D | Optare StarRider | B33FL | 1989 | Ex Jowitt, Tankersley, 1990 |
| 141 | G682KNW | Mercedes-Benz 811D | Optare StarRider | DP29FL | 1989 | Ex Jowitt, Tankersley, 1990 |
| 142 | E286OMG | Mercedes-Benz 709D | Reeve Burgess Beaver | B25F | 1988 | Ex Jowitt, Tankersley, 1990 |
| 143 | D522SKY | MCW MetroRider MF150/22 | MCW | B25F | 1987 | Ex Yorkshire Traction, 1992 |
| 144 | D524SKY | MCW MetroRider MF150/22 | MCW | B25F | 1987 | Ex Yorkshire Traction, 1992 |
| 145 | D525SKY | MCW MetroRider MF150/22 | MCW | B25F | 1987 | Ex Yorkshire Traction, 1993 |
| 146 | D526SKY | MCW MetroRider MF150/22 | MCW | B23F | 1987 | Ex Yorkshire Traction, 1994 |
| 150 | E703UEM | Renault-Dodge S56 | Alexander AM | B23F | 1987 | Ex Globe, Barnsley, 1995 |
| 151 | E704UEM | Renault-Dodge S56 | Alexander AM | B23F | 1987 | Ex Globe, Barnsley, 1995 |
| 155 | D528SKY | MCW MetroRider MF150/22 | MCW | B23F | 1987 | Ex Yorkshire Traction, 1996 |
| 156 | SGR117R | Leyland National 11351A/1R | | B49F | 1976 | Ex Andrews-Sheffield Omnibus, 1996 |
| 157 | NIL2457 | Scania K112CRB | East Lancashire Flyte(1997) | B53F | 1987 | Ex Yorkshire Terrier, 1996 |
| 158 | NIL2458 | Scania K112CRB | East Lancashire Flyte(1997) | B53F | 1987 | Ex Yorkshire Terrier, 1996 |
| 202 | EDT202V | Leyland National 2 NL116L11/1R | | B52F | 1980 | Ex Yorkshire Traction, 1994 |
| 203 | EDT203V | Leyland National 2 NL116L11/1R | | B52F | 1980 | Ex Yorkshire Traction, 1994 |
| 204 | PWY584W | Leyland National 2 NL106AL11/1R | | B44F | 1980 | Ex Keighley & District, 1996 |
| 205 | EDT205V | Leyland National 2 NL116L11/1R | | B52F | 1980 | Ex Yorkshire Traction, 1994 |
| 206 | EDT206V | Leyland National 2 NL116L11/1R | | B52F | 1980 | Ex Yorkshire Traction, 1994 |
| 208 | EDT208V | Leyland National 2 NL116L11/1R | | B52F | 1980 | Ex Yorkshire Traction, 1995 |
| 212 | EDT212V | Leyland National 2 NL116L11/1R | | B52F | 1980 | Ex Yorkshire Traction, 1995 |
| 213 | SWX539W | Leyland National 2 NL116AL11/1R | | B52F | 1981 | Ex Harrogate & District, 1996 |

**Previous Registrations:**

| | | | | | |
|---|---|---|---|---|---|
| JBN947N | MAN15D | NIL2457 | D87ALX | NIL2458 | D91ALX |

**Livery:** Blue, white and red

*Opposite, top:* **In response to competition on service 325 between Barnsley and Hoyland, Barnsley and District now operate a high frequency service over the route. Four Volvo B6 saloons were purchased for the route and all carry Hoyland Bus branding. The odd vehicle of the four is former demonstrator 137, M630NAC which carries the same East Lancashire EL2000 body style as a batch of eight bought for sister company RoadCar,** *Richard Godfrey*

*Opposite, bottom:* **Barnsley & District is a low cost operating subsidiary of Yorkshire Traction formed from the acquisition of a number of other operations in the Barnsley area. The minibus operation is provided with buses acquired with the businesses of Jowitt of Tankersley and Globe of Barnsley as well as being supported by MetroRiders from Yorkshire Traction. One of the latter is 143, D522SKY seen on route 216 to Hoyland.** *Lee Whitehead*

*The Yorkshire Bus Handbook*

The Scania K112 airside buses of the Yorkshire Terrier fleet are being re-bodied and re-allocated to other Yorkshire Traction group companies. Two are now in the Barnsley and District fleet having received new East Lancashire Flyte bodies. Number 158, NIL2458 was formerly D85ALX, having gained a dateless index mark. *Tony Wilson*

The Leyland National still dominates the Barnsley and District fleet with mark 2 versions purchased from various sources. Seen passing over the level crossing in the centre of Barnsley when operating route 279 to Mexborough was 212, EDT212V which came from parent company Yorkshire Traction. *Richard Godfrey*

# BIBBY'S OF INGLETON

Bibby's of Ingleton Ltd, New Road, Ingleton, North Yorkshire, LA6 3NU

| | | | | | |
|---|---|---|---|---|---|
| ACC629 | Bedford OB | Duple Vista | C29F | 1950 | Ex Turner, Lockerbie, 1976 |
| BIB5428 | DAF MB200DKTL600 | Plaxton Supreme V | C51F | 1982 | Ex Braithwaite & Inliff, Tebay, 1992 |
| FFV807Y | Leyland Leopard PSU5/2L | Plaxton Paramount 3200 | C53F | 1983 | |
| BIB7670 | Volvo B10M-56 | Plaxton Paramount 3200 | C53F | 1983 | Ex Silver Badge, Bowness, 1989 |
| BIB3994 | Leyland Tiger TRCTL11/3R | Plaxton Paramount 3500 | C53F | 1984 | |
| BIB728 | Leyland Tiger TRCTL11/3R | Plaxton Paramount 3200 II | C53F | 1985 | |
| BIB4884 | DAF MB200DKFL600 | Plaxton | C53F | 1986 | Ex Paul S Winson, Loughborough, 1995 |
| BIB5740 | Leyland Tiger TRCTL11/3R | Plaxton Paramount 3200 III | C55F | 1987 | |
| F911DRN | Freight Rover Sherpa | Made-to-Measure | C16F | 1989 | |
| VWU529 | DAF SB3000DKV601 | Plaxton Paramount 3500 III | C53F | 1989 | |
| BIB9842 | Leyland-DAF 400 | Made-to-Measure | C16F | 1990 | Ex Independent, Burnley, 1994 |
| BIB5491 | DAF SB2305SDHS585 | Plaxton Paramount 3200 III | C53F | 1991 | |
| BIB7667 | DAF SB3000DKV601 | Van Hool Alizée | C53FT | 1993 | Ex Hallmark, Luton, 1994 |
| BIB4843 | DAF SB2700HS585 | Van Hool Alizée | C49FT | 1993 | |
| N47FWU | DAF DE33WSSB3000 | Plaxton Première 320 | C53F | 1996 | |
| N241YRJ | LDV 400 | Olympic | M16 | 1996 | |
| P885KNF | LDV 400 | Olympic | M16 | 1996 | |
| P896PWW | DAF DE33WSSB3000 | Plaxton Première 350 | C53F | 1997 | |
| P213RWR | EOS E180Z | EOS 90 | C49FT | 1997 | |

**Previous Registrations:**

| | | | |
|---|---|---|---|
| ACC629 | ACC629, J3617, ACC629, TRN618A | BIB5740 | D105MEC |
| BIB728 | B891OEC | BIB7667 | K522RJX |
| BIB3994 | A281GEC | BIB7670 | A64BEC, ABM351A |
| BIB4843 | L525EHD | BIB9842 | G53VVM |
| BIB4884 | C991PNU | F911DRN | F294GNB, BIB7667 |
| BIB5428 | TND426X | FFV807Y | VWU529 |
| BIB5491 | H550YCX | VWU529 | F656OHD |

**Named vehicles:**
ACC629 *Old Faithful*; BIB728 *Dales Ambassador*; BIB5428 *Dales Conquest*; FFV807Y *Dales Endeavour*; BIB3994 *Dales Cruiser*; BIB4884 *Dales Hunter*; BIB5740 *Dales Drifter*; VWU529 *Dales Princess*; BIB9842 *Dales Revival*; BIB5491 *Dales Viking*; BIB4943 *Dales Diplomat*; N47FWU *Dales Majestic*; N48FWU *Dales Legend* ; N241YRJ *Dales Renown* .

**Livery:** Grey, white and red

Bibbys of Ingleton have obtained BIB index marks for many of their vehicles in order to reflect their ownership. BIB728 carries a Plaxton Paramount 3200 body on a Leyland Tiger chassis. Formerly B891OEC, this coach carries the name Dales Ambassador and is seen in Keswick, on the west of the Pennines.
*Donald Akrigg*

# BIGFOOT

M.C.Geldard, 1 Chapel Lane, Armley, Leeds, West Yorkshire, LS12 2DJ

**Depot:** Unit 14, Whitehall Industrial Estate, Leeds.

|  | | | | | | |
|---|---|---|---|---|---|---|
|  | H590UUA | Renault Trafic | Steedrive | M15 | 1991 | |
|  | J980AKY | Ford Transit VE6 | Advanced Vehicle Bodies | M14 | 1992 | Ex Kennings, 1994 |
|  | J992XKU | Ford Transit VE6 | Advanced Vehicle Bodies | M14 | 1992 | Ex Kennings, 1995 |
| 3 | J550RJA | Mercedes-Benz 609D | Crustals | C16F | 1992 | |
| 5 | F443LGX | Talbot Express | Crystals | M14 | 1992 | Ex Smith, Liss, 1993 |
| 6 | N214ENW | Ford Transit VE6 | Advanced Vehicle Bodies | M14 | 1995 | |
| 11 | L931UGA | Mercedes-Benz L408D | Deansgate | M16 | 1993 | Ex Jackson, Colwick, 1994 |
| 12 | M994CYS | Mercedes-Benz 410D | Deansgate | M16 | 1994 | |
| 401 | KMA404T | Leyland National 11351A/1R(6HLX) | | B49F | 1979 | Ex Constable, Long Melford, 1995 |
| 402 | MMB975P | Leyland National 11351/1R/SC(6HLX) | | DP48F | 1976 | Ex Constable, Long Melford, 1995 |
| 403 | CFM357S | Leyland National 11351A/1R(6HLX) | | B49F | 1978 | Ex Constable, Long Melford, 1995 |
| 404 | UPB306S | Leyland National 10351/1R | | B41F | 1977 | Ex West Midlands Travel, 1996 |
| 405 | PJI3671 | Leyland National 11351A/1R/SC | | DP48F | 1975 | Ex Constable, Long Melford, 1995 |
| 406 | NPK251R | Leyland National 10351A/1R | | B41F | 1976 | Ex West Midlands Travel, 1996 |
| 407 | LPB213P | Leyland National 10351/1R | | B41F | 1976 | Ex West Midlands Travel, 1996 |
| 409 | UPB319S | Leyland National 10351/1R | | B41F | 1977 | Ex West Midlands Travel, 1996 |
|  | NOE609R | Leyland National 11351A/1R | | B49F | 1977 | Ex K Line, Leeds, 1997 |
|  | PUK650R | Leyland National 11351A/1R | | B49F | 1977 | Ex K Line, Leeds, 1997 |
| 502 | MAB160X | Mercedes-Benz L508D | Devon Conversions | C19F | 1982 | Ex Pelter, Whittington, 1995 |
| 507 | M930SWX | Ford Transit VE6 | Ford | M11 | 1994 | |
| 701 | M848RCP | DAF SB220LT550 | Northern Counties Paladin | B49F | 1995 | Ex Speedlink, 1996 |
| 702 | J53GCX | DAF SB220LC550 | Ikarus CitiBus | B48F | 1992 | Ex Williams, Emsworth, 1996 |
| 703 | J54GCX | DAF SB220LC550 | Ikarus CitiBus | B48F | 1992 | Ex Williams, Emsworth, 1996 |
| 704 | M605RCP | DAF SB220LC550 | Ikarus CitiBus | B49F | 1992 | Ex Clarkson, South Elmsall, 1996 |
|  | L511EHD | DAF SB220LC550 | Ikarus CitiBus | B48F | 1993 | Ex K Line, Leeds, 1996 |
|  | P2BFB | Scania L113CRL | East Lancashire Flyte | B49F | 1997 | |
|  | B889AJX | DAF MB200DKFL600 | Duple 340 | C53F | 1985 | |
| 901 | XXI8968 | Scania K112CRS | Jonckheere Jubilee P599 | C51FT | 1984 | Ex Birmingham Coach Company, 1994 |
| 904 | PVB800S | Leyland Leopard PSU3E/4R | Duple Dominant I | C49F | 1978 | Ex Beeston, Hadleigh, 1995 |
|  | GDZ9114 | DAF MB230DKFL615 | Van Hool Alizée | C44FT | 1986 | Ex Pride of the Road, Huddersfield, 1996 |

**Livery:** Yellow and green

**Previous Registrations:**

| | | | |
|---|---|---|---|
| GDZ9114 | C761CWX | PJI3671 | GLJ678N |
| MAB160X | XDD183X, 8053KR | XXI8968 | B69MLT, C892WEA |

Leyland Nationals have provided the backbone of the Bigfoot fleet since the bus operation was started in 1995. Now carrying number 401, KMA404T was purchased from Constable of Long Melford but was new to Crosville as SNL404. The fleet livery incorporates black feet on the rear section of the bodywork as shown in this view taken at the Corn Exchange, Leeds. *Tony Wilson*

# BLACK PRINCE

B Crowther, York Cottage, Texas Street, Morley,
West Yorkshire  LS27 0HG

**Depot:** Fountain Street, Morley.

| | | | | | | |
|---|---|---|---|---|---|---|
| u | EHL335 | Leyland Tiger PS2/13A | Roe | C35F | 1952 | Ex Gra'Cars, Featherstone, 1992 |
| u | RTC822 | Leyland Titan PD2/12 | Leyland | H31/25R | 1953 | Ex Rossendale, 1992 |
| V1 u | A101SUU | Volvo B55-10 MkIII | Alexander RV | H47/31D | 1984 | Ex Merseybus, 1996 |
| V2 u | A102SUU | Volvo B55-10 MkIII | Alexander RV | H47/31D | 1984 | Ex Merseybus, 1996 |
| 60 | ALM60B | AEC Routemaster 52RH | Park Royal | H36/28R | 1964 | Ex Ribble, 1997 |

| | | | | | | |
|---|---|---|---|---|---|---|
| 71 | M71WYG | MAN 11.190 | Optare Vecta | B41F | 1995 | |
| 72 | M73WYG | MAN 11.190 | Optare Vecta | B41F | 1995 | |
| 74 | M74WYG | MAN 11.190 | Optare Vecta | B41F | 1995 | |
| 75 | M75WYG | MAN 11.190 | Optare Vecta | B41F | 1995 | |

| | | | | | |
|---|---|---|---|---|---|
| *82-101* | | Scania BR112DH | Marshall | H45/31F | 1981-82 *Ex Newport, 1996-97 |
| | | | | | * 85/7-91 ex Redby, Sunderland 1996 |

| | | | | | | | | | |
|---|---|---|---|---|---|---|---|---|---|
| 82 | JBO82W | 86 | JBO86W | 90 | JBO90W | 94 | PTG94Y | 98 | PTG98Y |
| 83 | JBO83W | 87 | JBO87W | 91 | JBO91W | 95 | PTG95Y | 99 | PTG99Y |
| 84 | JBO84W | 88 | JBO88W | 92 | JBO92W | 96 | PTG96Y | 100 | PTG100Y |
| 85 | JBO85W | 89 | JBO89W | 93 | PTG93Y | 97 | PTG97Y | 101 | PTG101Y |

| | | | | | | |
|---|---|---|---|---|---|---|
| C101 | C101CUL | Volvo Citybus B10M-50 | Alexander RV | H43/37F | 1985 | Ex A1 (McMenemy), Ardrossan, 1989 |
| 103u | A103SUU | Volvo B55-10 MkIII | Alexander RV | H36/30F | 1984 | Ex London Buses, 1992 |
| S113 | F113OMJ | Scania N113CRB | Alexander PS | B51F | 1989 | Ex London Buses, 1991 |
| 122 | CUV122C | AEC Routemaster 52RH | Park Royal | H36/28R | 1965 | Ex Ribble, 1997 |
| 167 | K167FYG | Optare MetroRider MR01 | Optare | B31F | 1992 | Ex Heatons Travel, Leigh, 1995 |
| 168 | K168FYG | Optare MetroRider MR01 | Optare | B31F | 1992 | Ex Heatons Travel, Leigh, 1995 |
| 213 | 213ONU | Leyland National 11351A/1R(V) | East Lancs Greenway(1993) | B49F | 1978 | Ex National Welsh, 1993 |
| 289 | N289DWY | Optare MetroRider MR17 | Optare | B29F | 1996 | Ex Optare Demonstrator, 1996 |

With the demise of White Rose, Black Prince is now the only operator of Routemasters in West Yorkshire. These London veterans are deployed on the service to the Royal Armouries in Leeds. LDS341A lost its original London index mark while operating in Scotland but, with Black Prince, it regained the original London Transport fleet number RM441. *Tony Wilson*

LUF549 is a Leyland National that has been re-built by East Lancashire Coachbuilders. The Greenway conversion involved considerable re-working of the entire vehicle and a new bus was the result. This Black Prince vehicle started as member of the Ribble fleet in dual-doored format. *Richard Godfrey*

| | | | | | | |
|---|---|---|---|---|---|---|
| **RM441** | LDS341A | AEC Routemaster 52RH | Park Royal | H36/28R | 1960 | Ex Western Scottish, 1990 |
| **549** | LUF549 | Leyland 1151/2R/0402(Volvo) | East Lancs Greenway(1993) | B49F | 1973 | Ex Ribble, 1993 |
| **577** | N577EUG | Mercedes-Benz 0405 | Optare Prisma | B49F | 1996 | |
| **568** | NJA568W | Leyland Olympian B45/TL11/1R | Northern Counties | H43/30F | 1980 | Ex Stagecoach, Manchester, 1997 |
| **653** | P653VWX | Scania L113CRL | East Lancashire Flyte | B49F | 1997 | |
| **654** | P654VWX | Scania L113CRL | East Lancashire Flyte | B49F | 1997 | |
| **655** | P655VWX | Scania L113CRL | East Lancashire Flyte | B49F | 1997 | |
| **702** | FTF702F | Leyland Titan PD3/4 | East Lancashire | H41/32F | 1967 | Ex Alpha, Bootle, 1984 |
| **704** | ACM704X | Leyland Olympian ONTL11/1R | Eastern Coachworks | H46/31F | 1981 | Ex MTL (Fareway), 1996 |
| **712** | ACM712X | Leyland Olympian ONTL11/1R | Eastern Coachworks | H46/31F | 1981 | Ex MTL (Fareway), 1996 |
| **766** | BVP766V | Leyland National 11351A/1R ( Volvo) | | B49F | 1979 | Ex Cherry, Aintree, 1997 |

**Previous Registrations:**

| | | | | |
|---|---|---|---|---|
| 213ONU | SKG924S | | LUF549 | PTF743L |
| LDS341A | WLT441 | | PWR256P | LES48P |

**Livery:** Red and yellow; green and white; blue, 249/50, 783

*Opposite, top:* **Black Prince 654, P654VWX** is one of a trio of Scania L113 saloons bought new for the fleet in 1997. All carry the latest East Lancashire Flyte bodywork which is of Alusuisse aluminium construction. This vehicle is seen in Eastgate, Leeds on route 53 to Morley *Tony Wilson*
*Opposite, bottom:* **Having favoured Ailsa double-deckers for a number of years, Black Prince recently changed policy and bought twenty Marshall-bodied Scania BR112DH vehicles this last year. This represents the entire 1981-82 deliveries to Newport. Several of this batch carry blue and green based liveries as well as the traditional red and yellow colours displayed by 91, JBO91W.** *Tony Wilson*

# CLARKSONS

Ken Clarkson Ltd, 52 Doncaster Road, South Elmsall, West Yorkshire, WF9 2JN

| | | | | | |
|---|---|---|---|---|---|
| NEL123P | Leyland National 11351A/1R | | B49F | 1976 | Ex Trent, 1994 |
| UHG726R | Leyland National 11351A/1R(Volvo) | | B49F | 1976 | Ex Ribble, 1994 |
| ACW920R | Leyland National 11351A/2R(Volvo) | | B52F | 1977 | Ex Halton, 1994 |
| SKF19T | Leyland National 11351A/2R(Volvo) | | B49F | 1977 | Ex Angloblue, Leeds, 1996 |
| H210CVU | Mercedes-Benz 811D | Plaxton Beaver | B33F | 1990 | Ex Dennis's Ashton-under-Lyne, 1996 |
| H83PTG | Mercedes-Benz 811D | Optare StarRider | B33F | 1991 | Ex Walls, Sharston, 1995 |
| J120LKO | Iveco Daily 49.10 | Dormobile Routemaker | B23F | 1992 | Ex East Kent, 1996 |
| J411NCP | DAF SB220LC550 | Ikarus CitiBus | B49F | 1992 | Ex Highland Country, 1996 |
| L974OWY | Volvo B10M-62 | Plaxton Excalibur | C49FT | 1994 | |
| L975OWY | Volvo B10M-62 | Plaxton Excalibur | C49FT | 1994 | |
| M291SBT | Volvo B10M-62 | Plaxton Premiére | C49FT | 1995 | |
| M292SBT | Mercedes-Benz 814D | Plaxton Beaver | C33F | 1995 | |
| N993BWJ | Volvo B10M-62 | Van Hool Alizée | C49FT | 1996 | |
| P542RGG | Mercedes-Benz 711D | Crest | C24F | 1997 | |
| P881PWW | Dennis Dart | Plaxton Pointer | B40F | 1997 | |
| P843WUG | Volvo B10M-62 | Van Hool Alizée | C49FT | 1997 | |

**Livery:** White and blue

**Named vehicles:** M291SBT *Lilly*

**Clarksons operate a mixture of high specification coaches and service buses. The bus services are concentrated on the village of Hemsworth with routes serving the nearby town of Pontefract. Former Halton Leyland National ACW920R is used on these routes and has now been fitted with a Volvo engine in place of a Leyland 510 unit.** *Tony Wilson*

# CYGNET

Cygnet Travel Ltd, Majestic Garage, Station Road, Darton, South Yorkshire, S75 5HT

| 3 | D460CKV | Freight Rover Sherpa | Rootes | B16F | 1986 | Ex Midland Red South, 1995 |
|---|---------|---------------------|--------|------|------|---------------------------|
| 7 | ERB534T | Leyland Leopard PSU3E/4R | Plaxton Supreme IV Express | C53F | 1979 | Ex Trent (Barton), 1995 |
| 8 | C405VVN | Mercedes-Benz L608D | Reeve Burgess | B20F | 1985 | Ex United, 1996 |
| 9 | C420VVN | Mercedes-Benz L608D | Reeve Burgess | B20F | 1985 | Ex United (Tees & District), 1996 |
| 11 | LPT706T | Bristol LH6L | Eastern Coach Works | B43F | 1979 | Ex United (Teeside), 1996 |
| 15 | LPY457W | Leyland Leopard PSU3E/4R | Duple Dominant | B55F | 1981 | Ex United, 1996 |
| 16 | ARB132T | Leyland Leopard PSU3E/4R | Plaxton Supreme III Express | C49F | 1978 | Ex Trent (Barton), 1996 |
| 17 | PTV585X | Leyland Leopard PSU3F/4R | Plaxton Supreme IV Express | C51F | 1981 | Ex Trent (Barton), 1996 |
| 19 | PTV591X | Leyland Leopard PSU3F/4R | Plaxton Supreme IV Express | C51F | 1981 | Ex Trent (Barton), 1996 |
| 20 | VRC612Y | Leyland Leopard PSU3G/4R | Plaxton Supreme V Express | C53F | 1982 | Ex Trent (Barton), 1996 |
| 21 | MFR306P | Leyland Leopard PSU3C/2R | Alexander AYS | B53F | 1976 | Ex Clydeside, 1996 |
| 22 | WCW308R | Leyland Leopard PSU3D/2R | Alexander AYS | B53F | 1977 | Ex Clydeside, 1996 |
|  | E497HHN | Renault-Dodge S56 | Alexander AM | B25F | 1987 | Ex Yorkshire, 1997 |

**Livery**:  Red and cream

Cygnet have established a route to serve Bretton Hall College which lies between Wakefield and Barnsley. LPY457W, seen here in Barnsley, carries promotional lettering for the college. This Duple Dominant-bodied Leyland Leopard was part of the Trimdon fleet acquired by United and passed to Cygnet in 1996. *Tony Wilson*

# EYMS Group

East Yorkshire Motor Services Ltd & National Holidays Ltd,
252 Anlaby Road, Hull, HU3 2RS

**Depots** : Springfield Way, Anlaby; Mill Lane, Beverley; Sheilds Road, Byker; St John Street, Bridlington; Middle Street, Driffield; Back Street, Easington; Stockbridge Road, Elloughton; Cliff Road, Hornsea; Anlaby Road, Hull; Hedon Road, Hull (store); Wilmslow Road, Manchester; Outgang Road, Pickering; Railway Street, Pocklington; Dunslow Road, Scarborough; Crofton Road, Stockton on Tees; Charles Street, Stockport; Bannister Street, Withernsea.

*National Holidays vehicles are identified at the end of the list.*

| | | | | | | |
|---|---|---|---|---|---|---|
| 1 | NBD101Y | Leyland Tiger TRCTL11/3R | Plaxton Paramount 3200 E | C48F | 1983 | Ex Luton & District, 1991 |
| 4 | GRH4Y | Leyland Tiger TRCTL11/3R | Plaxton Paramount 3200 E | C48FT | 1983 | |
| 5 | A573SRH | Leyland Tiger TRCTL11/3R | Plaxton Paramount 3200 E | C53F | 1983 | |
| 6 | 165DKH | Leyland Tiger TRCTL11/3R | Plaxton Paramount 3200 E | C53F | 1983 | |
| 14 | 6627VF | LAG G355Z | LAG Panoramic | C49FT | 1988 | Ex Hollings Coaches, Wallsend, 1996 |
| 21 | 421CKH | Leyland Tiger TRCTL11/2R | Plaxton Paramount 3200 E | C49F | 1983 | Ex United, 1986 |
| 22 | A520EVN | Leyland Tiger TRCTL11/2R | Plaxton Paramount 3200 E | C49F | 1983 | Ex United, 1986 |
| 23 | NDC239W | Leyland Leopard PSU3E/4RT | Plaxton Supreme IV Express | C49F | 1981 | Ex United, 1986 |
| 25 | NJI1255 | Leyland Tiger TRCTL11/3R | Plaxton Paramount 3200 E | C51F | 1983 | Ex Yorkshire Coastliner, 1995 |
| 27 | TXY978 | Leyland Tiger TRCTL11/3R | Duple Dominant IV | C49F | 1982 | Ex Vanguard, Bedworth, 1991 |
| 28 | OJI7078 | Leyland Tiger TRCTL11/2R | Duple Dominant IV | C49F | 1983 | Ex Kinch, Barrow-on-Soar, 1991 |
| 32 | EYD1T | Volvo B10M-61 | Duple 340 | C55F | 1987 | |
| 35 | F53EAT | Dennis Javelin 12SDA1907 | Plaxton Paramount 3200 III | C48FT | 1989 | Ex Kingstonian, 1997 |
| 36 | F55EAT | Dennis Javelin 12SDA1907 | Plaxton Paramount 3200 III | C48FT | 1989 | Ex Kingstonian, 1997 |
| 37 | P837XAG | Volvo B10M-62 | Plaxton Première 320 | C44FT | 1997 | |
| 43w | D43OKH | Iveco Daily 49-10 | Robin Hood City Nippy | DP19F | 1987 | |
| 45 | 32CHY | Leyland Tiger TRCTL11/3ARZ | Plaxton Paramount 3500 II | C51F | 1989 | Ex Fishwick, Leyland, 1995 |
| 46 | 271CLT | Leyland Tiger TRCTL11/3RZ | Plaxton Paramount 3200 II | C53F | 1986 | Ex Hornsby, Ashby, 1994 |
| 47 | 95EYM | Volvo B10M-61 | Plaxton Paramount 3200 II | C53F | 1985 | Ex Excelsior, Bournemouth, 1987 |
| 48 | YUU556 | Volvo B10M-61 | Plaxton Paramount 3200 II | C53F | 1985 | Ex Capital, West Drayton, 1988 |
| 49 | 834EYD | Volvo B10M-61 | Plaxton Paramount 3200 II | C53F | 1985 | Ex Capital, West Drayton, 1988 |
| 50 | 80EYC | Volvo B10M-61 | Plaxton Paramount 3200 II | C53F | 1985 | Ex Capital, West Drayton, 1988 |
| 51 | 334EYL | Leyland Tiger TRCTL11/3RZ | Duple 340 | C48FT | 1988 | |
| 52 | 152FRH | Leyland Tiger TRCTL11/3RZ | Duple 340 | C51FT | 1988 | |
| 53 | 546EYB | Leyland Tiger TRCTL11/3RZ | Duple 340 | C51FT | 1988 | |
| 57 | H157AKH | Volvo B10M-60 | Plaxton Expressliner | C46FT | 1991 | |
| 59 | J159HAT | Volvo B10M-60 | Plaxton Expressliner | C46FT | 1992 | |
| 60 | J160HAT | Volvo B10M-60 | Plaxton Expressliner | C46FT | 1992 | |
| 61 | K161TKH | Volvo B10M-60 | Plaxton Expressliner II | C46FT | 1993 | |
| 62 | L62VAG | Volvo B10M-60 | Plaxton Expressliner II | C46FT | 1993 | |
| 64 | L64CKH | Volvo B10M-60 | Plaxton Expressliner II | C46FT | 1994 | |
| 65 | 39EYD | Volvo B10M-61 | Plaxton Paramount 3200 III | C53F | 1988 | Ex Cambridge Coach Services, 1994 |
| 66 | 46EYB | Volvo B10M-61 | Plaxton Paramount 3200 III | C53F | 1988 | Ex Cambridge Coach Services, 1994 |
| 67 | M67LAG | Scania K113CRB | Van Hool Alizée | C49FT | 1995 | |
| 68 | M68LAG | Scania K113CRB | Van Hool Alizée | C49FT | 1995 | |
| 69 | F349JAT | Leyland Tiger TRCTL11/3ARZ | Plaxton Paramount 3500 III | C53F | 1989 | Ex Skills, Nottingham, 1995 |
| 70 | N170AAG | Scania K113CRB | Van Hool Alizée | C49FT | 1995 | |
| 71 | N171AAG | Scania K113CRB | Van Hool Alizée | C49FT | 1995 | |
| 72 | N172AAG | Scania K113CRB | Van Hool Alizée | C49FT | 1995 | |
| 73 | N173AAG | Scania K113CRB | Van Hool Alizée | C49FT | 1995 | |
| 74 | 665EYL | Leyland Tiger TRCL10/3RZM | Plaxton Paramount 3200 III | C53F | 1989 | Ex Emblings, Guyhirn, 1995 |
| 75 | 865EYT | Leyland Tiger TRCTL11/3ARZ | Plaxton Paramount 3500 III | C51F | 1989 | Ex Waughs, Greenhead, 1995 |
| 76 | GGD671T | Volvo B58-61 | Duple Dominant II | C57F | 1979 | Ex Connor & Graham, 1994 |
| 77 | F776GNA | Leyland Tiger TRCTL11/3ARZA | Plaxton Paramount 3200 III | C53F | 1989 | Ex Craig Lewis, Thringstone, 1995 |
| 78 | J343KTT | Volvo B10M-60 | Plaxton Paramount 3500 III | C53F | 1991 | Ex Plymouth, 1996 |
| 79 | IIL7075 | Leyland Tiger TRCL10/3ARZM | Plaxton Paramount 3200 III | C53F | 1989 | Ex Skills, Nottingham, 1996 |
| 80 | IIL7077 | Leyland Tiger TRCL10/3ARZM | Plaxton Paramount 3200 III | C53F | 1989 | Ex Skills, Nottingham, 1996 |
| 81 | FAZ2781 | Leyland Tiger TRCTL11/3R | Plaxton Paramount 3500 | C49FT | 1983 | Ex Connor & Graham, 1994 |
| 82 | 787EYC | Leyland Tiger TRCTL11/3ARZA | Plaxton Paramount 3200 III | C53F | 1989 | Ex Birds, Hunstanton, 1996 |
| 83 | G536LWU | Volvo B10M-60 | Plaxton Paramount 3500 III | C53F | 1990 | Ex Woodstones, Kidderminster, 1996 |
| 84 | G537LWU | Volvo B10M-60 | Plaxton Paramount 3500 III | C53F | 1990 | Ex Woodstones, Kidderminster, 1996 |
| 85 | 926BWV | Leyland Tiger TRCTL11/3ARZ | Plaxton Paramount 3500 III | C53F | 1989 | Ex Rolyn Travel, Bedford, 1996 |
| 86 | IIL9170 | Leyland Tiger TRCL10/3ARZM | Plaxton Paramount 3500 III | C51F | 1989 | Ex Moor-Dale, Newcastle, 1996 |

The National Holidays name was allowed to become dormant when the tour company was purchased from the National Bus Company by Shearings. East Yorkshire have now registered the National Holidays name in a new company which encompasses the coaching units in Hull, Manchester, Teeside and Tyneside. In order to build the new company's image, a striking grey, orange and blue livery has been adopted as displayed here on former Harry Shaw Volvo B10M 91, J631WWK.
*Lee Whitehead*

| 87 | 741DYE | Volvo B10M-61 | Van Hool Alizée | C49FT | 1984 | Ex Connor & Graham, 1994 |
|---|---|---|---|---|---|---|
| 88 | JSV486 | Volvo B10M-60 | Plaxton Paramount 3500 III | C53F | 1989 | Ex Snowdon, Peterlee, 1996 |
| 89 | H646UWR | Volvo B10M-60 | Plaxton Paramount 3200 III | C53F | 1991 | Ex Wallace Arnold, 1996 |
| 90 | TND123X | Volvo B58-61 | Duple Dominant II | C53F | 1982 | Ex Connor & Graham, 1994 |
| 91 | J631WWK | Volvo B10M-60 | Plaxton Paramount 3500 III | C53F | 1991 | Ex Harry Shaw, Coventry, 1996 |
| 92 | IIL7076 | Leyland Tiger TRCL10/3ARZM | Plaxton Paramount 3200 III | C53F | 1989 | Ex Skills, Nottingham, 1996 |
| 93 | KSU455 | Leyland Tiger TRCL10/3ARZM | Plaxton Paramount 3200 III | C53F | 1989 | Ex Busways (Armstrong Galley), 1997 |
| 94 | 491JVX | Leyland Tiger TRCL10/3ARZM | Plaxton Paramount 3200 III | C53F | 1989 | Ex Busways (Armstrong Galley), 1997 |
| 95 | 552UTE | Leyland Tiger TRCL10/3ARZM | Plaxton Paramount 3200 III | C53F | 1989 | Ex Busways (Armstrong Galley), 1997 |
| 96 | HIL8426 | DAF SB230DHS585 | Van Hool Alizée | C51F | 1987 | Ex Busways (Armstrong Galley), 1997 |
| 97 | HIL8427 | DAF SB230DHS585 | Van Hool Alizée | C51F | 1988 | Ex Busways (Armstrong Galley), 1997 |
| 98 | H344EOD | Volvo B10M-60 | Plaxton Paramount 3500 III | C53F | 1991 | Ex Plymouth, 1996 |
| 99 | DV7890 | Leyland Lion LT2 | Burlingham (1947) | C31F | 1931 | Ex preservation, 1989 |
| 100 | KSU381 | Bedford OB | Duple Vista | C29F | 1949 | Ex Tours, Isle of Man, 1990 |
| 104 | TPX884 | Leyland Tiger TRCTL11/3RH | Plaxton Paramount 3500 II | C49FT | 1985 | Ex Charterplan, 1996 |
| 114 | SIB2014 | Volvo B10M-61 | Plaxton Paramount 3500 II | C49FT | 1986 | Ex Charterplan, 1996 |
| 115 | PXI7915 | Volvo B10M-61 | Plaxton Paramount 3500 III | C49FT | 1988 | Ex Charterplan, 1996 |
| 116 | PJI8916 | Volvo B10M-61 | Plaxton Paramount 3500 III | C49FT | 1988 | Ex Charterplan, 1996 |
| 117 | OIW1317 | Leyland Tiger TRCTL11/3RZ | Plaxton Paramount 3500 III | C49FT | 1989 | Ex Charterplan, 1996 |
| 118 | OIW1318 | Volvo B10M-60 | Plaxton Paramount 3500 III | C49FT | 1989 | Ex Charterplan, 1996 |
| 119 | OIW1319 | Volvo B10M-60 | Plaxton Paramount 3500 III | C49FT | 1989 | Ex Charterplan, 1996 |
| 120 | 583TD | Kässbohrer Setra S215HD | Kässbohrer Tornado | C49FT | 1990 | Ex Charterplan, 1996 |
| 124 | J73VTG | Kässbohrer Setra S215HD | Kässbohrer Tornado | C49FT | 1992 | Ex Charterplan, 1996 |
| 125 | L543YUS | Volvo B10M-60 | Van Hool Alizée | C40FT | 1993 | Ex Charterplan, 1996 |
| 126 | SDZ9026 | Volvo B10M-60 | Jonckheere Deauville P599 | C51FT | 1990 | Ex Charterplan, 1996 |
| 130 | 515VTB | Kässbohrer Setra S215HD | Kässbohrer Tornado | C49FT | 1983 | Ex Charterplan, 1996 |
| 132 | OTK802 | Kässbohrer Setra S215HD | Kässbohrer Tornado | C49FT | 1983 | Ex Charterplan, 1996 |
| 133 | OXK373 | Kässbohrer Setra S215HD | Kässbohrer Tornado | C49FT | 1983 | Ex Charterplan, 1996 |
| 134 | KSU454 | Leyland Tiger TRCTL11/3R | Van Hool Alizée | C48T | 1985 | Ex Busways (Armstrong Galley), 1997 |
| 135 | KSU456 | Leyland Tiger TRCTL11/3R | Van Hool Alizée | C48T | 1985 | Ex Busways (Armstrong Galley), 1997 |
| 136 | KSU459 | Leyland Tiger TRCTL11/3RH | Van Hool Alizée | C48T | 1986 | Ex Busways (Armstrong Galley), 1997 |
| 137 | KSU457 | Leyland Tiger TRCTL11/3RZ | Plaxton Paramount 3500 III | C51T | 1988 | Ex Busways (Armstrong Galley), 1997 |
| 138 | KSU465 | Leyland Tiger TRCTL11/3ARZ | Plaxton Paramount 3500 III | C51T | 1989 | Ex Busways (Armstrong Galley), 1997 |

| 139 | KSU460 | Volvo B10M-60 | Van Hool Alizée | C49FT | 1992 | Ex Busways (Armstrong Galley), 1997 |
|---|---|---|---|---|---|---|
| 140 | K457PNR | Volvo B10M-60 | Plaxton Paramount 3500 III | C49FT | 1992 | Ex Busways (Armstrong Galley), 1997 |
| 141 | K458PNR | Volvo B10M-60 | Plaxton Paramount 3500 III | C49FT | 1992 | Ex Busways (Armstrong Galley), 1997 |
| 142 | J447HDS | Volvo B10M-60 | Plaxton Premiére 350 | C49FT | 1992 | Ex Busways (Armstrong Galley), 1997 |
| 143 | J448HDS | Volvo B10M-60 | Plaxton Premiére 350 | C49FT | 1992 | Ex Busways (Armstrong Galley), 1997 |
| 144 | 813VPU | Volvo B10M-60 | Plaxton Excalibur | C49FT | 1992 | Ex Busways (Armstrong Galley), 1997 |
| 145 | IIL1319 | Volvo B10M-61 | Plaxton Paramount 3200 II | C50FT | 1986 | Ex Kingstonian, 1997 |
| 146 | E52WAG | Volvo B10M-61 | Plaxton Paramount 3200 III | C50FT | 1988 | Ex Kingstonian, 1997 |
| 147 | 508DKH | Volvo B10M-60 | Plaxton Paramount 3500 III | C49FT | 1990 | Ex Kingstonian, 1997 |
| 148 | F108NRT | Volvo B10M-61 | Plaxton Paramount 3500 III | C49FT | 1988 | Ex Kingstonian, 1997 |
| 149 | J204JKH | Volvo B10M-60 | Plaxton Paramount 3500 III | C51FT | 1992 | Ex Kingstonian, 1997 |
| 150 | J205JKH | Volvo B10M-60 | Plaxton Paramount 3500 III | C51FT | 1992 | Ex Kingstonian, 1997 |
| 151 | H656UWR | Volvo B10M-60 | Plaxton Paramount 3500 III | C53F | 1991 | Ex Moor-Dale, 1997 |
| 152 | H620UWR | Volvo B10M-60 | Plaxton Paramount 3500 III | C53F | 1991 | Ex Lochs & Glens, Aberfoyle, 1997 |
| 153 | H621UWR | Volvo B10M-60 | Plaxton Paramount 3500 III | C53F | 1991 | Ex Lochs & Glens, Aberfoyle, 1997 |
| 188 | OBT693M | Leyland Leopard PSU3B/4R | Plaxton Elite III | C53F | 1973 | Ex Connor & Graham, 1994 |
| 189 | CPT822S | Leyland Leopard PSU3E/4R | Plaxton Supreme III Express | C53F | 1978 | Ex Connor & Graham, 1994 |
| 192 | JKH192V | Leyland Leopard PSU3E/4R | Plaxton Supreme IV Express | C49F | 1979 | |
| 195 | BUR443T | Leyland Leopard PSU5C/4R | Plaxton Supreme IV | C53F | 1978 | Ex Metro, Hull, 1992 |
| 196 | YOI7898 | Leyland Leopard PSU3C/4R | Plaxton Supreme IV Express | C53F | 1977 | Ex Thornton Dale, Pickering, 1992 |
| 197 | EGR571S | Leyland Leopard PSU3E/4R | Plaxton Supreme IV Express | C49F | 1978 | Ex Thornton Dale, Pickering, 1992 |
| 198 | GWV935V | Leyland Leopard PSU3E/4R | Plaxton Supreme IV Express | C48F | 1980 | Ex Thornton Dale, Pickering, 1992 |
| 199 | MIJ999 | Leyland Leopard PSU5E/4R | Plaxton Supreme V | C50F | 1982 | Ex Thornton Dale, Pickering, 1992 |
| 200 | OAT822V | Leyland National 2 NL116L11/1R | | B49F | 1980 | |
| 202 | 202YTE | Leyland Titan PD2/37 | East Lancashire | O37/28F | 1962 | Ex Sykes, Barnsley, 1989 |
| 207 | XAG207X | Leyland Leopard PSU3F/4R | Willowbrook 003 | C49F | 1981 | |
| 208 | XAG208X | Leyland Leopard PSU3G/4R | Duple Dominant IV Express | C49F | 1981 | |
| 209 | PNW309W | Leyland Leopard PSU3F/4R | Plaxton Supreme IV | C49F | 1981 | Ex Hardwicks, 1988 |
| 214 | 3277KH | Mercedes-Benz 811D | Whittaker | C19F | 1990 | |

| *215-221* | | Volvo B10M-55 | Alexander PS | DP48F | 1994 | Ex Finglands, 1997 |
|---|---|---|---|---|---|---|
| 215 | M415RRN | **217** | M417RRN | **219** | M419RRN | **220** | M420RRN | **221** | M421RRN |
| 216 | M416RRN | **218** | M418RRN | | | | | | |

| 232 | PNW332W | Leyland Leopard PSU3F/4R | Plaxton Supreme IV | C49F | 1981 | Ex Hardwicks, 1988 |
|---|---|---|---|---|---|---|
| 236 | DDZ236 | Leyland Leopard PSU5D/4R | East Lancs EL2000 (1991) | DP47F | 1981 | Ex Hardwicks, 1988 |
| 255 | IIL2155 | Leyland National 10351B/1R | East Lancs Greenway(1992) | B41F | 1978 | |
| 256 | IIL2156 | Leyland National 10351B/1R | East Lancs Greenway(1992) | B41F | 1978 | |
| 257 | IIL2157 | Leyland National 10351A/2R | East Lancs Greenway(1992) | B41F | 1979 | Ex Lucky Bus, Watford, 1991 |
| 258 | IIL2158 | Leyland National 10351B/1R | East Lancs Greenway(1992) | B41F | 1979 | |
| 259 | IIL2159 | Leyland National 10351B/1R | East Lancs Greenway(1992) | B41F | 1979 | |
| 260 | IIL2160 | Leyland National 10351B/1R | East Lancs Greenway(1992) | B41F | 1979 | |
| 261 | L261AKH | Volvo B6-9.9M | Northern Counties Paladin | B40F | 1994 | |
| 262 | P262NRH | Dennis Dart SLF | Plaxton Pointer | B41F | 1996 | |
| 263 | P263NRH | Dennis Dart SLF | Plaxton Pointer | B41F | 1996 | |
| 264 | P264NRH | Dennis Dart SLF | Plaxton Pointer | B41F | 1996 | |

| *265-272* | | Mercedes-Benz 0405 | Optare Prisma | B49F | 1996 | |
|---|---|---|---|---|---|---|
| 265 | N265KAG | **267** | N267KAG | **269** | N269KKH | **271** | P271NRH | **272** | P272NRH |
| 266 | N266KAG | **268** | N268KAG | **270** | N270KKH | | | | |

| *273-281* | | Optare L1150 | Optare Excel | B45F | 1996-97 | |
|---|---|---|---|---|---|---|
| 273 | P273NRH | **275** | P275NRH | **277** | P277NRH | **279** | R279EKH | **281** | R281EKH |
| 274 | P274NRH | **276** | P276NRH | **278** | R278EKH | **280** | R280EKH | | |

| *282-286* | | Mercedes-Benz 0405 | Optare Prisma | DP49F* | 1997 | *285/6 are B49F |
|---|---|---|---|---|---|---|
| 282 | R282EKH | **283** | R283EKH | **284** | R284EKH | **285** | P285WAT | **286** | P286WAT |

| 341 | E101XVM | Mercedes-Benz 609D | PMT | DP21F | 1988 | Ex Finglands, 1992 |
|---|---|---|---|---|---|---|
| 342 | E102XVM | Mercedes-Benz 609D | PMT | DP24F | 1988 | Ex Finglands, 1992 |
| 343 | F303JNC | Mercedes-Benz 609D | PMT | DP24F | 1989 | Ex Finglands, 1997 |
| 345 | D905RVM | Mercedes-Benz 609D | Reeve Burgess | DP19F | 1987 | Ex Finglands, 1992 |
| 352 | CIB3202 | Leyland Tiger TRCTL11/3R | Plaxton Paramount 3200 | C57F | 1984 | Ex Finglands, 1997 |
| 353 | WLT694 | Leyland Tiger TRCTL11/3R | Plaxton Paramount 3200 | C53F | 1984 | Ex Finglands, 1993 |
| 355 | 8225KH | Leyland Tiger TRCTL11/3RZ | Plaxton Paramount 3200 II | C53F | 1985 | Ex Finglands, 1997 |
| 356 | HIL7923 | Leyland Tiger TRCTL11/3RZ | Plaxton Paramount 3200 II | C57F | 1985 | Ex Finglands, 1997 |

**A trio of Mercedes-Benz 609D minibuses have been transferred from Finglands in Manchester to the parent company, East Yorkshire. Now numbered 342, E102XVM was converted from a van shell by PMT, the Potteries based bus company that has since ceased to be involved in minibus construction.**
*Lee Whitehead*

### 406-419

| | | | | | | | | | |
|---|---|---|---|---|---|---|---|---|---|
| Mercedes-Benz L608D | | Reeve Burgess | | B20F | | 1986 | Ex United, 1986 *406/7 are DP19F | | |
| **406** | C406VVN | **409** | C409VVN | **412** | C412VVN | **415** | C415VVN | **418** | C418VVN |
| **407** | C407VVN | **410** | C410VVN | **413** | C413VVN | **416** | C416VVN | **419** | C419VVN |
| **408** | C408VVN | **411** | C411VVN | **414** | C414VVN | **417** | C417VVN | | |

### 420-437

| | | | | | | | | | |
|---|---|---|---|---|---|---|---|---|---|
| Mercedes-Benz 811D | | Reeve Burgess Beaver | | B31F* | | 1989 | *435-7 are DP31F | | |
| **420** | F420GAT | **424** | F424GAT | **428** | F428GAT | **431** | F431GAT | **435** | F435GAT |
| **421** | F421GAT | **425** | F425GAT | **429** | F429GAT | **433** | F433GAT | **436** | F436GAT |
| **422** | F422GAT | **426** | F426GAT | **430** | F430GAT | **434** | F434GAT | **437** | F437GAT |
| **423** | F423GAT | **427** | F427GAT | | | | | | |

### 438-445

| | | | | | | | | | |
|---|---|---|---|---|---|---|---|---|---|
| Mercedes-Benz 709D | | Reeve Burgess Beaver | | B25F* | | 1989 | *438/9 are DP25F; 443-5 are B23F | | |
| **438** | F438GAT | **440** | F440GAT | **442** | F442GAT | **444** | F444GAT | **445** | F445GAT |
| **439** | F439GAT | **441** | F441GAT | **443** | F443GAT | | | | |

| | | | | | |
|---|---|---|---|---|---|
| **446** | H446YKH | Iveco Daily 49-10 | Reeve Burgess Beaver | B25F | 1990 |
| **447** | H447YKH | Iveco Daily 49-10 | Reeve Burgess Beaver | B25F | 1990 |
| **448** | K448RRH | Mercedes-Benz 811D | Plaxton Beaver | B31F | 1993 |

### 501-510

| | | | | | | | | | |
|---|---|---|---|---|---|---|---|---|---|
| Bristol VRT/SL3/501* | | Eastern Coach Works | | H43/31F | | 1979 | *508 is VRT/SL3/501(6LXB) | | |
| **501** | JKH501V | **503** | JKH503V | **506** | JKH506V | **508** | JKH508V | **510** | JKH510V |
| **502** | JKH502V | **505** | JKH505V | **507** | JKH507V | **509** | JKH509V | | |

Seen in York is East Yorkshire's 529, GRH3Y. This Leyland Olympian carries an Eastern Coach Works body fitted with high-backed seats for comfort on long distance bus services such as service 746. It carries the latest East Yorkshire livery of deep red and cream. Of note is the shaded EY logo behind the fleetname on the sides of this bus. *Tony Wilson*

### 511-527

Bristol VRT/SL3/6LXB    Eastern Coach Works    H43/31F    1980-81

| 511 | PAG511W | 514 | PAG514W | 518 | PAG518W | 522 | WKH522X | 525 | WKH525X |
|-----|---------|-----|---------|-----|---------|-----|---------|-----|---------|
| 512 | PAG512W | 515 | PAG515W | 519 | PAG519W | 523 | WKH523X | 526 | WKH526X |
| 513 | PAG513W | 517 | PAG517W | 520 | WKH520X | 524 | WKH524X | 527 | WKH527X |

| 528 | GRH2Y | Leyland Olympian ONLXB/1R | Eastern Coach Works | H45/32F | 1983 |
|-----|-------|---------------------------|---------------------|----------|------|
| 529 | GRH3Y | Leyland Olympian ONLXB/1R | Eastern Coach Works | DPH41/29F | 1983 |

### 530-535

Leyland Olympian ONLXB/1R    Eastern Coach Works    DPH42/28F*  1984-85  *533-5 are DPH42/30F

| 530 | A530OKH | 532 | A532OKH | 533 | B533WAT | 534 | B534WAT | 535 | B535WAT |
|-----|---------|-----|---------|-----|---------|-----|---------|-----|---------|
| 531 | A531OKH |     |         |     |         |     |         |     |         |

| 536 | C536DAT | Leyland Olympian ONLXB/1RH | Eastern Coach Works | DPH42/29F | 1986 | |
|-----|---------|----------------------------|---------------------|-----------|------|--|
| 537 | C537DAT | Leyland Olympian ONLXB/1RH | Eastern Coach Works | DPH42/29F | 1986 | |
| 539 | A239GHN | Leyland Olympian ONLXB/1R  | Eastern Coach Works | H41/29F | 1984 | Ex United, 1986 |
| 540 | B249NVN | Leyland Olympian ONLXB/1R  | Eastern Coach Works | H45/32F | 1985 | Ex United, 1986 |
| 541 | B250NVN | Leyland Olympian ONLXB/1R  | Eastern Coach Works | H45/32F | 1985 | Ex United, 1986 |
| 542 | B254RAJ | Leyland Olympian ONLXB/1R  | Eastern Coach Works | H42/30F | 1985 | Ex United, 1986 |

### 547-552

Leyland Olympian ON2R56C13Z4 Northern Counties Palatine  H51/34F    1990

| 547 | H547VAT | 549 | H549VAT | 550 | H550VAT | 551 | H551VAT | 552 | H552VAT |
|-----|---------|-----|---------|-----|---------|-----|---------|-----|---------|
| 548 | H548VAT |     |         |     |         |     |         |     |         |

*Opposite, top:* **Having favoured double-decks for many years, East Yorkshire have recently changed their new vehicle buying policy in favour of single-decks. Experience is now being gained in operating two types of low-floor, easy-access buses. A Plaxton Pointer Dart SLF is illustrated on the rear cover of this edition while the other type, the Optare Excel, is illustrated by 273, P273NRH, seen in Hull bound for Boothferry Estate.** *Tony Wilson*

*Opposite, bottom:* **In 1995, the East Yorkshire trunk route between Hull, Beverley, Bridlington and Scarborough was upgraded and branded Classic Line. A batch of Volvo Olympians fitted with Alexander Royale bodies to a high specification were purchased for the service enhancement. Seen in Bridlington is 602, N602BRH, one of the type.** *Tony Wilson*

| 553 | F261RHJ | Leyland Olympian ONCL10/1RZ | Alexander RL | H45/30F | 1989 | Ex Southend, 1991 |
|---|---|---|---|---|---|---|

### 554-570

Leyland Olympian ON2R50G13Z4 Northern Counties Palatine  H47/29F  1991-92

| | | | | | | | | |
|---|---|---|---|---|---|---|---|---|
| 554 | H154BKH | 558 | H158BKH | 562 | J562HAT | 565 | J565HAT | 568 | J568HAT |
| 555 | H155BKH | 559 | H159BKH | 563 | J563HAT | 566 | J566HAT | 569 | J569HAT |
| 556 | H156BKH | 560 | H160BKH | 564 | J564HAT | 567 | J567HAT | 570 | J570HAT |
| 557 | H157BKH | 561 | J561HAT | | | | | | |

| 571 | A1EYD | DAF DB250WB505 | Optare Spectra | H44/27F | 1992 |
|---|---|---|---|---|---|

### 572-583

Leyland Olympian ON2R50G13Z4 Northern Counties Palatine  H47/29F*  1993   *572/3 are DPH43/25F

| | | | | | | | | |
|---|---|---|---|---|---|---|---|---|
| 572 | K572RRH | 575 | K575RRH | 578 | K578RRH | 580 | K580RRH | 582 | K582RRH |
| 573 | K573RRH | 576 | K576RRH | 579 | K579RRH | 581 | K581RRH | 583 | K583RRH |
| 574 | K574RRH | 577 | K577RRH | | | | | | |

### 584-589

Volvo Olympian YN2RV18Z4   Northern Counties Palatine II  H43/29F  1995

| | | | | | | | | |
|---|---|---|---|---|---|---|---|---|
| 584 | N584BRH | 586 | N586BRH | 587 | N587BRH | 588 | N588BRH | 589 | N589BRH |
| 585 | N585BRH | | | | | | | |

### 590-603

Volvo Olympian YN2RV18Z4   Alexander Royale   DPH45/29F  1995

| | | | | | | | | |
|---|---|---|---|---|---|---|---|---|
| 590 | N590BRH | 593 | N593BRH | 596 | N596BRH | 599 | N599BRH | 602 | N602BRH |
| 591 | N591BRH | 594 | N594BRH | 597 | N597BRH | 600 | A10EYD | 603 | N603BRH |
| 592 | N592BRH | 595 | N595BRH | 598 | N598BRH | 601 | N601BRH | | |

### 604-611

Volvo Olympian YN2RV18Z4   Northern Counties Palatine  H47/30F  1996

| | | | | | | | | |
|---|---|---|---|---|---|---|---|---|
| 604 | P604SAT | 606 | P606SAT | 608 | P608SAT | 610 | P610SAT | 611 | P611SAT |
| 605 | P605SAT | 607 | P607SAT | 609 | P609SAT | | | | |

| 636 | VDV136S | Bristol VRT/SL3/6LXB | Eastern Coach Works | CO43/31F | 1977 | Ex Devon General, 1992 |
|---|---|---|---|---|---|---|
| 637 | DRB307H | Bristol VRT/SL6G | Eastern Coach Works | O39/31F | 1969 | Ex Trent, 1991 |
| 638 | VDV138S | Bristol VRT/SL3/6LXB | Eastern Coach Works | O43/31F | 1978 | Ex Devon General, 1992 |
| 639 | VDV139S | Bristol VRT/SL3/6LXB | Eastern Coach Works | CO43/31F | 1978 | Ex Devon General, 1992 |
| 640 | VDV140S | Bristol VRT/SL3/6LXB | Eastern Coach Works | CO43/31F | 1978 | Ex Devon General, 1992 |
| 644 | VKH44 | AEC Regent V MD3RV | Willowbrook | H30/26RD | 1956 | Ex preservation, 1990 |
| 658 | CYC658A | Leyland Atlantean AN68/1R | Park Royal | O43/32F | 1972 | Ex Hardwicks, 1988 |
| 659 | WBN959L | Leyland Atlantean AN68/1R | Park Royal | O43/32F | 1972 | Ex Hardwicks, 1988 |
| 708 | PUF584R | Bristol VRT/SL3/6LXB | Eastern Coach Works | H43/31F | 1977 | Ex United, 1992 |
| 710 | PUF591R | Bristol VRT/SL3/6LXB | Eastern Coach Works | H43/31F | 1977 | Ex United, 1986 |
| 711 | PUF592R | Bristol VRT/SL3/6LXB | Eastern Coach Works | H43/31F | 1977 | Ex United, 1986 |
| 712 | PUF593R | Bristol VRT/SL3/6LXB | Eastern Coach Works | H43/31F | 1977 | Ex United, 1986 |
| 714 | XAK914T | Bristol VRT/SL3/501(6LXB) | Eastern Coach Works | H43/31F | 1979 | Ex Yorkshire Traction, 1993 |
| 716 | AUP716S | Bristol VRT/SL3/6LXB | Eastern Coach Works | H43/31F | 1978 | Ex United, 1986 |
| 717 | PKM117R | Bristol VRT/SL3/6LX | Eastern Coach Works | H43/31F | 1977 | Ex Stagecoach South, 1993 |
| 718 | BPT918S | Bristol VRT/SL3/6LX | Eastern Coach Works | H43/31F | 1978 | Ex United, 1986 |
| 721 | BPT921S | Bristol VRT/SL3/6LX | Eastern Coach Works | H43/31F | 1978 | Ex United, 1986 |
| 725 | BPT925S | Bristol VRT/SL3/6LX | Eastern Coach Works | H43/31F | 1978 | Ex United, 1986 |
| 729 | CPT729S | Bristol VRT/SL3/6LX | Eastern Coach Works | H43/31F | 1978 | Ex United, 1986 |
| 730 | WRC830S | Bristol VRT/SL3/501(6LXB) | Eastern Coach Works | H43/31F | 1978 | Ex Trent, 1993 |

### 732-764

Bristol VRT/SL3/6LXB   Eastern Coach Works  H43/31F  1978   Ex United, 1986

| | | | | | | | | |
|---|---|---|---|---|---|---|---|---|
| 732 | CPT732S | 741 | DUP741S | 750 | DUP750S | 754 | DUP754S | 764 | HUP764T |
| 733 | CPT733S | 748 | DUP748S | | | | | | |

| 765 | PPH461R | Bristol VRT/SL3/501(6LXB) | Eastern Coach Works | H43/31F | 1977 | Ex Western National, 1993 |
|---|---|---|---|---|---|---|
| 767 | PPH467R | Bristol VRT/SL3/501(6LXB) | Eastern Coach Works | H43/31F | 1977 | Ex Western National, 1993 |
| 775 | XAK903T | Bristol VRT/SL3/501(6LXB) | Eastern Coach Works | H43/31F | 1978 | Ex RoadCar, 1994 |
| 776 | XAK907T | Bristol VRT/SL3/501(6LXB) | Eastern Coach Works | H43/31F | 1978 | Ex RoadCar, 1994 |
| 777 | XAK910T | Bristol VRT/SL3/501(6LXB) | Eastern Coach Works | H43/31F | 1979 | Ex RoadCar, 1994 |
| 778 | KTL28V | Bristol VRT/SL3/6LXB | Eastern Coach Works | H43/31F | 1979 | Ex RoadCar, 1994 |
| 779 | KTL29V | Bristol VRT/SL3/6LXB | Eastern Coach Works | H43/31F | 1979 | Ex RoadCar, 1994 |
| 787 | LAK937W | Bristol VRT/SL3/6LXB | Eastern Coach Works | H43/31F | 1981 | Ex Yorkshire Traction, 1992 |
| 788 | LAK938W | Bristol VRT/SL3/6LXB | Eastern Coach Works | H43/31F | 1981 | Ex Yorkshire Traction, 1992 |
| 789 | MWG939X | Bristol VRT/SL3/6LXB | Eastern Coach Works | H43/31F | 1981 | Ex Yorkshire Traction, 1992 |
| 790 | RUA450W | Bristol VRT/SL3/6LXB | Eastern Coach Works | H43/31F | 1980 | Ex Yorkshire, 1994 |
| 791 | MWG941X | Bristol VRT/SL3/6LXB | Eastern Coach Works | H43/31F | 1981 | Ex Yorkshire Traction, 1992 |
| 792w | BRF692T | Bristol VRT/SL3/501 | Eastern Coach Works | H43/31F | 1978 | Ex PMT, 1992 |
| 793 | SGR793V | Bristol VRT/SL3/6LXB | Eastern Coach Works | H43/31F | 1980 | Ex United, 1986 |

**While the Routemaster operation in Hull has been discontinued, seven of this model have been retained by East Yorkshire. Some have been converted to open-top for services in Scarborough including 816, CUV210C which carries appropriate Scarborough and District fleeetnames. This vehicle came into the East Yorkshire fleet from Black Prince.** *David Longbottom*

| | | | | | | |
|---|---|---|---|---|---|---|
| 795 | HWJ930W | Bristol VRT/SL3/501(6LXB) | Eastern Coach Works | H43/31F | 1981 | Ex Yorkshire Traction, 1992 |
| 796 | HWJ931W | Bristol VRT/SL3/501(6LXB) | Eastern Coach Works | H43/31F | 1981 | Ex Yorkshire Traction, 1993 |
| 799 | JYG433V | Bristol VRT/SL3/6LXB | Eastern Coach Works | H43/31F | 1979 | Ex Yorkshire, 1994 |
| 801 | NRH801A | AEC Routemaster 2R2RH | Park Royal | H36/28R | 1961 | Ex London Buses, 1988 |
| 802 | NRH802A | AEC Routemaster 2R2RH | Park Royal | H36/28R | 1961 | Ex London Buses, 1988 |
| 808 | VLT188 | AEC Routemaster R2RH | Park Royal | H36/28R | 1960 | Ex Kingston-upon-Hull, 1989 |
| 812 | ALM65B | AEC Routemaster R2RH | Park Royal | O36/28R | 1964 | Ex RoadCar, 1989 |
| 816 | CUV210C | AEC Routemaster R2RH | Park Royal | O36/28R | 1965 | Ex Black Prince, Morley, 1992 |
| 817 | LDS239A | AEC Routemaster R2RH | Park Royal | H36/28R | 1961 | Ex Western Scottish, 1992 |
| 819 | EDS221A | AEC Routemaster R2RH | Park Royal | O36/28R | 1962 | Ex Blue Triangle, Rainham, 1994 |
| 821 | MEF821W | Bristol VRT/SL3/6LXB | Eastern Coach Works | H43/31F | 1981 | Ex United, 1986 |
| 871 | PRH244G | Leyland Atlantean PDR1A/1 | Roe | H44/31F | 1968 | Ex Connor & Graham, 1994 |
| 872 | PRH246G | Leyland Atlantean PDR1A/1 | Roe | H44/31F | 1968 | Ex Connor & Graham, 1993 |
| 878 | KSA186P | Leyland Atlantean AN68A/1R | Alexander AL | H45/29D | 1976 | Ex GM, Cefn Cribwr, 1992 |
| 882 | GAK482N | Bristol VRT/SL2/6G | Eastern Coach Works | H43/31F | 1974 | Ex Yorkshire Traction, 1990 |
| 884 | PHE814M | Bristol VRT/SL2/6G | Eastern Coach Works | H43/34F | 1974 | Ex Yorkshire Traction, 1990 |
| 889 | VFT189T | Leyland Atlantean AN68/2R | MCW | H49/37F | 1979 | Ex Thornton Dale, Pickering, 1992 |
| 902 | ANC918T | Leyland Atlantean AN68A/1R | Park Royal | H43/32F | 1978 | Ex GM Buses, 1992 |
| 917 | NJI1250 | Leyland Atlantean PDR1A/1R | Northern Counties (1984) | H43/31F | 1970 | Ex Cleveland Transit, 1990 |
| 918 | NJI1251 | Leyland Atlantean PDR1A/1R | Northern Counties (1984) | H43/31F | 1970 | Ex Cleveland Transit, 1990 |
| 919 | NJI1252 | Leyland Atlantean PDR1A/1R | Northern Counties (1986) | H43/34F | 1970 | Ex Cleveland Transit, 1990 |
| 920 | NJI1253 | Leyland Atlantean PDR1A/1R | Northern Counties (1985) | H43/31F | 1970 | Ex Cleveland Transit, 1990 |
| 921w | NJI1254 | Leyland Atlantean PDR1A/1R | Northern Counties (1984) | H43/31F | 1970 | Ex Cleveland Transit, 1990 |
| 931 | FBZ2931 | Leyland Atlantean PDR1A/1 | Northern Counties (1984) | H43/31F | 1970 | Ex Cleveland Transit, 1990 |
| 932 | FBZ2932 | Leyland Atlantean PDR1A/1 | Northern Counties (1984) | H43/31F | 1970 | Ex Cleveland Transit, 1990 |
| 933 | FBZ2933 | Leyland Atlantean PDR1A/1 | Northern Counties (1985) | H43/31F | 1970 | Ex Cleveland Transit, 1990 |
| 958 | PVO821R | Bristol VRT/SL3/501(6LXB) | Eastern Coach Works | H43/31F | 1977 | Ex Trent, 1991 |
| 960 | RAU810R | Bristol VRT/SL3/501(6LXB) | Eastern Coach Works | H43/31F | 1976 | Ex Trent, 1991 |

| 973 | UKH973R | Bristol VRT/SL3/501 | Eastern Coach Works | H43/31F | 1977 | |
| 975 | WAG975S | Bristol VRT/SL3/501 | Eastern Coach Works | H43/31F | 1977 | |
| 979w | RTH928S | Bristol VRT/SL3/501 | Eastern Coach Works | H43/31F | 1978 | Ex The Bee Line, 1992 |
| 985 | EKH985T | Bristol VRT/SL3/501 | Eastern Coach Works | H43/31F | 1979 | |
| 987 | EKH987T | Bristol VRT/SL3/501 | Eastern Coach Works | H43/31F | 1979 | |
| 990 | EKH990T | Bristol VRT/SL3/501 | Eastern Coach Works | H43/31F | 1979 | |
| 995 | WTU487W | Bristol VRT/SL3/501(6LXB) | Eastern Coach Works | H43/31F | 1981 | Ex PMT, 1992 |
| 996 | GRF696V | Bristol VRT/SL3/501 | Eastern Coach Works | H43/31F | 1979 | Ex PMT, 1992 |
| 997 | PPH462R | Bristol VRT/SL3/501(6LXB) | Eastern Coach Works | H43/31F | 1977 | Ex Badgerline, 1992 |
| 998 | PPH464R | Bristol VRT/SL3/501(6LXB) | Eastern Coach Works | H43/31F | 1977 | Ex Badgerline, 1992 |
| 999 | PPH470R | Bristol VRT/SL3/501(6LXB) | Eastern Coach Works | H43/31F | 1977 | Ex Badgerline, 1992 |
| 1707 | YNA297M | Daimler Fleetline CRG6LXB | Northern Counties | H434/32F | 1973 | Ex Finglands,1996 |

**Operating Companies:**

| National Holidays: | 11/4, 45-50, 65/6/9, 74/5/7-80, 82-6/8/9, 91-98, 104-44/9-53, 355. |
| East Yorkshire: | Remainder. |

**Previous Registrations:**

| | | | |
|---|---|---|---|
| 152FRH | E52URH | IIL2156 | BRH180T |
| 165DKH | A106MKH | IIL2157 | AYR326T |
| 1918KH | NPD124L | IIL2158 | EAT185T |
| 202YTE | From new | IIL2159 | EAT186T |
| 271CLT | C178BFE, 2732RH | IIL2160 | EAT187T |
| 32CHY | BAJ639Y,9975VT,DFP495Y | IIL7075 | F711ENE |
| 3277KH | G214RKH | IIL7076 | F712ENE |
| 334EYL | E51URH | IIL7077 | F713ENE |
| 39EYD | E365NEG | J631WWK | J31SDU, 84COV |
| 421CKH | A521EVN | JSV486 | G837VAY |
| 46EYB | E366NEG | KSU381 | SS7376, 1949MN |
| 491JVX | F716ENE | KSU454 | B104DVK |
| 508DKH | G56SAG | KSU455 | F715ENE |
| 515VTB | From new | KSU456 | B103DVK |
| 546EYB | E53URH | KSU457 | From new |
| 552UTE | F717ENE | KSU459 | C109PLU |
| 583TD | H170DVL | KSU460 | IJVK, F900JRG |
| 665EYL | F705ENE | KSU465 | J462HDS, LSK502, J691LGA |
| 6627VF | E398MVV | L543YUS | XIA257, KSK954 |
| 741DYE | A605UGD | LDS239A | WLT727 |
| 787EYC | F782GNA | MIJ999 | EGV367Y |
| 794EYD | B111WAT | NJI1250 | SDC138H |
| 80EYC | B932MLN | NJI1251 | SXG50H |
| 813VPU | J423HDS | NJI1252 | SXG52H |
| 8225KH | B88WRJ, HIL774, B76XBU | NJI1253 | SDC144H |
| 834EYD | B930MLN, B931MLN | NJI1254 | SDC145H |
| 865EYT | F59GCW | NJI1255 | BGR4S, 334EYL, BAG96S |
| 926BWV | E880HFW, PS2045, E511RFU | NRH801A | WLT732 |
| 95EYM | B902SPR | NRH802A | WLT798 |
| A10EYD | N660BRH | NRH803A | WLT871 |
| A573SRH | A105MKH, 95EYM | NRH805A | 41CLT |
| B111WAT | B107LPH | NVS804 | WLT982 |
| CIB3202 | A402HRJ | NVS855 | WLT757 |
| CYC656A | VNB108L | OAT822V | NAT200V |
| DDZ236 | PNW336W | OIW1317 | F853JVR |
| DV7980 | From new | OIW1318 | F33HGG |
| EDS221A | 10CLT | OTK802 | A32KBA |
| EGV267Y | HHC365Y, RPN11 | OXK373 | A33KBA |
| EYD1T | D32OKH | PJI8916 | E578UHS |
| F349JAT | F772GNA, IIL7073 | PXI7915 | E574UHS |
| FAZ2781 | UTN954Y | SDZ9026 | G174RBD |
| FBZ2931 | SXG48H | SIB2014 | C106AFX |
| FBZ2932 | SXG49H | TPX884 | B371VBA |
| FBZ2933 | SDC143H | TXY978 | OHE278X, 6253VC, CRH182X |
| GRH2Y | GRH528Y | VKH44 | From new |
| GRH3Y | A529MAT | VLT188 | From new |
| HIL8426 | D274YCX, 5516PP, D397EDX | WLT694 | A403HRJ |
| HIL8427 | E666KCX | YOI7898 | VAB829R |
| IIL2155 | BRH179T | YUU556 | B931MLN, B930MNL |

**Named   Vehicles:** 22 *Ryedale Star;* 188 *Mrs Marjorie Graham.*

**Liveries:** Crimson and cream; light grey orange and blue (National Holidays); red, cream and blue (Connor and Graham); National Express (57/9-62/4/7/8 70-3).

The batch of Leyland Atlanteans that had been re-bodied by Cleveland Transit in 1984-86 are now in their seventh year of service with East Yorkshire and seem destined for a long term role in view of their repaint into the latest livery. One of these vehicles, 918, NJI1251 carries a 1984 Northern Counties body on a 1970 Leyland Atlantean chassis. *Lee Whitehead*

The Bristol VR is now being disposed of in large numbers by East Yorkshire, with the Leyland engined ones being preferred for early withdrawal. Of those that remain, 958, PVO821R is a former Trent vehicle which was converted to Gardner power some years ago and therefore continues in service. *David Longbottom*

# EDDIE BROWN

Eddie Brown Tours Ltd, Coach Garage, Brafferton, Helperby, North Yorkshire, YO6 2NY

**Depots:** Helperby and Kinoulton Road, Cropwell Bishop, Nottinghamshire.

| | | | | | |
|---|---|---|---|---|---|
| LDW362P | Leyland National 10351/1R | | B41F | 1976 | Ex Constable, Long Melford, 1996 |
| WGY594S | Leyland National 11351A/1R | | B49F | 1976 | Ex Constable, Long Melford, 1996 |
| KAZ7305 | Volvo B58-61 | Plaxton Supreme IV | C53F | 1979 | Ex Kirkham, Doncaster, 1996 |
| ODJ579W | Volvo B58-61 | Duple Dominant IV | C53F | 1981 | Ex Bradshaw, Alkrington, 1995 |
| B165XVU | Leyland Cub CU435 | Wadham Stringer Vanguard | B32F | 1985 | Ex LB Southwark, 1995 |
| WIJ551 | Volvo B10M-61 | Van Hool Alizée | C53F | 1987 | Ex Park's, Hamilton, 1992 |
| NJI5510 | Volvo B10M-61 | Van Hool Alizée | C50FT | 1987 | |
| MIB658 | Volvo B10M-61 | Van Hool Alizée | C53F | 1988 | Ex Park's, Hamilton, 1994 |
| JBZ551 | Volvo B10M-61 | Van Hool Alizée | C49FT | 1988 | Ex Clarke's of London, 1997 |
| UXI551 | Volvo B10M-61 | Van Hool Alizée | C49FT | 1988 | Ex Clarke's of London, 1997 |
| 551ALW | Volvo B10M-60 | Van Hool Alizée | C49FT | 1989 | |
| G840VAY | Dennis Javelin 8.5SDL1903 | Duple 320 | C34F | 1989 | Ex Selwyn's, Runcorn, 1994 |
| G580TVR | Leyland-DAF 200 | Leyland-DAF | M12 | 1990 | Ex Bradshaw, Alkrington, 1995 |
| H551SWY | Scania K113CRB | Van Hool Alizée | C51FT | 1991 | |
| J551BWW | Scania K113CRB | Van Hool Alizée | C52FT | 1992 | |
| J635MCU | Toyota Coaster HDB30R | Caetano Optimo II | C21F | 1992 | Ex Gardiner, Lower Prudhoe, 1997 |
| J869JNS | Volvo B10M-60 | Van Hool Alizée | C52FT | 1992 | Ex Clyde Coast, Ardrossan, 1993 |
| L915NWW | Volvo B10M-60 | Van Hool Alizée | C48FT | 1994 | Ex Wallace Arnold, 1997 |
| L551OUM | Scania K113CRB | Van Hool Alizée | C48FT | 1994 | |
| M51WWT | Volvo B10M-62 | Plaxton Premiére 350 | C53F | 1995 | |
| M551WWT | Volvo B10M-62 | Plaxton Premiére 350 | C53F | 1995 | |
| N51FWX | Volvo B10M-62 | Plaxton Premiére 350 | C53F | 1996 | |
| N551FWX | Volvo B10M-62 | Plaxton Premiére 350 | C53F | 1996 | |

**Previous Registrations:**

| | | | |
|---|---|---|---|
| 551ALW | F51BWY | NJI5510 | D51LWW |
| JBZ551 | E310UPR | UXI551 | E311UPR |
| KAZ7305 | GHS8T, SSV799 | WIJ551 | D609MVR |
| MIB658 | E628UNE, LSK807 | | |

**Livery:** White, brown, red and orange

**Eddie Brown have recently set up an operation in the Nottinghamshire village of Cropwell Bishop and have secured some school contract work for the vehicles based there. Operating out of the main base at Helperby is J869JNS, a Van Hool-bodied Volvo B10M. it is seen passing under the York city walls.**
*Les Peters*

# FAIRWAY RHODES

B L Barnett, 308 Wincolmlee, City of Kingston-upon-Hull, HU2 0QE

| | | | | | |
|---|---|---|---|---|---|
| TMU846Y | Leyland Leopard PSU3E/4R | Duple Dominant IV(1983) | C53F | 1972 | Ex Capitol, Cwmbran, 1992 |
| GUG539N | Leyland Atlantean AN68/1R | Roe | H43/33F | 1974 | Ex Yorkshire Rider, 1994 |
| GUG558N | Leyland Atlantean AN68/1R | Roe | H43/33F | 1975 | Ex Yorkshire Rider, 1994 |
| GUG561N | Leyland Atlantean AN68/1R | Roe | H43/33F | 1975 | Ex Yorkshire Rider, 1996 |
| HWT28N | Leyland Atlantean AN68/1R | Roe | H43/33F | 1975 | Ex Yorkshire Rider, 1994 |
| LUG84P | Leyland Atlantean AN68/1R | Roe | H43/33F | 1975 | Ex Yorkshire Rider, 1997 |
| LUG99P | Leyland Atlantean AN68/1R | Roe | H43/33F | 1975 | Ex Yorkshire Rider, 1994 |
| SFV434P | Leyland Atlantean AN68/1R | Eastern Coach Works | H43/31F | 1976 | Ex Glossopdale, 1994 |
| SUA136R | Leyland Atlantean AN68/1R | Roe | H43/33F | 1977 | Ex Yorkshire Rider, 1994 |
| WNW151S | Leyland Atlantean AN68/1R | Roe | H43/33F | 1977 | Ex Yorkshire Rider, 1994 |
| ARB131T | Leyland Leopard PSU3E/4R | Plaxton Supreme III Express | C49F | 1978 | Ex Trent (Barton), 1996 |
| BRC137T | Leyland Leopard PSU3E/4R | Plaxton Supreme III Express | C49F | 1979 | Ex Trent (Barton), 1996 |
| PDN236T | Ford R1114 | Duple Dominant II | C53F | 1979 | Ex Barnett & Lord, Bilton, 1992 |
| JDG283V | Leyland Leopard PSU5C/4R | Duple Dominant II | C50F | 1980 | Ex Greenslades, Exeter, 1992 |
| VSM783V | Leyland Leopard PSU3E/4R | Duple Dominant II | C53F | 1980 | Ex City Traveller, Hull, 1997 |
| RNG824W | Leyland Leopard PSU3F/4R | Duple Dominant IV | C53F | 1981 | Ex City Traveller, Hull, 1997 |
| EIL3018 | Leyland Tiger TRCTL11/3R | Plaxton Paramount 3500 | C46FT | 1983 | Ex Thomas, Wokingham, 1992 |
| 1918KH | Leyland Tiger TRCTL11/3RZ | Duple Caribbean | C48FT | 1985 | Ex East Yorkshire Travel, 1996 |
| E778TPW | Mercedes-Benz L307D | Mercedes-Benz | M12 | 1988 | Ex Skoda GB, Kings Lynn, 1993 |

**Livery:** Cream and red

**Previous Registrations:**

| | | | | | |
|---|---|---|---|---|---|
| 1918KH | B137ACK | EIL3018 | A512HVT | TMU846Y | JRK618K |

**Named vehicles:**
GUG539N *Tanya Grace*; GUG561N *Amy Charlotte*; HWT28N *Emma Caroline*; LUG99P *Benjamin*; SFV434P *Chantelle*; SUA136R *Lesley Marie*; WNW151S *Sapphire Marie*; LUG84P *Suzanne Margarete*; GUG558N *Peggy*

**Fairway Rhodes uses the fleetname Fairway Rider on the double deck vehicles in the fleet. Former Yorkshire Rider Atlanteans are preferred as typified by GUG539N, a Roe-bodied example which carries the name Tanya Grace.** *David Longbottom.*

# FRODINGHAM COACHES

Frodingham Coaches Ltd, 52 Main Street, North Frodingham, YO25 8LG

**Depot** : Kelleythorpe Industrial Estate, Driffield

| 26 | TJI4026 | Van Hool T815 | Van Hool Acron | C53FT | 1986 | Ex Wide Horizon, Burbage, 1996 |
|---|---|---|---|---|---|---|
| 36 | E36VKP | Iveco Daily 49.10 | Dormobile Routemaker | B25F | 1987 | Ex Dalybus, Eccles, 1995 |
| 174 | P174NAK | Mercedes-Benz 711D | Plaxton Beaver | B27F | 1997 | |
| 399 | P399MDT | Mercedes-Benz 814D | Plaxton Beaver | C32F | 1997 | |
| 567 | D567MVR | Volvo B10M-61 | Plaxton Paramount 3200 III | C53F | 1987 | Ex Longstaff, Mirfield, 1994 |
| 698 | DSV698 | Volvo B10M-61 | Berkhof Esprite 350 | C53F | 1985 | Ex Wallace Arnold, 1991 |
| 702 | F702PAY | Mercedes-Benz O303-15R | Mercedes-Benz | C53F | 1989 | Ex Redwing, London, 1997 |
| 703 | H703YUV | Iveco Daily 49.10 | Reeve Burgess Beaver | B20FL | 1990 | Ex London United, 1997 |
| 705 | F705PAY | Mercedes-Benz O303-15R | Mercedes-Benz | C53F | 1989 | Ex Redwing, London, 1997 |
| 706 | H706YUV | Iveco Daily 49.10 | Reeve Burgess Beaver | B20FL | 1990 | Ex London United, 1997 |

**Previous Registrations:**

| TJI4026 | C907YUE | DSV698 | ? |
|---|---|---|---|

**Livery**: Silver and white

*Opposite:* **Frodingham Coaches purchased a new Mercedes-Benz 711D minibus for local service work in 1997. A Plaxton Beaver body is carried by this latest addition to the fleet. This view of P174NAK shows the bus in service carrying the Frodingham white and silver colours.** *David Longbottom*

# GLENN COACHES

J Wreglesworth, 58 The Village, Wiggington, York, YO3 8PS

**Depot** : Cleveland Industrial Estate, Sutton-on-the-Forest

| UWW772R | Leyland Leopard PSU3E/4R | Plaxton Supreme III | C49F | 1977 | Ex Ingleby's, York, 1994 |
|---|---|---|---|---|---|
| XPC15S | Leyland National 10351A/1R | | B41F | 1978 | Ex Sovereign, 1995 |
| WUH172T | Leyland National 11351A/1R | | B49F | 1978 | Ex PMT, 1995 |
| BPL488T | Leyland National 10351B/1R | | B41F | 1979 | Ex City Bus Lines, Birmingham, 1995 |
| BPL496T | Leyland National 10351B/1R | | B41F | 1979 | Ex Sovereign, 1995 |
| DPH499T | Leyland National 10351B/1R | | B41F | 1979 | Ex City Bus Lines, Birmingham, 1995 |
| SKF6T | Leyland National 11351A/1R | | B49F | 1979 | Ex MTL, Manchester, 1995 |
| GWY970T | Leyland Leopard PSU3E/4R | Duple Dominant II | C53F | 1979 | Ex Ford, Ackworth, 1986 |
| TFG154 | Volvo B58-56 | Duple Dominant II | C53F | 1980 | Ex Irvine, Law, 1992 |
| FPR64V | Leyland National 11351A/1R | | B49F | 1980 | Ex Solent Blueline, 1996 |
| GGM74W | Leyland Leopard PSU3F/4R | Plaxton Supreme IV Express | C49F | 1981 | Ex Ladyline, Rawmarsh, 1993 |
| PNW333W | Leyland Leopard PSU3F/4R | Plaxton Supreme IV Express | C53F | 1981 | Ex Scarborough & District, 1993 |
| RPE556X | Leyland Tiger TRCTL11/3R | Plaxton Supreme IV | C53F | 1981 | Ex Frost & Heath, Leigh-on-Sea, 1990 |
| YKR702 | Volvo B10M-61 | Plaxton Paramount 3500 | C49FT | 1984 | Ex Wallace Arnold, 1990 |
| LIL9412 | Leyland Tiger TRCTL11/3R | Plaxton Paramount 3500 | C53F | 1984 | Ex Yorkshire Traction, 1996 |
| LIL.... | Leyland Tiger TRCTL11/3R | Plaxton Paramount 3500 | C53F | 1984 | Ex Yorkshire Traction, 1996 |

**Previous Registrations:**

| LIL9412 | A712SKH, YTC858, A259BHL | TFG154 | FWJ820V |
|---|---|---|---|
| LIL... | A713SKH, PHE692, A258BHL | YKR702 | From new |

**Livery:** Red, cream and yellow

*Opposite:* **Glenn Coaches operate the service from the village of Wiggington, where the vehicles are based, to York. WUH172T, a Leyland National, is seen arriving in York and was originally part of the National Welsh fleet. York Minster is visible in the distance.** *Tony Wilson*

# GODSONS

J M Godson, 3 Sandbed Lane, Crossgates, Leeds, West Yorkshire, LS15 8JH

**Depot** : Lowfields Road, Elland Road, Leeds.

| | | | | |
|---|---|---|---|---|
| K136KUM | Volvo B10M-60 | Plaxton Première 350 | C53F | 1993 |
| M391UWT | Dennis Javelin 12SDA2131 | Plaxton Première 320 | C53F | 1994 |
| M955HRY | Volvo B6-9.5m | Caetano Algarve II | C34F | 1994 |
| M230VHE | Bova FHD12.340 | Bova Futura | C55F | 1995 |
| M636RCP | DAF MB230LT615 | Van Hool Alizée | C51FT | 1989 |
| M763RCP | DAF DE02LTSB220 | Ikarus CitiBus | B41F | 1995 |
| M764RCP | DAF DE02LTSB220 | Ikarus CitiBus | B41F | 1995 |
| N37EUG | Bova FLD12.270 | Bova Futura Club | C53F | 1995 |
| N935EUG | Volvo B10M-62 | Plaxton Première 320 | C53F | 1996 |
| N972EUG | Bova FHD12.340 | Bova Futura Club | C53F | 1996 |
| N973EUG | Volvo B10M-62 | Van Hool Alizée | C51FT | 1996 |
| N128DDT | Volvo B10M-62 | Plaxton Première 350 | C53F | 1996 |
| N73FWU | DAF DE33WSSB3000 | Plaxton Première 350 | C53F | 1996 |
| N786ORY | Volvo B10M-62 | Caetano Algarve II | C53F | 1996 |
| N796ORY | Volvo B10M-62 | Caetano Algarve II | C53F | 1996 |
| N987FWT | DAF DE33WSSB3000 | Ikarus Blue Danube | C55F | 1996 |
| P183NAK | Volvo B10M-62 | Plaxton Première 350 | C49FT | 1997 |
| P184NAK | Volvo B10M-62 | Plaxton Première 350 | C53F | 1997 |
| P185NAK | Volvo B10M-62 | Plaxton Première 350 | C53F | 1997 |
| P201RWR | DAF DE33WSSB3000 | Plaxton Première 350 | C53F | 1997 |
| P202RWR | DAF DE33WSSB3000 | Van Hool Alizée | C55F | 1997 |
| P203RWR | DAF DE33WSSB3000 | Van Hool Alizée | C51FT | 1997 |

**Livery:** White (Buses), white, red and gold (coaches)

**Godsons operate a modern fleet of coaches but have entered the bus market by securing the tender to operate a service to Leeds/Bradford Airport. DAF powered coaches feature markedly in the fleet, and this has led to the purchase of Ikarus-bodied DAF buses for the route. Seen at the Corn Exchange in Leeds is M764RCP.** *Tony Wilson*

# GORDONS

D J & R Gordon, Chesterton Road, Eastwood Trading Estate, Rotherham,
South Yorkshire, S65 1SU
Billies Coaches Ltd, 100 Doncaster Road, Mexborough South Yorkshire, S64 0JS
Ronald Hague (Coaches) Ltd, 313 Coleford Road, Darnall, Sheffield
South Yorkshire, S9 5NF

| | | | | | | |
|---|---|---|---|---|---|---|
| | JLS456V | Volvo B58-61 | Plaxton Supreme IV | C57F | 1980 | Ex Rennie, Dunfermline, 1981 |
| H | SFD255W | Leyland Leopard PSU5C/4R | Plaxton Supreme IV | C57F | 1981 | Ex Hague, Sheffield, 1996 |
| | HAS716X | Volvo B58-56 | Plaxton Supreme V | C46FT | 1981 | Ex Skill, Nottingham, 1988 |
| | NDW139X | Leyland Tiger TRCTL11/3R | Plaxton Supreme V Express | C53F | 1982 | Ex Butler Bros, Kirkby-in-Ashfield, 1992 |
| | VET721Y | Leyland Tiger TRCTL11/3R | Plaxton Paramount 3200 | C51F | 1983 | Ex Hague, Sheffield, 1985 |
| | FIL7486 | Volvo B10M-61 | Plaxton Paramount 3500 | C53FT | 1984 | |
| | A445YWG | Volvo B10M-61 | Plaxton Paramount 3200 | C57FT | 1984 | |
| | B910UPW | Leyland Tiger TRCTL11/3R | Plaxton Paramount 3200 | C53F | 1985 | Ex Ambassador, 1992 |
| | FIL7485 | Volvo B10M-61 | Van Hool Alizée | C49FT | 1987 | Ex Premier Travel, 1989 |
| | E316UUB | Volvo B10M-61 | Plaxton Paramount 3500 III | C48FT | 1988 | Ex Wallace Arnold, 1991 |
| B | E770HJF | Volvo B10M-61 | Plaxton Paramount 3200 III | C57F | 1988 | |
| H | E996NMK | Leyland Tiger TRCTL11/3ARZ | Plaxton Paramount 3200 III | C57F | 1988 | Ex Smith, Pylle, 1996 |
| | E170OMD | Volvo B10M-61 | Plaxton Paramount 3200 III | C57F | 1988 | Ex Longmynd, Pontesbury, 1997 |
| | F370MUT | Dennis Javelin 12SDA1906 | Plaxton Paramount 3200 III | C53F | 1988 | Ex Patterson, Birmingham, 1994 |
| H | F462YOK | Dennis Javelin 11SDA1906 | Plaxton Paramount 3200 III | C53F | 1988 | Ex Hague, Sheffield, 1996 |
| | F743LOD | Dennis Javelin 8.5SDL1903 | Plaxton Paramount 3200 III | C53F | 1989 | Ex Seward, Dalwood, 1992 |
| | G513EFX | Volvo B10M-60 | Plaxton Paramount 3200 III | C57F | 1990 | Ex Excelsior, Bournouth, 1991 |
| | G344OWE | Volvo B10M-60 | Plaxton Paramount 3200 III | C55DL | 1990 | |
| | G303RJA | Dennis Javelin 12SDA1907 | Plaxton Paramount 3200 III | C53F | 1990 | Ex Star Line, Knutsford, 1994 |
| | H660AST | Dennis Javelin 11SDL1905 | Plaxton Paramount 3200 III | C53F | 1991 | Ex Mayne, Buckie, 1993 |
| B | H157HAC | Dennis Javelin 8.5SDA1926 | Plaxton Paramount 3200 III | C35F | 1991 | Ex Supreme, Coventry, 1994 |
| | H688UAK | Dennis Javelin 8.5SDA1926 | Plaxton Paramount 3200 III | C33FT | 1991 | |
| | H689UAK | Volvo B10M-60 | Plaxton Paramount 3200 III | C55DL | 1991 | |
| | J1EXC | Volvo B10M-60 | Plaxton Excalibur | C49FT | 1992 | Ex Anderson, Horsforth, 1993 |
| H | K390PJU | Dennis Javelin 12SDA2117 | Plaxton Première 320 | C53F | 1988 | Ex Hague, Sheffield, 1996 |
| | M113XWB | Volvo B10M-62 | Plaxton Première 320 | C55FL | 1995 | |
| | P407MDT | Volvo B10M-62 | Plaxton Première 350 | C49FT | 1997 | |
| | P408MDT | Volvo B10M-62 | Plaxton Première 320 | C57F | 1997 | |
| | P409MDT | Dennis Javelin | Plaxton Première 320 | C45F | 1997 | |

Previous Registrations:
| | | | |
|---|---|---|---|
| E996NMK | E996NMK, 217NYA | FIL7486 | A910XHE |
| FIL7485 | D849KVE | HAS716X | WJS840X, 3692NT |

Livery:   Red and cream (Gordons & Hague), White and black (Billies) - Operations:   Billes, B; Hague, H; Gordons - rest

Gordon's of
Rotherham
comprises a group
of companies,
having added
Hagues of Sheffield
to the business
which incorporated
Billie's of
Mexborough some
time ago. One of the
latest arrivals in the
fleet is Volvo B10
P408MDT, one of a
pair delivered in
1997 with Plaxton
Première 320
bodywork.

# HALIFAX JOINT COMMITTEE

A R Blackman, 1 Vicar Park Road, Norton Tower, Halifax, HX2 0NL

**Depot** : Thrum Hall Industrial Park, Halifax.

| | | | | | | |
|---|---|---|---|---|---|---|
| BCP671 | AEC Regent III | Park Royal | H33/26R | 1950 | Ex preservation, 1995 |
| WLT324 | AEC Routemaster 5RM | Park Royal | H36/28R | 1960 | Ex London Buses, 1997 |
| 104CLT | AEC Routemaster 5RM | Park Royal | H36/28R | 1962 | Ex London Central, 1997 |

**Previous Registrations:**

| | | | | | |
|---|---|---|---|---|---|
| 104CLT | From new | BCP671 | From new | WLT324 | From new |

**Livery:** Orange, green and cream


# HARROGATE & DISTRICT

Harrogate & District Travel Ltd, Petroleum House, Camwall Road, Starbeck, Harrogate,
North Yorkshire HG1 4PT

A subsidiary of Blazefield Holdings Ltd.

**Depots:** Dairycrest Yard, Camwal Road, Starbeck; Manse Lane, Knaresborough and Nidderdale High School, Pateley Bridge.

| | | | | | | |
|---|---|---|---|---|---|---|
| 172 | F172SMT | Leyland Swift LBM6T/2RA | Wadham Stringer Vanguard II | B39F | 1988 | Ex County, 1992 |
| 173 | F173SMT | Leyland Swift LBM6T/2RA | Wadham Stringer Vanguard II | B39F | 1988 | Ex County, 1992 |
| 204 | G111VMM | Leyland Swift LBM6T/2RA | Wadham Stringer Vanguard II | B37F | 1989 | Ex Harrogate Independent, 1993 |
| 205 | G112VMM | Leyland Swift LBM6T/2RA | Wadham Stringer Vanguard II | B37F | 1989 | Ex Yorkshire Coastliner, 1996 |
| 206 | G113VMM | Leyland Swift LBM6T/2RA | Wadham Stringer Vanguard II | B37F | 1989 | Ex Harrogate Independent, 1993 |
| 207 | G114VMM | Leyland Swift LBM6T/2RA | Wadham Stringer Vanguard II | B37F | 1989 | Ex Harrogate Independent, 1993 |
| 219 | G914UPP | Mercedes-Benz 709D | Reeve Burgess Beaver | B23F | 1989 | Ex Sovereign, 1996 |
| 220 | G912UPP | Mercedes-Benz 709D | Reeve Burgess Beaver | B23F | 1989 | Ex Sovereign, 1996 |
| 221 | G913UPP | Mercedes-Benz 709D | Reeve Burgess Beaver | B23F | 1989 | Ex Sovereign, 1996 |
| 222 | G922WGS | Mercedes-Benz 709D | Reeve Burgess Beaver | B23F | 1990 | Ex Welwyn-Hatfield Line, 1993 |
| 223 | G923WGS | Mercedes-Benz 709D | Reeve Burgess Beaver | B23F | 1990 | Ex Welwyn-Hatfield Line, 1993 |
| 234 | G434MWU | Leyland Tiger TRCL10/3ARZA | Plaxton Paramount 3200 III | C55F | 1990 | Ex Yorkshire Coastliner, 1996 |
| 244 | JIL2215 | Leyland Tiger TRCTL11/3R | Plaxton Paramount 3200 E | C49F | 1983 | Ex Keighley & District, 1996 |
| 307 | JIL2216 | Leyland Tiger TRCTL11/3RH | Plaxton Paramount 3200 E | C53F | 1983 | Ex Keighley & District, 1996 |
| 314 | B514UWW | Leyland Olympian ONLXB/1R | Eastern Coach Works | DPH41/29F | 1985 | Ex Keighley & District, 1993 |
| 316 | B516UWW | Leyland Olympian ONLXB/1R | Eastern Coach Works | H45/32F | 1985 | Ex York City & District, 1990 |
| 324 | E324SWY | Leyland Lynx LX112LXCTZR1R | Leyland Lynx | B49F | 1987 | Ex Keighley & District, 1996 |
| 325 | E325SWY | Leyland Lynx LX112LXCTZR1R | Leyland Lynx | B49F | 1987 | Ex Keighley & District, 1996 |

| | | | | | |
|---|---|---|---|---|---|
| *361-365* | | Volvo B10B-58 | Alexander Strider | DP49F | 1995 |

| | | | | | | | | | |
|---|---|---|---|---|---|---|---|---|---|
| **361** | M388VWX | **362** | M389VWX | **363** | M391VWX | **364** | M392VWX | **365** | M393VWX |

| | | | | | |
|---|---|---|---|---|---|
| 366 | P366UUG | Volvo B10B-58 | Wright Endurance | DP49F | 1996 |
| 367 | P367UUG | Volvo B10B-58 | Wright Endurance | DP49F | 1996 |
| 368 | P368UUG | Volvo B10B-58 | Wright Endurance | DP49F | 1996 |

**42**

Tony Blackman is a long standing preservationist. He now operates a *Heritage Trail* service in the Calderdale area with his 1950 AEC Regent III. This former Halifax vehicle is restored to its original owner's livery and the operators licence held by the proprietor appropriately indicates that the service was run by the Halifax Joint Committee. BCP671 carries Halifax fleet number, 277. *David Longbottom*

Harrogate & District acquired the business of Harrogate Independent in 1993 together with a number of Leyland Swift midibuses. All carry Wadham Stringer Vanguard bodies as can be seen in this view of 207, G114VMM. *Lee Whitehead*

The Blazefield group have favoured Volvo/Wright combinations for recent purchases. The first low floor midibuses in the Harrogate and District fleet are therefore Wright Crusader Volvo B6LEs. Carrying 642, P642UUG, is one of the batch and is seen in Harrogate. *Graham Crawshaw*

| 381 | G381MWU | Leyland Lynx LX112L10ZR1R | Leyland Lynx | DP47F | 1990 | |
| 382 | G382MWU | Leyland Lynx LX112L10ZR1R | Leyland Lynx | DP47F | 1990 | |
| 383 | G383MWU | Leyland Lynx LX112L10ZR1R | Leyland Lynx | DP47F | 1990 | |
| 392 | C481YWY | Leyland Olympian ONLXB/1R | Eastern Coach Works | DPH42/29F | 1985 | Ex Yorkshire Coastliner, 1994 |

### 394-398

| | | Leyland Olympian ON2R50G13Z4 | Northern Counties Palatine | H43/30F | 1990 | Ex Keighley & District, 1996 |

| 394 | H514RWX | 395 | H515RWX | 396 | H516RWX | 397 | H517RWX | 398 | H12SDW |
|-----|---------|-----|---------|-----|---------|-----|---------|-----|--------|

| 641 | P641UUG | Volvo B6LE | | Wright Crusader | DP38F | 1997 | |
| 642 | P642UUG | Volvo B6LE | | Wright Crusader | DP38F | 1997 | |
| 643 | P643UUG | Volvo B6LE | | Wright Crusader | DP38F | 1997 | |
| 644 | M876NWK | Volvo B6-9.9M | | Alexander Dash | DP40F | 1995 | Ex Volvo demonstrator, 1996 |

### 645-654

| | | Volvo B6-9.9M | | Alexander Dash | B40F | 1994 | |

| 645 | L645OWY | 647 | L647OWY | 649 | L649OWY | 651 | L651OWY | 653 | L653OWY |
|-----|---------|-----|---------|-----|---------|-----|---------|-----|---------|
| 646 | L646OWY | 648 | L648OWY | 650 | L650OWY | 652 | L652OWY | 654 | L654OWY |

| 664 | M384VWX | Volvo B6-9.9M | Alexander Dash | B40F | 1995 |
| 665 | M385VWX | Volvo B6-9.9M | Alexander Dash | B40F | 1995 |
| 781 | M386VWX | Volvo B6-9.9M | Alexander Dash | B40F | 1995 |
| 782 | M387VWX | Volvo B6-9.9M | Alexander Dash | B40F | 1995 |

**Previous Registrations:**
H12SDW       H281SWW

**Livery:** Red, cream and black

*Opposite, top:* **Harrogate & District have vehicles branded for service 36 running between Ripon, Harrogate and Leeds. Seen at Ripon bus station, the outer terminus of the route, is 363, M391VWX. This is a Volvo B10B carrying the Alexander Strider type of body which is to be replaced in production by the new ALX series introduced by Alexanders owners, Mayflower.** *Tony Wilson*
*Opposite, bottom:* **The Harrogate & District double deck fleet is totally Olympian. 394, H514RWX was built by Leyland and carries a Northern Counties Palatine body. It was previously No 332 in the fleet of Keighley & District, a fellow member of the Blazefield Holdings group. This view was taken in Harrogate.** *Richard Godfrey*

# HUDDERSFIELD TOWN BUS

D Haigh & A Williams, 10 Slaithwaite Road, Meltham, Huddersfield, HD7 3NY

**Depots** : Savile Street, Milnsbridge; Meltham Mills Industrial Estate, Meltham ; Peel Street, Marsden

| *1-7* | | Seddon Pennine 7 | | Alexander AYS | | B53F*<br>*4-7 are DP49F | 1979 | Ex Western, 1996 | |
|---|---|---|---|---|---|---|---|---|---|
| 1 | ASD826T | 3 | ASD837T | 5 | BSD862T | 6 | BSD863T | 7 | BSD864T |
| 2 | ASD834T | 4 | BSD860T | | | | | | |

**Livery:** Red, black and cream

*Opposite:* **Huddersfield Town Bus provide service 324 in Huddersfield. Only Seddon Pennine 7 buses formerly operated by Western are presently operated. All carry Alexander AYS-type bodies with four of the vehicles having high-backed seating as is seen in this view of 4, BSD860T.** *Tony Wilson*

# INGLEBY'S

Ingleby's Luxury Coaches Ltd, 24 Hospital Fields Road, Fulford, York,
North Yorkshire, YO1 4DZ

| TRN731 | Leyland Leopard PSU3/3R | Plaxton Panorama | C49F | 1964 | Ex Ribble, 1975 |
|---|---|---|---|---|---|
| B872FWA | Volvo B10M-61 | Plaxton Paramount 3500 II | C53F | 1985 | Ex Clarke's of London, 1989 |
| C486HAK | Volvo B10M-61 | Plaxton Paramount 3500 II | C53F | 1985 | Ex Clarke's of London, 1992 |
| C352DND | Volvo B10M-61 | Plaxton Paramount 3200 II | C53F | 1986 | Ex Shearings, 1994 |
| E515CDS | Volvo B10M-60 | Van Hool Alizée | C53F | 1988 | Ex Park's, Hamilton, 1994 |
| F277MGB | Volvo B10M-61 | Van Hool Alizée | C53F | 1989 | Ex Park's, Hamilton, 1995 |
| J43UFL | Volvo B10M-60 | Van Hool Alizée | C52F | 1992 | Ex Kenzies, Shepreth, 1996 |
| M948JJU | Volvo B6-9M | Jonckheere Ascot | C35F | 1995 | |
| R901WLG | Mercedes-Benz 811D | Onyx | C24F | 1997 | |

**Previous Registrations:**

| | | | |
|---|---|---|---|
| C486HAK | C484HAK | F277MGB | F755ENE, LSK512 |
| E515CDS | E640UNE, UOT648 | | |

**Livery:** Light blue and cream

*Opposite:* **Ingleby's operate a coach only fleet from their base at Fulford south of York. C352DND is a Volvo B10M that was originally in the Shearings touring fleet. It has Plaxton Paramount 3200 coachwork and is seen parked up at the Lightwater Valley theme park.** *Graham Crawshaw*

# JARONDA TRAVEL

C S Barwick & P Aspinall, 32 Wistowgate, Cawood, Selby, North Yorkshire, YO8 0SH

| | | | | | |
|---|---|---|---|---|---|
| OFB968R | Bristol LH6L | Eastern Coach Works | B43F | 1977 | Ex Bristol, 1985 |
| DTL544T | Bristol LH6L | Eastern Coach Works | B43F | 1978 | Ex RoadCar, 1989 |
| WAE189T | Bristol LH6L | Eastern Coach Works | B43F | 1979 | Ex United (Teeside), 1996 |
| YAE515V | Bristol LH6L | Eastern Coach Works | B43F | 1979 | Ex United (Tees & District), 1996 |
| WDX396X | Bedford YMT | Duple Dominant | B63F | 1982 | Ex Lincolnshire CC, 1997 |
| G140GOL | Dennis Dart 9SDL3002 | Duple Dartline | B39F | 1990 | |
| H878LOX | Dennis Dart 9SDL3002 | Carlyle Dartline | B39F | 1990 | |
| K601HWR | Dennis Dart 9SDL3017 | Plaxton Pointer | B43F | 1992 | |
| P212RWR | Dennis Dart | Plaxton Pointer | B40F | 1997 | |

**Livery:** White and two-tone blue

# JOHN SMITH & SONS

AM, JG & AN Smith, The Airfield, Dalton, Thirsk, North Yorkshire, YO7 3HE

| | | | | | |
|---|---|---|---|---|---|
| UNA799S | Leyland Atlantean AN68A/1R | Northern Counties | H43/32F | 1977 | Ex Yorkshire Rider, 1996 |
| RBT505T | Bedford YMT | Duple Dominant II | C53F | 1979 | |
| RBT506T | Bedford YMT | Duple Dominant II | C53F | 1979 | |
| CDN650V | Bedford YMT | Duple Dominant II | C53F | 1980 | |
| JSK268 | Bedford YMT | Duple Dominant II | C53F | 1980 | |
| KAD344V | Leyland Leopard PSU5C/4R | Plaxton Supreme IV | C57F | 1980 | Ex Miller, Calderbank, 1997 |
| DSU708 | Bedford YNT | Plaxton Supreme IV | C53F | 1980 | |
| 902DCV | Ford R1014 | Plaxton Supreme IV | C35F | 1981 | Ex Stott, Milnsbridge, 1995 |
| SND301X | Leyland Leopard PSU5C/4R | Plaxton Supreme V | C57F | 1981 | Ex Miller, Calderbank, 1997 |
| DNE74Y | Ford Transit | Deansgate | M16 | 1982 | Ex Holloway, Bristol, 1994 |
| JIL4381 | Mercedes-Benz L508D | Reeve Burgess | C19F | 1983 | Ex Fishwick, Carlton Husthwaite, 1997 |
| B375KUT | Bedford VAS5 | Plaxton Supreme IV | C29F | 1984 | Ex Myall, Bassingbourne, 1988 |
| JSV476 | DAF MB200DKFL600 | Plaxton Paramount 3200 | C51F | 1983 | Ex Shearings, 1987 |
| WJV980 | MAN MT8.136 | Reeve Burgess Riviera | C32F | 1986 | Ex Smith, Liss, 1992 |
| MIL1163 | Freight Rover Sherpa | Freight Rover | M12 | 1986 | Ex Humberside CC, 1995 |
| D829NRH | Freight Rover Sherpa | Freight Rover | M12 | 1986 | Ex Humberside CC, 1995 |
| HUI9710 | Iveco Daily 49-10 | Robin Hood City Nippy | B21F | 1986 | Ex United, 1996 |
| HUI9706 | Iveco Daily 49-10 | Robin Hood City Nippy | B19F | 1987 | Ex East Kent, 1996 |
| LIL7960 | Volkswagen LT55 | Optare City Pacer | B25F | 1987 | Ex ?, 1997 |
| D933XMV | Ford Transit | Coachcraft | M12 | 1987 | Ex Barfoot, West End, 1994 |
| E74JEG | Freight Rover Sherpa | Whittaker | C17F | 1987 | Ex Curtis, Gorefield, 1996 |
| HUI9714 | Iveco Daily 49-10 | Robin Hood City Nippy | B21F | 1988 | Ex Midland Fox, 1996 |
| F496THN | DAF MB230LB615 | Plaxton Paramount 3500 III | C53FT | 1988 | |
| F497THN | DAF SB2305DHTD585 | Duple 320 | C57F | 1988 | |
| H449VVN | LAG E180Z | LAG Panoramic | C53FT | 1991 | |
| J193BNW | Leyland-DAF 400 | Leyland DAF | M12 | 1992 | |
| M424TWF | Dennis Javelin 12SDA2144 | Neoplan Transliner | C48FT | 1995 | |
| M425TWF | Dennis Javelin 12SDA2144 | Neoplan Transliner | C48FT | 1995 | |

**Previous Registrations:**

| | | | |
|---|---|---|---|
| 902DCV | FCX578W | JIL4381 | FNM736Y |
| DSU708 | UUM943W | JSK268 | BDN114V |
| HUI9706 | E587TKJ | LIL7960 | ? |
| HUI9710 | D471WPM | MIL1163 | D827NRH |
| HUI9714 | E253ACC | WJV980 | C122BTP |
| JSV476 | ANA440Y | | |

**Livery:** Cream, green and gold

Jaronda Travel operate the service from Selby to York over the River Ouse at Cawood. The bridge at this point has a weight limit that allows the operation of Bristol LH and Dennis Dart buses. DTL544T was once a member of the large RoadCar fleet of Bristol LHs and is seen in the bus station in Selby. *Tony Wilson*

Neoplan are noted for their proven integral coaches which are assembled mostly in Germany. However, Neoplan coachwork has recently been fitted onto Dennis Javelin chassis. A pair of these vehicles were added to the John Smith & Sons fleet in 1995. Proudly proclaiming 60 years of service by the company is M425TWF. *David Longbottom*

# JOLLY ROGER

R G Flatt & J Smith, 36 Calf Close, Haxby, York, North Yorkshire  YO3 3NS

**Depots** : Willow Tree Farm, Gowthorpe, Townend Business Park, New Road, Newport, Hull and Thornton Road Industrial Estate, Pickering.

| | | | | | |
|---|---|---|---|---|---|
| LJX102N | Leyland Leopard PSU3C/4R | Plaxton Elite III | C53F | 1975 | Ex Rowland, North Dalton, 1996 |
| GOG560N | Daimler Fleetline CRL6(6LXB) | Park Royal | H43/33F | 1975 | Ex  Curtis Coaches, 1992 |
| TJI3374 | Leyland Fleetline FE30ALR | MCW | H44/24D | 1976 | Ex Taylor, Widnes, 1996 |
| KON304P | Leyland Fleetline FE30ALR | MCW | H43/33F | 1976 | Ex Kingsley, Birtley, 1995 |
| PAU208R | Daimler Fleetline CRG6LX | Northern Counties | H47/30D | 1976 | Ex Darlington, 1995 |
| OJD128R | Leyland Fleetline FE30AGR | Park Royal | H43/32F | 1976 | Ex Hornsby, Ashby, 1994 |
| OJD175R | Leyland Fleetline FE30AGR | MCW | H44/24D | 1976 | Ex Eddie Brown, Helperby, 1993 |
| WUM134S | Leyland Fleetline FE30ALR | Roe | H43/33F | 1976 | Ex Yorkshire Rider, 1996 |
| WUM134S | Leyland Fleetline FE30ALR | Roe | H43/33F | 1976 | Ex Yorkshire Rider, 1995 |
| SDA525S | Leyland Fleetline FE30AGR | MCW | H43/33F | 1977 | Ex Stort Valley, Bishops Stortford, 1996 |
| ANA43T | Leyland Fleetline FE30AGR | Northern Counties | H43/32F | 1978 | Ex Stagecoach Manchester, 1996 |
| ANA234T | Leyland Atlantean AN68A/1R | Northern Counties | H43/32F | 1979 | Ex Stagecoach Manchester, 1996 |
| BVR61T | Leyland Fleetline FE30AGR | Northern Counties | H43/32F | 1979 | Ex Stagecoach Manchester, 1996 |
| B379PAJ | Aüwaerter Neoplan N122/3 | Aüwaerter Skyliner | CH57/20CT | 1985 | Ex Black & White, Scunthorpe, 1995 |
| D102UJC | Freight Rover Sherpa | Dormobile | B16F | 1986 | Ex Lincoln, South Cave, 1996 |
| D453KWR | Freight Rover Sherpa | Dormobile | B20F | 1987 | Ex Barnacre, Blackpool, 1995 |
| D230TBW | Volkswagen LT55 | Optare CityPacer | B25F | 1987 | Ex Churchhouse, Harpenden, 1996 |
| F479UPB | TAZ Dubrava | TAZ D3200 | C47FT | 1989 | Ex MCH, Uxbridge, 1995 |
| F873ONR | TAZ Dubrava | TAZ D3200 | C57F | 1989 | Ex Aron, Northolt, 1995 |
| G577WUT | TAZ Dubrava | TAZ D3200 | C53F | 1990 | Ex Clews Travel, Wolverhampton, 1996 |

**Previous Registrations:**

| | | | |
|---|---|---|---|
| F479UPB | F863OWR, MCH384 | TJI3374 | KUC989P |
| LJX102N | HWU66N, 7222EZ | | |

**Livery:**  Two-tone green

**Named  vehicles**: LJX102N *Captain Pugwash*; GOG560N *Captain Morgan*; TJI3374 *Captain Jack Rackham*; PAU208R *Long John Silver;* WUM134S *Captain Calico Jack;* WUM135S *Captain Nathaniel Gordon;* OJD128R *Captain Hook*; OJD175R *Captain Billy Bones*; D102UJC *The Cabin Boy;* D453KWR *Captain Barnacle Bill;* F479UPB *Captain Providence.*

**Jolly Roger have a number of Fleetlines for school bus operations. OJD128R is a former London DMS which joined the Jolly Rodger fleet from the Scunthorpe area operator Hornsby. In keeping with the piratical theme of the company, the bus is named Captain Hook.**
*David Longbottom*

# KEIGHLEY & DISTRICT

Keighley & District Travel Ltd, 20 Devonshire Street, Keighley, West Yorkshire, BD21 2AU

A subsidiary of Blazefield Holdings Ltd

**Depots:** Suresnes Road, Keighley

### 101-108

| | | | | | | | | | |
|---|---|---|---|---|---|---|---|---|---|
| | | Mercedes-Benz 711D | | Plaxton Beaver | | B25F | 1993 | | |
| 101 | L652MYG | 103 | L654MYG | 105 | L656MYG | 107 | L658MYG | 108 | L659MYG |
| 102 | L653MYG | 104 | L655MYG | 106 | L657MYG | | | | |

| | | | | | |
|---|---|---|---|---|---|
| 121 | L660MYG | Mercedes-Benz 811D | Plaxton Beaver | B33F | 1993 |
| 122 | L661MYG | Mercedes-Benz 811D | Plaxton Beaver | B33F | 1993 |
| 123 | L662MYG | Mercedes-Benz 811D | Plaxton Beaver | B33F | 1993 |
| 124 | L663MYG | Mercedes-Benz 811D | Plaxton Beaver | B33F | 1993 |
| 125 | L664MYG | Mercedes-Benz 811D | Plaxton Beaver | B33F | 1993 |

### 201-208

| | | | | | | | | | |
|---|---|---|---|---|---|---|---|---|---|
| | | Leyland Lynx LX112L10ZR1R | | Leyland Lynx | | B49F | 1989 | | |
| 201 | G293KWY | 203 | G295KWY | 206 | G298KWY | 207 | G299KWY | 208 | G300KWY |
| 202 | G294KWY | | | | | | | | |

| | | | | | | |
|---|---|---|---|---|---|---|
| 221 | L642OWY | Volvo B6-9.9M | Alexander Dash | B40F | 1994 | |
| 222 | L643OWY | Volvo B6-9.9M | Alexander Dash | B40F | 1994 | |
| 223 | L644OWY | Volvo B6-9.9M | Alexander Dash | B40F | 1994 | |
| 224 | M259KWK | Volvo B6-9.9M | Alexander Dash | B40F | 1995 | Ex Volvo demonstrator, 1996 |
| 231 | G431MWU | Leyland Tiger TRCL10/3ARZA | Plaxton Paramount 3200 III | C55F | 1990 | Ex Yorkshire Coastliner, 1996 |
| 232 | G432MWU | Leyland Tiger TRCL10/3ARZA | Plaxton Paramount 3200 III | C55F | 1990 | Ex Yorkshire Coastliner, 1996 |
| 233 | G433MWU | Leyland Tiger TRCL10/3ARZA | Plaxton Paramount 3200 III | C55F | 1990 | Ex Yorkshire Coastliner, 1996 |
| 241 | A16KDT | Volvo B10M-61 | Plaxton Paramount 3500 III | C49FT | 1989 | Ex Cambridge Coach Services, 1994 |
| 250 | G435MWU | Leyland Tiger TRCL10/3RZA | Plaxton Paramount 3200 III | C55F* | 1990 | Ex Yorkshire Coastliner, 1994 |
| 252 | DNW840T | Leyland National 10351B/1R | | B44F | 1978 | Ex West Yorkshire, 1989 |
| 253 | DNW841T | Leyland National 10351B/1R | | B44F | 1978 | Ex West Yorkshire, 1989 |
| 260w | FUG324T | Leyland National 10351B/1R | | B44F | 1979 | Ex West Yorkshire, 1989 |
| 261 | FUG325T | Leyland National 10351B/1R | | B44F | 1979 | Ex West Yorkshire, 1989 |
| 263w | EPD542V | Leyland National 10351B/1R | | B41F | 1979 | Ex Sovereign, 1992 |
| 336 | H519RWX | Leyland Olympian ON2R50G13Z4 | Northern Counties Palatine | H43/30F | 1990 | |
| 345 | A605NYG | Leyland Olympian ONLXB/1R | Eastern Coach Works | H41/29F | 1984 | Ex Harrogate & District, 1996 |
| 347 | A604NYG | Leyland Olympian ONLXB/1R | Eastern Coach Works | H41/29F | 1984 | Ex Harrogate & District, 1992 |
| 348 | A602NYG | Leyland Olympian ONLXB/1R | Eastern Coach Works | H45/29F | 1984 | Ex Harrogate & District, 1992 |
| 349 | B517UWW | Leyland Olympian ONLXB/1R | Eastern Coach Works | H45/32F | 1985 | Ex Harrogate & District, 1992 |
| 350 | FUM485Y | Leyland Olympian ONLXB/1R | Eastern Coach Works | H45/32F | 1983 | Ex Harrogate & District, 1992 |

**Keighley & District have now replaced all their Iveco minibuses with Mercedes-Benz types. Numbered 125, L664MYG is a model 811D with a Plaxton Beaver body which works alongside smaller 711D types on town services.**
*Lee Whitehead*

### 351-373

Leyland Olympian ONLXB/1R    Eastern Coach Works    H45/32F    1982-85 Ex West Yorkshire, 1989
*370 is DPH41/29F; 361/8/9 are H45/29F

| | | | | | | | | | |
|---|---|---|---|---|---|---|---|---|---|
| 351 | DWW926Y | 356 | DWW931Y | 360 | FUM488Y | 364 | FUM500Y | 369 | A603NYG |
| 352 | DWW927Y | 357 | DWW932Y | 361 | FUM490Y | 365 | A92KWW | 370 | B91SWX |
| 353 | DWW928Y | 358 | FUM483Y | 362 | FUM493Y | 367 | A95KWW | 371 | B515UWW |
| 354 | DWW929Y | 359 | FUM484Y | 363 | FUM497Y | 368 | A96KWW | 373 | C484YWY |
| 355w | DWW930Y | | | | | | | | |

| | | | | | | |
|---|---|---|---|---|---|---|
| 372 | C482YWY | Leyland Olympian ONLXB/1R | Eastern Coach Works | H45/32F | 1985 | Ex Harrogate & District, 1996 |

### 381-388

Leyland Olympian ONLXB/1R    Eastern Coach Works    H45/32F    1983-84 Ex York City & District, 1990
*384 is DPH41/29F

| | | | | | | | | | |
|---|---|---|---|---|---|---|---|---|---|
| 381 | A683MWX | 383 | A685MWX | 385 | B92SWX | 387 | A17KDT | 388 | FUM496Y |
| 382 | A684MWX | 384 | B90SWX | 386 | A189RUM | | | | |

### 389-393

Leyland Olympian ONLXB/1R    Eastern Coach Works    DPH42/29F    1985    Ex Yorkshire Coastliner, 1992-94

| | | | | | | | | | |
|---|---|---|---|---|---|---|---|---|---|
| 389 | B521UWW | 390 | B522UWW | 391 | B524UWW | 392 | C479YWY | 393 | C480YWY |

### 501-510

Volvo B10B-58    Alexander Strider    DP49F    1996

| | | | | | | | | | |
|---|---|---|---|---|---|---|---|---|---|
| 501 | N501HWY | 503 | N503HWY | 505 | N505HWY | 507 | N507HWY | 509 | N509HWY |
| 502 | N502HWY | 504 | N504HWY | 506 | N506HWY | 508 | N508HWY | 510 | N510HWY |

### 511-515

Volvo B10B-58    Wright Endurance    DP47F    1997

| | | | | | | | | | |
|---|---|---|---|---|---|---|---|---|---|
| 511 | P511UUG | 512 | P512UUG | 513 | P513UUG | 514 | P514UUG | 515 | P515UUG |

| | | | | | | |
|---|---|---|---|---|---|---|
| 901 | L648MYG | Leyland Olympian ON2R50C13Z4 | Alexander RH | H45/29F | 1993 | |
| 902 | L649MYG | Leyland Olympian ON2R50C13Z4 | Alexander RH | H45/29F | 1993 | |
| 903 | L650MYG | Leyland Olympian ON2R50C13Z4 | Alexander RH | H45/29F | 1993 | |
| 904 | L651MYG | Leyland Olympian ON2R50C13Z4 | Alexander RH | H45/29F | 1993 | |
| 905 | K2YCL | Leyland Olympian ON2R50C13Z4 | Northern Counties Palatine | DPH43/27F | 1992 | Ex Yorkshire Coastliner, 1995 |
| 906 | K6YCL | Leyland Olympian ON2R50C13Z4 | Northern Counties Palatine | DPH43/27F | 1992 | Ex Yorkshire Coastliner, 1995 |
| 907 | K7YCL | Leyland Olympian ON2R50C13Z4 | Northern Counties Palatine | DPH43/27F | 1992 | Ex Yorkshire Coastliner, 1995 |
| 913 | K3YCL | Leyland Olympian ON2R50C13Z4 | Northern Counties Palatine | DPH43/27F | 1992 | Ex Yorkshire Coastliner, 1997 |
| 914 | K4YCL | Leyland Olympian ON2R50C13Z4 | Northern Counties Palatine | DPH43/27F | 1992 | Ex Yorkshire Coastliner, 1997 |
| 915 | K5YCL | Leyland Olympian ON2R50C13Z4 | Northern Counties Palatine | DPH43/27F | 1992 | Ex Yorkshire Coastliner, 1997 |
| 973 | BPF134Y | Leyland Olympian ONTL11/1R | Roe | H43/29F | 1983 | Ex Sovereign, 1992 |
| 974 | B261LPH | Leyland Olympian ONTL11/1R | Eastern Coach Works | H43/29F | 1985 | Ex County, 1990 |
| 975 | B264LPH | Leyland Olympian ONTL11/1R | Eastern Coach Works | H43/29F | 1985 | Ex County, 1990 |
| 976 | B265LPH | Leyland Olympian ONTL11/1R | Eastern Coach Works | H43/29F | 1985 | Ex County, 1990 |
| KDG26 | CWX671 | Bristol K5G | Roe (1950) | L27/28R | 1938 | Ex preservation, 1993 |

**Livery:** White, blue, red and yellow (buses); dark blue and silver (coaches).

**Previous Registrations:**
A16KDT        F884RFP

**Named vehicles**: 501 *Red Star*, 502 *Rising Star*, 503 *Royal Star*, 504 *Shooting Star*, 505 *Silver Star*, 506 *Lode Star*, 507 *North Star*, 508 *Polar Star*, 509 *Morning Star*, 510 *Evening Star*, 511 *Bright Star*, 512 *Sun Star*, 513 *Craven Star*, 514 *White Star*, 515 *Star of Elendil.*

*Opposite, top:* **Leyland Olympian 901, L648MYG, carries a full height Alexander RH body and is one of a batch of four which were bought by Keighley & District to operate service 760. The route details are carried boldly on the vehicles side as is the large K which was introduced to the fleet livery on these buses.** *Tony Wilson*

*Opposite, bottom:* **Keighley & District operate high standard services under the Star Bus banner. For these routes a number of Alexander Strider-bodied Volvo B10B saloons were built and they carry a brighter blue, white, red and yellow livery. This scheme has seen the ending of the use of grey for the Harrogate and District fleet. 505, N505HWY is seen in Bradford.** *Tony Wilson*

# LEISUREWAYS

M Crowcroft, 68 Raley Street, Kingstone, Barnsley, South Yorkshire, S70 6LH

**Depot** : Dodworth Hall Farm, Green Road, Dodworth

| | | | | | |
|---|---|---|---|---|---|
| 225KUO | Leyland Tiger TRCTL11/3R | Plaxton Paramount 3200 | C50F | 1983 | Ex Majestic, Darton, 1997 |
| WHK81W | Bova EL26/581 | Bova Europa | C50F | 1981 | Ex Pride of the Road, Huddersfield, 1995 |

**Previous Registrations:**
225KUO    SOH553Y, RFE482

# LEON

Leon Motor Services Ltd, Finningley House, Old Bawtry Road, Finningley,
South Yorkshire, DN9 3DD

| | | | | | | |
|---|---|---|---|---|---|---|
| 96 | XKU903T | Leyland Fleetline FE30ALR(6LXB) | Northern Counties | H43/32F | 1978 | |
| 99 | GWF571V | Bedford YMT | Duple Dominant II Express | C53F | 1980 | |
| 101 | HKU361W | Leyland Fleetline FE30AGR | Alexander AD | H44/31F | 1980 | |
| 102w | BGY606T | Bedford YMT | Duple Dominant II | C53F | 1979 | Ex National Travel London, 1982 |
| 103w | MHE50P | Leyland Fleetline FE30AGR | Roe | H44/34F | 1976 | Ex South Yorkshire PTE, 1983 |
| 104 | LEO163 | Leyland Tiger TRCTL11/3R | Van Hool Alizée | C48F | 1983 | |
| 108 | MPL135W | Leyland Leopard PSU3E/4R | Duple Dominant IV Express | C53F | 1981 | Ex London Country, 1986 |
| 109 | D734PWF | Mercedes-Benz 609D | Reeve Burgess | DP19F | 1987 | |
| 110 | D736PWF | Mercedes-Benz 609D | Reeve Burgess | DP19F | 1987 | |
| 111 | PRJ500R | Daimler Fleetline CRG6LXB | Northern Counties | H43/32F | 1976 | Ex Greater Manchester, 1987 |
| 112 | C809KBT | Leyland Cub CU435 | Optare | B33F | 1986 | Ex Yorkshire Rider, 1987 |
| 116 | 4395EL | Leyland Tiger TRCTL11/3R | Duple Caribbean | C51F | 1983 | Ex Hirdle, Boscombe, 1988 |
| 117 | GSD723V | Leyland Fleetline FE30AGR | Alexander AL | H45/33F | 1980 | Ex AA (Dodds), Troon, 1988 |
| 118 | GSD724V | Leyland Fleetline FE30AGR | Alexander AL | H45/33F | 1980 | Ex AA (Dodds), Troon, 1988 |
| 120 | MSU174 | Leyland Tiger TRCTL11/3R | Van Hool Alizée | C53F | 1983 | Ex BRC, Tockington, 1989 |
| 121 | NAK322R | Leyland Atlantean AN68A/1R | East Lancashire | H43/32F | 1976 | Ex South Yorkshire, 1989 |
| 122 | C171AWK | Leyland Royal Tiger RT | Van Hool Alizée | C49FT | 1986 | Ex Harry Shaw, Coventry, 1990 |

Leon operate the service between the company's home base of Finningley and Doncaster. Fleetlines have been used on this route for many years. Seen in service in Doncaster is 128, TWH700T, a Northern Counties-bodied example which came to Leon from GM Buses in 1991.
*Richard Godfrey*

The most modern vehicle in the Leon fleet is newly delivered 144, P144RWR. This Dennis Dart was photographed in Doncaster while operating service 89 to West Bessacarr. Plaxton Pointer bodywork is carried by this vehicle and the other Dart in the fleet that was acquired in 1996. *Lee Whitehead*

| 123 | NOC435R | Leyland Fleetline FE30AGR | MCW | H43/33F | 1977 | Ex West Midlands Travel, 1990 |
|-----|---------|---------------------------|-----|---------|------|-------------------------------|
| 124 | NOC465R | Leyland Fleetline FE30AGR | MCW | H43/33F | 1977 | Ex West Midlands Travel, 1990 |
| 125 | NOC391R | Leyland Fleetline FE30ALR | MCW | H43/33F | 1976 | Ex West Midlands Travel, 1990 |
| 126 | SDA561S | Leyland Fleetline FE30AGR | MCW | H43/33F | 1978 | Ex West Midlands Travel, 1990 |
| 127 | GDZ885 | Leyland Tiger TRCTL11/3RZ | Van Hool Alizée | C51D | 1985 | Ex Travellers, Hounslow, 1991 |
| 128 | TWH700T | Leyland Fleetline FE30AGR | Northern Counties | H43/32F | 1979 | Ex GM Buses, 1991 |
| 129 | ANA49T | Leyland Fleetline FE30AGR | Northern Counties | H43/32F | 1979 | Ex GM Buses, 1991 |
| 130 | F101RTR | Leyland Lynx LX112L10ZR1S | Leyland Lynx | B49F | 1989 | Ex Southampton, 1991 |
| 131 | F103RTR | Leyland Lynx LX112L10ZR1S | Leyland Lynx | B49F | 1989 | Ex Southampton, 1991 |
| 132 | FIL4145 | Leyland Tiger TRCTL11/3R | Van Hool Alizée | C50FT | 1984 | Ex Supreme, Southend, 1992 |
| 133 | FIL4146 | Leyland Tiger TRCTL11/3R | Van Hool Alizée | C50FT | 1984 | Ex Supreme, Southend, 1992 |
| 134 | TSJ34S | Leyland Fleetline FE30AGR | Northern Counties | H44/31F | 1978 | Ex Western Scottish, 1992 |
| 135 | G473PGE | Leyland Lynx LX112L10ZR1R | Leyland Lynx 2 | B51F | 1989 | Ex Whitelaw, Stonehouse, 1993 |
| 136 | M926TYG | Optare MetroRider | Optare | B31F | 1994 | |
| 137 | M927TYG | Optare MetroRider | Optare | B31F | 1994 | |
| 138 | ASA24T | Leyland Fleetline FE30AGR | Eastern Coach Works | H43/32F | 1978 | Ex Western, 1995 |
| 139 | ASA26T | Leyland Fleetline FE30AGR | Eastern Coach Works | H43/32F | 1978 | Ex Western, 1995 |
| 140 | LMS160W | Leyland Fleetline FE30AGR | Alexander AD | H44/31F | 1980 | Ex Western, 1995 |
| 141 | ECS887V | Leyland Fleetline FE30AGR | Alexander AD | H44/31F | 1979 | Ex Western, 1995 |
| 142 | LMS170W | Leyland Fleetline FE30AGR | Alexander AD | H44/31F | 1980 | Ex Clydeside, 1995 |
| 143 | N528DWY | Dennis Dart 9.8SDL3054 | Plaxton Pointer | B40F | 1995 | Ex Bookham Coaches, 1996 |
| 144 | P144RWR | Dennis Dart | Plaxton Pointer | B40F | 1997 | |
| 145 | D319NEC | Leyland Tiger TRCTL11/3RH | Plaxton Paramount 3200 III | C53F | 1987 | Ex Blackburn, 1997 |
| 146 | D320NEC | Leyland Tiger TRCTL11/3RH | Plaxton Paramount 3200 III | C53F | 1987 | Ex Blackburn, 1997 |

Previous Registrations:

| | | | | | |
|---|---|---|---|---|---|
| 4395EL | KGS482Y | FIL4146 | B331ANY | LEO163 | VKY541Y |
| C171AWK | HS8882 | GDZ885 | B327AMH | MSU174 | NYS61Y |
| FIL4145 | B332ANY | | | | |

Livery: Two-tone blue and grey.

# LONGSTAFF

J J Longstaff & Sons Ltd, 2 Shillbank Lane, Mirfield, West Yorkshire, WF13 1LH

Depot: Eastfield Garage, Stoney Lane, Ravensthorpe

| LPY734 | Volvo B10M-61 | Plaxton Paramount 3500 III | C53F | 1987 | |
|--------|---------------|----------------------------|------|------|---|
| E479UOF | MCW Metrobus DR102/65 | MCW | H43/30F | 1988 | Ex London Buses, 1991 |
| F694ACX | Volvo B10M-60 | Van Hool Alizée | C53F | 1989 | |
| M123SKY | Volvo B10M-62 | Van Hool Alizée | C49F | 1994 | |
| M70JJL | Volvo B10M-62 | Van Hool Alizée | C53F | 1995 | |
| P2JJL | Dennis Lance 11SDA3113 | Plaxton Verde | B49F | 1996 | |

**Previous Registrations:**
LPY374        D51YVH

**Livery:**  Blue, grey and white

Longstaff provide a service between Dewsbury and Mirfield. A single-decker and a double-decker are in the fleet for this route with the single-decker having been renewed in 1996. The new addition to the fleet is P2JJL, a Dennis Lance with Plaxton Verde bodywork seen in Dewsbury bus station. Dewsbury is also the location for this picture of double-deck Metrobus E479UOF that was new to London Buses.
*Lee Whitehead/ Richard Godfrey*

# MAINLINE

Mainline Group Ltd, 8 Riverside Court, Newhall Road, South Yorkshire, S9 1BX

**Depots** : Leger Way, Doncaster; Bootham Lane, Dunscroft; Station Road, Halfway; Midland Road, Rotherham; Greenland Road, Sheffield and Olive Grove, Sheffield.

| | | | | | | |
|---|---|---|---|---|---|---|
| 22 | KWA22W | Leyland National 2 NL116L11/1R | | B48F | 1980 | |
| 63 | YPD103Y | Leyland Tiger TRCTL11/2R | Duple Dominant IV Express | C53F | 1983 | Ex Sheafline, Sheffield, 1990 |
| 66u | G566SNN | Mercedes-Benz 811D | Carlyle | B33F | 1990 | Ex Skills, Nottingham, 1991 |
| 98 | FWA498V | Leyland Leopard PSU3E/4R | Duple Dominant I | DP53F | 1980 | |

### 112-122

| | | | | | |
|---|---|---|---|---|---|
| | Mercedes-Benz 709D | Plaxton Beaver | DP12FL | 1996 | |

| 112 | N112DWE | 115 | N115DWE | 117 | N117DWE | 119 | N119DWE | 121 | N121DWE |
|---|---|---|---|---|---|---|---|---|---|
| 113 | N113DWE | 116 | N116DWE | 118 | N118DWE | 120 | N120DWE | 122 | N122DWE |
| 114 | N114DWE | | | | | | | | |

### 192-219

| | Renault-Dodge S56 | Reeve Burgess Beaver | B25F | 1988 | |
|---|---|---|---|---|---|

| 192 | E192XWG | 197 | E197XWG | 202 | E202XWG | 206 | E206XWG | 216 | E216XWG |
|---|---|---|---|---|---|---|---|---|---|
| 193 | E193XWG | 198 | E198XWG | 203 | E203XWG | 209 | E209XWG | 217 | E217XWG |
| 194 | E194XWG | 199 | E199XWG | 204 | E204XWG | 210 | E210XWG | 218 | E218XWG |
| 196 | E196XWG | 201 | E201XWG | 205 | E205XWG | 211 | E211XWG | 219 | E219XWG |

### 222-238

| | Renault-Dodge S56 | Northern Counties | B23F* | 1989 | *229-38 are B25F |
|---|---|---|---|---|---|

| 222 | F222EWG | 227 | F227EWG | 230 | F230EWG | 233 | F233EWG | 238 | F238EWG |
|---|---|---|---|---|---|---|---|---|---|
| 226 | F226EWG | 229 | F229EWG | | | | | | |

**The minibus fleet operated by Mainline has dwindled in number in recent years. The Reeve Burgess Beaver-bodied Renault-Dodge S56 type are now starting to be sold, though still in service is 196, E196XWG. The type was joined in 1989 by several of the same model from Lincoln City Transport.**

**The latest batch of minibuses are a batch of eleven Mercedes-Benz 709Ds that provide access lifts at their rear. Illustrating the use is 116, N116DWE which is seen in Doncaster town centre loading passengers through this facility.** *Lee Whitehead*

### 240-254

| | | | | | | | | | | | |
|---|---|---|---|---|---|---|---|---|---|---|---|
| | | Renault-Dodge S56 | | Reeve Burgess Beaver | | B25F | | 1988 | Ex Lincoln, 1989 | | |
| **240** | E425XKU | **243** | E403BCT | **246** | E406BCT | **249** | E409BCT | **252** | E412BCT |
| **241** | E401BCT | **244** | E404BCT | **247** | E407BCT | **250** | E410BCT | **253** | E413BCT |
| **242** | E402BCT | **245** | E405BCT | **248** | E408BCT | **251** | E411BCT | **254** | E414BCT |

| | | | | | | |
|---|---|---|---|---|---|---|
| **287** | SWB287L | Leyland Atlantean AN68/1R | Alexander AL | O43/31F | 1973 |

### 301-350

| | | | | | | | | | | | |
|---|---|---|---|---|---|---|---|---|---|---|---|
| | | Renault-Dodge S56 | | Reeve Burgess Beaver | | B23F | | 1990 | | | |
| **301** | G301NWB | **311** | G311NWB | **321** | G321NWB | **331** | G331NWB | **341** | G341NWB |
| **302** | G302NWB | **312** | G312NWB | **322** | G322NWB | **332** | G332NWB | **342** | G342NWB |
| **303** | G303NWB | **313** | G313NWB | **323** | G323NWB | **333** | G333NWB | **343** | G343NWB |
| **304** | G304NWB | **314** | G314NWB | **324** | G324NWB | **334** | G334NWB | **344** | H344RKU |
| **305** | G305NWB | **315** | G315NWB | **325** | G325NWB | **335** | G335NWB | **345** | H345RKU |
| **306** | G306NWB | **316** | G316NWB | **326** | G326NWB | **336** | G336NWB | **346** | H346RKU |
| **307** | G307NWB | **317** | G317NWB | **327u** | G327NWB | **337** | G337NWB | **347** | H347RKU |
| **308** | G308NWB | **318** | G318NWB | **328** | G328NWB | **338** | G338NWB | **348** | H348RKU |
| **309** | G309NWB | **319** | G319NWB | **329** | G329NWB | **339** | G339NWB | **349** | H349RKU |
| **310** | G310NWB | **320** | G320NWB | **330** | G330NWB | **340** | G340NWB | **350** | H569SWJ |

### 351-389

| | | | | | | | | | | | |
|---|---|---|---|---|---|---|---|---|---|---|---|
| | | Renault-Dodge S56 | | Reeve Burgess Beaver | | B23F | | 1991 | 387-9 are B21F | | |
| **351** | H351UWB | **359** | H359UWB | **367** | H367UWB | **375** | H375UWB | **383** | H383UWB |
| **352** | H352UWB | **360** | H390UWB | **368** | H368UWB | **376** | H376UWB | **384** | H384UWB |
| **353** | H353UWB | **361** | H361UWB | **369** | H369UWB | **377** | H377UWB | **385** | H385UWB |
| **354** | H354UWB | **362** | H362UWB | **370** | H370UWB | **378** | H378UWB | **386** | H386UWB |
| **355** | H355UWB | **363** | H363UWB | **371** | H371UWB | **379** | H379UWB | **387** | H387UWB |
| **356** | H356UWB | **364** | H364UWB | **372** | H372UWB | **380** | H380UWB | **388** | H388UWB |
| **357** | H357UWB | **365** | H365UWB | **373** | H373UWB | **381** | H381UWB | **389** | H389UWB |
| **358** | H358UWB | **366** | H366UWB | **374** | H374UWB | **382** | H382UWB | | |

Of the latest delivery of B6BLEs several are liveried for the Tesco park and ride service along Abbeydale Road, including two purchased by the superstore. Pictured arriving at the store is 455, *P455LWE.* *Lee Whitehead*

| 400 | M918MRW | Volvo B6BLE | Wright Crusader | B36F | 1995 | Ex Volvo demonstrator, 1996 |
| 401 | K401EDT | Volvo B6-8.5M | Plaxton Pointer | B34F | 1992 | |

### 411-440                    Volvo B6-9.9M            Plaxton Pointer        B40F    1995

| 411 | M411VHE | 417 | M417VHE | 423 | M423VHE | 429 | M429VHE | 435 | M435VHE |
| 412 | M412VHE | 418 | M418VHE | 424 | M424VHE | 430 | M430VHE | 436 | M436VHE |
| 413 | M413VHE | 419 | M419VHE | 425 | M425VHE | 431 | M431VHE | 437 | M437VHE |
| 414 | M414VHE | 420 | M420VHE | 426 | M426VHE | 432 | M432VHE | 438 | M438VHE |
| 415 | M415VHE | 421 | M421VHE | 427 | M427VHE | 433 | M433VHE | 439 | M439VHE |
| 416 | M416VHE | 422 | M422VHE | 428 | M428VHE | 434 | M434VHE | 440 | M440VHE |

### 441-455                    Volvo B6BLE              Wright Crusader        B36F*   1995-97 *450/1 are B32F
*452-5 are DP36F of which two were purchased by Tesco.

| 441 | N441BKY | 444 | N144BWG | 447 | N447BKY | 450 | N450DWJ | 453 | P453LWE |
| 442 | N442BKY | 445 | N445BKY | 448 | N448BKY | 451 | N451DWJ | 454 | P454LWE |
| 443 | N443BKY | 446 | N446BKY | 449 | N449BKY | 452 | P452LWE | 455 | P455LWE |

### 601-650                    Volvo B10M-55            Alexander PS           B51F    1990

| 601 | G601NWA | 611 | G611NWA | 621 | G621NWA | 631 | G631NWA | 641 | G641NWA |
| 602 | G602NWA | 612 | G612NWA | 622 | G622NWA | 632 | G632NWA | 642 | H642RKU |
| 603 | G603NWA | 613 | G613NWA | 623 | G623NWA | 633 | G633NWA | 643 | H643RKU |
| 604 | G604NWA | 614 | G614NWA | 624 | G624NWA | 634 | G634NWA | 644 | H644RKU |
| 605 | G605NWA | 615 | G615NWA | 625 | G625NWA | 635 | G635NWA | 645 | H645RKU |
| 606 | G606NWA | 616 | G616NWA | 626 | G626NWA | 636 | G636NWA | 646 | H646RKU |
| 607 | G607NWA | 617 | G617NWA | 627 | G627NWA | 637 | G637NWA | 647 | H647RKU |
| 608 | G608NWA | 618 | G618NWA | 628 | G628NWA | 638 | G638NWA | 648 | H648RKU |
| 609 | G609NWA | 619 | G619NWA | 629 | G629NWA | 639 | G639NWA | 649 | H649RKU |
| 610 | G610NWA | 620 | G620NWA | 630 | G630NWA | 640 | G640NWA | 650 | H650RKU |

## 651-690 — Volvo B10M-55 — Alexander PS — B51F — 1991

| | | | | | | | | | |
|---|---|---|---|---|---|---|---|---|---|
| 651 | H651THL | 659 | H659THL | 667 | H667THL | 675 | H675THL | 683 | H683THL |
| 652 | H652THL | 660 | H660THL | 668 | H668THL | 676 | H676THL | 684 | H684THL |
| 653 | H653THL | 661 | H661THL | 669 | H669THL | 677 | H677THL | 685 | H685THL |
| 654 | H654THL | 662 | H662THL | 670 | H670THL | 678 | H678THL | 686 | H686THL |
| 655 | H655THL | 663 | H663THL | 671 | H671THL | 679 | H679THL | 687 | H687THL |
| 656 | H656THL | 664 | H664THL | 672 | H672THL | 680 | H680THL | 688 | H688THL |
| 657 | H657THL | 665 | H665THL | 673 | H673THL | 681 | H681THL | 689 | J689XAK |
| 658 | H658THL | 666 | H691THL | 674 | H674THL | 682 | H682THL | 690 | J690XAK |

## 691-715 — Volvo B10M-55 — Alexander PS — B51F — 1992

| | | | | | | | | | |
|---|---|---|---|---|---|---|---|---|---|
| 691 | J691AWF | 696 | J696AWF | 701 | J701AWF | 706 | K706EDT | 711 | K711EDT |
| 692 | J692AWF | 697 | J697AWF | 702 | J702AWF | 707 | K707EDT | 712 | K712EDT |
| 693 | J693AWF | 698 | J698AWF | 703 | J703AWF | 708 | K708EDT | 713 | K713EDT |
| 694 | J694AWF | 699 | J699AWF | 704 | J704AWF | 709 | K709EDT | 714 | K714EDT |
| 695 | J695AWF | 700 | J794AWF | 705 | J705AWF | 710 | K710EDT | 715 | K715EDT |

## 716-740 — Volvo B10M-55 — Alexander PS — B49F — 1995

| | | | | | | | | | |
|---|---|---|---|---|---|---|---|---|---|
| 716 | M716VET | 721 | M721VET | 726 | M726VET | 731 | M731VET | 736 | M736VET |
| 717 | M717VET | 722 | M722VET | 727 | M727VET | 732 | M732VET | 737 | M737VET |
| 718 | M718VET | 723 | M723VET | 728 | M728VET | 733 | M733VET | 738 | M738VET |
| 719 | M719VET | 724 | M724VET | 729 | M729VET | 734 | M734VET | 739 | M739VET |
| 720 | M720VET | 725 | M725VET | 730 | M730VET | 735 | M735VET | 740 | M740VET |

## 741-780 — Volvo B10M-55 — Alexander PS — B49F* — 1996 — *741-8 are DP49F

| | | | | | | | | | |
|---|---|---|---|---|---|---|---|---|---|
| 741 | N741CKY | 749 | N749CKY | 757 | N757CKY | 765 | N765CKY | 773 | N773CKY |
| 742 | N742CKY | 750 | N750CKY | 758 | N758CKY | 766 | N766CKY | 774 | N774CKY |
| 743 | N743CKY | 751 | N751CKY | 759 | N759CKY | 767 | N767CKY | 775 | N775CKY |
| 744 | N744CKY | 752 | N752CKY | 760 | N760CKY | 768 | N768CKY | 776 | N776CKY |
| 745 | N745CKY | 753 | N753CKY | 761 | N761CKY | 769 | N769CKY | 777 | N277CKY |
| 746 | N746CKY | 754 | N754CKY | 762 | N762CKY | 770 | N770CKY | 778 | N778CKY |
| 747 | N247CKY | 755 | N755CKY | 763 | N763CKY | 771 | N771CKY | 779 | N779CKY |
| 748 | N748CKY | 756 | N756CKY | 764 | N764CKY | 772 | N772CKY | 780 | N780CKY |

Mainline have bought substantial numbers of single deck buses to replace Atlanteans and Leyland Nationals. The Volvo B10M chassis bodied by Alexander is now a familiar sight throughout Mainline's South Yorkshire operating area. Photographed at Lady's Bridge is 727, M727VET, one of 25 buses of this type purchased in 1995. *Lee Whitehead*

| 940 | 3904WE | Leyland Titan PD3/1 | Roe | | H39/30R | 1959 | |
|---|---|---|---|---|---|---|---|
| **1001** | YPD126Y | Leyland Tiger TRCTL11/2R | Duple Dominant IV Express | C53F | 1983 | Ex London Country, 1991 |
| **1156** | 3156WE | Leyland Titan PD2/30 | Roe | | H33/26RD | 1958 | |

### 1854-1887
MCW Metrobus DR104/6 — MCW — H46/31F — 1981

| 1854 | JHE154W | 1859 | JHE159W | 1866 | JHE166W | 1874 | JHE174W | 1883 | JHE183W |
|---|---|---|---|---|---|---|---|---|---|
| 1855 | JHE155W | 1861 | JHE161W | 1868 | JHE168W | 1876 | JHE176W | 1887 | JHE187W |
| 1858u | JHE158W | 1865 | JHE165W | | | | | | |

### 1901-1919
MCW Metrobus DR104/11 — MCW — H47/33F — 1983

| 1901 | UKY901Y | 1906 | A106XWE | 1910 | A110XWE | 1914 | A114XWE | 1917 | A117XWE |
|---|---|---|---|---|---|---|---|---|---|
| 1902 | UKY902Y | 1907 | A107XWE | 1911 | A111XWE | 1915 | A115XWE | 1918 | A118XWE |
| 1903 | UKY903Y | 1908 | A108XWE | 1912 | A112XWE | 1916 | A116XWE | 1919 | A119XWE |
| 1904 | UKY904Y | 1909 | A109XWE | 1913 | A113XWE | | | | | |

### 1921-1940
MCW Metrobus DR104/12 — MCW — H47/33F — 1984-85

| 1921 | B921CDT | 1926 | B926CDT | 1930 | B930CDT | 1934 | B934CDT | 1938 | B938CDT |
|---|---|---|---|---|---|---|---|---|---|
| 1922 | B922CDT | 1927 | B927CDT | 1931 | B931CDT | 1935 | B935CDT | 1939 | B939CDT |
| 1923 | B923CDT | 1928 | B928CDT | 1932 | B932CDT | 1936 | B936CDT | 1940 | B940CDT |
| 1924 | B924CDT | 1929 | B929CDT | 1933 | B933CDT | 1937 | B937CDT | | |

### 1941-1950
MCW Metrobus DR102/50 — MCW — DPH42/28F — 1985

| 1941 | B941FET | 1943 | B943FET | 1945 | B945FET | 1947 | C947HWF | 1949 | C949HWF |
|---|---|---|---|---|---|---|---|---|---|
| 1942 | B942FET | 1944 | B944FET | 1946 | B946FET | 1948 | C948HWF | 1950 | C950HWF |

### 1951-1960
MCW Metrobus DR102/53 — MCW — DPH42/28F* 1986 — * 1951 is DPH38/28F

| 1951 | C951LWJ | 1953 | C953LWJ | 1955 | C955LWJ | 1957 | C957LWJ | 1959 | C959LWJ |
|---|---|---|---|---|---|---|---|---|---|
| 1952 | C952LWJ | 1954 | C954LWJ | 1956 | C956LWJ | 1958 | C958LWJ | 1960 | C960LWJ |

**Until the introduction of articulated coaches onto the Stagecoach Express network, Mainline was the only major operator of bendi-buses in Britain. One of the 13 articulated Leyland DAB types is 2010, C110HDT. The batch have now been working for Mainline for 12 years and many carry the latest version of fleet livery.** *Richard Godfrey*

## 2001-2010

Leyland-DAB 07-1735B-222054    DAB                    AB60T    1985

| 2001 | C101HDT | 2003 | C103HDT | 2005 | C105HDT | 2007 | C107HDT | 2009 | C109HDT |
|------|---------|------|---------|------|---------|------|---------|------|---------|
| 2002 | C102HDT | 2004 | C104HDT | 2006 | C106HDT | 2008 | C108HDT | 2010 | C110HDT |

| 2011 | C111HDT | Leyland-DAB 07-1735L-222054 | DAB | ADP67D | 1985 |
|------|---------|-----------------------------|-----|--------|------|
| 2012 | C112HDT | Leyland-DAB 07-1735L-222054 | DAB | ADP67D | 1985 |
| 2013 | C113HDT | Leyland-DAB 07-1735L-222054 | DAB | ADP67D | 1985 |

## 2101-2140

Dennis Dominator DDA133    Alexander RH    H46/32F    1981

| 2101 | KKU101W | 2108 | KKU108W | 2119 | KKU119W | 2127 | KKU127W | 2135 | MWB855W |
|------|---------|------|---------|------|---------|------|---------|------|---------|
| 2102 | KKU102W | 2109 | KKU109W | 2120 | KKU120W | 2128 | KKU128W | 2136 | MWB856W |
| 2103 | KKU103W | 2111 | KKU111W | 2121 | KKU121W | 2129 | MWB849W | 2137 | OWE137X |
| 2104 | KKU104W | 2113 | KKU113W | 2122 | KKU122W | 2131 | MWB851W | 2138 | OWE138X |
| 2105 | KKU105W | 2116 | KKU116W | 2123 | KKU123W | 2132 | MWB852W | 2139 | OWE139X |
| 2106 | KKU106W | 2117 | KKU117W | 2124 | KKU124W | 2133 | MWB853W | 2140 | OWE140X |
| 2107 | KKU107W | 2118 | KKU118W | 2126 | KKU126W | 2134 | MWB854W |      |         |

## 2141-2220

Dennis Dominator DDA133    Alexander RH    H46/32F    1981-82

| 2141 | NKU141X | 2159 | NKU159X | 2175 | NKU175X | 2191 | NKU191X | 2206 | NKU206X |
|------|---------|------|---------|------|---------|------|---------|------|---------|
| 2142 | NKU142X | 2160 | NKU160X | 2176 | NKU176X | 2192 | NKU192X | 2207 | NKU207X |
| 2143 | NKU143X | 2161 | NKU161X | 2177 | NKU177X | 2193 | NKU193X | 2208 | NKU208X |
| 2145 | NKU145X | 2162 | NKU162X | 2179 | NKU179X | 2194 | NKU194X | 2209 | NKU209X |
| 2146 | NKU146X | 2163 | NKU163X | 2180 | NKU180X | 2195 | NKU195X | 2210 | NKU210X |
| 2147 | NKU147X | 2164 | NKU164X | 2181 | NKU181X | 2196 | NKU196X | 2211 | NKU211X |
| 2148 | NKU148X | 2165 | NKU165X | 2182 | NKU182X | 2197 | NKU197X | 2212 | NKU212X |
| 2149 | NKU149X | 2166 | NKU166X | 2183 | NKU183X | 2198 | NKU198X | 2213 | NKU213X |
| 2150 | NKU150X | 2167 | NKU167X | 2184 | NKU184X | 2199 | NKU199X | 2214 | NKU214X |
| 2151 | NKU151X | 2168 | NKU168X | 2185 | NKU185X | 2200 | NKU200X | 2215 | NKU215X |
| 2152 | NKU152X | 2169 | NKU169X | 2186 | NKU186X | 2201 | NKU201X | 2216 | NKU216X |
| 2154 | NKU154X | 2170 | NKU170X | 2187 | NKU187X | 2202 | NKU202X | 2217 | NKU217X |
| 2155 | NKU155X | 2171 | NKU171X | 2188 | NKU188X | 2203 | NKU203X | 2218 | NKU218X |
| 2156 | NKU156X | 2172 | NKU172X | 2189 | NKU189X | 2204 | NKU204X | 2219 | NKU219X |
| 2157 | NKU157X | 2174 | NKU174X | 2190 | NKU190X | 2205 | NKU205X | 2220 | NKU220X |
| 2158 | NKU158X |      |         |      |         |      |         |      |         |

## 2221-2274

Dennis Dominator DDA133    Alexander RH    H46/32F    1982-83

| 2221 | SDT221Y | 2232 | SDT232Y | 2243 | SDT243Y | 2254 | SDT254Y | 2264 | SDT264Y |
|------|---------|------|---------|------|---------|------|---------|------|---------|
| 2222 | SDT222Y | 2233 | SDT233Y | 2244 | SDT244Y | 2255 | SDT255Y | 2265 | SDT265Y |
| 2223 | SDT223Y | 2234 | SDT234Y | 2245 | SDT245Y | 2256 | SDT256Y | 2266 | SDT266Y |
| 2224 | SDT224Y | 2235 | SDT235Y | 2247 | SDT247Y | 2257 | SDT257Y | 2267 | SDT267Y |
| 2225 | SDT225Y | 2236 | SDT236Y | 2248 | SDT248Y | 2258 | SDT258Y | 2268 | SDT268Y |
| 2226 | SDT226Y | 2237 | SDT237Y | 2249 | SDT249Y | 2259 | SDT259Y | 2270 | SDT270Y |
| 2227 | SDT227Y | 2238 | SDT238Y | 2250 | SDT250Y | 2260 | SDT260Y | 2271 | SDT271Y |
| 2228 | SDT228Y | 2239 | SDT239Y | 2251 | SDT251Y | 2261 | SDT261Y | 2272 | SDT272Y |
| 2229 | SDT229Y | 2240 | SDT240Y | 2252 | SDT252Y | 2262 | SDT262Y | 2273 | SDT273Y |
| 2230 | SDT230Y | 2241 | SDT241Y | 2253 | SDT253Y | 2263 | SDT263Y | 2274 | SDT274Y |
| 2231 | SDT231Y | 2242 | SDT242Y |      |         |      |         |      |         |

## 2275-2304

Dennis Dominator DDA165    Alexander RH    H46/32F*    1983    *2275 is H46/33F

| 2275 | UWJ275Y | 2281 | UWJ281Y | 2287 | UWJ287Y | 2293 | UWJ293Y | 2299 | A299XAK |
|------|---------|------|---------|------|---------|------|---------|------|---------|
| 2276 | UWJ276Y | 2282 | UWJ282Y | 2288 | UWJ288Y | 2294 | UWJ294Y | 2300 | A300XAK |
| 2277 | UWJ277Y | 2283 | UWJ283Y | 2289 | UWJ289Y | 2295 | A295XAK | 2301 | A301XAK |
| 2278 | UWJ278Y | 2284 | UWJ284Y | 2290 | UWJ290Y | 2296 | A296XAK | 2302 | A302XAK |
| 2279 | UWJ279Y | 2285 | UWJ285Y | 2291 | UWJ291Y | 2297 | A297XAK | 2303 | A303XAK |
| 2280 | UWJ280Y | 2286 | UWJ286Y | 2292 | UWJ292Y | 2298 | A298XAK | 2304 | A304XAK |

*Opposite, top:* **The double deck layout is now forming a smaller proportion of the Mainline fleet as new deliveries are single deckers, a trend likely to continue as double-deck buses fall from favour. As well as Dennis Dominators there are small batches of MCW Metrobuses in service. A mark II Metrobus is 1950, C950HWF, an example which is fitted with high-backed seats.** *Richard Godfrey Opposite, bottom:* **The Volvo product is the standard midibus in the Mainline fleet. For the first batch the Plaxton Pointer design were specified but for the low-floor B6BLE examples Wright Crusader model was chosen. Two of the B6BLE easy access buses are dedicated to the Goole town service which is operated on tender for the East Riding of Yorkshire. Number 450, N450DWJ, is one of the pair.** *Tony Wilson*

The Dennis Dominator is the standard double-deck in the Mainline fleet. Most, like 2469, C889JWE were bodied by Alexander though there are also small batches with Northern Counties and East Lancashire bodies. Here, 2469 is seen climbing East Bank Road on service 43. *Lee Whitehead*

### 2311-2320     Dennis Dominator DDA165    Northern Counties    H47/33F    1983

| 2311 | A311XAK | 2313 | A313XAK | 2315 | A315XAK | 2317 | A317XAK | 2319 | A319XAK |
|------|---------|------|---------|------|---------|------|---------|------|---------|
| 2312 | A312XAK | 2314 | A314XAK | 2316 | A316XAK | 2318 | A318XAK | 2320 | A320XAK |

### 2351-2363     Dennis Dominator DDA901    East Lancashire    H46/33F    1984

| 2351 | B351CDT | 2354 | B354CDT | 2357 | B357CDT | 2360 | B360CDT | 2362 | B362CDT |
|------|---------|------|---------|------|---------|------|---------|------|---------|
| 2352 | B352CDT | 2355 | B355CDT | 2358 | B358CDT | 2361 | B361CDT | 2363 | B363CDT |
| 2353 | B353CDT | 2356 | B356CDT | 2359 | B359CDT |  |  |  |  |

### 2401-2449     Dennis Dominator DDA901    Alexander RH    H46/32F    1984

| 2401 | A401YAK | 2410 | A410YAK | 2419 | A419YAK | 2430 | A430YAK | 2439 | B439CKW |
|------|---------|------|---------|------|---------|------|---------|------|---------|
| 2402 | A402YAK | 2411 | A411YAK | 2421 | A421YAK | 2431 | A431YAK | 2441 | B441CKW |
| 2403 | A403YAK | 2412 | A412YAK | 2423 | A423YAK | 2432 | A432YAK | 2442 | B442CKW |
| 2404 | A404YAK | 2413 | A413YAK | 2424 | A424YAK | 2433 | A433YAK | 2445 | B445CKW |
| 2405 | A405YAK | 2414 | A414YAK | 2425 | A425YAK | 2434 | A434YAK | 2446 | B446CKW |
| 2406 | A406YAK | 2415 | A415YAK | 2426 | A426YAK | 2435 | A435YAK | 2447 | B447CKW |
| 2407 | A407YAK | 2416 | A416YAK | 2427 | A427YAK | 2436 | A436YAK | 2448 | B448CKW |
| 2408 | A408YAK | 2417 | A417YAK | 2428 | A428YAK | 2437 | A437YAK | 2449 | B449CKW |
| 2409 | A409YAK | 2418 | A418YAK | 2429 | A429YAK | 2438 | A438YAK |  |  |

### 2451-2470     Dennis Dominator DDA910    Alexander RH    H46/32F    1986

| 2451 | C871JWE | 2455 | C875JWE | 2459 | C879JWE | 2463 | C883JWE | 2467 | C887JWE |
|------|---------|------|---------|------|---------|------|---------|------|---------|
| 2452 | C872JWE | 2456 | C876JWE | 2460 | C880JWE | 2464 | C884JWE | 2468 | C888JWE |
| 2453 | C873JWE | 2457 | C877JWE | 2461 | C881JWE | 2465 | C885JWE | 2469 | C889JWE |
| 2454 | C874JWE | 2458 | C878JWE | 2462 | C882JWE | 2466 | C886JWE | 2470 | C890JWE |

In the spring of 1997, Mainline took over the Wilfreda-Beehive bus operation in Doncaster. The Don Valley unit of Mainline has been allocated the work and eight buses have been purchased from Wilfreda-Beehive. All are Plaxton Pointer-bodied Dennis Darts. Seen here is 4006, L970NET which still carried Wilfreda-Beehive livery in May 1997 though with Don Valley fleetnames applied. *Richard Godfrey*

### 2471-2485    Dennis Dominator DDA1011    Alexander RH    DPH45/33F*  1986    *Seating varies

| | | | | | | | | |
|---|---|---|---|---|---|---|---|---|
| 2471 | D471OWE | 2474 | D474OWE | 2477 | D477OWE | 2480 | D480OWE | 2483 | D483OWE |
| 2472 | D472OWE | 2475 | D475OWE | 2478 | D478OWE | 2481 | D481OWE | 2484 | D484OWE |
| 2473 | D473OWE | 2476 | D476OWE | 2479 | D479OWE | 2482 | D482OWE | 2485 | D485OWE |

| | | | | | |
|---|---|---|---|---|---|
| 2486 | D486OWE | Dennis Dominator DDA1013 | Alexander RH | DPH40/33F | 1986 |
| 2487 | D487OWE | Dennis Dominator DDA1013 | Alexander RH | DPH40/33F | 1986 |
| 2488 | D488OWE | Dennis Dominator DDA1013 | Alexander RH | DPH45/24F | 1986 |
| 2489 | D489OWE | Dennis Dominator DDA1013 | Alexander RH | DPH45/33F | 1986 |
| 2490 | D490OWE | Dennis Dominator DDA1013 | Alexander RH | DPH45/24F | 1986 |
| 4000 | K945JWE | Dennis Dart 9.8SDL3035 | Plaxton Pointer | B36F | 1993 | Ex Wilfreda-Beehive, 1997 |
| 4001 | K946JWE | Dennis Dart 9.8SDL3035 | Plaxton Pointer | B36F | 1993 | Ex Wilfreda-Beehive, 1997 |
| 4002 | K947JWE | Dennis Dart 9.8SDL3035 | Plaxton Pointer | B36F | 1993 | Ex Wilfreda-Beehive, 1997 |
| 4003 | K948JWE | Dennis Dart 9.8SDL3035 | Plaxton Pointer | B36F | 1993 | Ex Wilfreda-Beehive, 1997 |
| 4004 | L129OWF | Dennis Dart 9.8SDL3035 | Plaxton Pointer | B36F | 1994 | Ex Wilfreda-Beehive, 1997 |
| 4005 | L130OWF | Dennis Dart 9.8SDL3035 | Plaxton Pointer | B36F | 1994 | Ex Wilfreda-Beehive, 1997 |
| 4006 | L970NET | Dennis Dart 9.8SDL3035 | Plaxton Pointer | B36F | 1993 | Ex Wilfreda-Beehive, 1997 |
| 4007 | L971NET | Dennis Dart 9.8SDL3035 | Plaxton Pointer | B36F | 1993 | Ex Wilfreda-Beehive, 1997 |

**Named Vehicles:**
287 *Catherine Howard*; 431 *Vice Admiral Sir Hilary Briggs*; 2001 *Cutty Sark*; 2002 *Samuel Plimsoll*; 2003 *Storm King*; 2004 *Fiery Cross*; 2005 *Sir Lancelot*; 2006 *Flying Cloud*; 2007 *Pegasus*; 2008 *Queen of Clippers*; 2009 *Challenger*; 2010 *The Great Republic*;

**Liveries:** Yellow, red, silver and blue;  (Don Valley) 2103/5/7, 2211, 2353/64/5, 4000-5.

# NORTH BANK TRAVEL

Fleetjet Ltd, Unit 3, Century Road, Newfield Industrial Estate,
Hedon Road, City of Kingston-upon-Hull, HU12 8FB.

| | | | | | |
|---|---|---|---|---|---|
| OKJ514M | Leyland National 1151/1R | | B49F | 1974 | Ex Good News Travels, Hull, 1993 |
| LPB203P | Leyland National 10351A/1R | | B41F | 1976 | Ex Lawrenson, Earlestown, 1995 |
| JJG889P | Leyland National 11351A/1R | | B49F | 1976 | Ex Yorkshire Rider, 1993 |
| MFN119R | Leyland National 11351A/1R | | B49F | 1976 | Ex Good News Travels, Hull, 1993 |
| MFN121R | Leyland National 11351A/1R | | B49F | 1976 | Ex Blue Triangle, Rainham, 1997 |
| UPB296S | Leyland National 10351A/1R | | B41F | 1977 | Ex Lawrenson, Earlestown, 1995 |
| EPT876S | Leyland National 11351A/1R | | B49F | 1978 | Ex Good News Travels, Hull, 1993 |
| NCW800T | Leyland National NL11390/1R | | B50F | 1978 | Ex Lawrenson, Earlstown, 1995 |
| AKY611T | Leyland National 10351B/1R | | B41F | 1979 | Ex MTL, Manchester, 1995 |
| XEU860T | Leyland National 10351B/1R | | B41F | 1979 | Ex MTL, Manchester, 1995 |
| TTC538T | Leyland National 11351A/1R | | B49F | 1979 | Ex MTL, Manchester, 1995 |
| ANJ311T | Leyland Leopard PSU3E/4RT | Plaxton Supreme III Express | C49F | 1979 | Ex Good News Travels, Hull, 1995 |
| ANJ316T | Leyland Leopard PSU3E/4RT | Plaxton Supreme III Express | C49F | 1979 | Ex Good News Travels, Hull, 1995 |
| EPD504V | Leyland National 10351B/1R | | B41F | 1979 | Ex Sovereign, 1994 |
| DOC34V | Leyland National 2 NL116L11/1R | | B50F | 1980 | Ex West Midlands Travel, 1996 |
| DOC44V | Leyland National 2 NL116L11/1R | | B50F | 1980 | Ex West Midlands Travel, 1996 |
| UWY81X | Leyland Leopard PSU3F/4R | Duple Dominant IV Express | C49F | 1981 | Ex K-Line, Huddersfield, 1997 |
| A11NBT | DAF SB3000DKSB585 | Van Hool Alizée | C48FT | 1985 | Ex Harris Coach, Grays, 1996 |

**Named Vehicles**: A11NBT *Jemima Lucy*.

**Previous Registrations:**
A11NBT        B89CNO, 6306FH, B231FHK

**Livery:** Light blue and cream

**North Bank Travel are the successor to Pride of The Road in the city of Kingston-upon-Hull where a cream and purple livery has been adopted. OKJ514M, a Leyland National which was new to Maidstone and District, is the oldest member of the fleet.  It is seen in near Princes Quay in Hull bound for the Orchard Park estate.** *Lee Whitehead*

# NORTHERN BUS

Northern Bus Co Ltd, Northern Garage, Houghton Road, North Anston,
South Yorkshire, S31 7JJ

| | | | | | | |
|---|---|---|---|---|---|---|
| ....p | NFM67 | Bristol KSW6B | Eastern Coach Works | H32/28R | 1952 | Ex Classic Buses, Winchester, 1993 |
| ....p | 782EFM | Bristol SC4LK | Eastern Coach Works | B35F | 1957 | Ex Crosville Cymru, 1995 |
| ....p | 644LFM | Bristol SC4LK | Eastern Coach Works | B35F | 1960 | Ex preservation, 1993 |
| 0113p | AFM113G | Bristol RELL6G | Eastern Coach Works | B53F | 1969 | Ex Crosville Cymru, 1990 |
| 0234p | JFM234D | Bristol Lodekka FS6G | Eastern Coach Works | H33/27RD | 1966 | Ex Crosville Cymru, 1994 |
| 0375 | 222WFM | Daimler Fleetline CRG6LX | Northern Counties | O40/31F | 1970 | Ex Crosville Cymru, 1995 |
| 0376 | 223FWW | Daimler Fleetline CRG6LX | Northern Counties | O40/31F | 1970 | Ex Crosville Cymru, 1995 |
| 0530p | AFM105B | Bristol RELH6G | Eastern Coach Works | C47F | 1964 | Ex preservation, 1994 |
| 0594p | HFM594D | Bristol RELL6G | Eastern Coach Works | DP50F | 1966 | Ex Liverpool Community Transport, 1990 |
| 0978p | 627HFM | Bristol Lodekka LD6B | Eastern Coach Works | CO33/27RD | 1959 | Ex Dunn-Line, Nottingham, 1991 |
| 1064 | C64JTU | Leyland Tiger TRCTL11/3RH | Duple 340 | C51F | 1986 | Ex Crosville Cymru, 1995 |
| 1216 | SPT216V | Leyland Leopard PSU3E/4R | Plaxton Supreme IV Express | C49F | 1979 | Ex Northumbria, 1995 |
| 1217 | SPT217V | Leyland Leopard PSU3E/4R | Plaxton Supreme IV Express | C49F | 1979 | Ex Northumbria, 1995 |
| 1265 | OWJ165X | Leyland Leopard PSU3G/4R | Eastern Coach Works B51 | C49F | 1982 | Ex Curtis, 1995 |
| 1278 | FAZ4478 | Leyland Tiger TRCTL11/2RH | Plaxton Paramount 3200 E | C53F | 1983 | Ex Crosville Cymru, 1995 |
| 1305 | EBW105Y | Leyland Tiger TRCTL11/3R | Duple Dominant IV Express | C51F | 1983 | Ex City of Oxford, 1995 |
| 1310 | EBW110Y | Leyland Tiger TRCTL11/3R | Duple Dominant IV Express | C51F | 1983 | Ex City of Oxford, 1995 |
| .... | SKY32Y | Leyland Tiger TRCTL11/3R | Eastern Coach Works B51 | C51F | 1983 | Ex East Midland, 1997 |
| 2112 | YFM282L | Bristol RELL6G | Eastern Coach Works | B52F | 1973 | Ex Crosville Cymru, 1990 |
| 2191 | GEF191N | Bristol RELL6G | Eastern Coach Works | B46D | 1974 | Ex Harlepool, 1995 |
| 2205 | TPC105X | Leyland Tiger TRCTL11/2R | Eastern Coach Works B51 | DP53F | 1982 | Ex Davies Bros, Pencader, 1992 |
| 2221 | MHE213M | Bristol RELH6G | Eastern Coach Works | DP49F | 1974 | Ex Vale of Manchester, 1992 |
| 2229 | 929CVJ | Bristol RELH6G | Eastern Coach Works B51 | DP49F | 1972 | Ex Badgerline, 1992 |
| 2230 | WPD30Y | Leyland Leopard PSU3G/4R | Eastern Coach Works B51 | DP49F | 1982 | Ex The Bee Line, 1992 |
| 2261 | JOX461P | Leyland Leopard PSU3C/4R | Plaxton Supreme III Express | DP49F | 1976 | Ex Crosville Cymru, 1994 |
| 2270 | WWY70X | Leyland Leopard PSU3F/4R | Willowbrook 003 | C49F | 1982 | Ex United, 1992 |
| 2277 | MMB977P | Leyland National 11351A/1R/SC(Gardner) | | DP48F | 1976 | Ex Barnsley & District, 1995 |
| 2287 | RKA887T | Leyland National 11351A/1R/SC | | DP45F | 1978 | Ex Merseybus, 1995 |
| 2313 | CHH213T | Leyland National 10351B/1R | | B44F | 1979 | Ex MTL Manchester, 1995 |
| 2355 | GMB655T | Leyland National 10351B/1R | | B44F | 1978 | Ex Crosville Cymru, 1995 |
| 2365 | EMB365S | Leyland National 11351A/1R | | B49F | 1978 | Ex Stagecoach Midland Red, 1996 |
| 2369 | GMB669T | Leyland National 10351B/1R | | B44F | 1978 | Ex Crosville Cymru, 1995 |
| 2378 | JTU578T | Leyland National 10351B/1R | | B40F | 1979 | Ex Crosville Cymru, 1996 |
| 2383 | YPL383T | Leyland National 10351B/1R | | B41F | 1978 | Ex Crosville Cymru, 1995 |
| 2398 | JTU598T | Leyland National 10351B/1R | | B44F | 1979 | Ex Crosville Cymru, 1995 |
| 2399 | JTU599T | Leyland National 10351B/1R | | B44F | 1979 | Ex Crosville Cymru, 1995 |
| 2414 | LMA414T | Leyland National 11351A/1R | | B49F | 1979 | Ex Mainline, 1995 |
| 2494 | BHN694N | Bristol RELH6L | Eastern Coach Works | DP49F | 1974 | Ex preservation, 1992 |
| 2507 | HRN107N | Bristol RESL6L | Eastern Coach Works | DP44F | 1975 | Ex Fylde, 1993 |
| 2508 | HRN108N | Bristol RESL6L | Eastern Coach Works | B38F | 1975 | Ex Fylde, 1993 |
| 2554 | THU354G | Bristol RESL6L | Eastern Coach Works | B43F | 1969 | Ex preservation, 1992 |
| 2601 | UKK335X | Bedford JJL | Marshall | B27F | 1981 | Ex Brighton, 1992 |
| | AVS903T | Bedford JJL | Marshall | B27F | 1978 | Ex Brighton, 1992 |
| 2602 | F221EWG | Renault-Dodge S56 | Northern Counties | B25F | 1988 | Ex Mainline, 1996 |
| 2807 | GMB387T | Leyland National 11351A/1R | | B49F | 1978 | Ex Constable, Long Melford, 1996 |
| 2813 | LMA413T | Leyland National 11351A/1R(6HLX) | | B49F | 1979 | Ex Hedingham & District, 1996 |
| 2835 | TTC535T | Leyland National 11351A/1R | | B52F | 1978 | Ex MTL Manchester, 1995 |
| 2845 | CFM345S | Leyland National 11351A/1R(6HLX) | | B49F | 1978 | Ex Hedingham & District, 1996 |
| 2847 | CFM347S | Leyland National 11351A/1R(6HLX) | | B49F | 1978 | Ex Hedingham & District, 1996 |
| 2849 | CFM349S | Leyland National 11351A/1R | | B49F | 1978 | Ex Constable, Long Melford, 1996 |
| 2870 | YFB970V | Leyland National 11351A/1R | | B52F | 1979 | Ex MTL Manchester, 1996 |
| 2882 | UTU982R | Leyland National 11351A/1R(6HLX) | | B49F | 1977 | Ex Mainline, 1996 |
| 2887 | VFX987S | Leyland National 11351A/1R | | B52F | 1978 | Ex MTL Manchester, 1995 |
| 2893 | PCK193P | Leyland National 11351/1R | | B49F | 1976 | Ex MTL Manchester, 1996 |

| | | | | | | |
|---|---|---|---|---|---|---|
| ? | AAK111T | Leyland National 10351B/1R | | B44F | 1977 | Ex Mainline, 1996 |
| ? | XAK452T | Leyland National 11351A/1R | | B49F | 1978 | Ex Mainline, 1996 |
| ? | CFM355S | Leyland National 11351A/1R | | B49F | 1978 | Ex Constable, Long Melford, 1996 |
| ? | EMB363S | Leyland National 11351A/1R | | B49F | 1978 | Ex Constable, Long Melford, 1996 |
| ? | WBN477T | Leyland National 11351A/1R | | B49F | 1979 | Ex East Midland, 1997 |
| 3000 | CPU979G | Bristol VRT/SL/6G | Eastern Coach Works | H39/31F | 1969 | Ex preservation, 1993 |
| 3003 | ODM413V | Bristol VRT/SL3/501 | Eastern Coach Works | H43/31F | 1979 | Ex Crosville Cymru, 1995 |
| 3006 | XAK906T | Bristol VRT/SL3/501(6LXB) | Eastern Coach Works | H43/31F | 1978 | Ex RoadCar, 1994 |
| 3007 | KAU327N | Bristol VRT/SL3/501 | Eastern Coach Works | H43/34F | 1974 | Ex Trent, 1993 |
| 3008 | XAK908T | Bristol VRT/SL3/501(6LXB) | Eastern Coach Works | H43/31F | 1978 | Ex RoadCar, 1994 |
| 3013 | VDV113S | Bristol VRT/SL3/6LXB | Eastern Coach Works | H45/29F | 1978 | Ex Crosville Cymru, 1994 |
| 3017 | VHB677S | Bristol VRT/SL3/6LXB | Eastern Coach Works | CO43/29F | 1978 | Ex Crosville Cymru, 1995 |
| 3018 | VHB678S | Bristol VRT/SL3/6LXB | Eastern Coach Works | CO43/29F | 1978 | Ex Crosville Cymru, 1995 |
| 3023 | YBW603R | Bristol VRT/SL3/6LXB | Eastern Coach Works | H43/29F | 1976 | Ex Crosville Cymru, 1995 |
| 3024 | YBW604R | Bristol VRT/SL3/6LXB | Eastern Coach Works | H43/29F | 1976 | Ex Crosville Cymru, 1995 |
| 3026 | YRC126M | Bristol VRT/SL2/6G | Eastern Coach Works | H43/34F | 1974 | Ex Trent, 1991 |
| 3034 | RMA434V | Bristol VRT/SL3/501 | Eastern Coach Works | H43/31F | 1980 | Ex Crosville Cymru, 1994 |
| 3041 | XMO541H | Bristol VRT/SL2/6G | Eastern Coach Works | H39/31F | 1970 | Ex The Bee Line, 1993 |
| 3051 | AYG851S | Bristol VRT/SL3/6LXB | Eastern Coach Works | H43/29F | 1978 | Ex Crosville Cymru, 1994 |
| 3070 | BTU370S | Bristol VRT/SL3/501 | Eastern Coach Works | H43/31F | 1978 | Ex East Midland, 1993 |
| 3076 | XRR176S | Bristol VRT/SL3/6LXB | Eastern Coach Works | H43/31F | 1978 | Ex East Midland, 1993 |
| 3081 | MDM281P | Bristol VRT/SL3/6LXB | Eastern Coach Works | H43/29F | 1975 | Ex Crosville Cymru, 1994 |
| 3083 | AET183T | Bristol VRT/SL3/6XLB | Eastern Coach Works | H43/34F | 1979 | Ex East Midland, 1993 |
| 3089 | FTU389T | Bristol VRT/SL3/501 | Eastern Coach Works | H43/31F | 1978 | Ex Crosville Cymru, 1994 |
| 3090 | FTU390T | Bristol VRT/SL3/501(6LXB) | Eastern Coach Works | H43/31F | 1978 | Ex Crosville Cymru, 1995 |
| 3092 | DWF192V | Bristol VRT/SL3/6LXB | Eastern Coach Works | H43/31F | 1979 | Ex East Midland, 1993 |
| ? | AUD462R | Bristol VRT/SL3/6LXB | Eastern Coach Works | H43/29F | 1977 | Ex Crosville Cymru, 1995 |
| ? | DCA531X | Bristol VRT/SL3/6LXB | Eastern Coach Works | H43/29F | 1981 | Ex Crosville Cymru, 1996 |
| 3112 | KKU112W | Dennis Dominator DDA133 | Alexander RH | H46/32F | 1981 | Ex Mainline, 1996 |
| 3114 | KKU114W | Dennis Dominator DDA133 | Alexander RH | H46/32F | 1981 | Ex Mainline, 1996 |
| 3115 | KKU115W | Dennis Dominator DDA133 | Alexander RH | H46/32F | 1981 | Ex Mainline, 1996 |
| 3500 | FBV500W | Leyland Atlantean AN68B/1R | Eastern Coach Works | H43/31F | 1981 | Ex North Western, 1996 |
| 3515 | FBV515W | Leyland Atlantean AN68B/1R | Eastern Coach Works | H43/31F | 1981 | Ex North Western, 1996 |
| 3592 | FBV492W | Leyland Atlantean AN68B/1R | Eastern Coach Works | H43/31F | 1980 | Ex North Western, 1996 |
| 3601 | HJI3932 | Leyland Olympian ONTL11/2RSp | Eastern Coach Works | CH45/28F | 1983 | Ex The Bee Line, 1992 |
| 3602 | B782FOG | Leyland Olympian ONTL11/2RSp | Eastern Coach Works | CH45/24F | 1985 | Ex East Yorkshire, 1997 |
| 3603 | B161AKH | Leyland Olympian ONTL11/2RSp | Eastern Coach Works | CH45/24F | 1985 | Ex East Yorkshire, 1997 |
| 3604 | B109LPH | Leyland Olympian ONTL11/2RSp | Eastern Coach Works | CH45/24F | 1985 | Ex East Yorkshire, 1997 |
| 3605 | B162AKH | Leyland Olympian ONTL11/2RSp | Eastern Coach Works | CH45/24F | 1985 | Ex East Yorkshire, 1997 |

**Named Vehicles:** 0234 *Happy Dragon*; 0375 *Beaumaris Castle*; 0376 *Rhuddlan Castle*; 1064 *Clarence*; 1216 *Rock*; 1217 *Gravel*; 1265 *George*; 2191 *Brian*; 2221 *The Soup Dragon*; 2261 *Jock*; 2383 *Sherpa Tensing*; 2554 *Thug*; 2601 *Hattie*; 2602 *Droopy*; 3000 *Good King Henry*; 3003 *The Ant Hill Mob*; 3006 *Mungo*; 3008 *Midge*; 3013 *Pippin*; 3026 *Sage the Owl*; 3034 *Tog*; 3041 *Constable Knapweed*; 3051 *Pogle*; 3070 *Belladonna/Andy4*; 3076 *Aunt Mint*; 3081 *Dick Dastardly*; 3083 *Devils Mitt*; 3089 *The Turbo Terrific*; 3092 *Miss Jessup*; 3601 *Zorba*.

**Previous Registrations:**

| | | | | | |
|---|---|---|---|---|---|
| 222WFM | TCD375J | 929CVJ | VHK177L | HJI3932 | YPJ502Y |
| 223FWW | TCD376J | B161AKH | B108LPH, 334EYL | KAU327N | ORC256N, YRC181 |
| 627HFM | From new | B162AKH | B110LPH, 546EYB | MHE213M | RPU869M, 223FWW |
| 644LFM | From new | B782FOG | B107LPH, B111WAT | NFM67 | From new |
| 782EFM | From new | FAZ4478 | A102EPA | | |

**Livery:** Cream, dark blue and red.

*Opposite, top:* **The Bristol VR was once the standard double decker in the Northern Bus fleet though this is now being phased out. Replacements have come in the form of Leyland Olympians, Atlanteans and Dennis Dominators. Previously in the Mainline fleet 3112, KKU112W, is an Alexander-bodied Dennis Dominator seen here entering the interchange in Sheffield.** *Tony Wilson*
*Opposite, bottom:* **Northern Bus have replaced Mainline as the "Sheffield end" operator of the White Rose express services. These services between Sheffield, Barnsley, Wakefield, Bradford and Leeds are jointly operated with Yorkshire Bus Group, Yorkshire Rider and Yorkshire Traction. Pictured passing through Barnsley while bound for Leeds is 1064, C64JTU, a Duple 340-bodied Leyland Tiger purchased from Crosville Wales, as are many vehicles in the Northern Bus fleet.** *Tony Wilson*

# PENNINE

ND J & M Simpson, Grouse Garage, Gargrave, Skipton,
North Yorkshire, BD23 3RB

**Depots:** West Close Garage, Barnoldswick; Grouse Garage, Gargrave; New Road Garage, Ingleton; White Friars Garage, Settle and Red Lion Garage, Skipton.

| | | | | | | |
|---|---|---|---|---|---|---|
| u | MTD235 | Leyland Royal Tiger PSU1/15 | Leyland | C41C | 1951 | Ex Leyland demonstrator, 1952 |
| | HHU636N | Leyland National 10351/1R | | B44F | 1975 | Ex Yorkshire Terrier, 1995 |
| | XPD234N | Leyland National 10351/1R/SC | | DP39F | 1974 | Ex East Yorkshire, 1995 |
| L12 | JIL4698 | Leyland Leopard PSU3E/4R | Plaxton Supreme IV Express | C49F | 1980 | |
| | JIL2427 | Leyland Leopard PSU3F/4R | Plaxton Supreme IV | C49F | 1981 | Ex Southdown, 1990 |
| L14 | JIL2428 | Leyland Leopard PSU3E/4R | Plaxton Supreme IV Express | C49F | 1981 | Ex London Country, 1986 |
| | JIL2426 | Leyland Leopard PSU3E/4R | Plaxton Supreme IV | C53F | 1981 | Ex Wings, Sleaford, 1984 |
| LN1 | JIL2794 | Leyland National 10351A/1R(Volvo) | | B41F | 1977 | Ex Northumbria, 1994 |
| LN2 | RIB5081 | Leyland National 10351A/1R(Volvo) | | B41F | 1978 | Ex R&I Buses, Milton Keynes, 1994 |
| LN3 | JIL7422 | Leyland National 10351A/1R(Volvo) | | B41F | 1977 | Ex Northumbria, 1994 |
| LN4 | JIL2793 | Leyland National 10351A/2R | | DP42F | 1977 | Ex London United, 1994 |
| LN5 | JIL2795 | Leyland National 1051/1R/0501(Volvo) | | B44F | 1973 | Ex Executive Minibuses, Greasby, 1994 |
| LN6 | JIL8353 | Leyland National 2 NL106L11/1R | | B44F | 1980 | Ex Harrogate & District, 1995 |
| LN7 | JIL6502 | Leyland National 10351B/1R | | B44F | 1978 | Ex Ribble, 1995 |
| LN8 | JIL7417 | Leyland National 10351B/1R | | B44F | 1978 | Ex Ribble, 1995 |
| LN9 | JIL4653 | Leyland National 1051/1R/SC | | B44F | 1975 | Ex Kingsman, Sheffield, 1995 |
| LN10 | JIL7416 | Leyland National 10351/1R | | B41F | 1975 | Ex Kingsman, Sheffield, 1995 |
| LN | JCK847W | Leyland National 2 NL106AL11/1R | | B44F | 1980 | Ex Ribble, 1997 |

**Previous Registrations:**

| | | | | | |
|---|---|---|---|---|---|
| JIL2426 | BTL485X | JIL2795 | XDL800L | JIL7417 | OLS809T |
| JIL2427 | MAP347W, 400DCD, OUF50W | JIL4653 | HPF311N | JIL7422 | SPC276R |
| JIL2428 | NPA220W | JIL4698 | NWT839V | JIL8353 | PWY583W |
| JIL2793 | OJD879R | JIL6502 | OLS807T | RIB5081 | YPF767T |
| JIL2794 | SPC282R | JIL7416 | JNA589N | | |

**Livery:** Orange, black and grey

# PRIDE OF THE ROAD

Pride of the Road (Travel) Ltd, Station Yard, Station Road, Honley,
Huddersfield, West Yorkshire, HD7 2LJ.

| | | | | | |
|---|---|---|---|---|---|
| RCC512S | Ford R1114 | Duple Dominant II Express | C53F | 1978 | Ex Sel's Llanrwst, 1997 |
| WDR274V | Fiat 55-10 | Hawton | C25F | 1980 | Ex Richardson, Stevenage, 1996 |
| PIA2192 | Volvo B10M-61 | Duple Goldliner | C53F | 1982 | Ex Taj, Batley, 1997 |
| FSU359 | DAF MB230LB615 | Caetano Algarve | C53F | 1988 | Ex Catteralls, Southam, 1992 |
| F237RJX | DAF MB230LB615 | Caetano Algarve | C53F | 1989 | Ex Moxon, Oldcoates, 1994 |
| J798KHD | DAF MB230LT615 | Van Hool Alizeé | C51FT | 1992 | |
| K520RJX | DAF MB230LT615 | Van Hool Alizée | C57F | 1993 | Ex Landtourers, Farnham, 1994 |
| K529RJX | DAF MB230LT615 | Van Hool Alizée | C57F | 1993 | Ex Landtourers, Farnham, 1994 |
| K538RJX | DAF MB230LT615 | Van Hool Alizée | C51FT | 1993 | Ex Armchair, Brentford, 1997 |

**Previous Registrations:**

| | | | | |
|---|---|---|---|---|
| FSU359 | F877TNH | | PIA2192 | FHS755X, 12EWO, HAS843X |

**Livery:** White

*The Yorkshire Bus Handbook*

Pennine is a long established operator of bus services in the Skipton and Ingleton areas. Having favoured Leyland Leopards for many years, the latest policy is to purchase Leyland Nationals which are then refurbished. Seen in the market town of Settle is LN3, JIL7422, a 10.3 metre long example acquired from Northumbria. The vehicle was new to London Country, passing from that operator to Kentishbus, *Tony Wilson*

The Pride of The Road fleet is now considerably reduced with the bus operations now in the Ambermile and North Bank operations. A white livery has been adopted as can be seen in this view of J798KHD, a Van Hool-bodied DAF depicted in Tower Street, York. *Tony Wilson*

# PONTEFRACT MOTORWAYS

S Stringer, 102 Southgate, Pontefract, West Yorkshire, WF8 1PN

| | | | | | |
|---|---|---|---|---|---|
| IBZ5892 | Daimler Fleetline CRL6-30 | Northern Counties | H44/31F | 1975 | Ex City of Nottingham, 1993 |
| IBZ5893 | Daimler Fleetline CRL6-30 | Northern Counties | H44/31F | 1975 | Ex City of Nottingham, 1993 |
| 63XMD | Leyland Leopard PSU3C/4R | Plaxton Supreme III | C53F | 1976 | |
| NFB115R | Bristol VRT/SL3/6LXB | Eastern Coach Works | H43/27D | 1976 | Ex City Line, 1993 |
| WCW310R | Leyland Leopard PSU3D/2R | Alexander AYS | B53F | 1977 | Ex Blue Bus, Huddersfield, 1996 |
| DWX395T | Leyland Fleetline FE30ALR | Northern Counties | H39/31F | 1978 | Ex Wealden, Five Oak Green, 1997 |
| BSJ892T | Leyland Leopard PSU3E/4R | Alexander AY | B53F | 1979 | Ex Clydeside, 1997 |
| TJI2804 | Volvo B10M-61 | Duple Caribbean 2 | C53F | 1985 | Ex Ludlow, Halesowen, 1995 |
| B461WTC | Ford Transit | Dormobile | B16F | 1986 | Ex Eastern National, 1995 |
| D766MUR | Iveco Daily 49-10 | Robin Hood City Nippy | B19F | 1986 | Ex The Shires, 1995 |
| TJI2805 | DAF SB2305DHTD585 | Plaxton Paramount 3200 III | C55F | 1987 | Ex Nelson, Glyn Neath, 1995 |
| F78CJC | Iveco Daily 49-10 | Carlyle Dailybus 2 | B25F | 1988 | Ex Crosville Cymru, 1995 |
| F64SMC | Mercedes-Benz 407D | Reeve Burgess | M15 | 1988 | |
| F356BWU | Mercedes-Benz 811D | Reeve Burgess Beaver | C25F | 1988 | |
| F706ENE | Leyland Tiger TRCL10/3ARZM | Plaxton Paramount 3200 III | C53F | 1989 | Ex Shearings, 1993 |
| G649DKC | Ford Transit | Dormobile | B16F | 1990 | Ex Trafford MBC, 1997 |
| P794TGK | Mercedes-Benz 711D | Crest | C24F | 1996 | |
| P795TGK | Mercedes-Benz 412D | Crest | M16 | 1996 | |
| P740UNW | Mercedes-Benz 711D | Crest | C24F | 1997 | |
| P6SYD | Mercedes-Benz 814D | Plaxton Beaver | C33F | 1997 | |

**Previous Registrations:**

| | | | |
|---|---|---|---|
| 63XMD | PYG581R | TJI2804 | C118KDD, GJI2223, C437LOJ |
| IBZ5892 | HRC788N | TJI2805 | E350EVH, PJI3548, E552WEP |
| IBZ5893 | HRC789N | | |

**Livery:** White, red and black

**IBZ5892 is one of a pair of Northern Counties-bodied Daimler Fleetline buses from the City of Nottingham fleet in 1993. It is seen in Pontefract bus station before heading for Brotherton.**
*Tony Wilson*

# POWELL BUS

JS, P and J Powell; Powells Bus Co Ltd, 176 Bawtry Road, Wickersley, Rotherham, South Yorkshire, S66 0AG

**Depot:** Hellaby Lane, Hellaby

|     |          |                           |                        |          |      |                                          |
|-----|----------|---------------------------|------------------------|----------|------|------------------------------------------|
|     | 260ERY   | Leyland Tiger TRCTL11/3R  | Duple Dominant IV      | C51F     | 1982 | Ex Warner, Tewksbury, 1988               |
|     | RIB1727  | DAF MB200DKTL600          | Jonckheere Bermuda     | C49FT    | 1981 | Ex Taylor, Dinnington, 1997              |
| 1   | 240HYU   | Scania K112CRS            | Van Hool Alizée        | C49F     | 1984 |                                          |
| 2   | MIL7798  | Leyland Tiger TRCTL11/3RH | Berkhof Everest 370    | C49FT    | 1986 | Ex Speedlink, 1993                       |
| 3   | 91RTO    | Leyland Tiger TRCTL11/3R  | Plaxton Paramount 3500 | C49F     | 1983 | Ex Yelloway, 1986                        |
| 5   | A805RNW  | DAF MB200DKTL600          | Caetano Algarve        | C53F     | 1983 | Ex Howie, Roberttown, 1995               |
| 6   | XBF976   | Leyland Tiger TRCTL11/2R  | Plaxton Viewmaster IV Exp | C53F  | 1982 | Ex Williams, Brecon, 1993                |
| 7   | FNA927T  | Leyland Leopard PSU5C/4R  | Duple Dominant II      | C50F     | 1978 | Ex Rothwell, Heywood, 1994               |
| 8   | P2BUS    | Mercedes-Benz 814D        | Plaxton Beaver         | DP32F    | 1996 |                                          |
| 21  | KOM797P  | Leyland National 11351/2R |                        | B46D     | 1976 | Ex London & Country, 1996                |
| 22  | HPF316N  | Leyland National 10351/1R/SC |                     | DP39F    | 1975 | Ex Greater Manchester, 1996              |
| 24  | GPD295N  | Leyland National 10351/1R/SC |                     | DP39F    | 1974 | Ex Greater Manchester, 1996              |
| 25  | TPD178M  | Leyland National 1051/1R/0402 |                    | B41F     | 1973 | Ex London & Country, 1996                |
| 26  | DAR128T  | Leyland National 11351A/1R |                       | B49F     | 1979 | Ex Thamesway, 1996                       |
| 27  | JHJ145V  | Leyland National 11351A/1R |                       | B49F     | 1979 | Ex Thamesway, 1996                       |
| 28  | DAR125T  | Leyland National 11351A/1R |                       | B49F     | 1979 | Ex Thamesway, 1996                       |
| 29  | BNO666T  | Leyland National 11351A/1R |                       | B49F     | 1978 | Ex Thamesway, 1996                       |
| 31  | E99OUH   | Freight Rover Sherpa      | Carlyle Citybus 2      | B20F     | 1987 | Ex Stagecoach Midland Red (G&G), 1996    |
| 36  | YEV305S  | Leyland National 11351A/1R |                       | B49F     | 1978 | Ex Thamesway, 1996                       |
| 37  | E913NEW  | Volkswagen LT55           | Optare CityPacer       | B25F     | 1988 | Ex Goodwin, Eccles, 1996                 |
| 38  | OCY907R  | Bristol VRT/SL3/501       | Eastern Coach Works    | H43/31F  | 1977 | Ex Hulley, Baslow, 1996                  |
| 39  | UNW929R  | Bristol VRT/SL3/6LXB      | Eastern Coach Works    | H43/31F  | 1977 | Ex Happy Days, Woodseaves, 1996          |
| 40  | E109JPL  | Renault-Dodge S56         | Northern Counties      | B25F     | 1988 | Ex London & Country, (Guildford), 1996   |
| 41  | H701YUV  | Iveco Daily 49-10         | Reeve Burgess Beaver   | B20FL    | 1990 | Ex London United, 1997                   |
|     | E195XWG  | Renault-Dodge S56         | Reeve Burgess Beaver   | B25F     | 1989 | Ex Mainline, 1997                        |
|     | F220EWG  | Renault-Dodge S56         | Northern Counties      | B23F     | 1989 | Ex Mainline, 1997                        |
|     | F224EWG  | Renault-Dodge S56         | Northern Counties      | B23F     | 1989 | Ex Mainline, 1997                        |
|     | F237EWG  | Renault-Dodge S56         | Northern Counties      | B23F     | 1989 | Ex Mainline, 1997                        |

**Previous Registrations:**

| | | | |
|---|---|---|---|
| 91RTO | A579KVU | FNA927T | BUR425T, 9195RH |
| 260ERY | NTG18X, 8921WF | MIL7798 | C139SPB |
| 240HYU | A536YHE | RIB1727 | KRW865W, YRX481, FBK945W |
| A805RNW | A474OYA, A5SDH | XBF976 | GCA123X, 3810VT, XAY875X, WSV490, LES991X |

**Livery:** Blue, orange and red

Powell of Wickersley, near Rotherham, have recently developed a network of bus routes centred on Rotherham. While the majority of vehicles in the bus fleet are Leyland Nationals, there are two Bristol VR double-deckers. One of these, OCY907R was new to South Wales Transport and this example is seen in Dinnington.
*Tony Wilson*

# PROCTERS

JJ & KJ Procter, 6 Oaktree Road, Bedale, North Yorkshire, DL8 1UE

**Depots:** Leeming Bar Industrial Estate, Bat Garage, Robin Hoods Bay.

| | | | | | |
|---|---|---|---|---|---|
| YFR496R | Leyland Leopard PSU3E/4R | Duple Dominant I | C49F | 1977 | Ex Hyndburn, 1995 |
| KIB7257 | Leyland Leopard PSU3E/4R | Duple Dominant II | C49F | 1978 | Ex Hyndburn, 1995 |
| BKJ150T | Leyland Leopard PSU3E/4R | Duple Dominant II | C47F | 1979 | Ex Hyndburn, 1995 |
| SWH127T | Volvo B58-61 | Plaxton Supreme IV | C49FT | 1979 | Ex Hyndburn, 1995 |
| KSD104W | Ailsa B55-10 MkII | Alexander AV | H44/35F | 1980 | Ex Clydeside 2000, 1993 |
| KSD105W | Ailsa B55-10 MkII | Alexander AV | H44/35F | 1980 | Ex Clydeside 2000, 1993 |
| NSU611 | Volvo B58-61 | Duple Dominant IV | C57F | 1981 | Ex Battersby-Silver Grey, Morecambe, 1994 |
| LCW980W | Volvo B58-61 | Duple Dominant IV | C57F | 1981 | Ex Battersby-Silver Grey, Morecambe, 1994 |
| HFB845X | Volvo B58-61 | Duple Dominant IV | C53F | 1981 | Ex Hyndburn, 1996 |
| MAX261X | Leyland Tiger TRCTL11/3R | Plaxton Supreme IV | C57F | 1981 | Ex Daisy, Broughton, 1994 |
| BUA751X | Leyland Tiger TRCTL11/3R | Plaxton Supreme V | C50F | 1983 | Ex Dodsworth, Boroughbridge, 1994 |
| MHW197Y | Fiat 60-10 | Caetano Viana | C18F | 1982 | Ex Hall, Robin Hood's Bay, 1997 |
| A574HNE | Ford Transit | Dixon Lomas | M12 | 1983 | Ex Hall, Robin Hood's Bay, 1997 |
| YSU912 | Leyland Royal Tiger B50 | Roe Doyen | C44FT | 1983 | Ex Gypsy Queen, Langley Park, 1994 |
| GSU230 | Leyland Tiger TRCTL11/3RZ | Duple 320 | C49FT | 1987 | Ex Trumans, Pontypool, 1995 |
| B256ADM | Mercedes-Benz L608D | PMT | C21F | 1984 | Ex Hall, Robin Hoods Bay, 1997 |
| C28CAJ | Ford Transit | Ford | M9 | 1987 | Ex Private owner, 1989 |
| C356PUJ | Volvo B10M-61 | Plaxton Paramount 3500 II | C53F | 1987 | Ex Elcock Reisen, Telford, 1997 |
| D894EVN | Ford Transit | Ford | M8 | 1987 | Ex Private owner, 1989 |
| D586MVR | Leyland Tiger TRCTL11/3RZ | Plaxton Paramount 3200 III | C53F | 1987 | Ex ?, 1996 |
| E639DPD | Mercedes-Benz 609D | Advanced Vehicle Bodies | C24F | 1987 | Ex Cropper, Kirkstall, 1996 |
| E603JEF | Renault-Dodge S56 | Customline | B16FL | 1987 | Ex North Yorkshire County Council, 1996 |
| E604JEF | Renault-Dodge S56 | Customline | B16FL | 1987 | Ex North Yorkshire County Council, 1996 |
| E607JEF | Renault-Dodge S56 | Customline | B16FL | 1987 | Ex North Yorkshire County Council, 1996 |

**Procters of Bedale operate the town service in Ripon. Seen in the bus station is K396NGG. This Mercedes-Benz 709D was built in Kent by the now defunct Dormobile company with their Routemaker minibus body.** *Tony Wilson*

Representing the Procters coach fleet is HFB845X, a Volvo B58 with Duple Dominant bodywork which was previously operated by Hyndburn. *David Longbottom*

| | | | | | |
|---|---|---|---|---|---|
| E150LAJ | Renault-Dodge S56 | Customline | B16FL | 1988 | Ex North Yorkshire County Council, 1996 |
| E419FNB | Mazda E2200 | Mazda | M12 | 1988 | Ex ?, 1997 |
| GIJ8319 | DAF SB2305DHTD585 | Plaxton Paramount 3200 III | C57F | 1988 | Ex Shaw Hadwin, Silverdale, 1997 |
| E462ANC | Mercedes-Benz 609D | Made-to-Measure | C24F | 1988 | Ex Hall, Robin Hood's Bay, 1997 |
| MSU462 | LAG G355Z | LAG Panoramic | C49FT | 1988 | Ex Black Prince, Morley, 1996 |
| F702UHD | Ford Transit | Ford | M8 | 1988 | Ex Hall, Robin Hood's Bay, 1997 |
| F893XOE | Freight Rover Sherpa | Carlyle Citybus 2 | B15FL | 1988 | Ex ?, 1995 |
| F520BHD | Ford Transit | Crystals | M14 | 1989 | Ex Hall, Robin Hood's Bay, 1997 |
| RIA7809 | Mercedes-Benz 811D | Carlyle | C29F | 1989 | Ex Skills, Nottingham, 1995 |
| H201FSK | Ford Transit | Deansgate | M14 | 1990 | Ex Hall, Robin Hood's Bay, 1997 |
| G512NHH | Volvo B10M-60 | Plaxton Paramount 3500 III | C54F | 1989 | Ex Messenger, Aspatria, 1997 |
| G357BHN | Ford Transit | Ford | M8 | 1990 | Ex Private owner, 1994 |
| K396NGG | Mercedes-Benz 709D | Dormobile Routemaker | B29F | 1989 | Ex Thompson, South Bank, 1996 |
| M183BFE | Ford Transit | Ford | M | 1995 | Ex ?, 1996 |

**Previous Registrations:**

| | | | |
|---|---|---|---|
| BUA751X | XPP293X, JSV328 | MSU462 | E641LNV |
| C356PUJ | C177LWB, 1577NT | NSU611 | HHG922W, 7144FN, LCW979W |
| GIJ8319 | E652EEO | RIA7809 | F79KRA, MSU462 |
| GSU230 | D23NWO | SWH127T | CJF7T, 9874ND |
| KIB7257 | LWC5S | YSU912 | A212XJR, PCN762, A272DCU |
| LCW980W | HHG920W, 5096WF | | |

**Livery:** Silver, blue and red.

**Photographed while on lay-over in the Meadowhall coach park, F992BFR from the Relaince fleet is a Leyland Swift with Elme Orion coachwork. This vehicle has the smallest capacity in the fleet where Leyland products dominate.** *Donald Akrigg*

**Ross Travel are based in the former mining town of Featherstone which once had a substantial West Riding depot. As well as operating a bus route which serves Featherstone, the company also has a number of coaches. HIL 7643 was new to Ross in 1986 and is a Bova Futura which has a distinctive rounded front.** *Tony Wilson*

# RELIANCE

JH & M Duff, The Garage, Wigginton Road, Sutton-on-the-Forest,
North Yorkshire, YO6 1ES

| | | | | | |
|---|---|---|---|---|---|
| CWG761V | Leyland Atlantean AN68A/1R | Roe | H45/29D | 1979 | Ex Your Bus, Alcester, 1993 |
| TCK200X | Leyland Atlantean AN68D/2R | East Lancashire | H50/36F | 1982 | Ex Ribble, 1997 |
| TCK212X | Leyland Atlantean AN68D/2R | East Lancashire | H50/36F | 1982 | Ex Ribble, 1997 |
| C76XWK | Leyland Tiger TRCTL11/3RZ | Plaxton Paramount 3200 II | C51F | 1986 | Ex Midland Red South, 1993 |
| F992BFR | Leyland Swift LBM6T/1RS | Elme Orion | C27F | 1989 | Ex Kinnaird, Edinburgh, 1992 |
| F702ENE | Leyland Tiger TRCL10/3ARZM | Plaxton Paramount 3200 III | C53F | 1989 | Ex Blue Bus, Horwich, 1997 |
| H940DRJ | Volvo B10M-61 | Plaxton Paramount 3500 III | C53F | 1991 | Ex Capital, Heathrow, 1997 |
| R26GNW | DAF SB220LC550 | Optare Delta | B53F | 1997 | |

Livery: Green and cream

**Named Vehicles**: CWG761V *Moonlight Legend;* C76XWK *Desert Surprise;* F702ENE *Sally's Choice;* R26GNW *Far Ahead.*

# ROSS TRAVEL

P E Ross, The Garage, Allinson Street, Station Road, Featherstone
West Yorkshire, WF7 5BC

| | | | | | | |
|---|---|---|---|---|---|---|
| 2 | HSC170X | Leyland Cub CU435 | Duple Dominant | B31F | 1981 | Ex Lothian, 1993 |
| 3 | HSC169X | Leyland Cub CU435 | Duple Dominant | B31F | 1981 | Ex Lothian, 1993 |
| 5 | HSC173X | Leyland Cub CU435 | Duple Dominant | B31F | 1981 | Ex Lothian, 1993 |
| 6 | F139HNC | Renault-Dodge S56 | Northern Counties | B23F | 1988 | Ex Trafalgar Travel, Hindley Green, 1995 |
| 7 | F33CWY | Mercedes-Benz 811D | Optare StarRider | B26F | 1989 | Ex Cowie Leaside, 1996 |
| 8 | H933DBU | Mercedes-Benz 811D | Reeve Burgess Beaver | B31F | 1990 | Ex Dennis's Ashton-under-Lyne, 1996 |
| 9 | F909YWY | Mercedes-Benz 811D | Optare StarRider | B26F | 1988 | Ex Cowie Leaside, 1996 |
| | GGB640L | Bedford J2SZ10 | Plaxton Embassy | C20F | 1972 | Ex Sutton, Sunderland, 1986 |
| | BPJ77H | Van Hool T815H | Van Hool Alicron | C54F | 1984 | Ex Wood, Billericay, 1993 |
| | A739PUS | Leyland Cub CU435 | Wadham Stringer Vanguard | B24FL | 1986 | Ex Cowell & Hamilton, Johnstone, 1995 |
| | A63FNU | Bova FHD12.280 | Bova Futura | C36DT | 1984 | Ex Nottigham CC, 1995 |
| | C808KBT | Leyland Cub CU435 | Optare | B33F | 1988 | Ex McAinsh, Redding, 1996 |
| | HIL7643 | Bova FHD12.280 | Bova Futura | C53F | 1986 | |
| | D506GEN | Volvo B10M-61 | Plaxton Paramount 3200 III | C53F | 1987 | Ex Shearings, 1992 |
| | HIL7642 | Volvo B10M-61 | Duple 340 | C49FT | 1987 | Ex Bleanch, Hetton le Hole, 1988 |
| | HIL7644 | Scania K92CRB | Plaxton Paramount 3200 II | C53F | 1987 | Ex Aston, Kempsey, 1991 |
| | E507YSU | Mercedes-Benz L307D | North West Coach Sales | M15 | 1988 | |
| | F161FWY | Mercedes-Benz 811D | Optare StarRider | B26F | 1989 | Ex Pauls, Huddersfield, 1997 |
| | HIL7641 | LAG G355Z | LAG Panoramic | C49FT | 1989 | Ex Wood, Buckfastleigh, 1992 |
| | G836RDS | Mercedes-Benz 609D | North West Coach Sales | C24F | 1990 | |
| | K23GVC | Scania K113CRB | Van Hool Alizée | C48FT | 1993 | Ex Harry Shaw, Coventry, 1996 |

**Previous Registrations:**

| | | | |
|---|---|---|---|
| BPJ77H | A103TVW | HIL7642 | D530YCK |
| D506GEN | D571MVR, ESU121 | HIL7643 | D202XUT |
| HIL7641 | F620VNH | HIL7644 | D662XCT |

**Livery:** Blue and white

# SOUTH YORKSHIRE SUPERTRAM

South Yorkshire Supertram Ltd, 11 Arundel Gate, Sheffield, S1 2PN.

**Depot:** Nunnery, Sheffield

| *01-25* | | Siemens | | Duewag | | ST88T | 1993-94 | | |
|---------|----|---------|----|--------|----|-------|----|----|----|
| 01 | 04 | 07 | 10 | 13 | 16 | 18 | 20 | 22 | 24 |
| 02 | 05 | 08 | 11 | 14 | 17 | 19 | 21 | 23 | 25 |
| 03 | 06 | 09 | 12 | 15 | | | | | |

**Livery:** Silver

The Supertram has been a controversial addition to the South Yorkshire transport scene, though the benefits of this mode of operation have been slow to gain acceptance from a British population where pre-war impressions remain. Within the city the tram runs along sections of roadway but at Crystal Peaks, where this picture was taken, the tram runs on reserved track. Unit 25 is numerically the last one of the German-built cars. *Lee Whitehead*

# SHORELINE SUNCRUISERS

J Stephenson and A E & C E Spalding, 1 Maple Avenue, Keelby, Grimsby,
North East Lincolnshire, DN41 8EN

**Depot:** Scalby Road, Scarborough

| | | | | | | |
|---|---|---|---|---|---|---|
| SS1 | KON327P | Leyland Fleetline FE30ALR | MCW | O43/33F | 1976 | Ex West Midlands Travel, 1991 |
| SS2 | MOM573P | Leyland Fleetline FE30ALR | Park Royal | O43/33F | 1976 | Ex West Midlands Travel, 1991 |
| SS3 | UWA155S | Leyland Fleetline FE30AGR | Roe | H42/29D | 1978 | Ex East Midland (Chesterfield), 1997 |
| SS4 | HPK507N | Bristol VRT/SL2/6G | Eastern Coach Works | O43/31F | 1975 | Ex Alder Valley South, 1991 |
| SS5 | NHR165M | Daimler Fleetline CRG6LX | MCW | O43/31F | 1973 | Ex Thamesdown, 1991 |
| SS7 | KBE108P | Daimler Fleetline CRG6LX | Roe | O43/31F | 1976 | Ex Grimsby-Cleethorpes, 1993 |

**Livery:** Turquoise and yellow

There are three operators of open-top services along Scarborough sea front. Applebys are based in
Lincolnshire and feature in our East Midlands edition. The two other operators are East Yorkshire
and Shoreline Suncruisers. The latter fleet is mainly open-top and until recently included LFS296F,
a Bristol VRT which was one of many new to the Scottish Bus Group that were quickly exchanged
with Bristol Lodekka FLFs from the National Bus Company fleets. *Tony Wilson*

Shoreline Suncruisers SS2, MOM573P, is seen on SS Seafront Service at Scrborough. The vehicle spent its earlier years with West Midlands PTE, currently known as Travel West Midlands. It is seen in its convert open-top form. The latest arrival in the fleet has taken number SS3, and was previously with East Midlans Grimsby operation. That bus is expected to be converted to open-top form also.
*Tony Wilson*

Now a rare sight is the MCW Metroliner, the integral coach built by MCW at Birmingham. Seen here in the Stephensons fleet is PJI9142 where the rounded lines of this model may be seen.
*David Longbottom*

# STEPHENSONS

HJ Stephenson, Nine Acre, Stillington Road, Easingwold,
North Yorkshire, YO6 3OZ

**Depot & outstations**: Unit 16, Moor Lane Industrial Estate, Tholthorpe and Easingwold.

| | | | | | |
|---|---|---|---|---|---|
| RKO820M | Bristol VRT/SL2/6LX | Eastern Coach Works | H43/34F | 1974 | Ex Scutt, Owston Ferry, 1994 |
| YNJ434 | Leyland Leopard PSU3C/4R | Duple 320 (1990) | C53F | 1975 | Ex Blackpool (BlueBus), 1997 |
| TRN772 | Leyland Leopard PSU3C/4R | Duple 320 (1989) | C53F | 1977 | Ex Blackpool (BlueBus), 1997 |
| EGR708S | Leyland Leopard PSU3E/4RT | Plaxton Supreme III Express | C51F | 1979 | Ex ?, 1997 |
| FUS23T | Leyland Leopard PSU3E/4R | Plaxton Supreme IV Express | C51F | 1979 | Ex Midland Fox, 1996 |
| NUE594V | Leyland Leopard PSU5C/4R | Duple Dominant II | C53F | 1980 | Ex Portrest, Southam, 1995 |
| EUY532W | Leyland Leopard PSU5D/4R | Duple Dominant IV | C51FT | 1980 | Ex Amberley Travel, Pudsey, 1994 |
| HIL5669 | DAF MB200DKFL600 | Van Hool Alizée | C48FT | 1983 | Ex Hodson, Bilborough, 1995 |
| AAL587A | Leyland Tiger TRCTL11/3R | Plaxton Paramount 3200 E | C48FT | 1983 | Ex Rhondda, 1997 |
| AAL622A | Leyland Tiger TRCTL11/3R | Plaxton Paramount 3200 E | C48FT | 1983 | Ex Rhondda, 1997 |
| C710FKE | Ford Transit | Dormobile | B16F | 1986 | Ex Riversdale, Brighouse, 1997 |

**Previous Registrations:**

| | | | | | |
|---|---|---|---|---|---|
| AAL587A | SDW920YY | HIL5569 | VKU743Y, 8087WE, CHN952Y | TRN772 | XRN36R |
| AAL622A | SDW919YY | NUE594V | NLD6V, YBJ403 | YNJ434 | HRN97N |
| EUY532W | KUX246W, YFU846 | | | | |

**Livery:** Cream, orange and red

In 1989 the original Duple bodywork of TRN772, then operated by Fylde Transport was replaced with a new Duple 320 body along with sister vehicle YNJ434. These vehicles are now in the Stephensons fleet where they are mostly used on school duties. Photographed in the Lightwater Valley in July 1997 is TRN772. *Graham Crawshaw*

# STOTTS

EM & C Stott, Colne Valley Garage, off Savile Street, Milnsbridge,
Huddersfield, West Yorkshire, HD3 4PG

| | | | | | |
|---|---|---|---|---|---|
| NAH137P | Bristol VRT/SL3/501 | Eastern Coach Works | H43/31F | 1976 | Ex MK Metro, 1996 |
| CBV12S | Bristol VRT/SL3/501 | Eastern Coach Works | H43/31F | 1977 | Ex East Yorkshire, 1996 |
| PJI6617 | Bristol LHS6L | Plaxton Supreme V | C33F | 1982 | Ex Acorn Coaches, York, 1997 |
| XWK618X | Ford R1114 | Plaxton Supreme | C53F | 1982 | Ex Inland Travel, Flumwell, 1995 |
| A337HNX | Ford R1115 | Plaxton Paramount 3200 | C53F | 1983 | Ex Fairway-Rhodes, Hull, 1995 |
| A14ESS | Leyland Tiger TRCTL11/3RH | Berkhof Everest 370 | C53F | 1984 | Ex Speedlink, 1996 |
| B933NSX | Ford R1115 | Plaxton Paramount 3200 | C35F | 1985 | Ex McVay, Edinburgh, 1996 |
| B592XWW | Leyland Tiger TRCTL11/3RH | Plaxton Paramount 3200 II | C50FT | 1985 | Ex Midland Fox, 1995 |
| MIL7901 | Leyland Tiger TRCTL11/3R | Van Hool Alizeé | C50FT | 1985 | Ex Busways, 1996 |
| C343VVN | Mercedes-Benz L608D | Reeve Burgess | DP19F | 1986 | Ex United, 1996 |
| C428VVN | Mercedes-Benz L608D | Reeve Burgess | B20F | 1986 | Ex United, 1996 |
| FIW738 | Leyland Tiger TRCTL11/3RH | Berkhof Everest 370 | C49F | 1986 | Ex Speedlink, 1996 |
| D300OKM | Mercedes-Benz 709D | Dormobile | B20F | 1987 | Ex Formby Coaches, 1997 |
| E919HHG | Mercedes-Benz 609D | Reeve Burgess | B19F | 1987 | Ex Whitehead, Darwen, 1997 |
| F78TDE | Mercedes-Benz 609D | PMT | B24F | 1988 | Ex Pauls, Huddersfield, 1997 |
| MIL7902 | DAF SB2305DHS585 | Van Hool Alizeé | C51FT | 1989 | Ex Happy Als, Birkenhead, 1996 |
| G107RNC | Mercedes-Benz 609D | Reeve Burgess | B19F | 1989 | Ex Timeline, Leigh, 1996 |
| G108RNC | Mercedes-Benz 609D | Reeve Burgess | B19F | 1989 | Ex Timeline, Leigh, 1996 |
| G118SNV | Toyota Coaster HB31R | Caetano Optimo | C18F | 1990 | Ex Pauls, Huddersfield, 1997 |
| H109DVM | Mercedes-Benz 609D | Reeve Burgess | B19F | 1990 | Ex Timeline, Leigh, 1996 |

**Previous Registrations:**

| | | | |
|---|---|---|---|
| A14ESS | B113KPF | MIL7901 | B105DVK, KSU455, A7ESS |
| B592XWW | B103LJU, FIL3451, B369RJV, 82EV | MIL7902 | F272RJX, F48ALS |
| B933NSX | B396VRJ, LIB3899 | PJI6617 | GOW464X |
| FIW738 | C138SPB | | |

**Livery:** White red and black.

Stotts operate a
network of tendered
minibus routes
centred on Holmfirth
and marketed as the
Holme Valley
Hopper. Three
Reeve Burgess
converted
Mercedes-Benz
midibuses have
been purchased
from Timeline of
Leigh for these
routes. G107RNC is
seen in Holmfirth.
*Tony Wilson*

# SYKES

JH Sykes, Southfield, Appleton Roebuck, North Yorkshire, YO5 7DG

| | | | | | |
|---|---|---|---|---|---|
| RAH132M | Bristol VRT/SL2/6G | Eastern Coach Works | H43/31F | 1974 | Ex The Bee Line, 1994 |
| RGF231P | Bristol LHS6L | Plaxton Supreme III | C33F | 1976 | Ex Goodwin, Stockport, 1981 |
| VUP731V | Leyland Leopard PSU3E/4R | Duple Dominant II | C53F | 1980 | Ex The Eden, 1996 |
| A501WGF | Volvo B10M-61 | Plaxton Paramount 3500 | C50F | 1984 | Ex Epsom Coaches, 1993 |
| NBZ9148 | Leyland Tiger TRCTL11/3R | Van Hool Alizée | C53FT | 1984 | Ex J S Perry & Sons, Slingsby, 1996 |
| D459TWE | Bedford YNV | Plaxton Paramount 3200 III | C53F | 1987 | Ex Larrat Pepper, Thurnscoe, 1995 |
| F846YJX | DAF SB2305DHTD585 | Duple 320 | C57F | 1989 | Ex Hanson Coach, Halifax, 1991 |
| G690ORM | Mercedes-Benz 609D | Coachcraft | B23F | 1989 | Ex Dodsworth, Boroughbridge, 1997 |
| BAZ7053 | Volvo B10M-60 | Van Hool Alizée | C53F | 1989 | Ex Shearings, 1997 |

**Previous Registrations:**

| | | | |
|---|---|---|---|
| BAZ7053 | G853RNC | NBZ9148 | B333TNW |
| D549TWE | 8466PH, THU514 | | |

**Named vehicles:** NBZ9148 *Roebuck Rambler.*

**Livery:** Blue and cream

Sykes provide a bus service from the operator's home village of Appleton Roebuck to York. The City of York is the location of this view of Leyland Leopard VUP731V which is fitted with Duple Dominant II coachwork. The vehicle was new to The Eden, West Auckland. *Les Peters*

# T J WALSH

N Walsh, 5 Well Head Drive, Well Head, Halifax, West Yorkshire, HX1 2QX

**Depot:** Union Street South, Halifax

| | | | | | | |
|---|---|---|---|---|---|---|
| TJ1 | F817XUG | Ford Transit | Dormobile | B16F | 1988 | Ex Coates, Haxby, 1992 |
| TJ2 | TJI9142 | Ford Transit | Rootes | B16F | 1986 | Ex Midland Fox, 1994 |
| TJ3 | TJI9143 | Freight Rover Sherpa | Dormobile | B16F | 1986 | Ex Denby Dale Lions, 1994 |
| TJ4 | TJI9144 | Ford Transit | Alexander | B16F | 1985 | Ex ?, 1995 |
| TJ5 | TJI5590 | Ford Transit | Carlyle | B20F | 1986 | Ex Vale of Manchester, 1996 |
| TJ6 | TJI9146 | Ford Transit | Carlyle | B16F | 1985 | Ex Avondale Coaches, Greenock, 1995 |
| TJ7 | TJI9147 | Ford Transit | Carlyle | B20F | 1985 | Ex Keighley & District, 1996 |
| TJ8 | TJI9148 | Ford Transit | Carlyle | B16F | 1985 | Ex Haylands Farm Project, Ryde, 1995 |
| TJ9 | B9TJW | Ford Transit | Carlyle | B20F | 1986 | Ex Happy Days, Woodseaves, 1996 |
| TJ10 | B10TJW | Freight Rover Sherpa | Carlyle Citybus 2 | B20F | 1986 | Ex Acorn, Chester, 1995 |
| TJ11 | B11TJW | Ford Transit | Dormobile | B16F | 1986 | Ex Oldfield, Hoyland, 1996 |
| TJ12 | B12TJW | Ford Transit | Carlyle | B20F | 1986 | Ex West Midlands Travel, 1996 |
| TJ14 | B14TJW | Ford Transit | Carlyle | B18F | 1986 | Ex Community Routes, Hattersley |
| TJ15 | B15TJW | Ford Transit | Carlyle | B20F | 1986 | Ex Rhondda, 1997 |
| TJ?? | C430SJU | Ford Transit | Robin Hood | B16F | 1985 | Ex Sapphire, Middlesbrough, 1997 |
| TJ17 | B17TJW | Ford Transit | Carlyle | B20F | 1986 | Ex ?? |
| TJ?? | D528HNW | Ford Transit | Carlyle | B18F | 1986 | Ex Brown, East Kilbride, 1996 |
| TJ?? | C82AUB | Ford Transit | Carlyle | B18F | 1986 | Ex Buchanan, Fenton, 1997 |
| TJ20 | B20TJW | Ford Transit | Carlyle | OB16F | 1985 | Ex M Travel, Newport, 1997 |
| TJ?? | C318OFL | Ford Transit | Dormobile | B16F | 1986 | Ex Red & White, 1997 |

**Previous Registrations:**

| | | | |
|---|---|---|---|
| B9TJW | D526HNW | TJI5590 | B739YUD |
| B10TJW | E93OUH | TJI9142 | C532TJF |
| B11TJW | C516BFB | TJI9143 | D205KWT |
| B12TJW | D554NOE | TJI9144 | B206GNL |
| B14TJW | D553NOE | TJI9146 | C25NVV |
| B15TJW | D525HNW | TJI9147 | C63LHL |
| B17TJW | ? | TJI9148 | B258MDL |
| B20TJW | B261MDL | | |

**Named vehicles**: TJ1 *Little Bertha;* TJ2 *Betsy;* TJ3 *Ethel;* TJ5 *Pussy Galore;* TJ6 *Bry Rose;* TJ7 *Flash;* TJ8 *The Shuttle Bug;* TJ9 *Jean;* TJ10 *Maureen;* TJ11 *Peggy;* TJ12 *Gladys;* TJ14 *Herbie;* TJ15 *Babe;* TJ17 *Red Dwarf.;* TJ20 *Benjamin*

**Livery:** Grey, red and maroon

*Opposite:* **T J Walsh number their fleet of minibuses with TJ prefix and have secured a number of cherished TJW marks which complement several purchased TJI plates originating from Ireland. TJ7, TJI9147 is a Ford Transit converted by Carlyle. Previously with the West Riding and the now disbanded Ingfield- Northern Rose companies, this 20-seat minibus is depicted in Halifax on the 400 service to Elland. The lower picture shows TJ20, B20TJW which is the open-top version of the Transit that once operated on the Isle of Wight.** *Lee Whitehead/ Tony Wilson*

# THOMPSON TRAVEL

C,H,M & T Thompson and D Vickers , 524 Wortley Road, Rotherham,
South Yorkshire, S62 6BP

**Depot:** Naylor Street, Parkgate, Rotherham

| | | | | | | |
|---|---|---|---|---|---|---|
| w | MSF125P | Leyland Leopard PSU3C/4R | Alexander AY | DP49F | 1975 | Ex Ladyline, Rawmarsh, 1993 |
| | YFC14R | Leyland Leopard PSU3E/4R | Duple Dominant I | C49F | 1977 | Ex Ladyline, Rawmarsh, 1993 |
| | WCK133V | Leyland Leopard PSU3E/4R | Duple Dominant II Express | C51F | 1979 | Ex Ladyline, Rawmarsh, 1993 |
| w | COF707V | Leyland Leopard PSU3E/4R | Plaxton Supreme IV Express | C51F | 1979 | Ex Hodgkinson, Langley Mill, 1994 |
| | JNJ31V | Leyland Leopard PSU3E/4R | Plaxton Supreme IV Express | C49F | 1980 | Ex Armstrong, Inverkeithing, 1993 |
| | MPL133W | Leyland Leopard PSU3E/4R | Duple Dominant IV Express | C53F | 1980 | Ex Goodwin, Stockport, 1994 |
| | ALZ3260 | Leyland Tiger TRCTL11/3R | Plaxton Paramount 3200 E | C55F | 1983 | Ex United Counties, 1997 |
| | LIL8050 | Leyland Tiger TRCTL11/3R | Plaxton Paramount 3200 | C55F | 1983 | Ex The Bee Line, 1995 |
| | SXU708 | Leyland Tiger TRCTL11/3R | Plaxton Paramount 3500 | C49FT | 1983 | Ex Greenhalgh, Ottershaw, 1994 |

**Previous Registrations:**

| | | | |
|---|---|---|---|
| ALZ3260 | NBD102Y | LIL8050 | A211DPB |
| JNJ31V | GWV932V, YLJ332 | SXU708 | A369HNC |

**Named vehicles**: MSF125P *Annamarie.*

**Livery:** Red, black and gold.

**The Thompson Travel red and black livery has recently gained yellow stripes. Displaying this new scheme is LIL8050, a Plaxton Paramount-bodied Leyland Tiger which has migrated north from the former Alder Valley Bee Line fleet.** *Tony Wilson*

# THORNES / INDEPENDENT

Thornes Motor Services Ltd, Derwent Garage, Bubwith, Selby,
North Yorkshire, YO8 7LT
Independent Coachways Ltd; Edwards Coachways Ltd, Low Fold Garage,
New Road Side, Horsforth, Leeds, West Yorkshire, LS18 4DR

**Depot** : Derwent Garage, Bubwith and Low Fold Garage, Horsforth.

| | | | | | | |
|---|---|---|---|---|---|---|
| 32w | OKP980 | Beadle-Leyland | Beadle | B39F | 1952 | Ex Maidstone & District, 1960 |
| 35 | VHO200 | Seddon Mk19 | Harrington Wayfarer | C41F | 1959 | Ex Liss & District, 1961 |
| 46 | GSL906N | Daimler Fleetline CRG6LXB | Alexander AL | H49/34D | 1975 | Ex Tayside, 1985 |
| 71w | EWT386C | Bristol SUL6P | Eastern Coach Works | B36F | 1965 | Ex West Yorkshire Road Car, 1974 |
| 74 | JCV385N | Bristol LHS6L | Plaxton Supreme III | C35F | 1975 | Ex Pollard, Ruan Minor, 1994 |
| 76w | MBO1F | Bristol LHS6L | Weymann | DP30F | 1968 | Ex Western Welsh, 1975 |
| 79 | VBT379V | Bedford YMT(Perkins) | Plaxton Supreme V Express | C53F | 1979 | |
| 81w | JHP810N | Bedford YRT | Plaxton Elite III | C53F | 1975 | Ex Parr, Liverpool, 1981 |
| 85 | WWW33 | Volvo B10M-61 | Plaxton Paramount 3500 | C49FT | 1984 | |
| 86 | LBT380N | AEC Reliance 6U3ZR | Plaxton Derwent | B66F | 1975 | Ex Premier, Stainforth, 1984 |
| 93 | VFN53 | Volvo B10M-46 | Plaxton Paramount 3200 II | C43F | 1987 | Ex Courtlands, Horley, 1989 |
| 94 | F467WFX | Volvo B10M-60 | Plaxton Paramount 3200 III | C53F | 1989 | Ex Excelsior, Bournemouth, 1990 |
| 101 | SMV24 | Scania K93CRB | Plaxton Paramount 3200 III | C57F | 1990 | Ex Premier Coaches, Dunnington, 1992 |
| 102 | F427DUG | Volvo B10M-60 | Plaxton Paramount 3200 III | C53F | 1989 | Ex Wallace Arnold, 1992 |
| 103 | HBT378S | Freight Rover Sherpa | Carlyle | B18F | 1987 | Ex Ribble, 1992 |
| 107 | K500TMS | Volvo B10M-60 | Plaxton Paramount 3200 III | C53F | 1993 | |

**The Independent of Horsforth company is owned by Thornes of Bubwith. The Single-deck fleet has gained a batch of Plaxton Bustler-bodied Scanias. These former airside buses were used by British Airways at Heathrow and have been extensively re-furbished. Now numbered 119 in the Independent fleet is C936VLB.** *David Longbottom*

The number of AEC Reliances still in service in Britain continues to diminish, though continuing to work for Thornes is 86, LBT380N. This vehicle carries a Plaxton Derwent body and has a high capacity of 66 seats as a result of 3+2 seating towards the rear of the bus. *Tony Wilson*

| | | | | | | |
|---|---|---|---|---|---|---|
| 111 | M600TMS | Volvo B10M-62 | Plaxton Premiére 320 | C53F | 1995 | |
| 112 | M700TMS | Volvo B10M-62 | Plaxton Premiére 320 | C53F | 1995 | |
| 113 | BBT380V | Bedford CFL | Plaxton Mini Supreme | C17F | 1980 | Ex Jervis Bros, Margam, 1994 |
| 114 | NHN260K | Daimler Fleetline CRG6LX | Park Royal | B48D | 1972 | Ex Darlington, 1995 |
| 115 | C930VLB | Scania K112CRB | Plaxton Bustler | DP49F | 1986 | Ex British Airways, 1995 |
| 116 | C931VLB | Scania K112CRB | Plaxton Bustler | DP45DL | 1986 | Ex British Airways, 1995 |
| 117 | C932VLB | Scania K112CRB | Plaxton Bustler | DP49F | 1986 | Ex British Airways, 1995 |
| 118 | C935VLB | Scania K112CRB | Plaxton Bustler | DP49F | 1986 | Ex British Airways, 1995 |
| 119 | C936VLB | Scania K112CRB | Plaxton Bustler | DP49F | 1986 | Ex British Airways, 1995 |
| 120w | JJG9P | Leyland Atlantean AN68/1R | Eastern Coach Works | H43/31F | 1976 | Ex Kingsley, Birtley, 1995 |
| 121 | C933VLB | Scania K112CRB | Plaxton Bustler | DP49F | 1986 | Ex British Airways, 1996 |
| 122 | C938VLB | Scania K112CRB | Plaxton Bustler | DP49F | 1986 | Ex British Airways, 1996 |
| 123 | CBV307S | Leyland Atlantean AN68A/2R | East Lancashire | H50/36F | 1977 | Ex Hedingham & District, 1996 |
| 124 | CBV308S | Leyland Atlantean AN68A/2R | East Lancashire | H50/36F | 1977 | Ex Hedingham & District, 1996 |
| 125 | CBV309S | Leyland Atlantean AN68A/2R | East Lancashire | H50/36F | 1977 | Ex Hedingham & District, 1996 |
| 126 | YHD599V | Volvo B58-56 | Duple Dominant | B63F | 1979 | Ex Longstaff, Mirfield, 1996 |
| 135 | M200VHO | Volvo B10M-62 | Plaxton Excalibur | C49FT | 1995 | |
| 136 | N200VHO | Volvo B10M-62 | Plaxton Premiére 350 | C57F | 1996 | |
| 137 | R200TMS | Volvo B10M-62 | Plaxton Premiére 350 | C57F | 1997 | |

**Operating companies**: Independent 107/11/12/15-19/22/26;  Edwards: 94, 102/21;  Thornes: remainder

**Previous Registrations:**

| | | | |
|---|---|---|---|
| BAG150S | HBT378S | OKP980 | From new |
| BBT380V | KNT815W | SMV24 | G27HKY |
| HBT378S | D829PUK | VFN53 | D866YPH |
| JCV385N | LBT380N, KKH101N, WRL270 | VHO200 | From new |
| LBT380N | HUM951N | WWW33 | B385JVY |

**Livery:** Blue, grey and red

**Named vehicles**: 74 *Derwent Pioneer*; 79 *Derwent Phaser*; 85 *Derwent Explorer*; 86 *Derwent Reliance*; 93 *Derwent Ambassador*; 101 *Derwent Adventurer*; 102 *Derwent Challenger*; 113 *The Breighton Belle*; 126 *Derwent Crusader*; 135 *Derwent Excalibur* ; 136 *The Spirit of Drumcondra*.

# VIKING TOURS

D Turner, 74, Skeldergate, York, North Yorkshire, YO1 1DN

**Depots** : Brockett Park Industrial Estate, Acaster Malbis & Stainsacre Industrial Estate, Whitby.

| | | | | | |
|---|---|---|---|---|---|
| WJY758 | Leyland Atlantean PDR1/1 | Metro Cammell | O44/33F | 1962 | Ex SS Suncruisers, Scarborough, 1992 |
| LFS288F | Bristol VRT/LL/6G | Eastern Coach Works | O43/31F | 1968 | Ex SS Suncruisers, Scarborough, 1992 |
| RNV811M | Bristol VRT/SL2/6G | Eastern Coach Works | O43/31F | 1974 | Ex United Counties, 1992 |
| MDS687P | Leyland Atlantean AN68A/1R | Alexander AL | O45/31F | 1976 | Ex Jorvik, Market Weighton, 1992 |
| LRA798P | Bristol VRT/SL3/501(6LXB) | Eastern Coach Works | O43/34F | 1976 | Ex Trent, 1992 |
| WTH962T | Bristol VRT/SL3/501 | Eastern Coach Works | O43/31F | 1979 | Ex Battrick & Brown, Clayton-le-Dale, 1991 |

**Previous Registrations:**
WJY758          From new

**Livery:** Two-tone blue and cream

**Viking operate open-top services in Whitby and York. MDS687P is allocated to the York city tour service. This Alexander-bodied Leyland Atlantean was new to the Glasgow-based Strathclyde Buses fleet. The front section of the roof has been left in place in give protection on windy or damp days.** *Tony Wilson*

# WALLACE ARNOLD

Wallace Arnold Coaches Ltd, Gelderd Road, Leeds, West Yorkshire, LS12 6DH
Wallace Arnold Coaches Ltd, Barton Hill Way, Barton, Torquay, Devon, TQ2 8JG

**Note**: Fleet numbers are not displayed on any of the vehicles.

| | | | | | |
|---|---|---|---|---|---|
| 101 | 4WA | Volvo B10M-62 | Plaxton Excalibur | C28FT | 1995 |
| 102 | 8665WA | Volvo B10M-62 | Plaxton Première 350 | C48FT | 1995 |
| 103 | 8980WA | Volvo B10M-62 | Plaxton Première 350 | C48FT | 1995 |
| 104 | M104UWY | Volvo B10M-62 | Plaxton Première 350 | C48FT | 1995 |
| 105 | M105UWY | Volvo B10M-62 | Plaxton Première 350 | C48FT | 1995 |

### 108-116
Volvo B10M-62 — Plaxton Première 320 — C50F — 1995

| | | | | | | | | | |
|---|---|---|---|---|---|---|---|---|---|
| 108 | M108UWY | 110 | M110UWY | 113 | M113UWY | 115 | M115UWY | 116 | M116UWY |
| 109 | M109UWY | 112 | M112UWY | 114 | M114UWY | | | | |

### 117-124
Volvo B10M-62 — Plaxton Première 350 — C50F — 1995

| | | | | | | | | | |
|---|---|---|---|---|---|---|---|---|---|
| 117 | M117UWY | 119 | M119UWY | 121 | M121UWY | 123 | M123UWY | 124 | M124UWY |
| 118 | M118UWY | 120 | M120UWY | 122 | M122UWY | | | | |

### 132-136
Volvo B10M-62 — Plaxton Excalibur — C50F — 1995

| | | | | | | | | | |
|---|---|---|---|---|---|---|---|---|---|
| 132 | M132UWY | 133 | M133UWY | 134 | M134UWY | 135 | M135UWY | 136 | M136UYG |

The Toyota Coaster minicoach is often used by tour companies to operate feeder services. Wallace Arnold N253HWX carries the Portugese-built Caetano Optimo body which is now a common sight throughout Britain today. 253 is seen on tour feeder duties at South Mimms services where Wallace Arnold interchange passengers. *Les Peters*

**The 1995 intake of coaches was dominated by the Plaxton 350 bodied Volvo B10M though there were variants in bodywork interior to suit the tour on which the coach was used. Pictured in Newcastle, 204, N204HWX was working as a feeder when pictured.** *Donald Akrigg*

### 201-252

| | Volvo B10M-62 | | Plaxton Première 350 | | C48FT* | | 1996-97 *216-52 are C50F | |
|---|---|---|---|---|---|---|---|---|
| 201 | N201HWX | 212 | N212HWX | 223 | N223HWX | 233 | N233HWX | 243 | N243HWX |
| 202 | N202HWX | 213 | N213HWX | 224 | N224HWX | 234 | N234HWX | 244 | N244HWX |
| 203 | N203HWX | 214 | N214HWX | 225 | N225HWX | 235 | N235HWX | 245 | N245HWX |
| 204 | N204HWX | 215 | N215HWX | 226 | N226HWX | 236 | N236HWX | 246 | N246HWX |
| 205 | N205HWX | 216 | N216HWX | 227 | N227HWX | 237 | N237HWX | 247 | N247HWX |
| 206 | N206HWX | 217 | N217HWX | 228 | N228HWX | 238 | N238HWX | 248 | N248HWX |
| 207 | N207HWX | 218 | N218HWX | 229 | N229HWX | 239 | N239HWX | 249 | N249HWX |
| 208 | N208HWX | 219 | N219HWX | 230 | N230HWX | 240 | N240HWX | 250 | N250HWX |
| 209 | N209HWX | 220 | N220HWX | 231 | N231HWX | 241 | N241HWX | 251 | N251HWX |
| 210 | N210HWX | 221 | N221HWX | 232 | N232HWX | 242 | N242HWX | 252 | N252HWX |
| 211 | N211HWX | | | | | | | | |

| 253 | N253HWX | Toyota Coaster HZB50R | Caetano Optimo III | C21F | 1996 |
|---|---|---|---|---|---|
| 254 | N254HWX | Toyota Coaster HZB50R | Caetano Optimo III | C21F | 1996 |

### 301-315

| | Volvo B10M-62 | | Van Hool Alizée | | C46FT | 1997 | | |
|---|---|---|---|---|---|---|---|---|
| 301 | P301VWR | 304 | P304VWR | 307 | P307VWR | 310 | P310VWR | 313 | P313VWR |
| 302 | P302VWR | 305 | P305VWR | 308 | P308VWR | 311 | P311VWR | 314 | P314VWR |
| 303 | P303VWR | 306 | P306VWR | 309 | P309VWR | 312 | P312VWR | 315 | P315VWR |

### 316-352

| | Volvo B10M-62 | | Plaxton Première 350 | | C50F* | | 1997 *316-26 are C48FT | |
|---|---|---|---|---|---|---|---|---|
| 316 | P316VWR | 324 | P324VWR | 331 | P331VWR | 339 | P339VWR | 346 | P346VWR |
| 317 | P317VWR | 325 | P325VWR | 332 | P332VWR | 340 | P340VWR | 347 | P347VWR |
| 318 | P318VWR | 326 | P326VWR | 334 | P333VWR | 341 | P341VWR | 348 | P348VWR |
| 319 | P319VWR | 327 | P327VWR | 335 | P334VWR | 342 | P342VWR | 349 | P349VWR |
| 320 | P320VWR | 328 | P328VWR | 336 | P335VWR | 343 | P343VWR | 350 | P350VWR |
| 321 | P321VWR | 329 | P329VWR | 337 | P336VWR | 344 | P344VWR | 351 | P351VWR |
| 322 | P322VWR | 330 | P330VWR | 338 | P337VWR | 345 | P345VWR | 352 | P352VWR |
| 323 | P323VWR | | | | | | | | |

## 353-357 — Volvo B10M-62 — Jonckheere Mistral — C50F — 1997

| 353 | P353VWR | 354 | P354VWR | 355 | P355VWR | 356 | P356VWR | 357 | P357VWR |
|---|---|---|---|---|---|---|---|---|---|

| 425 | BUF425C | Leyland Titan PD3/4 | Northern Counties | FCO39/30F | 1965 | Ex Harris Bus, West Thurrock, 1994 |
|---|---|---|---|---|---|---|
| 426 | D426STT | Mercedes-Benz L307D | Yeates | M12 | 1987 | |
| 427 | BUF267C | Leyland Titan PD3/4 | Northern Counties | FCO39/30F | 1965 | Ex Weardale, Stanhope, 1995 |
| | WA3399 | Ailsa B55-10 | Alexander AV | DPH--/24D | 1976 | Ex Yeates, Loughborough, 1996 |
| 436 | CSU936 | Leyland Leopard PSU4E/4R | Plaxton Paramount 3200 II(1987) | C45F | 1977 | |
| 437 | CSU937 | Leyland Leopard PSU4E/4R | Plaxton Paramount 3200 II(1987) | C45F | 1977 | |
| 438 | CSU938 | Leyland Leopard PSU4E/4R | Plaxton Paramount 3200 II(1987) | C45F | 1977 | |
| 728 | J728CWT | Volvo B10M-60 | Plaxton Excalibur | C50F | 1992 | |
| 730 | J730CWT | Volvo B10M-60 | Plaxton Excalibur | C50F | 1992 | |
| 733 | J733CWT | Volvo B10M-60 | Plaxton Excalibur | C50F | 1992 | |
| 763 | J763CWT | Mercedes-Benz 308D | Devon Conversion | C12F | 1992 | |
| 764 | J764CWT | Mercedes-Benz 308D | Devon Conversion | C12F | 1992 | |
| 765 | J765CWT | Volkswagen Transporter | Advanced Vehicle Bodies | M7 | 1992 | |
| 766 | J766CWT | Volkswagen Transporter | Advanced Vehicle Bodies | M7 | 1992 | |
| 802 | 4030WA | Volvo B10M-60 | Van Hool Alizée | C48FT | 1993 | |
| 803 | 7243WA | Volvo B10M-60 | Van Hool Alizée | C48FT | 1993 | |
| 804 | 7820WA | Volvo B10M-60 | Van Hool Alizée | C48FT | 1993 | |

## 901-905 — Volvo B10M-62 — Jonckheere Deauville 45 — C50F — 1994

| 901 | L901NWW | 902 | L902NWW | 903 | L903NWW | 904 | L904NWW | 905 | L905NWW |
|---|---|---|---|---|---|---|---|---|---|

| 921 | 3333WA | Volvo B10M-62 | Plaxton Excalibur | C46FT | 1994 |
|---|---|---|---|---|---|

## 925-930 — Volvo B10M-60 — Plaxton Excalibur — C50F — 1994

| 925 | L925NWW | 927 | L927NWW | 928 | L928NWW | 929 | L929NWW | 930 | L930NWW |
|---|---|---|---|---|---|---|---|---|---|
| 926 | L926NWW | | | | | | | | |

| 942 | L942NWW | Volvo B10M-60 | Jonckheere Deauville 45 | C50FT | 1994 |
|---|---|---|---|---|---|
| 943 | L943NWW | Volvo B10M-60 | Jonckheere Deauville 45 | C50FT | 1994 |
| 944 | L944NWW | Volvo B10M-60 | Jonckheere Deauville 45 | C50FT | 1994 |

## 947-963 — Volvo B10M-62 — Jonckheere Deauville 45 — C50F — 1994

| 947 | L947NWW | 952 | L952NWW | 955 | L955NWW | 958 | L958NWW | 961 | L961NWW |
|---|---|---|---|---|---|---|---|---|---|
| 948 | L948NWW | 953 | L953NWW | 956 | L956NWW | 959 | L959NWW | 962 | L962NWW |
| 951 | L951NWW | 954 | L954NWW | 957 | L957NWW | 960 | L960NWW | 963 | L963NWW |

| 8332 | 8332U | AEC Reliance MU3RA | Plaxton Consort | C41C | 1958 | Ex preservation, 1989 |
|---|---|---|---|---|---|---|

**Previous Registrations:**

| 4WA | M101UWY | 7820WA | K804HUM | CSU937 | WUG127S |
|---|---|---|---|---|---|
| 3333WA | L921NWW | 8665WA | M102UWY | CSU938 | WUG128S |
| 4030WA | K802HUM | 8980WA | M103UWY | WA3399 | NET520R, CVS999, TUT101 |
| 7243WA | K803HUM | CSU936 | SWW126R | 8332U | From new |

**Livery:** Cream, orange and brown. 425 is named *Uncle Wally*

*Opposite, top*: **The 1994 delivery of new coaches for the Wallace Arnold fleet included a number bodied at Roeselare in Belgium by Jonckheere. L943NWW is a Volvo B10M-62 which carries the attractive Deauville 45 body style which dominated the 1994 vehicle intake. It is seen on tour in the historic city of Chester, having just passed under the city walls.** *Ralph Stevens*
*Opposite, bottom*: **M119UWY is a Volvo B10M-62 added to the Wallace Arnold fleet in 1995. This coach carries a Plaxton Première 350 body built in Yorkshire at the Scarborough factory. The figure 350 indicates that the vehicle is 3.50 metres high.** *Terry Wightman*

*The Yorkshire Bus Handbook*

# WILFREDA-BEEHIVE

Wilfreda Luxury Coaches Ltd, Apex House, Church Lane, Adwick-le-Street, Doncaster,
South Yorkshire, DN6 7AY
E A Hart Ltd, Apex House, Church Lane, Adwick-le-Street, Doncaster, South Yorkshire.
Roeville Tours Ltd, Apex House, Church Lane, Adwick-le-Street, Doncaster
South Yorkshire, DN6 7AY

|    | CGF313S  | Leyland Leopard PSU5C/4R      | Plaxton Supreme III         | C55F  | 1978 | Ex West Sussex, Chichester, 1997 |
|----|----------|-------------------------------|-----------------------------|-------|------|----------------------------------|
| 25 | F89CWG   | Scania K92CRB                 | Duple 320                   | C55F  | 1988 |                                  |
| 26 | JIL3716  | Bova FHD12.290                | Bova Futura                 | C49FT | 1989 |                                  |
| 27 | WIB4393  | Scania K92CRB                 | Duple 320                   | C55F  | 1989 |                                  |
| 31 | F371CHE  | Scania K92CRB                 | Duple 320                   | C55F  | 1988 | Ex BTS, Borehamwood, 1989        |
| 32 | F372CHE  | Scania K92CRB                 | Duple 320                   | C55F  | 1988 | Ex BTS, Borehamwood, 1989        |
| 34 | JIL3715  | Scania K113CRB                | Plaxton Paramount 3500 III  | C49FT | 1989 |                                  |
| 37 | WIB5749  | Scania K93CRB                 | Duple 320                   | C56F  | 1989 |                                  |
| 38 | WIB8371  | Scania K93CRB                 | Duple 320                   | C56F  | 1989 |                                  |
| 66 | PIJ5017  | Leyland National 11351/2R     | East Lancs Greenway (1992)  | B44DL | 1975 | Ex CityLine, 1990                |
| 70 | G211YDL  | Mercedes-Benz 811D            | Phoenix                     | B31F  | 1990 | Ex Solent Blueline, 1996         |
| 71 | G212YDL  | Mercedes-Benz 811D            | Phoenix                     | B31F  | 1990 | Ex Solent Blueline, 1996         |
| 72 | G205YDL  | Mercedes-Benz 811D            | Phoenix                     | B31F  | 1990 | Ex Solent Blueline, 1995         |
| 73 | G207YDL  | Mercedes-Benz 811D            | Phoenix                     | B31F  | 1990 | Ex Solent Blueline, 1995         |
| 74 | F40CWY   | Mercedes-Benz 811D            | Optare StarRider            | B26F  | 1989 | Ex Cowie Leaside, 1996           |
| 75 | F37CWY   | Mercedes-Benz 811D            | Optare StarRider            | B26F  | 1989 | Ex Rest & Ride, Smethwick, 1996  |
| 76 | F39CWY   | Mercedes-Benz 811D            | Optare StarRider            | B26F  | 1989 | Ex Cowie Leaside, 1996           |
| 77 | G99CUB   | Mercedes-Benz 811D            | Optare StarRider            | B26F  | 1989 | Ex Cowie Leaside, 1996           |

**Wilfreda-Beehive have disposed of their bus service network in Doncaster to Mainline and now
concentrate on coach work, although a limited number of journeys are still registered with the traffic
commissioners under the Roeville name.** Now numbered 25, F89CWG is one of several Scanias in
the fleet carrying Duple 320 coachwork. *Richard Godfrey*

In 1989 two further examples of the Duple-bodies Scania K92s were purchased from BTS of Borehamwood in north London. Photographed near its old haunts 32, F372CHE was heading for Wembley Stadium when seen. Latest deliveries to Wilfreda-Beehive are Bova Futura coaches one of which is the lower style known as the Club. *Keith Grimes*

| 81 | ONV746 | Leyland Tiger TRCTL11/3R | Plaxton Paramount 3500 | C48FT | 1983 | Ex Funston, Chrishall, 1989 |
|----|--------|--------------------------|------------------------|-------|------|------------------------------|
| 82 | JIL3711 | Leyland Tiger TRCTL11/3R | Plaxton Paramount 3200 | C53F | 1983 | Ex Mashford, Doncaster, 1991 |
| 83 | F647CDT | Mercedes-Benz 609D | Reeve Burgess Beaver | C19F | 1988 | |
| 87 | L335PWX | Bova FLD12.270 | Bova Futura Club | C53F | 1994 | Ex Bova demonstrator, 1995 |
| 88 | OHL893X | Mercedes-Benz 207D | Whittaker | M12 | 1982 | Ex Nicholson, Farnsfield, 1992 |
| 90 | M875FVK | Mercedes-Benz 811D | Autobus Classique | C24F | 1994 | |
| | H511SWE | Mercedes-Benz 609D | Whittaker-Europa | B19F | 1990 | |
| | N71EAK | Bova FHD12.340 | Bova Futura | C49FT | 1996 | |
| | P157XNW | Bova FLD12.270 | Bova Futura Club | C53F | 1997 | |
| | P563XNW | Bova FHD12.340 | Bova Futura | C53F | 1997 | |
| | P564XNW | Bova FHD12.340 | Bova Futura | C53F | 1997 | |

**Named Vehicles**: ONV746 *Angela Maria*.

**Previous Registrations:**

| | | | | | |
|---|---|---|---|---|---|
| F371CHE | F372CHE | JIL3716 | F648EET | WIB5749 | G21HKY |
| F372CHE | F371CHE | ONV746 | BRN3Y | WIB8371 | G22HKY |
| JIL3711 | RNY310Y | PIJ5017 | GEU361N | | |
| JIL3715 | F601GET | WIB4393 | F90CWG | | |

**Livery:** White and two-tone blue

# WRAY'S OF HARROGATE

A Wray & Son Ltd, 2 Montpelier Street, Harrogate, North Yorkshire, HG1 2TQ

**Depots** : Main Street, Dacre Banks and Ashville College, Harrogate

| | | | | | |
|---|---|---|---|---|---|
| PJI4315 | Leyland Tiger TRCTL11/2R | Duple | C53F | 1984 | Ex Westercroft Cs, Queensbury, 1995 |
| A20MCW | Volvo B10M-61 | Plaxton Paramount 3500 III | C49FT | 1989 | |
| F156GWR | Volvo B10M-61 | Plaxton Paramount 3500 III | C49FT | 1989 | Ex Wallace Arnold, 1993 |
| H854AHS | Volvo B10M-60 | Plaxton Paramount 3500 III | C53F | 1991 | Ex Park's, Hamilton, 1993 |
| H172EJF | MAN 10.180 | Caetano Algarve II | C35F | 1991 | Ex Britannia Travel, Otley, 1994 |
| J814EBU | Volvo B10M-60 | Plaxton Premiére 350 | C48FT | 1992 | Ex Wallace Arnold, 1994 |
| MIW5839 | Volvo B10M-60 | Plaxton Premiére 350 | C48FT | 1992 | Ex Wallace Arnold, 1994 |
| K413GAV | Ford Transit | Ford | M14 | 1993 | Ex private owner, 1996 |
| K814HUM | Volvo B10M-60 | Van Hool Alizée | C48FT | 1993 | Ex Wallace Arnold, 1996 |
| K818HUM | Volvo B10M-60 | Van Hool Alizée | C48FT | 1993 | Ex Wallace Arnold, 1996 |
| L50MCW | Volvo B10M-60 | Plaxton Premiére 350 | C49FT | 1994 | |
| M580JBC | Volvo B6-9M | Caetano Algarve II | C34F | 1994 | |
| M583DSJ | Volvo B9M | Van Hool Alizée | C38FT | 1995 | Ex Park's, Hamilton, 1996 |
| N937RBC | Volvo B10M-60 | Plaxton Premiére 350 | C49FT | 1996 | |
| N761HWW | Volkswagen Transporter | Volkswagen | M8 | 1996 | |

**Livery:** Grey and red

**Previous Registrations:**

| | | | | | |
|---|---|---|---|---|---|
| A20MCW | F21CWW | L50MCW | L532XUT | MIW5839 | ? |
| HSV126 | C119DWR | M583DSJ | XIA257 | PJI4615 | A459FHH |
| F156GWR | F431DUG, YMW149 | | | | |

**Photographed in April 1997 was Wray's of Harrogate J814EUB, a Volvo B10M with Plaxton Première 350 bodywork. It is seen outside the York City walls. The plaque behind the door proclaims Harrogate to be *the conference city* and is now rivalling coastal resorts for conference business.** *Tony Wilson*

# YORK PULLMAN

York Pullman Ltd, Byron House, Seaham Grange Industrial Estate, Seaham,
County Durham, SR7 0PW

A subsidiary of Durham Travel Services

**Depot and outstations:** Halifax Way, Airfield Industrial Estate, Elvington and Harrogate.

| | | | | | | |
|---|---|---|---|---|---|---|
| 102 | H202CRH | Volvo B10M-60 | Plaxton Expressliner | C46FT | 1991 | Ex York Pullman Coach, 1993 |
| 104 | CAZ5104 | Dennis Javelin 12SDA1907 | Plaxton Paramount 3200 III | C50FT | 1989 | Ex York Pullman Coach, 1993 |
| 105 | B40UAG | Dennis Dorchester SDA805 | Plaxton Paramount 3200 | C50FT | 1984 | Ex York Pullman Coach, 1993 |
| 107 | IIL1317 | Volvo B10M-61 | Plaxton Paramount 3500 II | C50F | 1986 | Ex York Pullman Coach, 1993 |
| 108 | IIL1318 | Volvo B10M-61 | Plaxton Paramount 3500 II | C50F | 1986 | Ex York Pullman Coach, 1993 |
| 141 | A922LTM | Bedford YNT | Duple Laser | C53F | 1983 | Ex York Pullman Coach, 1993 |
| 143 | A875THS | Bedford YNT | Plaxton Paramount 3200 | C53F | 1984 | Ex York Pullman Coach, 1993 |
| 159 | F659GNL | Iveco Daily 49-10 | Carlyle Dailybus | B23F | 1989 | Ex Busways, 1996 |
| 161 | F661GNL | Iveco Daily 49-10 | Carlyle Dailybus | B23F | 1989 | Ex Busways, 1996 |
| 172 | D562RKW | Bedford YNV Venturer | Plaxton Paramount 3200 II | C54F | 1987 | Ex York Pullman Coach, 1993 |
| 173 | AWE53T | Bedford YMT | Plaxton Supreme IV | C53F | 1979 | Ex York Pullman Coach, 1993 |
| 175 | PKU78X | Bedford YNT | Plaxton Supreme V | C53F | 1982 | Ex York Pullman Coach, 1993 |
| 179 | AVK179V | Leyland Atlantean AN68A/2R | Alexander AL | H49/37F | 1980 | Ex Busways, 1997 |
| 193 | DRH319L | Leyland Atlantean AN68/1R | Roe | O43/29F | 1972 | Ex Kingston-upon-Hull, 1993 |
| 194 | DRH321L | Leyland Atlantean AN68/1R | Roe | O43/29F | 1972 | Ex York Pullman Coach, 1993 |
| 195 | NAT341M | Leyland Atlantean AN68/1R | Roe | O43/29F | 1973 | Ex York Pullman Coach, 1993 |
| 196 | NAT350M | Leyland Atlantean AN68/1R | Roe | O43/29F | 1974 | Ex York Pullman Coach, 1993 |
| 197 | GAT203N | Leyland Atlantean AN68/1R | Roe | H43/29F | 1975 | Ex York Pullman Coach, 1993 |

**The city tour in York is operated by several companies including Guide Friday, whose fleet can be found in our South Midlands edition. York Pullman have four former Kingston-upon-Hull Leyland Atlanteans for open-top tour work. They are painted all over maroon as typified by DRH319L.**
*Tony Wilson*

York Pullman, having for many years relied on Bedfords for service work, now operate three Leyland Nationals. WJN558S was purchased from Sovereign in 1996 and carries the latest cream and maroon livery. *Tony Wilson*

| | | | | | |
|---|---|---|---|---|---|
| GAT201N | Leyland Atlantean AN68/1R | Roe | H43/29F | 1975 | Ex Kingston-upon-Hull, 1993 |
| GAT204N | Leyland Atlantean AN68/1R | Roe | H43/29F | 1975 | Ex Kingston-upon-Hull, 1993 |
| FHE810L | Bristol VRT/SL2/6G | Eastern Coach Works | O43/34F | 1973 | Ex RoadCar, 1993 |
| NRD131M | Leyland National 1151/1R/0402 | | B49F | 1973 | Ex George Bell Travel, Seaham, 1996 |
| VKE564S | Leyland National 11351A/1R | | B49F | 1977 | Ex Welwyn & Hatfield, 1996 |
| WJN558S | Leyland National 11351A/1R | | B49F | 1978 | Ex Sovereign, 1996 |
| EAZ8409 | Van Hool T815 | Van Hool Acron | C53F | 1987 | Ex Woodcock Coaches, Felbridge, 1995 |
| G799FJX | Scania K93CRB | Van Hool Alizée | C55F | 1990 | Ex Lowland, 1995 |
| G801FJX | Scania K93CRB | Van Hool Alizée | C55F | 1990 | Ex Lowland, 1995 |
| H35CNL | Volvo B10M-60 | Plaxton Paramount 3500 III | C49FT | 1990 | Ex Durham Travel, 1997 |
| 2719DT | Volvo B10M-60 | Plaxton Paramount 3500 III | C49FT | 1990 | Ex Durham Travel, 1995 |

**Previous Registrations:**

| | | | | | |
|---|---|---|---|---|---|
| 2719DT | G65RGG | EAZ8409 | D145HMT | IIL1318 | C117DWR |
| CAZ5104 | F54EAT | IIL1317 | C107DWR | | |

**Named Vehicles:**
107 - *Neville Shute*; 141 - *Alcuin*; 143 - *James Fairfax*; 172 - *John Carr*; 175 - *Guy Fawkes*; 195 - *Archbishop Holgate*.

**Livery:** Cream and maroon.

# YORKSHIRE BUS

West Riding Automobile Co Ltd; South Yorkshire Road Transport Ltd;
Selby & District Bus Co Ltd,
24 Barnsley Road, Wakefield, West Yorkshire, WF1 5JX
Yorkshire Woollen District Transport Co Ltd, Mill Street East, Dewsbury,
West Yorkshire, WF12 9AG

Part of Cowie plc
**Depots:** Wheldon Road, Castleford; Mill Street East, Dewsbury; Beck Lane, Heckmondwike; Northgate, Pontefract; Chimes
Road, Selby and Belle Isle, Barnsley Road, Wakefield

| 31 | P31XUG | DAF DE33WSSB3000 | Van Hool Alizée | C FT | 1997 |
|----|--------|------------------|-----------------|------|------|

| *51-56* | | Scania K113CRB | Van Hool Alizée | C44FT | 1995 | | |
|---------|--------|----------------|-----------------|-------|--------|------|--------|
| **51** | M51AWW | **53** M53AWW | **54** M54AWW | **55** | M55AWW | **56** | M56AWW |
| **52** | M52AWW | | | | | | |

**National Express acquired the Flightlink services from Flights during 1996 and this service is now
being expanded to link more towns with the main airports. Photographed at Bradford Interchange,
Yorkshire's 54, M54AWW was photographed in the Flightlink livery in July 1994. It is a Scania K113
with Van Hool Alizée bodywork.** *Donald Akrigg*

For many years the Leyland National dominated the Yorkshire bus groups fleet and these were progressively replaced as large numbers of Lynx arrived. The last of the National 2s were withdrawn as the book was prepared with some the last examples passing to fellow Cowie group member, Crosville Wales. Photographed in Heckmondwike just prior to its withdrawal, 127, HED204V was one of the Gardner-engined models new to Halton in 1980. *Lee Whitehead*

### 170-199

| | | Dennis Dart SLF | | | Alexander ALX200 | | B40F | 1997 | | |
|------|----------|-----|----------|-----|----------|-----|----------|-----|----------|
| 170 | P170VUA | 176 | P176VUA | 182 | P182VUA | 188 | P188VUA | 194 | P194VUA |
| 171 | P171VUA | 177 | P177VUA | 183 | P183VUA | 189 | P189VUA | 195 | P195VUA |
| 172 | P172VUA | 178 | P178VUA | 184 | P184VUA | 190 | P190VUA | 196 | P196VUA |
| 173 | P173VUA | 179 | P179VUA | 185 | P185VUA | 191 | P191VUA | 197 | P197VUA |
| 174 | P174VUA | 180 | P180VUA | 186 | P186VUA | 192 | P192VUA | 198 | P198VUA |
| 175 | P175VUA | 181 | P181VUA | 187 | P187VUA | 193 | P193VUA | 199 | P199VUA |

| | | | | | | |
|------|---------|-------------------------|--------------|------|------|---------------------------|
| 252 | C920FMP | Leyland Lynx LX1126LXCTFR1 | Leyland Lynx | B51F | 1986 | Ex Leyland Bus, 1987 |
| 253 | D204FBK | Leyland Lynx LX112TL11ZR1 | Leyland Lynx | B51F | 1986 | Ex Solent Blue Line, 1987 |
| 254 | E254TUB | Leyland Lynx LX1126LXCTFR2 | Leyland Lynx | B50F | 1987 | |

### 255-264

| | | Leyland Lynx LX1126LXCTFR1S | Leyland Lynx | | | B49F | 1987-88 | | |
|------|---------|-----|---------|-----|---------|-----|---------|-----|---------|
| 255 | E255TUB | 257 | E257TUB | 259 | E259TUB | 261 | E261TUB | 263 | E263TUB |
| 256 | E256TUB | 258 | E258TUB | 260 | E260TUB | 262 | E262TUB | 264 | E264TUB |

*Opposite, top*: **The Yorkshire fleet received its first low floor buses in 1997. Numbered 176, P176VUA is a Dennis Dart SLF photographed in Dewsbury. The body on this vehicle is the new Alexander ALX200 which is constructed using revolutionary methods at the Falkirk plant. The sides are built complete with glazing before being attached to the chassis. This method is expected to be highly cost-effective, both for construction and accident repair.** *Tony Wilson*
*Opposite, bottom*: **While the Yorkshire fleet is painted red and cream, the West Riding vehicles carry a similar style in green and cream as displayed by 515, CWR515Y. This Eastern Coach Works-bodied Leyland Olympian is seen in Leeds operating the 163 service via Garforth and Kippax to the town of Castleford, where the bus is based.** *Tony Wilson*

In 1987 the total number of new Lynx licensed worldwide was some 60. Early in 1988, the Caldaire Group, which the Yorkshire Bus group was then known placed an order for 50 Lynx buses. Passing Leeds bus station is 287, F287AWW, a Leyland Lynx and represents this large number placed in service then. *Tony Wilson*

### 265-314

Leyland Lynx LX112L10ZR1S    Leyland Lynx    B49F    1988-89

| | | | | | | | | | |
|---|---|---|---|---|---|---|---|---|---|
| 265 | E265WUB | 275 | F275AWW | 285 | F285AWW | 295 | F295AWW | 305 | F305AWW |
| 266 | E266WUB | 276 | F276AWW | 286 | F286AWW | 296 | F296AWW | 306 | F306AWW |
| 267 | E267WUB | 277 | F277AWW | 287 | F287AWW | 297 | F297AWW | 307 | F307AWW |
| 268 | E268WUB | 278 | F278AWW | 288 | F288AWW | 298 | F298AWW | 308 | F308AWW |
| 269 | E269WUB | 279 | F279AWW | 289 | F289AWW | 299 | F299AWW | 309 | F309AWW |
| 270 | E270WUB | 280 | F280AWW | 290 | F290AWW | 300 | F300AWW | 310 | F310AWW |
| 271 | E271WUB | 281 | F281AWW | 291 | F291AWW | 301 | F301AWW | 311 | F311AWW |
| 272 | F272AWW | 282 | F282AWW | 292 | F292AWW | 302 | F302AWW | 312 | F312AWW |
| 273 | F273AWW | 283 | F283AWW | 293 | F293AWW | 303 | F303AWW | 313 | F313AWW |
| 274 | F274AWW | 284 | F284AWW | 294 | F294AWW | 304 | F304AWW | 314 | F314AWW |

| | | | | | | |
|---|---|---|---|---|---|---|
| 315 | E116UTX | Leyland Lynx LX112L10ZR1R | Leyland Lynx | B51F | 1988 | Ex Merthyr Tydfil, 1989 |
| 316 | F117XTX | Leyland Lynx LX112L10ZR1R | Leyland Lynx | B51F | 1988 | Ex Merthyr Tydfil, 1989 |
| 317 | F118XTX | Leyland Lynx LX112L10ZR1R | Leyland Lynx | B51F | 1988 | Ex Merthyr Tydfil, 1989 |

### 318-332

Leyland Lynx LX2R11C15Z4S    Leyland Lynx    B49F    1990

| | | | | | | | | | |
|---|---|---|---|---|---|---|---|---|---|
| 318 | G317NNW | 321 | G321NNW | 324 | G324NUM | 327 | G327NUM | 330 | G330NUM |
| 319 | G319NNW | 322 | G322NNW | 325 | G110OUG | 328 | G109OUG | 331 | G331NUM |
| 320 | G324NNW | 323 | G108OUG | 326 | G326NUM | 329 | G329NUM | 332 | G332NUM |

### 333-337

Leyland Lynx LX2R11C15Z4S    Leyland Lynx 2    B49F    1990

| | | | | | | | | | |
|---|---|---|---|---|---|---|---|---|---|
| 333 | H338TYG | 334 | H334TYG | 335 | H335TYG | 336 | H336TYG | 337 | H337TYG |

Seen passing through Morley en route for Bradford is West Riding's 363, J363YWX. This Leyland Lynx 2 is one on the 1991 intake which were actually produced by Volvo who, by then, had acquired the Leyland company. The successor to the Lynx is the Volvo B10B which includes many features of the Lynx chassis. *Lee Whitehead*

### 338-347

Leyland Lynx LX2R11C15Z4S    Leyland Lxnx 2        B49F        1990-91

| 338 | H338UWT | 340 | H343UWT | 342 | H342UWT | 344 | H344UWX | 346 | H346UWX |
| 339 | H339UWT | 341 | H341UWT | 343 | H343UWX | 345 | H345UWX | 347 | H347UWX |

| 348 | G542GAC | Leyland Lynx LX2R11C15Z4R | Leyland Lynx | B49F | 1990 | Ex Volvo Bus, Warwick, 1991 |
| 349 | G148CHP | Leyland Lynx LX2R11C15Z4R | Leyland Lynx | B49F | 1990 | Ex Volvo Bus, Warwick, 1991 |
| 350 | G149CHP | Leyland Lynx LX2R11C15Z4R | Leyland Lynx | B51F | 1990 | Ex Volvo Bus, Warwick, 1991 |
| 351 | G49CVC | Leyland Lynx LX112L10ZR1R | Leyland Lynx | B51F | 1990 | Ex Volvo Bus, Warwick, 1991 |

### 352-382

Leyland Lynx LX2R11C15Z4S*    Leyland Lxnx 2        B49F        1991        *378 is LX2R11V18Z4S

| 352 | H755WWW | 359 | H359WWY | 365 | J365YWX | 371 | J371YWX | 377 | J377AWT |
| 353 | H756WWW | 360 | H460WWY | 366 | J366YWX | 372 | J372AWT | 378 | J371AWT |
| 354 | H757WWW | 361 | H393WWY | 367 | J367YWX | 373 | J373AWT | 379 | J379BWU |
| 355 | H355WWX | 362 | J362YWX | 368 | J368YWX | 374 | J374AWT | 380 | J380BWU |
| 356 | H356WWX | 363 | J363YWX | 369 | J369YWX | 375 | J375AWT | 381 | J381BWU |
| 357 | H357WWX | 364 | J364YWX | 370 | J370YWX | 376 | J376AWT | 382 | J382BWU |
| 358 | H358WWY | | | | | | | | |

### 401-405

Volvo B10B-58        Alexander Strider        B51F        1993

| 401 | K401HWW | 402 | K402HWW | 403 | K403HWW | 404 | K404HWW | 405 | K405HWX |

| 406 | L406NUA | Volvo B10B-58 | Wright Endeavour | DP49F | 1993 |
| 407 | L407NUA | Volvo B10B-58 | Wright Endeavour | DP49F | 1993 |
| 408 | L408NUA | Volvo B10B-58 | Wright Endeavour | DP49F | 1993 |
| 409 | L409NUA | Volvo B10B-58 | Wright Endeavour | DP49F | 1993 |

## 410-433 — Volvo B10B-58 — Alexander Strider — B51F — 1994

| 410 | M410UNW | 415 | M415UNW | 420 | M420UNW | 425 | M425UNW | 430 | M430UNW |
|---|---|---|---|---|---|---|---|---|---|
| 411 | M411UNW | 416 | M416UNW | 421 | M421UNW | 426 | M426UNW | 431 | M431UNW |
| 412 | M412UNW | 417 | M417UNW | 422 | M422UNW | 427 | M427UNW | 432 | M432UNW |
| 413 | M413UNW | 418 | M418UNW | 423 | M423UNW | 428 | M428UNW | 433 | M433UNW |
| 414 | M414UNW | 419 | M419UNW | 424 | M424UNW | 429 | M429UNW | | |

## 508-552 — Leyland Olympian ONLXB/1R — Eastern Coach Works — H45/33F — 1982-83

| 508 | CWR508Y | 518 | CWR518Y | 528 | CWR528Y | 536 | EWX536Y | 544 | 544WRA |
|---|---|---|---|---|---|---|---|---|---|
| 510 | CWR510Y | 519 | CWR519Y | 529 | EWX529Y | 537 | EWX537Y | 545 | EWW545Y |
| 511 | CWR511Y | 520 | CWR520Y | 530 | EWX530Y | 538 | EWW538Y | 546 | EWW546Y |
| 512 | CWR512Y | 521 | CWR521Y | 531 | EWX531Y | 539 | EWW539Y | 547 | EWW547Y |
| 513 | CWR513Y | 522 | CWR522Y | 532 | EWX532Y | 540 | EWW540Y | 548 | EWW548Y |
| 514 | CWR514Y | 523 | CWR523Y | 533 | EWX533Y | 541 | EWW541Y | 550 | EWW550Y |
| 515 | CWR515Y | 524 | CWR524Y | 534 | EWX534Y | 542 | EWW542Y | 551 | EWW551Y |
| 516 | CWR516Y | 527 | CWR527Y | 535 | EWX535Y | 543 | EWW543Y | 552 | EWW552Y |
| 517 | CWR517Y | | | | | | | | |

## 560-612 — Leyland Olympian ONLXB/1R — Eastern Coach Works — H45/32F* — 1983-85 *seating varies

| 560 | A560KWY | 572 | A572NWX | 582 | A582NWX | 592 | B592SWX | 603 | B603UUM |
|---|---|---|---|---|---|---|---|---|---|
| 562 | A562KWY | 573 | A573NWX | 583 | A583NWX | 593 | B593SWX | 604 | B604UUM |
| 564 | A564KWY | 574 | A574NWX | 584 | A584NWX | 594 | B594SWX | 605 | B605UUM |
| 565 | A565NWX | 575 | A575NWX | 585 | A585NWX | 595 | B595SWX | 606 | B606UUM |
| 566 | A566NWX | 576 | A576NWX | 586 | A586NWX | 596 | B596SWX | 607 | B607UUM |
| 567 | A567NWX | 577 | A577NWX | 587 | A587NWX | 597 | B597SWX | 608 | B608UUM |
| 568 | A568NWX | 578 | A578NWX | 588 | A588NWX | 599 | B599SWX | 609 | B609UUM |
| 569 | A569NWX | 579 | A579NWX | 589 | A589NWX | 600 | B601UUM | 610 | C610ANW |
| 570 | A570NWX | 580 | A580NWX | 590 | A590NWX | 601 | B602UUM | 611 | C611ANW |
| 571 | A571NWX | 581 | A581NWX | 591 | B591SWX | 602 | B603UUM | 612 | C612ANW |

Photographed at Meadowhall, some 6 kilometres from the centre of Sheffield, is Yorkshire Bus' 410, M410UNW the first of two-dozen Alexander-bodied Volvo B10Bs delivered in 1994. It is seen in the livery style in which it was delivered. The latest liveries are shown in the colour section.
*Lee Whitehead*

| 613 | E205TUB | Leyland Olympian ONTL11/1RH | Northern Counties | H43/28F | 1988 | Ex South Yorkshire, Pontefract, 1995 |
|-----|---------|------------------------------|-------------------|---------|------|--------------------------------------|
| 614 | TWY7 | Leyland Olympian ONCL10/1RZ | Northern Counties | H43/28F | 1988 | Ex South Yorkshire, Pontefract, 1995 |
| 615 | H106RWT | Leyland Olympian ON2R50C13Z4 | Northern Counties | H43/28F | 1990 | Ex South Yorkshire, Pontefract, 1995 |
| 616 | H108RWT | Leyland Olympian ON2R50C13Z4 | Northern Counties | H43/28F | 1990 | Ex South Yorkshire, Pontefract, 1995 |
| 621 | N621KUA | Volvo Olympian YN2RV18Z4 | Northern Counties Palatine II | H43/30F | 1996 | |
| 622 | N622KUA | Volvo Olympian YN2RV18Z4 | Northern Counties Palatine II | H43/30F | 1996 | |
| 623 | N623KUA | Volvo Olympian YN2RV18Z4 | Northern Counties Palatine II | H43/30F | 1996 | |

### 701-713
Optare MetroRider MR09 — Optare — B23F — 1991

| 701w | H701UNW | 704w | H704UNW | 707w | H707UNW | 710w | H710UNW | 712w | H712UNW |
|------|---------|------|---------|------|---------|------|---------|------|---------|
| 702w | H702UNW | 705w | H705UNW | 708w | H708UNW | 711w | H711UNW | 713w | H713UNW |
| 703w | H703UNW | 706w | H706UNW | 709w | H709UNW | | | | |

### 714-729
Optare MetroRider MR05 — Optare — B31F — 1992-93

| 714 | J714CUM | 718 | J718CUM | 721 | J721CUM | 724 | K724HUG | 727 | K727HUG |
|-----|---------|-----|---------|-----|---------|-----|---------|-----|---------|
| 715 | J715CUM | 719 | J719CUM | 722 | J722CUM | 725 | K725HUG | 728 | K728HUG |
| 716 | J716CUM | 720 | J720CUM | 723 | K723HUG | 726 | K726HUG | 729 | K729HUG |
| 717 | J717CUM | | | | | | | | |

### 730-745
Optare MetroRider MR15 — Optare — B31F — 1993-94

| 730 | L730MWW | 734 | L734MWW | 737 | L737PUA | 740 | L740PUA | 743 | M743UUA |
|-----|---------|-----|---------|-----|---------|-----|---------|-----|---------|
| 731 | L731MWW | 735 | L735PUA | 738 | L738PUA | 741 | L741PUA | 744 | M744UUA |
| 732 | L732MWW | 736 | L736PUA | 739 | L739PUA | 742 | M742UUA | 745 | M745UUA |
| 733 | L733MWW | | | | | | | | |

### 746-750
Optare MetroRider MR15 — Optare — B31F — 1995

| 746 | M746WWX | 747 | M247WWX | 748 | M748WWX | 749 | M749WWR | 750 | M750WWR |
|-----|---------|-----|---------|-----|---------|-----|---------|-----|---------|

**Vehicles allocated to Selby depot are licenced to the Selby & District company and illustrated here is 623, N623KUA, one of three Volvo Olympians delivered in 1996. The designation of the Olympians changed shortly after this bus was delivered, the model now simply known as the Olympian now that the previously offered engine and gearbox options have been withdrawn.** *Les Peters*

| | | | | | | |
|---|---|---|---|---|---|---|
| 751 | M751WWR | Optare MetroRider MR31 | Optare | B25F | 1995 | |
| 752 | M752WWR | Optare MetroRider MR31 | Optare | B25F | 1995 | |
| 753 | M753WWR | Optare MetroRider MR31 | Optare | B25F | 1995 | |
| 754 | N754LWW | Optare MetroRider MR15 | Optare | B31F | 1996 | |
| 755 | N755LWW | Optare MetroRider MR15 | Optare | B31F | 1996 | |
| 756 | N756LWW | Optare MetroRider MR15 | Optare | B31F | 1996 | |
| 757 | N757LWW | Optare MetroRider MR15 | Optare | B31F | 1996 | |

### 758-770

Mercedes-Benz Vario O814    Plaxton Beaver 2    B27F    1997

| | | | | | | | | | |
|---|---|---|---|---|---|---|---|---|---|
| 758 | R758DUB | 761 | R761DUB | 764 | R764DUB | 767 | R767DUB | 769 | R769DUB |
| 759 | R758DUB | 762 | R762DUB | 765 | R765DUB | 768 | R768DUB | 770 | R770DUB |
| 760 | R760DUB | 763 | R763DUB | 766 | R766DUB | | | | |

### 771-778

Mercedes-Benz 811D    Plaxton Beaver    B31F    1994

| | | | | | | | | | |
|---|---|---|---|---|---|---|---|---|---|
| 771 | L771RWW | 773 | L773RWW | 775 | L775RWW | 777 | L779RWW | 778 | L778RWW |
| 772 | L772RWW | 774 | L774RWW | 776 | L776RWW | | | | |

### 779-784

Mercedes-Benz 811D    Plaxton Beaver    B31F*    1995    *779 is B27F

| | | | | | | | | | |
|---|---|---|---|---|---|---|---|---|---|
| 779 | N779EUA | 781 | N781EUA | 782 | N782EUA | 783 | N783EUA | 784 | N784EUA |
| 780 | N780EUA | | | | | | | | |

### 785-799

Mercedes-Benz Vario O814    Plaxton Beaver 2    B27F    1997

| | | | | | | | | | |
|---|---|---|---|---|---|---|---|---|---|
| 785 | R785DUB | 789 | R789DUB | 792 | R792DUB | 795 | R795DUB | 798 | R798DUB |
| 787 | R787DUB | 790 | R790DUB | 793 | R793DUB | 796 | R796DUB | 799 | R799DUB |
| 788 | R788DUB | 791 | R791DUB | 794 | R794DUB | 797 | R797DUB | | |

### 801-830

Dennis Lance 11SDA3107    Alexander Strider    B47F    1993

| | | | | | | | | | |
|---|---|---|---|---|---|---|---|---|---|
| 801 | K801HWW | 807 | L807NNW | 813 | L813NNW | 819 | L819NWY | 825 | L825NWY |
| 802 | K802HWW | 808 | L808NNW | 814 | L814NNW | 820 | L820NWY | 826 | L826NYG |
| 803 | K803HWW | 809 | L809NNW | 815 | L815NNW | 821 | L821NWY | 827 | L827NYG |
| 804 | K804HWW | 810 | L810NNW | 816 | L816NWY | 822 | L822NWY | 828 | L828NYG |
| 805 | K805HWX | 811 | L811NNW | 817 | L817NWY | 823 | L823NWY | 829 | L829NYG |
| 806 | L806NNW | 812 | L812NNW | 818 | L818NWY | 824 | L824NWY | 830 | L830NYG |

**Allocations August 1997**

Selby (Selby & District):  401-5/21/2, 512/20/34/5/42/91-4, 621-3, 712/3/51-3
Pontefract (South Yorkshire):  315-27, 508/10/8/9, 613-6, 749/50/4-7
Dewsbury (Yorkshire Woollen):  31, 51-4/6, 170-99, 275/7/9-81/4/5/7/8/91/5/6, 303/4/28/50/1, 771-84
Heckmondwike (Yorkshire Woollen):  406-18, 521/4/7/40/7/8/62/4/5/8-71/85-9, 600/1/3, 801-30
Castleford (Yorkshire Woollen):  267/9/76/89/90/3/4/9, 301/29-47/52-7/60/6-71, 515/28/9/37-9/41/95-9, 702/20-9/43-5
Belle Isle (West Riding):  Remainder.

**Previous Registrations:**

| | | | |
|---|---|---|---|
| 544WRA | EWX544Y | TWY7 | From new |

**Liveries:**
Cream and green (West Riding); cream and red (Yorkshire Bus); cream and green (Selby & District); cream and blue (South Yorkshire); cream and red (Flightlink) 31, 51-6.

*Opposite:* **Two buses from Cowie's Yorkshire subsidiary Yorkshire Bus Group are shown here, both delivered in the early 1990s. The upper picture of MetroRider 719, J719CUM, was taken in Wakefield where the vehicle is based, the depot being known as Belle Isle with the vehicle lattered for West Riding. The lower picture shows Dennis Lance 819, L819NWY which is one of thirty delivered in 1993. All are based at the Heckmondwike depot of Yorkshire Woollen and carry Yorkshire Bus names on their red and cream livery.**

# YORKSHIRE COASTLINER

Yorkshire Coastliner Ltd, Petroleum House, Camwall Road, Starbeck, Harrogate, North Yorkshire HG1 4PT

**Depot** : Railway Street, Malton

A subsidiary of Blazefield Holdings Ltd

| | | | | | | |
|---|---|---|---|---|---|---|
| 408 | L8YCL | Volvo Olympian YN2RV18Z4 | Alexander Royale | DPH45/29F | 1993 | |
| 409 | L9YCL | Volvo Olympian YN2RV18Z4 | Alexander Royale | DPH45/27F | 1994 | |
| 410 | G910UPP | Mercedes-Benz 709D | Reeve Burgess Beaver | B23F | 1990 | |
| 411 | G911UPP | Mercedes-Benz 709D | Reeve Burgess Beaver | B23F | 1990 | |
| 420 | G920WGS | Mercedes-Benz 709D | Reeve Burgess Beaver | B23F | 1990 | Ex Welwyn-Hatfield Line, 1993 |
| 421 | G921WGS | Mercedes-Benz 709D | Reeve Burgess Beaver | B23F | 1990 | Ex Welwyn-Hatfield Line, 1993 |
| 422 | M922UYG | Volvo Olympian YN2RV18Z5 | Alexander Royale | DPH45/27F | 1995 | |
| 423 | M923UYG | Volvo Olympian YN2RV18Z5 | Alexander Royale | DPH45/27F | 1995 | |
| 424 | M924UYG | Volvo Olympian YN2RV18Z5 | Alexander Royale | DPH45/27F | 1995 | |
| 425 | M925UYG | Volvo Olympian YN2RV18Z5 | Alexander Royale | DPH45/27F | 1995 | |
| 426 | P426UUG | Volvo Olympian | Alexander Royale | DPH45/27F | 1997 | |
| 427 | P427UUG | Volvo Olympian | Alexander Royale | DPH45/27F | 1997 | |
| 428 | P428UUG | Volvo Olympian | Alexander Royale | DPH45/27F | 1997 | |
| 429 | P429UUG | Volvo Olympian | Alexander Royale | DPH45/27F | 1997 | |

| *451-456* | | Volvo B10B | Wright Endurance | DP49F | 1996-97 |
|---|---|---|---|---|---|

| | | | | | | | | |
|---|---|---|---|---|---|---|---|---|
| **451** | N451HWY | **453** | N453HWY | **454** | N454HWY | **455** | N455HWY | **456** | P456UUG |
| **452** | N452HWY | | | | | | | |

| | | | | | | |
|---|---|---|---|---|---|---|
| **483** | E283TWW | Mercedes-Benz 811D | Optare StarRider | DP33F | 1988 | Ex Rover, Bromsgrove, 1994 |

*Opposite, top*: **The Yorkshire Coastliner double-deck fleet comprises only one type. The Alexander Royale body fitted to Olympian chassis is suited to the long routes operated from Leeds to the east coast resorts which operate through the City of York. All these buses are fitted to a high specification to ensure passenger comfort. Seen in York is 423, M923UYG, en-route for Leeds.** *Tony Wilson*
*Opposite, bottom*: **Yorkshire Coastliner 456, P456UUG is a Volvo B10B. The Wright Endurance body was constructed in Ballymena, Northern Ireland, using the Alusuisse system. In keeping with the standards set with the Olympians, these recent additions to the Malton-based fleet are fitted out to a high specification. This view was taken as the bus ends its journey in Leeds.** *Tony Wilson*

Livery: Blue and cream

The Yorkshire Coastliner fleet contains a single Mercedes-Benz 811 and this vehicle carries a Optare StarRider body. It is lettered for service 81 between York and Malton which was operated when pictured.
*Lee Whitehead*

# YORKSHIRE RIDER

Bradford Traveller, MetroChange House, 61 Hall Ings, Bradford  BD1 5SQ
Calderline, Skircoat Road, Halifax  HX1 2RF
Kingfisher, Old Fieldhouse Lane, Huddersfield  HD2 1AG
Rider York, 7 James Street, York YO1 3DW
Leeds Citylink, Kirkstall Garage, Kirkstall Road, Leeds  LS3 1LH
Quickstep Travel, Kirkstall Garage, Kirkstall Road, Leeds  LS3 1LH

**Depots:** Hall Ings, Bradford; Henconner Lane, Bramley; Skircoat Road, Halifax; Old Fieldhouse Lane, Huddersfield; Cherry Row, Leeds; Kirkstall Road, Leeds; Millwood, Todmorden and James Street, York

| 16 | L516EHD | DAF SB220LC550 | Ikarus CitiBus | B48F | 1993 | |
|----|---------|----------------|----------------|------|------|---|
| 17 | L517EHD | DAF SB220LC550 | Ikarus CitiBus | B48F | 1994 | |
| 18 | L518EHD | DAF SB220LC550 | Ikarus CitiBus | B48F | 1994 | |
| 23 | UOI4323 | Volvo B10M-61 | East Lancashire (1993) | B51F | 1982 | Ex Rhodeservices, 1994 |
| 26 | K506RJX | DAF SB220LC550 | Ikarus CitiBus | B48F | 1993 | Ex Yorkshire Travel, 1994 |
| 27 | K507RJX | DAF SB220LC550 | Ikarus CitiBus | B48F | 1993 | Ex Yorkshire Travel, 1994 |
| 29 | F229FSU | Leyland Tiger TRBTL11/2RP | Plaxton Derwent II | B54F | 1988 | Ex Rhodeservices, 1994 |
| 332 | MNW132V | Leyland National 2 NL116L11/1R | | B52F | 1980 | Ex York City & District, 1990 |
| 333 | SWX533W | Leyland National 2 NL116AL11/1R | | B52F | 1981 | Ex York City & District, 1990 |
| 335 | SWX535W | Leyland National 2 NL116AL11/1R | | B52F | 1981 | Ex York City & District, 1990 |
| 338 | SWX538W | Leyland National 2 NL116AL11/1R | | B52F | 1981 | Ex York City & District, 1990 |
| 340 | SWX540W | Leyland National 2 NL116AL11/1R | | B52F | 1981 | Ex York City & District, 1990 |
| 363 | PNW603W | Leyland National 2 NL116L11/1R | | B52F | 1980 | Ex York City & District, 1990 |
| 368 | UWY68X | Leyland National 2 NL116AL11/1R | | B52F | 1982 | Ex York City & District, 1990 |
| 371 | UWY71X | Leyland National 2 NL116AL11/1R | | B52F | 1982 | Ex York City & District, 1990 |

**Photographed passing the Corn Exchange in Leeds is Leeds City Link 16, L516EHD, a 1993 DAF SB220 with Ikarus CitiBus bodywork. This model is imported into Britain through Hughes-DAF, which is part of the Cowie Group.** *Tony Wilson*

| 713-994 | | Bristol VRT/SL3/6LXB | | Eastern Coach Works | | H43/31F | | 1978-81 Ex West Yorkshire, 1989 | |
|---|---|---|---|---|---|---|---|---|---|
| 713 | DWU296T | 746 | PUM149W | 755 | PWY41W | 980 | SWW305R | 994 | WWY127S |
| 717 | EWR165T | | | | | | | | |

| 1001-1030 | | Volvo B10B-58 | | Alexander Strider | | B51F | | 1993-94 | |
|---|---|---|---|---|---|---|---|---|---|
| 1001 | K101HUM | 1007 | K107HUM | 1013 | K113HUM | 1019 | K119HUM | 1025 | L125PWR |
| 1002 | K102HUM | 1008 | K108HUM | 1014 | K114HUM | 1020 | K120HUM | 1026 | L126PWR |
| 1003 | K103HUM | 1009 | K109HUM | 1015 | K115HUM | 1021 | L121PWR | 1027 | L127PWR |
| 1004 | K104HUM | 1010 | K110HUM | 1016 | K116HUM | 1022 | L122PWR | 1028 | L128PWR |
| 1005 | K105HUM | 1011 | K211HUM | 1017 | K117HUM | 1023 | L123PWR | 1029 | L129PWR |
| 1006 | K106HUM | 1012 | K112HUM | 1018 | K118HUM | 1024 | L124PWR | 1030 | L130PWR |

| 1201-1208 | | DAF SB220LC550 | | Ikarus CitiBus | | B48F | | 1992 | |
|---|---|---|---|---|---|---|---|---|---|
| 1201 | J421NCP | 1203 | J423NCP | 1205 | J425NCP | 1207 | K527RJX | 1208 | K528RJX |
| 1202 | J422NCP | 1204 | J424NCP | 1206 | J426NCP | | | | |

| 1251-1255 | | DAF SB220LC550 | | Optare Delta | | B47F | | 1989 | |
|---|---|---|---|---|---|---|---|---|---|
| 1251 | G251JYG | 1252 | G252JYG | 1253 | G253JYG | 1254 | G254JYG | 1255 | G255JYG |

| 1256 | J994GCP | DAF SB220LC550 | Optare Delta | B49F | 1991 | Ex Yorkshire Travel, 1994 |
|---|---|---|---|---|---|---|

| 1317-1329 | | Leyland National 2 NL106L11/1R | | | | B41F | | 1980 | Ex WYPTE, 1986 |
|---|---|---|---|---|---|---|---|---|---|
| 1317 | LUA317V | 1318 | LUA318V | 1319 | LUA319V | 1321 | LUA321V | 1329 | LUA329V |

| 1331 | VWU331X | Leyland National 2 NL116AL11/1R | B49F | 1981 | Ex WYPTE, 1986 |
|---|---|---|---|---|---|
| 1332 | VWU332X | Leyland National 2 NL116AL11/1R | B49F | 1981 | Ex WYPTE, 1986 |
| 1333 | YWX333X | Leyland National 2 NL116AL11/1R | B49F | 1982 | Ex WYPTE, 1986 |
| 1343 | MNW130V | Leyland National 2 NL116L11/1R | B52F | 1980 | Ex West Yorkshire, 1989 |
| 1345 | PNW598W | Leyland National 2 NL116L11/1R | B49F | 1980 | Ex West Yorkshire, 1989 |
| 1348 | PNW601W | Leyland National 2 NL116L11/1R | B49F | 1980 | Ex West Yorkshire, 1989 |

| 1349-1354 | | Leyland National 2 NL116AL11/1R | | | | B52F | | 1981-82 Ex West Yorkshire, 1989 | |
|---|---|---|---|---|---|---|---|---|---|
| 1349 | SWX537W | 1351 | UWY72X | 1352 | UWY74X | 1353 | UWY75X | 1354 | UWY90X |
| 1350 | UWY69X | | | | | | | | |

| 1356 | PWY588W | Leyland National 2 NL106AL11/1R | B44F | 1981 | Ex West Yorkshire, 1989 |
|---|---|---|---|---|---|
| 1357 | FWA473V | Leyland National 2 NL116AL11/1R | B41F | 1980 | Ex Pride of the Road, 1993 |
| 1367 | MHJ723V | Leyland National 2 NL116AL11/1R | B49F | 1980 | Ex Eastern National, 1994 |
| 1368 | MHJ726V | Leyland National 2 NL116AL11/1R | B49F | 1980 | Ex Eastern National, 1994 |
| 1369 | MHJ729V | Leyland National 2 NL116AL11/1R | B49F | 1980 | Ex Eastern National, 1994 |
| 1370 | STW19W | Leyland National 2 NL116AL11/1R | B49F | 1980 | Ex Eastern National, 1994 |

| 1419 | G427PWW | Volvo B10M-60 | Plaxton Paramount 3500 III | C49FT | 1990 | Ex Park's, 1992 |
|---|---|---|---|---|---|---|
| 1420 | G76RGG | Volvo B10M-60 | Plaxton Paramount 3500 III | C49FT | 1990 | Ex Park's, 1992 |
| 1421 | H841AHS | Volvo B10M-60 | Plaxton Paramount 3500 III | C53F | 1991 | Ex Park's, 1993 |
| 1422 | L22YRL | Volvo B10M-60 | Jonckheere Deauville P599 | C49F | 1993 | |
| 1423 | L511NYG | Volvo B10M-60 | Plaxton Premiére 350 | C49FT | 1993 | |
| 1424 | L541XUT | Volvo B10M-60 | Plaxton Premiére 350 | C49FT | 1994 | |
| 1425 | L542XUT | Volvo B10M-60 | Plaxton Premiére 350 | C49FT | 1994 | |
| 1426 | L546XUT | Volvo B10M-62 | Plaxton Premiére 350 | C49FT | 1994 | |
| 1427 | H114UYG | Volvo B10M-60 | Plaxton Expressliner | C46FT | 1991 | Ex Angloblue, Leeds, 1997 |
| 1428 | H741WWU | Volvo B10M-60 | Plaxton Expressliner | C46FT | 1991 | Ex Angloblue, Leeds, 1997 |

| 1451-1460 | | Volvo B10M-55 | | Plaxton Derwent II | | B51F | | 1990 | |
|---|---|---|---|---|---|---|---|---|---|
| 1451 | G451JYG | 1453 | G453JYG | 1455 | G455JYG | 1457 | G457JYG | 1459 | G459JYG |
| 1452 | G452JYG | 1454 | G454JYG | 1456 | G456JYG | 1458 | G458JYG | 1460 | G460JYG |

Between 1994 and 1996 almost a hundred Mercedes-Benz 709D minibuses were supplied to the Rider fleet, all fitted with Plaxton Beaver bodies. Some have now departed for the Greater Manchester fleet but one which does remain is 2255, M255VWU seen here with Quickstep Travel names. *Lee Whitehead*

| | | | | | | | |
|---|---|---|---|---|---|---|---|
| 1594 | ABR868S | Leyland Leopard PSU3E/4R | Plaxton Derwent II (1990) | B55F | 1977 | Ex Reynard Buses, 1990 |
| 1595 | JKW215W | Leyland Leopard PSU3G/4R | Plaxton Derwent II (1990) | B55F | 1981 | Ex Reynard.Buses, 1990 |
| 1596 | JKW216W | Leyland Leopard PSU3G/4R | Plaxton Derwent II (1990) | B55F | 1981 | Ex Reynard Buses, 1990 |
| 1597 | ABR869S | Leyland Leopard PSU3E/4R | Plaxton Derwent II (1990) | B55F | 1977 | Ex Reynard Buses, 1990 |
| 1606 | HUA606Y | Leyland Tiger TRCTL11/2RH | Plaxton Paramount 3200 E | C49F | 1983 | Ex WYPTE, 1986 |
| 1607 | HUA607Y | Leyland Tiger TRCTL11/2RH | Plaxton Paramount 3200 E | C49F | 1983 | Ex WYPTE, 1986 |
| 1608 | WSV410 | Leyland Tiger TRCTL11/2RH | Plaxton Paramount 3200 | C49F | 1984 | Ex WYPTE, 1986 |
| 1610 | B610VWU | Leyland Tiger TRCTL11/3RH | Plaxton Paramount 3200 IIE | C53F | 1985 | Ex WYPTE, 1986 |
| 1615 | F615XWY | Leyland Tiger TRCTL11/3ARZA | Plaxton Paramount 3200 IIIE | C53F | 1988 | |
| 1616 | F616XWY | Leyland Tiger TRCTL11/3ARZA | Plaxton Paramount 3200 IIIE | C53F | 1988 | |
| 1619 | F619XWY | Leyland Tiger TRCTL11/3ARZA | Plaxton Paramount 3200 III | C53F | 1988 | |
| 1621 | F621XWY | Leyland Tiger TRCTL11/3ARZA | Plaxton Paramount 3200 IIIE | C53F | 1988 | |
| 1622 | F622XWY | Leyland Tiger TRCTL11/3ARZA | Plaxton Paramount 3200 III | C53F | 1988 | |

### 1659-1672

| | | | | | | |
|---|---|---|---|---|---|---|
| | | Leyland Tiger TRBTL11/2R | Duple Dominant | DP47F | 1983-84 Ex WYPTE, 1986 |

| | | | | | | | | | |
|---|---|---|---|---|---|---|---|---|---|
| 1659 | A659KUM | 1662 | A662KUM | 1669 | A669KUM | 1671 | A671KUM | 1672 | A672KUM |
| 1661 | A661KUM | | | | | | | | |

| | | | | | | |
|---|---|---|---|---|---|---|
| 1796 | D796KWR | Freight Rover Sherpa | Dormobile | B20F | 1987 | |
| 1869w | D869LWR | Freight Rover Sherpa | Dormobile | B20F | 1987 | |
| 2117 | D564FAE | Mercedes-Benz L608D | Dormobile | B20F | 1986 | Ex City Line, 1994 |

### 2201-2293

| | | | | | |
|---|---|---|---|---|---|
| | | Mercedes-Benz 709D | Plaxton Beaver | B25F | 1994-96 |

| | | | | | | | | | |
|---|---|---|---|---|---|---|---|---|---|
| 2201 | M201VWU | 2227 | M227VWU | 2252 | M252VWU | 2266 | N266JUG | 2280 | N280JUG |
| 2202 | M202VWU | 2228 | M228VWU | 2253 | M253VWU | 2267 | N267JUG | 2281 | N281JUG |
| 2203 | M203VWU | 2229 | M229VWU | 2254 | M254VWU | 2268 | N268JUG | 2282 | N282JUG |
| 2204 | M204VWU | 2230 | M230VWU | 2255 | M255VWU | 2269 | N269JUG | 2283 | N283JUG |
| 2205 | M205VWU | 2231 | M231VWU | 2256 | M256VWU | 2270 | N270JUG | 2284 | N284JUG |
| 2206 | M206VWU | 2232 | M232VWU | 2257 | M257VWU | 2271 | N271JUG | 2285 | N285JUG |
| 2208 | M208VWU | 2233 | M233VWU | 2258 | M258VWU | 2272 | N272JUG | 2286 | N286JUG |
| 2210 | M210VWU | 2235 | M235VWU | 2259 | M259VWU | 2273 | N273JUG | 2287 | N287JUG |
| 2216 | M216VWU | 2240 | M240VWU | 2260 | M260VWU | 2274 | N274JUG | 2288 | N288JUG |
| 2217 | M217VWU | 2241 | M241VWU | 2261 | M261VWU | 2275 | N275JUG | 2289 | N289JUG |
| 2219 | M219VWU | 2242w | M242VWU | 2262 | M262VWU | 2276 | N276JUG | 2290 | N290JUG |
| 2220 | M220VWU | 2243 | M243VWU | 2263 | M263VWU | 2277 | N277JUG | 2291 | N291JUG |
| 2221 | M221VWU | 2250 | M250VWU | 2264 | N264JUG | 2278 | N278JUG | 2292 | N292JUG |
| 2222 | M449VWW | 2251 | M251VWU | 2265 | N265JUG | 2279 | N279JUG | 2293 | N293JUG |

*Opposite, top*: **The FirstBus fleets of Yorkshire Rider and Greater Manchester have recently exchanged a number of vehicles. Rider York 3301, M107RRJ was numbered 1107 in the Greater Manchester fleet before crossing the Pennines. It is a Northern Counties Paladin-bodied Dennis Dart and carries the latest version of the cream and green livery used for the Rider York operations.** *Tony Wilson*
*Opposite, bottom*: **Scott Hall Road in Leeds has the most extensive guided busway in Britain. The Leeds City Link buses run on a reserved roadway and are held in position on the guideway by small wheels one of which can be seen just behind the entrance door. Buses used on the routes which use the busway are painted in a special blue and silver livery and are branded Superbus. Number 8642, L642PWR is a Scania N113 which carries an Alexander Strider body.** *Tony Wilson*

**Kingfisher Huddersfield names are carried by 3002, one of only six Volvo B6s supplied to the fleet. All are based at Huddersfield which also operates Dennis Darts and the first 48 Dennis Lances.**
*Lee Whitehead*

### 3001-3006     Volvo B6-9.8m     Alexander Dash     B40F     1994

| | | | | | | | | | |
|---|---|---|---|---|---|---|---|---|---|
| **3001** | L101PWR | **3003** | L103PWR | **3004** | L104PWR | **3005** | L105PWR | **3006** | L106PWR |
| **3002** | L102PWR | | | | | | | | |

### 3201-3218     Dennis Dart 9.8SDL3054     Plaxton Pointer     B40F     1995

| | | | | | | | | | |
|---|---|---|---|---|---|---|---|---|---|
| **3201** | M201VWW | **3205** | M205VWW | **3209** | M209VWW | **3213** | M213VWW | **3216** | M216VWW |
| **3202** | M202VWW | **3206** | M206VWW | **3210** | M210VWW | **3214** | M214VWW | **3217** | M217VWW |
| **3203** | M203VWW | **3207** | M207VWW | **3211** | M211VWW | **3215** | M215VWW | **3218** | M218VWW |
| **3204** | M204VWW | **3208** | M208VWW | **3212** | M212VWW | | | | |

### 3219-3268     Dennis Dart 9.8SDL3054     Alexander Dash     B40F     1995

| | | | | | | | | | |
|---|---|---|---|---|---|---|---|---|---|
| **3219** | M219VWW | **3229** | M229VWW | **3239** | M239VWW | **3249** | M249VWW | **3259** | M259VWW |
| **3220** | M220VWW | **3230** | M230VWW | **3240** | M240VWW | **3250** | M250VWW | **3260** | M260VWW |
| **3221** | M221VWW | **3231** | M231VWW | **3241** | M241VWW | **3251** | M251VWW | **3261** | M261VWW |
| **3222** | M450VWW | **3232** | M232VWW | **3242** | M242VWW | **3252** | M252VWW | **3262** | M262VWW |
| **3223** | M223VWW | **3233** | M233VWW | **3243** | M243VWW | **3253** | M253VWW | **3263** | M263VWW |
| **3224** | M224VWW | **3234** | M234VWW | **3244** | M244VWW | **3254** | M254VWW | **3264** | M264VWW |
| **3225** | M225VWW | **3235** | M235VWW | **3245** | M245VWW | **3255** | M255VWW | **3265** | M265VWW |
| **3226** | M226VWW | **3236** | M236VWW | **3246** | M246VWW | **3256** | M256VWW | **3266** | M266VWW |
| **3227** | M227VWW | **3237** | M237VWW | **3247** | M247VWW | **3257** | M257VWW | **3267** | M267VWW |
| **3228** | M228VWW | **3238** | M238VWW | **3248** | M248VWW | **3258** | M258VWW | **3268** | M268VWW |

In 1997 FirstBus undertook a survey of passengers to determine the types and colour of vehicle interior they found the most attractive. As part of that survey several buses including 3305, P305AUM, an all-white liveried Dennis Dart SLF with Plaxton Pointer bodywork have been shown to the public at various venues. The vehicle is one of four in this white colour scheme now with Rider York. *David Longbottom*

### 3269-3298 Dennis Dart · Plaxton Pointer · B40F · 1996

| | | | | | | | | | |
|---|---|---|---|---|---|---|---|---|---|
| 3269 | N269JUM | 3275 | N275JUM | 3281 | N281JUM | 3287 | N287JUM | 3293 | N293JUM |
| 3270 | N270JUM | 3276 | N276JUM | 3282 | N282JUM | 3288 | N288JUM | 3294 | N294JUM |
| 3271 | N271JUM | 3277 | N277JUM | 3283 | N283JUM | 3289 | N289JUM | 3295 | N295JUM |
| 3272 | N272JUM | 3278 | N278JUM | 3284 | N284JUM | 3290 | N290JUM | 3296 | N296JUM |
| 3273 | N273JUM | 3279 | N279JUM | 3285 | N285JUM | 3291 | N291JUM | 3297 | N297JUM |
| 3274 | N274JUM | 3280 | N299JUM | 3286 | N286JUM | 3292 | N292JUM | 3298 | N298JUM |

| | | | | | |
|---|---|---|---|---|---|
| 3299 | M615SBA | Dennis Dart 9.8SDL3054 | Northern Counties Paladin | B39F | 1995 | Ex Greater Manchester, 1996 |
| 3300 | M616SBA | Dennis Dart 9.8SDL3054 | Northern Counties Paladin | B39F | 1995 | Ex Greater Manchester, 1996 |
| 3301 | M107RRJ | Dennis Dart 9.8SDL3054 | Northern Countirs Paladin | B40F | 1995 | Ex Greater Manchester, 1996 |
| 3302 | P302AUM | Dennis Dart SLF | Plaxton Pointer | B39F | 1997 | |
| 3303 | P303AUM | Dennis Dart SLF | Plaxton Pointer | B39F | 1997 | |
| 3304 | P304AUM | Dennis Dart SLF | Plaxton Pointer | B39F | 1997 | |
| 3305 | P305AUM | Dennis Dart SLF | Plaxton Pointer | B39F | 1997 | |

### 4001-4048 Dennis Lance 11SDA3113 · Plaxton Verde · B49F · 1995

| | | | | | | | | | |
|---|---|---|---|---|---|---|---|---|---|
| 4001 | M401VWW | 4011 | M411VWW | 4021 | M421VWW | 4031 | M431VWW | 4040 | N440VWW |
| 4002 | M402VWW | 4012 | M412VWW | 4022 | M422VWW | 4032 | M432VWW | 4041 | N441ENW |
| 4003 | M403VWW | 4013 | M413VWW | 4023 | M423VWW | 4033 | M433VWW | 4042 | N442ENW |
| 4004 | M404VWW | 4014 | M414VWW | 4024 | M424VWW | 4034 | M434VWW | 4043 | N443ENW |
| 4005 | M405VWW | 4015 | M415VWW | 4025 | M425VWW | 4035 | M435VWW | 4044 | N544ENW |
| 4006 | M406VWW | 4016 | M416VWW | 4026 | M426VWW | 4036 | M436VWW | 4045 | N445ENW |
| 4007 | M407VWW | 4017 | M417VWW | 4027 | M427VWW | 4037 | M437VWW | 4046 | N446ENW |
| 4008 | M408VWW | 4018 | M418VWW | 4028 | M428VWW | 4038 | M438VWW | 4047 | M447VWW |
| 4009 | M409VWW | 4019 | M419VWW | 4029 | M429VWW | 4039 | M439VWW | 4048 | M448VWW |
| 4010 | M410VWW | 4020 | M420VWW | 4030 | M430VWW | | | | |

## 4049-4078

Dennis Lance — Plaxton Verde — B49F — 1996

| | | | | | | | |
|---|---|---|---|---|---|---|---|
| **4049** N449JUG | **4055** N455JUG | **4061** N461JUG | **4067** N467JUG | **4073** N473JUG |
| **4050** N450JUG | **4056** N456JUG | **4062** N462JUG | **4068** N468JUG | **4074** N474JUG |
| **4051** N451JUG | **4057** N457JUG | **4063** N463JUG | **4069** N469JUG | **4075** N475JUG |
| **4052** N452JUG | **4058** N458JUG | **4064** N464JUG | **4070** N470JUG | **4076** N476JUG |
| **4053** N453JUG | **4059** N459JUG | **4065** N465JUG | **4071** N471JUG | **4077** N477JUG |
| **4054** N454JUG | **4060** N460JUG | **4066** N466JUG | **4072** N472JUG | **4078** N478JUG |

**4079** M221EAF — Dennis Lance — Wright Pathfinder — B40F — 1995 — Ex Badgerline, 1996

## 5018-5081

Leyland Olympian ONLXB/1R — Roe — H47/29F — 1982-83 Ex WYPTE, 1986

| | | | | | | | |
|---|---|---|---|---|---|---|---|
| **5018** UWW18X | **5026** CUB26Y | **5034** CUB34Y | **5042** CUB42Y | **5052** CUB52Y |
| **5019** UWW19X | **5027** CUB27Y | **5035** CUB35Y | **5043** CUB43Y | **5053** CUB53Y |
| **5020** UWW20X | **5028** CUB28Y | **5036** CUB36Y | **5044** CUB44Y | **5054** CUB54Y |
| **5021** CUB21Y | **5029** CUB29Y | **5037** CUB37Y | **5045** CUB45Y | **5055** CUB55Y |
| **5022** CUB22Y | **5030** CUB30Y | **5038** CUB38Y | **5046** CUB46Y | **5065** CUB65Y |
| **5023** CUB23Y | **5031** CUB31Y | **5039** CUB39Y | **5047** CUB47Y | **5077** EWY77Y |
| **5024** CUB24Y | **5032** CUB32Y | **5040** CUB40Y | **5048** CUB48Y | **5081** EWY81Y |
| **5025** CUB25Y | **5033** CUB33Y | **5041** CUB41Y | **5051** CUB51Y | |

## 5082-5127

Leyland Olympian ONLXB/1R — Roe — H47/29F — 1982-83 Ex WYPTE, 1986

| | | | | | | | |
|---|---|---|---|---|---|---|---|
| **5082** A82KUM | **5092** A92KUM | **5101** A101KUM | **5110** A110KUM | **5119** A119KUM |
| **5083** A83KUM | **5093** A93KUM | **5102** A102KUM | **5111** A111KUM | **5120** A120KUM |
| **5084** A84KUM | **5094** A94KUM | **5103** A103KUM | **5112** A112KUM | **5121** A121KUM |
| **5085** A85KUM | **5095** A95KUM | **5104** A104KUM | **5113** A113KUM | **5122** B122RWY |
| **5086** A86KUM | **5096** A96KUM | **5105** A105KUM | **5114** A114KUM | **5123** B123RWY |
| **5087** A87KUM | **5097** A97KUM | **5106** A106KUM | **5115** A115KUM | **5124** B124RWY |
| **5088** A88KUM | **5098** A98KUM | **5107** A107KUM | **5116** A116KUM | **5125** B125RWY |
| **5089** A89KUM | **5099** A99KUM | **5108** A108KUM | **5117** A117KUM | **5126** B126RWY |
| **5090** A90KUM | **5100** A100KUM | **5109** A109KUM | **5118** A118KUM | **5127** B127RWY |
| **5091** A91KUM | | | | |

## 5128-5145

Leyland Olympian ONLXB/1R — Roe — H47/29F — 1984 — Ex WYPTE, 1986

| | | | | | | | |
|---|---|---|---|---|---|---|---|
| **5128** B128RWY | **5132** B132RWY | **5136** B136RWY | **5140** B501RWY | **5143** B504RWY |
| **5129** B129RWY | **5133** B133RWY | **5137** B137RWY | **5141** B502RWY | **5144** B505RWY |
| **5130** B130RWY | **5134** B134RWY | **5138** B138RWY | **5142** B503RWY | **5145** B140RWY |
| **5131** B131RWY | **5135** B135RWY | **5139** B139RWY | | |

| | | | | |
|---|---|---|---|---|
| **5146** C146KBT | Leyland Olympian ONLXB/1R | Optare | CO47/29F | 1985 | Ex WYPTE, 1986 |
| **5147** C147KBT | Leyland Olympian ONLXB/1R | Optare | CO47/29F | 1985 | Ex WYPTE, 1986 |
| **5148** C148KBT | Leyland Olympian ONLXB/1R | Optare | H47/29F | 1985 | Ex WYPTE, 1986 |
| **5149** C149KBT | Leyland Olympian ONLXB/1R | Optare | H47/29F | 1985 | Ex WYPTE, 1986 |
| **5150** C150KBT | Leyland Olympian ONLXB/1R | Optare | H47/29F | 1985 | Ex WYPTE, 1986 |

## 5156-5175

Leyland Olympian ONCL10/1RZ — Northern Counties — H45/29F* — 1988 — *5165 is H43/29F

| | | | | | | | |
|---|---|---|---|---|---|---|---|
| **5151** F151XYG | **5156** F156XYG | **5161** F161XYG | **5166** F166XYG | **5171** F171XYG |
| **5152** F152XYG | **5157** F157XYG | **5162** F162XYG | **5167** F167XYG | **5172** F172XYG |
| **5153** F153XYG | **5158** F158XYG | **5163** F163XYG | **5168** F168XYG | **5173** F173XYG |
| **5154** F154XYG | **5159** F159XYG | **5164** F164XYG | **5169** F169XYG | **5174** F174XYG |
| **5155** F155XYG | **5160** F160XYG | **5165** F165XYG | **5170** F170XYG | **5175** F175XYG |

## 5176-5185

Leyland Olympian ONCL10/1RZ — Northern Counties — H47/29F — 1990

| | | | | | | | |
|---|---|---|---|---|---|---|---|
| **5176** G176JYG | **5178** G178JYG | **5180** G180JYG | **5182** G182JYG | **5184** G184JYG |
| **5177** G177JYG | **5179** G179JYG | **5181** G181JYG | **5183** G183JYG | **5185** G185JYG |

## 5186-5199

Leyland Olympian ONLXB/1R — Eastern Coach Works — H45/32F — 1983-85 Ex West Yorkshire, 1989

| | | | | | | | |
|---|---|---|---|---|---|---|---|
| **5186** FUM486Y | **5189** FUM492Y | **5192** FUM498Y | **5195** A599NYG | **5198** C483YWY |
| **5187** FUM487Y | **5190** FUM494Y | **5193** FUM499Y | **5196** A600NYG | **5199** C484YWY |
| **5188** FUM491Y | **5191** FUM495Y | **5194** A686MWX | **5197** A601NYG | |

Pictured in Bradford Traveller's dual-tone blue and red livery is Leyland Olympian 5184, G184JYG. This vehicle carries a Northern Counties Palatine body. *Terry Wightman*

### 5200-5222
Leyland Olympian ONCL10/1RZ  Alexander RL          H47/32F*  1990  *5207-13 are H47/30F

| 5200 | G623OWR | 5205 | G605OWR | 5210 | G610OWR | 5215 | G615OWR | 5219 | G619OWR |
|------|---------|------|---------|------|---------|------|---------|------|---------|
| 5201 | G601OWR | 5206 | G606OWR | 5211 | G611OWR | 5216 | G616OWR | 5220 | G620OWR |
| 5202 | G602OWR | 5207 | G607OWR | 5212 | G612OWR | 5217 | G617OWR | 5221 | G621OWR |
| 5203 | G603OWR | 5208 | G608OWR | 5213 | G613OWR | 5218 | G618OWR | 5222 | G622OWR |
| 5204 | G604OWR | 5209 | G609OWR | 5214 | G614OWR |      |         |      |         |

### 5301-5315
Volvo Olympian YN2RV18Z4     Northern Counties Palatine  H47/29F    1994

| 5301 | L301PWR | 5304 | L304PWR | 5307 | L307PWR | 5310 | L310PWR | 5313 | L313PWR |
|------|---------|------|---------|------|---------|------|---------|------|---------|
| 5302 | L302PWR | 5305 | L305PWR | 5308 | L308PWR | 5311 | L311PWR | 5314 | L314PWR |
| 5303 | L303PWR | 5306 | L306PWR | 5309 | L309PWR | 5312 | L312PWR | 5315 | L315PWR |

### 5401-5405
Volvo Olympian YN2RC16Z4     Northern Counties Palatine  H47/29F    1994

| 5401 | L401PWR | 5402 | L402PWR | 5403 | L403PWR | 5404 | L404PWR | 5405 | L405PWR |
|------|---------|------|---------|------|---------|------|---------|------|---------|

| 5501 | B141RWY | Leyland Olympian ONLXB/1R | Roe | | H47/27F | 1984 | Ex WYPTE, 1986 |
|------|---------|---------------------------|--------|--|---------|------|----------------|
| 5502 | B142RWY | Leyland Olympian ONLXB/1R | Roe    | | H47/27F | 1984 | Ex WYPTE, 1986 |
| 5503 | B143RWY | Leyland Olympian ONLXB/1R | Roe    | | H47/27F | 1984 | Ex WYPTE, 1986 |
| 5505 | B145RWY | Leyland Olympian ONLXB/1R | Roe    | | H47/27F | 1984 | Ex WYPTE, 1986 |
| 5506 | B506RWY | Leyland Olympian ONLXB/1R | Roe    | | H47/27F | 1984 | Ex WYPTE, 1986 |
| 5507 | C507KBT | Leyland Olympian ONTL11/1R | Optare | | H47/27F | 1985 | Ex WYPTE, 1986 |
| 5508 | C508KBT | Leyland Olympian ONTL11/1R | Optare | | H47/27F | 1985 | Ex WYPTE, 1986 |
| 5509 | C509KBT | Leyland Olympian ONTL11/1R | Optare | | H47/27F | 1985 | Ex WYPTE, 1986 |
| 5510 | C510KBT | Leyland Olympian ONTL11/1R | Optare | | H47/27F | 1985 | Ex WYPTE, 1986 |
| 5512 | D512HUB | Leyland Olympian ONTL11/1R | Optare | | H43/27F | 1987 | |
| 5513 | D512HUB | Leyland Olympian ONTL11/1R | Optare | | DPH43/27F | 1987 | |
| 5514 | D512HUB | Leyland Olympian ONTL11/1R | Optare | | H43/27F | 1987 | |
| 5515 | D515HUB | Leyland Olympian ONTL11/1R | Optare | | H43/27F | 1987 | |
| 5516 | D516HUB | Leyland Olympian ONTL11/1R | Optare | | H43/27F | 1987 | |

| 5517 | FUM489Y | Leyland Olympian ONLXB/1R | Eastern Coach Works | H41/29F | 1983 | Ex West Yorkshire, 1989 |
| 5518 | B518UWW | Leyland Olympian ONLXB/1R | Eastern Coach Works | DPH42/29F | 1985 | Ex West Yorkshire, 1989 |
| 5519 | B519UWW | Leyland Olympian ONLXB/1R | Eastern Coach Works | DPH42/29F | 1985 | Ex West Yorkshire, 1989 |
| 5520 | B520UWW | Leyland Olympian ONLXB/1R | Eastern Coach Works | DPH42/29F | 1985 | Ex West Yorkshire, 1989 |
| 5521 | B523UWW | Leyland Olympian ONLXB/1R | Eastern Coach Works | DPH42/29F | 1985 | Ex West Yorkshire, 1989 |

### 5601-5605

Volvo Olympian YN2RV18Z4 — Northern Counties Palatine — H47/29F — 1994

| 5601 | L601PWR | 5602 | L602PWR | 5603 | L603PWR | 5604 | L604PWR | 5605 | L605PWR |

### 6001-6074

Leyland Atlantean AN68/1R — Roe — H43/33F — 1974-75 Ex WYPTE, 1986

| 6001 | GUG533N | 6027w | GUG554N | 6039 | GUG566N | 6047 | HWT33N | 6064 | HWT50N |
| 6005 | GUG535N | 6030 | GUG557N | 6040 | GUG567N | 6050w | HWT36N | 6068 | HWT54N |
| 6015 | GUG542N | 6032 | GUG559N | 6043 | HWT29N | 6058 | HWT44N | 6073 | HWT59N |
| 6017 | GUG544N | 6033 | GUG560N | 6044 | HWT30N | 6061 | HWT47N | 6074 | HWT60N |
| 6024 | GUG551N | 6038 | GUG565N | 6045 | HWT31N | | | | |

### 6113-6175

Leyland Atlantean AN68/1R — Roe — H43/33F — 1975-77 Ex WYPTE, 1986

| 6113 | LUG113P | 6132 | SUA132R | 6146 | SUA146R | 6159 | WNW159S | 6169 | WNW169S |
| 6116 | LUG116P | 6133 | SUA133R | 6147 | SUA147R | 6161 | WNW161S | 6171 | WNW171S |
| 6117 | LUG117P | 6134 | SUA134R | 6150 | SUA150R | 6162 | WNW162S | 6172 | WNW172S |
| 6118 | LUG118P | 6140 | SUA140R | 6152 | WNW152S | 6163 | WNW163S | 6173 | WNW173S |
| 6127 | SUA127R | 6142 | SUA142R | 6156 | WNW156S | 6164 | WNW164S | 6174 | WNW174S |
| 6128 | SUA128R | 6144 | SUA144R | 6158 | WNW158S | 6167 | WNW167S | 6175 | WNW175S |
| 6130 | SUA130R | | | | | | | | |

### 6176-6191

Leyland Atlantean AN68/1R — Roe — H43/33F — 1979 Ex WYPTE, 1986

| 6176 | GWR176T | 6180 | GWR180T | 6183 | GWR183T | 6187 | GWR187T | 6190 | GWR190T |
| 6177 | GWR177T | 6181 | GWR181T | 6185 | GWR185T | 6188 | GWR188T | 6191 | GWR191T |
| 6178 | GWR178T | 6182 | GWR182T | 6186 | GWR186T | 6189 | GWR189T | | |

### 6192-6207

Leyland Atlantean AN68A/1R — Roe — H43/32F — 1979 Ex WYPTE, 1986

| 6192 | JUM192V | 6196 | JUM196V | 6199 | JUM199V | 6202 | JUM202V | 6205 | JUM205V |
| 6193 | JUM193V | 6197 | JUM197V | 6200 | JUM200V | 6203 | JUM203V | 6206 | JUM206V |
| 6194 | JUM194V | 6198 | JUM198V | 6201 | JUM201V | 6204 | JUM204V | 6207 | JUM207V |
| 6195 | JUM195V | | | | | | | | |

### 6208-6266

Leyland Atlantean AN68A/1R — Roe — H43/32F — 1979-80 Ex WYPTE, 1986

| 6208 | JUM208V | 6220 | KWY220V | 6232 | KWY232V | 6245 | KWY245V | 6256 | PUA256W |
| 6209 | JUM209V | 6221 | KWY221V | 6233 | KWY233V | 6246 | KWY246V | 6257 | PUA257W |
| 6210 | JUM210V | 6222 | KWY222V | 6234 | KWY234V | 6247 | KWY247V | 6258 | PUA258W |
| 6211 | JUM211V | 6223 | KWY223V | 6236 | KWY236V | 6248 | KWY248V | 6259 | PUA259W |
| 6212 | JUM212V | 6224 | KWY224V | 6237 | KWY237V | 6249 | KWY249V | 6260 | PUA260W |
| 6213 | JUM213V | 6225 | KWY225V | 6238 | KWY238V | 6250 | KWY250V | 6261 | PUA261W |
| 6214 | JUM214V | 6226 | KWY226V | 6239 | KWY239V | 6251 | KWY251V | 6262 | PUA262W |
| 6215 | JUM215V | 6227 | KWY227V | 6241 | KWY241V | 6252 | PUA252W | 6263 | PUA263W |
| 6216 | KWY216V | 6228 | KWY228V | 6242 | KWY242V | 6253 | PUA253W | 6264 | PUA264W |
| 6217 | KWY217V | 6229 | KWY229V | 6243 | KWY243V | 6254 | PUA254W | 6265 | PUA265W |
| 6218 | KWY218V | 6230 | KWY230V | 6244 | KWY244V | 6255 | PUA255W | 6266 | PUA266W |
| 6219 | KWY219V | 6231 | KWY231V | | | | | | |

*Opposite, top*: **Bradford Traveller is the name used by Yorkshire Rider in the area which recently celebrated 100 years as a city. Carrying the blue and red livery for the Bradford operations is Leyland Olympian 5515, D515HUB. The body on this vehicle was constructed at the Optare factory in Crossgates, Leeds. The Leeds fleet carries a white, red, orange and yellow scheme as seen on the vehicle behind and also as depicted by the Plaxton Verdé-bodied Dennis Lance on the rear cover of this publication.** *Tony Wilson*

*Opposite, bottom*: **The Halifax operation of Yorkshire Rider are now branded Calderline and buses are rapidly being re-painted in this white, blue and yellow scheme. Seen leaving the bus station in Halifax is Northern Counties-bodied Leyland Olympian 5174, F174XYG. This example is built to the lower height of 4.20 metres as opposed to the normal height of 4.46 metres enabling the bus to traverse routes with height limitations.** *Les Peters*

The mainstay of the Rider double-deck fleet, especially in the West Yorkshire PTE time, was the Leyland Atlantean many of which still remain in full service. Photographed in Huddersfield is 6282, PUA282W which carries locally-built Roe bodywork. *Lee Whitehead*

## 6267-6326
Leyland Atlantean AN68C/1R · Roe · H43/32F · 1980-81 · Ex WYPTE, 1986

| | | | | | | | | | |
|---|---|---|---|---|---|---|---|---|---|
| 6267 | PUA267W | 6279 | PUA279W | 6292 | PUA292W | 6304 | PUA304W | 6316 | PUA316W |
| 6268 | PUA268W | 6280 | PUA280W | 6293 | PUA293W | 6305 | PUA305W | 6317 | PUA317W |
| 6269 | PUA269W | 6282 | PUA282W | 6294 | PUA294W | 6306 | PUA306W | 6318 | PUA318W |
| 6270 | PUA270W | 6283 | PUA283W | 6295 | PUA295W | 6307 | PUA307W | 6319 | PUA319W |
| 6271 | PUA271W | 6284 | PUA284W | 6296 | PUA296W | 6308 | PUA308W | 6320 | PUA320W |
| 6272 | PUA272W | 6285 | PUA285W | 6297 | PUA297W | 6309 | PUA309W | 6321 | PUA321W |
| 6273 | PUA273W | 6286 | PUA286W | 6298 | PUA298W | 6310 | PUA310W | 6322 | PUA322W |
| 6274 | PUA274W | 6287 | PUA287W | 6299 | PUA299W | 6311 | PUA311W | 6323 | PUA323W |
| 6275 | PUA275W | 6288 | PUA288W | 6300 | PUA300W | 6312 | PUA312W | 6324 | PUA324W |
| 6276 | PUA276W | 6289 | PUA289W | 6301 | PUA301W | 6313 | PUA313W | 6325 | PUA325W |
| 6277 | PUA277W | 6290 | PUA290W | 6302 | PUA302W | 6314 | PUA314W | 6326 | PUA326W |
| 6278 | PUA278W | 6291 | PUA291W | 6303 | PUA303W | 6315 | PUA321W | | |

## 6327-6361
Leyland Atlantean AN68C/1R · Roe · H43/32F · 1981 · Ex WYPTE, 1986

| | | | | | | | | | |
|---|---|---|---|---|---|---|---|---|---|
| 6327 | VWW327X | 6334 | VWW334X | 6341 | VWW341X | 6348 | VWW348X | 6355 | VWW355X |
| 6328 | VWW328X | 6335 | VWW335X | 6342 | VWW342X | 6349 | VWW349X | 6356 | VWW356X |
| 6329 | VWW329X | 6336 | VWW336X | 6343 | VWW343X | 6350 | VWW350X | 6357 | VWW357X |
| 6330 | VWW330X | 6337 | VWW337X | 6344 | VWW344X | 6351 | VWW351X | 6358 | VWW358X |
| 6331 | VWW331X | 6338 | VWW338X | 6345 | VWW345X | 6352 | VWW352X | 6359 | VWW359X |
| 6332 | VWW332X | 6339 | VWW339X | 6346 | VWW346X | 6353 | VWW353X | 6360 | VWW360X |
| 6333 | VWW333X | 6340 | VWW340X | 6347 | VWW347X | 6354 | VWW354X | 6361 | VWW361X |

| | | | | | | |
|---|---|---|---|---|---|---|
| 6423 | UNA800S | Leyland Atlantean AN68/1R | Northern Counties | H43/32F | 1978 | Ex G M Buses, 1988 |

## 6425-6435
Leyland Atlantean AN68B/1R · Roe · H43/30F · 1980-81 Ex Sovereign, 1989

| | | | | | | | | | |
|---|---|---|---|---|---|---|---|---|---|
| 6425 | EPH227V | 6427 | KPJ255W | 6430 | KPJ261W | 6432 | KPJ290W | 6434 | KPJ292W |
| 6426 | KPJ253W | 6428 | KPJ257W | 6431 | KPJ263W | 6433 | KPJ291W | 6435 | MPG293W |

After a period of some nine years further doble-deck buses from Manchester are again crossing the Pennines into Yorkshire. One of the earlier migrants is 7204, PTD642S, which now carries the latest Calderline livery. *Lee Whitehead*

| | | | | | | |
|---|---|---|---|---|---|---|
| 6436 | ORJ356W | Leyland Atlantean AN68A/1R | Northern Counties | H43/32F | 1981 | Greater Manchester, 1997 |
| 6437 | ORJ373W | Leyland Atlantean AN68A/1R | Northern Counties | H43/32F | 1981 | Greater Manchester, 1997 |
| 6438 | ORJ400W | Leyland Atlantean AN68A/1R | Northern Counties | H43/32F | 1981 | Greater Manchester, 1997 |
| 6439 | SND415X | Leyland Atlantean AN68A/1R | Northern Counties | H43/32F | 1981 | Greater Manchester, 1997 |
| 6440 | UNA834S | Leyland Atlantean AN68A/1R | Park Royal | H43/32F | 1977 | Greater Manchester, 1997 |
| 6441 | ANA209T | Leyland Atlantean AN68A/1R | Northern Counties | H43/32F | 1978 | Greater Manchester, 1997 |
| 6442 | FVR266V | Leyland Atlantean AN68A/1R | Northern Counties | H43/32F | 1979 | Greater Manchester, 1997 |
| 7033 | MNW33P | Leyland Fleetline FE30GR | Roe | H43/33F | 1976 | Ex WYPTE, 1986 |
| 7054w | RWU54R | Leyland Fleetline FE30AGR | Roe | H43/33F | 1976 | Ex WYPTE, 1986 |

### 7073-7088

| | | Leyland Fleetline FE30AGR | | Northern Counties | | H43/31F | | 1979-80 Ex WYPTE, 1986 | |
|---|---|---|---|---|---|---|---|---|---|
| 7073 | JNW73V | 7079 | JUM79V | 7082 | JUM82V | 7086 | JUM86V | 7088 | JUM88V |
| 7078 | JUM78V | | | | | | | | |

### 7092-7156

| | | Leyland Fleetline FE30AGR | | Roe | | H43/33F | | 1977-78 Ex WYPTE, 1986 | |
|---|---|---|---|---|---|---|---|---|---|
| 7092 | WUM92S | 7120 | WUM120S | 7126 | CWU136T | 7148 | CWU148T | 7153 | CWU153T |
| 7097 | WUM97S | 7121 | WUM121S | 7137 | CWU137T | 7149 | CWU149T | 7155 | CWU155T |
| 7109 | WUM109S | 7125 | WUM125S | 7144 | CWU144T | 7152 | CWU152T | 7156 | CWU156T |

### 7203-7211

| | | Leyland Fleetline FE30AGR | | Northern Counties | | H43/32F | | 1977-78 Ex Greater Manchester Transport, 1987/96 | |
|---|---|---|---|---|---|---|---|---|---|
| 7203 | PTD640S | 7205 | PTD646S | 7207 | PTD649S | 7209 | PTD651S | 7211 | PTD658S |
| 7204 | PTD642S | | | | | | | | |

### 7214-7234

| | | Leyland Fleetline FE30GR | | Northern Counties | | H43/32F | | 1978-79 Ex Greater Manchester Transport, 1987 | |
|---|---|---|---|---|---|---|---|---|---|
| 7214 | XBU5S | 7221 | XBU17S | 7228 | ANA34T | 7231 | ANA45T | 7233 | BVR53T |
| 7216 | XBU9S | 7223 | ANA25T | 7229 | ANA40T | 7232 | ANA48T | 7234 | BVR55T |
| 7219 | XBU15S | 7226 | ANA31T | 7230 | ANA44T | | | | |

## 7235-7243 Leyland Fleetline FE30AGR — Northern Counties — H43/32F — 1978-80 Ex Greater Manchester Transport, 1987

| | | | | | | | | |
|---|---|---|---|---|---|---|---|---|
| 7235 | TWH690T | 7237 | TWH692T | 7239 | TWH695T | 7242 | BCB611V | 7243 | BCB612V |
| 7236 | TWH691T | 7238 | TWH693T | 7241 | BCB610V | | | | |

## 7244-7253 Leyland Fleetline FE30GR — Northern Counties — H43/32F — 1979 Ex GM Buses, 1988

| | | | | | | | | |
|---|---|---|---|---|---|---|---|---|
| 7244 | BVR52T | 7246 | BVR67T | 7248 | BVR70T | 7250 | BVR85T | 7253 | BVR97T |
| 7245 | BVR65T | 7247 | BVR69T | 7249 | BVR71T | 7252 | BVR92T | | |

## 7521-7537 MCW Metrobus DR102/32 — MCW — H46/30F — 1983 Ex WYPTE, 1986

| | | | | | | | | |
|---|---|---|---|---|---|---|---|---|
| 7521 | CUB521Y | 7525 | CUB525Y | 7530 | CUB530Y | 7534 | CUB534Y | 7536 | CUB536Y |
| 7522 | CUB522Y | 7527 | CUB527Y | 7531 | CUB531Y | 7535 | CUB535Y | 7537 | CUB537Y |
| 7523 | CUB523Y | 7529 | CUB529Y | 7532 | CUB532Y | | | | |

## 7542-7580 MCW Metrobus DR102/38 — MCW — H46/30F — 1984 Ex WYPTE, 1986

| | | | | | | | | |
|---|---|---|---|---|---|---|---|---|
| 7542 | A542KUM | 7550 | A750LWY | 7556 | A756LWY | 7563 | B563RWY | 7575 | B575RWY |
| 7544 | A544KUM | 7551 | A751LWY | 7558 | A758LWY | 7566 | B566RWY | 7577 | B577RWY |
| 7545 | A545KUM | 7552 | A752LWY | 7560 | A760LWY | 7567 | B567RWY | 7578 | B578RWY |
| 7549 | A549KUM | 7554 | A754LWY | 7561 | B561RWY | 7570 | B570RWY | 7580 | B580RWY |

## 7581-7595 MCW Metrobus DR102/66 — MCW — H46/31F — 1988

| | | | | | | | | |
|---|---|---|---|---|---|---|---|---|
| 7581 | F581XWY | 7584 | F584XWY | 7587 | F587XWY | 7590 | F590XWY | 7593 | F593XWY |
| 7582 | F582XWY | 7585 | F585XWY | 7588 | F588XWY | 7591 | F591XWY | 7594 | F594XWY |
| 7583 | F583XWY | 7586 | F586XWY | 7589 | F589XWY | 7592 | F592XWY | 7595 | F595XWY |

## 7596-7600 MCW Metrobus DR102/67 — MCW — H46/31F — 1988

| | | | | | | | | |
|---|---|---|---|---|---|---|---|---|
| 7596 | F596XWY | 7597 | F597XWY | 7598 | F598XWY | 7599 | F599XWY | 7600 | F600XWY |

## 7601-7605 MCW Metrobus DR102/69 — MCW — H46/31F — 1988

| | | | | | | | | |
|---|---|---|---|---|---|---|---|---|
| 7601 | F601XWY | 7602 | F602XWY | 7603 | F603XWY | 7604 | F604XWY | 7605 | F605XWY |

**Leeds City Link operate all the Scania double-deck buses in the Rider fleet. Seen here is 8008, H808TWX, one of five Scania N113s delivered in 1990 which feature Northern Counties bodywork.**
*Lee Whitehead*

## 8001-8005
| | Scania N113DRB | | Alexander RH | | H47/33F | 1990 | | |
|---|---|---|---|---|---|---|---|---|
| **8001** | G801JYG | **8002** | G802JYG | **8003** | G803JYG | **8004** | G804JYG | **8005** G805JYG |

## 8006-8010
| | Scania N113DRB | | Northern Counties Palatine | H43/33F | 1990 | |
|---|---|---|---|---|---|---|
| **8006** | H806TWX | **8007** | H807TWX | **8008** H808TWX | **8009** H809TWX | **8010** H810TWX |

## 8011-8042
Scania N113DRB — Alexander RH — H47/31F — 1991

| | | | | | | | | | |
|---|---|---|---|---|---|---|---|---|---|
| **8011** | H611VNW | **8018** | H618VNW | **8025** | H625VNW | **8031** | H631VNW | **8037** | H637VNW |
| **8012** | H612VNW | **8019** | H619VNW | **8026** | H726VNW | **8032** | H632VNW | **8038** | H638VNW |
| **8013** | H613VNW | **8020** | H620VNW | **8027** | H627VNW | **8033** | H633VNW | **8039** | H639VNW |
| **8014** | H614VNW | **8021** | H621VNW | **8028** | H628VNW | **8034** | H634VNW | **8040** | H640VNW |
| **8015** | H615VNW | **8022** | H622VNW | **8029** | H629VNW | **8035** | H643VNW | **8041** | H641VNW |
| **8016** | H616VNW | **8023** | H623VNW | **8030** | H630VNW | **8036** | H636VNW | **8042** | H642VNW |
| **8017** | H617VNW | **8024** | H624VNW | | | | | | |

## 8401-8405
Scania L113CRL — Alexander Strider — B48F — 1994

| **8401** | M401UUB | **8402** | M402UUB | **8403** | M403UUB | **8404** | M404UUB | **8405** | M405UUB |
|---|---|---|---|---|---|---|---|---|---|

## 8411-8425
Scania L113CRL — Wright Axcess-ultralow — B48F — 1995-96

| **8411** | N411ENW | **8414** | N414ENW | **8417** | N417ENW | **8420** | N420MWY | **8423** | N423MWY |
|---|---|---|---|---|---|---|---|---|---|
| **8412** | N412ENW | **8415** | N415ENW | **8418** | N418ENW | **8421** | N421MWY | **8424** | N424MWY |
| **8413** | N413ENW | **8416** | N416ENW | **8419** | N419ENW | **8422** | N422MWY | **8425** | N425MWY |

## 8426-8431
Scania L113CRL — Wright Axcess-ultralow — B48F — 1997

| **8426** | P426GLS | **8428** | P428GLS | **8429** | P429GLS | **8430** | P430GLS | **8431** | P431GLS |
|---|---|---|---|---|---|---|---|---|---|
| **8427** | P427GLS | | | | | | | | |

| **8534** | RWT534R | Leyland Leopard PSU4D/4R | Plaxton Derwent | DP43F | 1976 | Ex WYPTE, 1986 |
|---|---|---|---|---|---|---|

## 8601-8634
Scania N113CRB — Alexander Strider — B50F — 1993

| **8601** | K601HUG | **8608** | K608HUG | **8615** | K615HUG | **8622** | K622HUG | **8629** | K629HUG |
|---|---|---|---|---|---|---|---|---|---|
| **8602** | K602HUG | **8609** | K609HUG | **8616** | K616HUG | **8623** | K623HUG | **8630** | K630HUG |
| **8603** | K603HUG | **8610** | K610HUG | **8617** | K617HUG | **8624** | K624HUG | **8631** | K631HUG |
| **8604** | K604HUG | **8611** | K611HUG | **8618** | K618HUG | **8625** | K625HUG | **8632** | K632HUG |
| **8605** | K605HUG | **8612** | K612HUG | **8619** | K619HUG | **8626** | K626HUG | **8633** | K633HUG |
| **8606** | K606HUG | **8613** | K613HUG | **8620** | K620HUG | **8627** | K627HUG | **8634** | K634HUG |
| **8607** | K607HUG | **8614** | K614HUG | **8621** | K621HUG | **8628** | K628HUG | | |

| **8635** | K1YRL | Scania N113CRB | Alexander Strider | DP50F | 1993 |
|---|---|---|---|---|---|

## 8636-8655
Scania N113CRB — Alexander Strider — B48F — 1994

| **8636** | L636PWR | **8640** | L640PWR | **8644** | L644PWR | **8648** | L648PWR | **8652** | L652PWR |
|---|---|---|---|---|---|---|---|---|---|
| **8637** | L637PWR | **8641** | L641PWR | **8645** | L645PWR | **8649** | L649PWR | **8653** | L653PWR |
| **8638** | L638PWR | **8642** | L642PWR | **8646** | L646PWR | **8650** | L650PWR | **8654** | L654PWR |
| **8639** | L639PWR | **8643** | L643PWR | **8647** | L647PWR | **8651** | L651PWR | **8655** | L655PWR |

| **8656** | 8995WY | Scania N113CRL | East Lancashire European | B46F | 1995 | Ex Scania demonstrator, 1997 |
|---|---|---|---|---|---|---|

Fleet information for each Yorkshire Rider operation is listed separately in the 1997 FirstBus Bus Handbook to allow readers to benefit from both styles of listing.

**Previous Registrations:**
| 8995WY | M78WKX | | UOI4323 | ? |
|---|---|---|---|---|

Only two Scanias that were formerly used as airside vehicles remain with Yorkshire Terrier, the others have been rebodied for service with other group companies. Photographed in April 1997 while heading for Sheffield's Halfway, 88, D88ALX illustrates the East Lancashire body style used for these buses. *Tony Wilson*

Yorkshire Terrier has become a popular operator on the competetive service to Crookes, to the west of Sheffield. Since de-regulation Terrier has continually increased its presence in this area with high bus useage. Pictured in Sheffield's High Street while heading for the Crookes district is 101, K1YTB the first of the Dennis Darts. *Tony Wilson*

# YORKSHIRE TERRIER

Yorkshire Terrier Ltd, Upper Sheffield Road, Barnsley,
South Yorkshire, S70 4PP

**Depot** : Rother Valley Way, Holbrook, Sheffield

Part of the Yorkshire Traction Group

| | | | | | | |
|---|---|---|---|---|---|---|
| 1 | TCY735M | Leyland National 11351/1R | | B52F | 1974 | Ex Shearings, 1988 |
| 2 | VPT948R | Leyland National 11351A/1R | | B49F | 1977 | Ex South Riding, 1995 |
| 6 | NFM844M | Leyland National 1151/1R | | B49F | 1973 | Ex Crosville, 1988 |
| 8 | LMO224L | Leyland National 1151/1R/0402 | | B49F | 1973 | Ex Crosville Wales, 1988 |
| 15w | NPD168L | Leyland National 1151/1R/0402 | | B49F | 1973 | Ex Shearings, 1988 |
| 18 | NPD138L | Leyland National 1151/1R/0402 | | B49F | 1973 | Ex Shearings, 1989 |
| 22 | MBO22P | Leyland National 11351A/1R | | B49F | 1976 | Ex Fletcher, Skelmersdale, 1989 |
| 23 | MBO23P | Leyland National 11351A/1R | | B49F | 1976 | Ex Fletcher, Skelmersdale, 1989 |
| 24 | BCD806L | Leyland National 1151/1R/0102 | | B49F | 1973 | Ex Thames Transit, 1991 |
| 25 | JNO195N | Leyland National 11351/1R | | B49F | 1975 | Ex East Midland, 1989 |
| 28 | NEV675M | Leyland National 1151/1R/0402 | | B49F | 1973 | Ex Hastings & Distrist, 1989 |
| 29 | MOD855P | Leyland National 11351A/1R | | B49F | 1976 | Ex Western National, 1990 |
| 30 | VOD602S | Leyland National 11351A/1R (Volvo) | | B52F | 1978 | Ex Western National, 1990 |
| 32 | KRE282P | Leyland National 11351/1R | | B52F | 1975 | Ex South Riding, 1995 |
| 33 | TUG813R | Leyland National 11351A/1R | | B49F | 1977 | Ex Rotherham & District, 1991 |
| 34 | AWT702S | Leyland National 11351A/1R (Volvo) | | B49F | 1978 | Ex Rotherham & District, 1991 |
| 36 | KRE276P | Leyland National 11351/1R | | B52F | 1975 | Ex South Riding, 1995 |
| 39 | RKA879T | Leyland National 11351A/1R | | B49F | 1978 | Ex Merseybus, 1991 |
| 40 | RKA881T | Leyland National 11351A/1R | | B49F | 1978 | Ex Merseybus, 1991 |
| 42 | RKA885T | Leyland National 11351A/1R | | B49F | 1978 | Ex Merseybus, 1991 |
| 43 | VRP528S | Leyland National 11351A/1R | | B49F | 1977 | Ex United Counties, 1991 |
| 44 | VRP529S | Leyland National (Volvo)11351A/1R | | B49F | 1977 | Ex United Counties, 1991 |
| 45 | VRP530S | Leyland National 11351A/1R | | B49F | 1977 | Ex United Counties, 1991 |
| 46 | XVV534S | Leyland National 11351A/1R | | B49F | 1978 | Ex United Counties, 1991 |
| 47 | CBV777S | Leyland National 11351A/1R(Volvo) | | B49F | 1977 | Ex Thames Transit, 1991 |
| 48 | CBV778S | Leyland National 11351A/1R | | B49F | 1977 | Ex Thames Transit, 1991 |
| 49 | CBV789S | Leyland National 11351A/1R | | B49F | 1977 | Ex Thames Transit, 1991 |
| 50 | CBV770S | Leyland National 11351A/1R(Volvo) | | B49F | 1977 | Ex Thames Transit, 1991 |
| 51 | CBV771S | Leyland National 11351A/1R(Volvo) | | B49F | 1977 | Ex Thames Transit, 1991 |
| 52 | OKJ507M | Leyland National 1151/1R/0102 | | B49F | 1973 | Ex Brighton, 1991 |
| 53 | OKJ511M | Leyland National 1151/1R/0102 | | B49F | 1973 | Ex Brighton, 1991 |
| 54 | CBV788S | Leyland National 11351A/1R | | B49F | 1977 | Ex Thames Transit, 1991 |
| 56 | YCD86T | Leyland National 11351A/2R | | B49F | 1978 | Ex Thames Transit, 1991 |
| 57 | MLJ921P | Leyland National 11351/1R | | B49F | 1976 | Ex Wilts & Dorset, 1992 |
| 58 | MLJ918P | Leyland National 11351/1R | | B49F | 1976 | Ex Wilts & Dorset, 1992 |
| 70 | LUA323V | Leyland National 2 NL106L11/1R | | B41F | 1980 | Ex AngloBlue, Leeds, 1996 |
| 71 | GHB225W | Leyland National 2 NL106L11/1R | | B44F | 1980 | Ex AngloBlue, Leeds, 1996 |
| 72 | PWY586W | Leyland National 2 NL106AL11/1R | | B41F | 1980 | Ex AngloBlue, Leeds, 1996 |
| 73 | UWY64X | Leyland National 2 NL116AL11/1R | | B52F | 1981 | Ex Harrogate & District, 1996 |
| 74 | APT124W | Leyland National 2 NL116AL11/1R | | B49F | 1980 | Ex Northumbria, 1997 |
| 75 | APT125W | Leyland National 2 NL116AL11/1R | | B49F | 1980 | Ex Northumbria, 1997 |
| 88 | D88ALX | Scania K112CRB | East Lancashire | DP51F | 1987 | Ex British Airways, Heathrow, 1992 |
| 93 | D93ALX | Scania K112CRB | East Lancashire | DP51F | 1987 | Ex British Airways, Heathrow, 1992 |
| 101 | K1YTB | Dennis Dart 9.8SDL3017 | Plaxton Pointer | B40F | 1993 | |
| 102 | K2YTB | Dennis Dart 9.8SDL3017 | Plaxton Pointer | B40F | 1993 | |
| 103 | K3YTB | Dennis Dart 9.8SDL3017 | Plaxton Pointer | B40F | 1993 | |
| 104 | L4YTB | Dennis Dart 9.8SDL3025 | Plaxton Pointer | B40F | 1993 | |
| 105 | N105CET | Dennis Dart 9.8SDL3054 | Northern Counties Paladin | B40F | 1995 | |
| 106 | N106CET | Dennis Dart 9.8SDL3054 | Northern Counties Paladin | B40F | 1995 | |
| 107 | N107CET | Dennis Dart 9.8SDL3054 | Northern Counties Paladin | B40F | 1995 | |
| 108 | N108CET | Dennis Dart 9.8SDL3054 | Northern Counties Paladin | B40F | 1995 | |
| 109 | K9YTB | Dennis Dart 9.8SDL3017 | Plaxton Pointer | B40F | 1993 | |
| 110 | N110CET | Dennis Dart 9.8SDL3054 | Northern Counties Paladin | B40F | 1995 | |
| 111 | N109CET | Dennis Dart 9.8SDL3054 | Northern Counties Paladin | B40F | 1995 | |

Yorkshire Terrier coaches used to carry the Kingsman Travel fleetname. In line with Yorkshire Traction group identity, the fleetname Yorkshire Terrier CoachlinK is now carried. Recently painted 128, 128NNU is one of four Plaxton-bodied Leyland Tigers in the Yorkshire Terrier fleet. *Lee Whitehead*

| 120 | L860WVC | Volvo B6-9.9M | Alexander Dash | B40F | 1994 | |
|-----|---------|---------------|----------------|------|------|--|
| 121 | M121UET | Volvo B6-9.9M | Alexander Dash | B40F | 1994 | |
| 122 | M122UET | Volvo B6-9.9M | Alexander Dash | B40F | 1994 | |
| 123 | M123UET | Volvo B6-9.9M | Alexander Dash | B40F | 1994 | |
| 124 | M124VAK | Volvo B6-9.9M | Alexander Dash | B40F | 1995 | |
| 125 | M125VAK | Volvo B6-9.9M | Alexander Dash | B40F | 1995 | |
| 128 | 128NNU | Leyland Tiger TRCTL11/3R | Plaxton Paramount 3500 | C49FT | 1983 | Ex Kingsman, Matlock, 1992 |
| 159 | A159EPA | Leyland Tiger TRCTL11/2RH | Plaxton Paramount 3200 E | C53F | 1984 | Ex Kingsman, Matlock, 1992 |
| 290 | THL290Y | Leyland Tiger TRCTL11/3R | Plaxton Paramount 3500 | C47FT | 1983 | Ex Kingsman, Matlock, 1992 |
| 918 | DBZ918 | Leyland Tiger TRCTL11/3R | Plaxton Paramount 3500 | C49FT | 1983 | Ex Kingsman, Matlock, 1992 |

**Previous Registrations**:

| 128NNU | LFE777Y | | M121UET | L860WVC |
|--------|---------|--|---------|---------|
| DBZ918 | BAJ637Y,2090VT,DFP492Y,MIA2192,YOI139 | | | |

**Livery**: Green yellow and white

**Operations**: Coachlink: THL290Y, 128NNU, DBZ918, A159EPA ; Yorkshire Terrier: Remainder.

**On Order**: 5 Dennis Dart SLF- East Lancashire Spryte with B39Fbodies

*Opposite, top*: **Mark I Leyland Nationals have provided the backbone of the Yorkshire Terrier fleet since the company was founded at de-regulation. Number 43, VRP528S, was purchased from United Counties in 1991 and continues in service. Some of these vehicles have been fitted with Volvo engines instead of the normal fixed head, turbocharged Leyland 510 unit. Gradually Leyland Nationals are being replaced by Dennis Darts and a Northern Counties Paladin-bodied example is on the cover of this publication.** *Lee Whitehead*

*Opposite, bottom*: **As well as new vehicles, Yorkshire Terrier have started acquiring Mk 2 Leyland Nationals as part of the buying policy of the Yorkshire Traction group. 73, UWY64X arrived from the Harrogate and District fleet in 1996. There are also former Harrogate and District National 2s in the group fleets of Barnsley & District, Andrews-Sheffield Omnibus, RoadCar and Lincoln City Transport.** *Tony Wilson*

# YORKSHIRE TRACTION

The Yorkshire Traction Co Ltd, Upper Sheffield Road, Barnsley,
South Yorkshire, S70 4PP

**Depots:** Upper Sheffield Road, Barnsley; Milethorn Lane, Doncaster; Penistone Road, Huddersfield; Dale Road, Rawmarsh; Weetshaw Lane, Shafton and Brampton Road, Wombwell.

| | | | | | | |
|---|---|---|---|---|---|---|
| 1 | 6078HE | Scania K93CRB | Plaxton Paramount 3500 III | C46FT | 1992 | |
| 2 | 5562HE | Scania K93CRB | Plaxton Paramount 3500 III | C46FT | 1992 | |
| 3 | 3030HE | Scania K93CRB | Plaxton Paramount 3500 III | C46FT | 1992 | |
| 4 | 6290HE | Scania K93CRB | Van Hool Alizée | C46FT | 1992 | Ex Barnsley & District, 1995 |
| 14 | 1737HE | Leyland Tiger TRCL10/3ARZM | Plaxton Paramount 3500 III | C49FT | 1989 | Ex Richardson, South Anston, 1994 |
| 15 | RHE353 | Leyland Tiger TRCTL11/3ARZ | Plaxton Paramount 3500 III | C46FT | 1988 | Ex Hills, Tredegar, 1992 |
| 16 | 6341HE | Leyland Tiger TRCTL11/3ARZ | Plaxton Paramount 3500 III | C48FT | 1988 | Ex Hills, Tredegar, 1992 |
| 17 | 6087HE | Leyland Tiger TRCTL11/3ARZ | Plaxton Paramount 3500 III | C46FT | 1988 | Ex Hills, Tredegar, 1992 |
| 41 | 374YTC | Hestair Duple 425 | Duple 425 | C57F | 1992 | |
| 48 | PHE692 | DAF SB3000DKV601 | Van Hool Alizée | C51FT | 1989 | Ex Barnsley & District, 1995 |
| 49 | HSV389 | DAF SB3000DKV601 | Van Hool Alizée | C51FT | 1988 | Ex Barnsley & District, 1995 |
| 50 | YTC49 | Volvo B10M-60 | Plaxton Paramount 3500 III | C47FT | 1990 | Ex Ambassador Travel, 1994 |
| 52 | NHE340 | Volvo B10M-61 | Plaxton Paramount 3500 III | C46FT | 1988 | Ex Shearings, 1992 |
| 53 | HE5362 | Volvo B10M-60 | Plaxton Premiére 350 | C46FT | 1993 | |
| 54 | RHE194 | Volvo B10M-60 | Plaxton Premiére 350 | C46FT | 1993 | |
| 55 | HE8054 | Volvo B10M-62 | Plaxton Premiére 350 | C46FT | 1995 | |
| 56 | 2316HE | Volvo B10M-62 | Plaxton Premiére 350 | C46FT | 1995 | |
| 57 | YTC838 | Volvo B10M-62 | Plaxton Premiére 350 | C46FT | 1995 | |
| 58 | P58KWG | Volvo B10M-62 | Plaxton Premiére 350 | C44FT | 1997 | |
| 59 | P59KWG | Volvo B10M-62 | Plaxton Premiére 350 | C44FT | 1997 | |
| 60 | P160MDT | Volvo B10M-62 | Plaxton Premiére 350 | C44FT | 1997 | |

**The Spartan chassis built in the USA was imported into Britain as a joint venture between Yorkshire Traction and East Lancashire Coachbuilders. Alusuisse constructed bodywork is fitted to an experimental Opus 2 style which has since evolved into the Flyte. While the chassis is fitted with a standard Cummins engine and Allison gearbox, there are unusual features such as 12-volt electrics. Two of type have been built, the first of which is 201, N201CKU.** *Tony Wilson*

Yorkshire Traction provide many of the coaches for National Express services radiating from South Yorkshire. Volvo and Scania chassis are preferred coupled with Van Hool or Plaxton coachwork. Number 54, RHE194, is a Volvo/Plaxton example which, in common with many of the Yorkshire Traction coach fleet, now bears a HE registration mark, traditionally issued by the Borough of Barnsley. *Terry Wightman*

| | | | | | | |
|---|---|---|---|---|---|---|
| 71 | 2542HE | Scania K93CRB | Plaxton Paramount 3500 III | C46FT | 1991 | |
| 75 | OHE50 | Scania K93CRB | Plaxton Paramount 3500 III | C46FT | 1991 | |
| 76 | YTC856 | Scania K113CRB | Plaxton Paramount 3500 III | C46FT | 1990 | |
| 77 | 2408HE | Scania K113CRB | Plaxton Paramount 3500 III | C46FT | 1990 | |
| 78 | 1619HE | Scania K113CRB | Plaxton Paramount 3500 III | C46FT | 1990 | |
| 79 | YHE91 | Scania K112CRB | Plaxton Paramount 3500 III | C48FT | 1988 | |
| 80 | FHE428 | Scania K113CRB | Plaxton Paramount 3500 III | C46FT | 1990 | Ex Shearings, 1993 |
| 81 | N281CAK | Scania K113CRB | Van Hool Alizée | C46FT | 1996 | |
| 82 | N282CAK | Scania K113CRB | Van Hool Alizée | C46FT | 1996 | |
| 95 | 4195HE | Auwaerter Neoplan N722/3 | Plaxton Paramount 4000 | CH53/18DT | 1986 | |
| 96 | 3141HE | Auwaerter Neoplan N722/3 | Plaxton Paramount 4000 | CH53/18DT | 1986 | Ex Yorkshire Voyager, 1991 |
| 98 | YTC858 | MCW Metroliner DR140/3 | MCW 400GT | CH53/20DT | 1988 | Ex West Midlands Travel, 1995 |
| 99 | HE8899 | MCW Metroliner DR140/3 | MCW 400GT | CH53/18DT | 1988 | |
| 108 | 1901HE | Leyland Leopard PSU5D/4R | Plaxton Supreme IV | DP32DL | 1981 | TL11 engine fitted |
| 109 | 1975HE | Leyland Leopard PSU5D/4R | Plaxton Supreme IV | DP32DL | 1981 | TL11 engine fitted |
| 201 | N201CKY | Spartan TXM2242 | East Lancashire Opus 2 | B53F | 1996 | |
| 202 | P202KKY | Spartan TXM2242 | East Lancashire Opus 2 | B53F | 1997 | |
| 203 | NIL5383 | Scania K112CRB | East Lancashire Flyte(1997) | B53F | 1987 | Ex Yorkshire Terrier, 1996 |
| 204 | D85ALX | Scania K112CRB | East Lancashire Flyte(1997) | B53F | 1987 | Ex Yorkshire Terrier, 1996 |

### 207-226

| | | | |
|---|---|---|---|
| | Leyland National 2 NL116L11/1R* | B52F | 1980 | *224 fitted with a Volvo engine |

| | | | | | | | | | |
|---|---|---|---|---|---|---|---|---|---|
| 207 | EDT207V | 215 | EDT215V | 219 | EDT219V | 222 | EDT222V | 225 | EDT225V |
| 209 | EDT209V | 217 | EDT217V | 220 | EDT220V | 223 | EDT223V | 226 | EDT226V |
| 213 | EDT213V | 218 | EDT218V | 221 | EDT221V | 224 | EDT224V | | |

The MCW MetroRider forms a large part of the Yorkshire Traction minibus fleet. This type is being heavily re-furbished at the groups Barnsley central works in order that they will remain in service for many years to come. Seen here is 328, F328FDT, one of twenty long wheelbase MetroRiders in the fleet with a seating capacity of 33. *Tony Wilson*

### 227-264

Leyland National 2 NL116AL11/1R*     B52F     1981-82     *252 fitted with DAF engine

| 227 | LWE227W | 235 | LWE235W | 243 | NKU243X | 251 | OHL251X | 258 | OHL258X |
|-----|---------|-----|---------|-----|---------|-----|---------|-----|---------|
| 228 | LWE228W | 236 | LWE236W | 244 | NKU244X | 252 | OHL252X | 259 | TWE259Y |
| 229 | LWE229W | 237 | LWE237W | 245 | NKU245X | 253 | OHL253X | 260 | TWE260Y |
| 230 | LWE230W | 238 | LWE238W | 246 | NKU246X | 254 | OHL254X | 261 | TWE261Y |
| 231 | LWE231W | 239 | MWE239W | 247 | NKU247X | 255 | OHL255X | 262 | TWE262Y |
| 232 | LWE232W | 240 | MWE240W | 248 | OHL248X | 256 | OHL256X | 263 | TWE263Y |
| 233 | LWE233W | 241 | MWE241W | 249 | OHL249X | 257 | OHL257X | 264 | TWE264Y |
| 234 | LWE234W | 242 | NKU242X | 250 | OHL250X |     |         |     |         |

### 265-269

Scania K93CRB     Wright Endurance     B53F     1993

| 265 | L265LHE | 266 | L266LHE | 267 | L267LHE | 268 | L268LHE | 269 | L269LHE |
|-----|---------|-----|---------|-----|---------|-----|---------|-----|---------|

### 270-274

Scania N113CRB     Alexander PS     B51F     1991

| 270 | H270THL | 271 | H271THL | 272 | H272THL | 273 | H273THL | 274 | H274THL |
|-----|---------|-----|---------|-----|---------|-----|---------|-----|---------|

### 275-279

Scania K93CRB     Wright Endurance     B53F     1992

| 275 | K275EWA | 276 | K276EWA | 277 | K277EWA | 278 | K278EWA | 279 | K279EWA |
|-----|---------|-----|---------|-----|---------|-----|---------|-----|---------|

### 281-288

Leyland Lynx LX112L10ZR1     Leyland Lynx     B49F     1987-88 Ex Shearings, 1991

| 281 | E21UNE | 283 | E23UNE | 285 | F41ENF | 287 | F43ENF | 288 | F44ENF |
|-----|--------|-----|--------|-----|--------|-----|--------|-----|--------|
| 282 | E22UNE | 284 | E24UNE | 286 | F42ENF |     |        |     |        |

### 290-294

Scania L113CRL     Northern Counties Paladin     B52F     1994

| 290 | M290TWB | 291 | M291TWB | 292 | M292TWB | 293 | M293TWB | 294 | M294TWB |
|-----|---------|-----|---------|-----|---------|-----|---------|-----|---------|

The Rawmarsh circular services from Rotherham run to a high frequency timetable and many vehicle types appear on the routes. Seen on service 109 is Yorkshire Traction 238, LWE238W, a Leyland National 2. This type is now being spread around the subsidiary companies with former Yorkshire Traction National 2s now being found in the Andrews-Sheffield Omnibus, Barnsley & District and RoadCar fleets. *Richard Godfrey*

### 295-299

| | | Scania L113CRL | | East Lancashire European | B53F | 1995 | | |
|---|---|---|---|---|---|---|---|---|
| 295 | M295TWB | 296 | M296TWB | 297 | M297TWB | 298 | M298TWB | 299 | M299TWB |

| 301 | F501EKY | Mercedes-Benz 811D | Optare StarRider | B33F | 1989 |
|---|---|---|---|---|---|

### 302-306

| | | Mercedes-Benz 811D | | Optare StarRider | B31F | 1989 | | |
|---|---|---|---|---|---|---|---|---|
| 302 | F302FWB | 303 | F303FWB | 304 | F304FWB | 305 | F305FWB | 306 | F306FWB |

| 307 | F479FUA | Mercedes-Benz 811D | Optare StarRider | B29F | 1989 | Ex Optare, 1989 |
|---|---|---|---|---|---|---|
| 308 | F369BUA | Mercedes-Benz 811D | Optare StarRider | B33F | 1987 | Ex Optare, 1989 |
| 309 | G123KUB | Mercedes-Benz 811D | Optare StarRider | B29F | 1990 | Ex Optare, 1990 |
| 310 | G841LWR | Mercedes-Benz 811D | Optare StarRider | DP33F | 1990 | Ex Optare, 1990 |
| 311 | H202TWE | Mercedes-Benz 811D | Reeve Burgess Beaver | B33F | 1990 | |
| 312 | H201TWE | Mercedes-Benz 811D | Reeve Burgess Beaver | B33F | 1990 | |
| 313 | H313TWE | Mercedes-Benz 811D | Europa Enterprise | B31F | 1990 | |
| 315 | H315TWE | Mercedes-Benz 811D | Carlyle | B31F | 1990 | |
| 316 | H319TWE | Mercedes-Benz 811D | Carlyle | B33F | 1991 | |
| 317 | H317TWE | Mercedes-Benz 811D | Carlyle | B31F | 1990 | |
| 318 | H98UWA | Mercedes-Benz 811D | Carlyle | B31F | 1991 | |
| 319 | F793DWT | Mercedes-Benz 811D | Optare StarRider | B33F | 1989 | Ex Barnsley & District, 1991 |
| 320 | J320AWB | Mercedes-Benz 811D | Autobus Classique | B31F | 1992 | |

### 321-330

| | | MCW MetroRider MF158 | | MCW | | B33F | 1989 | |
|---|---|---|---|---|---|---|---|---|
| 321 | F321FDT | 323 | F323FDT | 325 | F325FDT | 327 | F327FDT | 329 | F329FDT |
| 322 | F322FDT | 324 | F324FDT | 326 | F326FDT | 328 | F328FDT | 330 | F330FDT |

### 331-340

| | | MCW MetroRider MF154/17 | | MCW | | B33F | 1988 | Ex SUT, 1989 | |
|---|---|---|---|---|---|---|---|---|---|
| 331 | F701CWJ | 333 | F703CWJ | 335 | F705CWJ | 337 | F707CWJ | 339 | F709CWJ |
| 332 | F702CWJ | 334 | F704CWJ | 336 | F706CWJ | 338 | F708CWJ | 340 | F710CWJ |

The Dennis Dart is the standard Yorkshire Traction midibus, featuring a number of different body types. The first Dart in service with the company, 401, J401XHL, carries a Reeve Burgess Pointer body. The latest Darts to enter service are SLF types with East Lancashire Spryte bodywork. *Tony Wilson*

### 361-370

| | | | | | | | | Renault S75 | | Reeve Burgess Beaver | B31F | 1991 |

| 361 | H361TWJ | 363 | H363TWJ | 365 | H365TWJ | 367 | H367TWJ | 369 | H369TWJ |
|-----|---------|-----|---------|-----|---------|-----|---------|-----|---------|
| 362 | H362TWJ | 364 | H364TWJ | 366 | H366TWJ | 368 | H368TWJ | 370 | H370TWJ |

### 371-383

Renault S75  Reeve Burgess Beaver  B31F*  1990  Ex London Buses, 1994
*371 is DP29F

| 371 | G871WML | 374 | G874WML | 377 | G877WML | 380 | G880WML | 383 | H133AML |
|-----|---------|-----|---------|-----|---------|-----|---------|-----|---------|
| 372 | G872WML | 375 | G875WML | 378 | G878WML | 381 | H131AML | 384 | H130AML |
| 373 | G873WML | 376 | G876WML | 379 | G879WML | 382 | H132AML | | |

| 391 | J391AWB | Mercedes-Benz 811D | Autobus Classique | DP33F | 1992 |
|-----|---------|--------------------|-------------------|-------|------|
| 392 | J392AWB | Mercedes-Benz 811D | Autobus Classique | DP33F | 1992 |
| 393 | J393AWB | Mercedes-Benz 811D | Autobus Classique | DP33F | 1992 |

### 401-406

Dennis Dart 9.8SDL3012  Reeve Burgess Pointer  B41F  1991

| 401 | J401XHL | 403 | J403XHL | 404 | J404XHL | 405 | J405XHL | 406 | J406XHL |
|-----|---------|-----|---------|-----|---------|-----|---------|-----|---------|
| 402 | J402XHL | | | | | | | | |

*Opposite, top*: **East Lancashire bodywork has been favoured by Yorkshire Traction in recent times. The style demonstrated by 298, M298TWB is now being replaced by the Flyte. This Scania L113 is lettered for the Dearne Valley Link route 222 which serves Barnsley, Wombwell, Wath-upon-Dearne, Mexborough and Doncaster. It is seen leaving Barnsley for Doncaster.** *Tony Wilson*
*Opposite, bottom*: **Yorkshire Traction purchased seventy-three Eastern Coach Works-bodied Leyland Olympians when in the ownership of the National Bus Company. All remain in service, with 623, SHE623Y seen carrying the brighter red, white and blue livery applied to these vehicles under private ownership. Based at Huddersfield, 623 is seen in Neville Street, Leeds, while returning to its base on route 203.** *Tony Wilson*

As well as Olympians, the Yorkshire Traction double-deck fleet also features Volvo B10M and MCW Metrobus types. Seen in Eldon Street, Barnsley, 714, D714NKY, is a low-height example new to the company. The higher, former-West Midlands vehicles of this type are now migrating to Andrews-Sheffield Omnibus. *Tony Wilson*

### 407-415

| | | | | | | | | | | |
|---|---|---|---|---|---|---|---|---|---|---|
| | | Dennis Dart 9.8SDL3017 | | | Wright Handy-bus | | B41F | 1992 | | |
| 407 | K407EWA | 409 | K409EWA | 411 | K411EWA | 413 | K413EWA | 415 | K415EWA |
| 408 | K408EWA | 410 | K410EWA | 412 | K412EWA | 414 | K414EWA | | |

| | | | | | | | |
|---|---|---|---|---|---|---|---|
| 416 | J416CWF | Dennis Dart 9.8SDL3012 | Wright Handy-bus | B40F | 1992 | Ex Wright demonstrator, 1992 |

### 417-421

| | | | | | | | | | |
|---|---|---|---|---|---|---|---|---|---|
| | | Dennis Dart 9.8SDL3025 | | | Wright Handy-bus | | B41F | 1993 | |
| 417 | K417HWG | 418 | K418HWG | 419 | K419HWG | 420 | K420HWG | 421 | K421HWG |

### 422-426

| | | | | | | | | | |
|---|---|---|---|---|---|---|---|---|---|
| | | Dennis Dart 9.8SDL3035 | | | Wright Handy-bus | | B41F | 1993 | |
| 422 | L422LET | 423 | L423LET | 424 | L424LET | 425 | L425LET | 426 | L426LET |

| | | | | | | |
|---|---|---|---|---|---|---|
| 427 | L51ONW | Dennis Dart 9.8SDL3035 | Plaxton Pointer | B39F | 1994 | Ex South Yorkshire, 1994 |
| 428 | L52ONW | Dennis Dart 9.8SDL3035 | Plaxton Pointer | B39F | 1994 | Ex South Yorkshire, 1994 |
| 429 | L53ONW | Dennis Dart 9.8SDL3035 | Plaxton Pointer | B39F | 1994 | Ex South Yorkshire, 1994 |
| 430 | N430CHL | Dennis Dart 9.8SDL3054 | Northern Counties Paladin | B39F | 1995 | |
| 431 | N431CHL | Dennis Dart 9.8SDL3054 | Northern Counties Paladin | B39F | 1995 | |
| 432 | N432CHL | Dennis Dart 9.8SDL3054 | Northern Counties Paladin | B39F | 1995 | |
| 441 | P718WFR | Dennis Dart SLF | East Lancashire Spryte | B39F | 1997 | Ex East Lancashire Demonstrator, 1997 |
| 442 | R442THL | Dennis Dart SLF | East Lancashire Spryte | B39F | 1997 | |
| 492 | HE6762 | Leyland Tiger TS7 | Weymann (1950) | B34F | 1935 | |
| 533w | D533SKY | MCW MetroRider MF150/36 | MCW | B23F | 1987 | |

### 537-546

| | | | | | | | | | | |
|---|---|---|---|---|---|---|---|---|---|---|
| | | MCW MetroRider MF150/33 | | | MCW | | B23F | 1987 | | |
| 537w | E537VKY | 540 | E540VKY | 542 | E542VKY | 544 | E544VKY | 546 | E546VKY |
| 538w | E538VKY | 541 | E541VKY | 543 | E543VKY | 545 | E545VKY | | |

### 547-561

| | | | | | | | | | | |
|---|---|---|---|---|---|---|---|---|---|---|
| | | MCW MetroRider MF150/77 | | | MCW | | B23F | 1988 | | |
| 547 | E547XWG | 550 | E650XWG | 553w | E553YKW | 557 | E557YKW | 560 | E560AWF |
| 548w | E548XWG | 551 | E551XWG | 554 | E554YKW | 558 | E558AWF | 561 | E561AWF |
| 549 | E549XWG | 552 | E552YKW | 556 | E556YKW | 559w | E559AWF | | |

| 562-568 | | MCW MetroRider MF150/77* | MCW | | B23F | 1988 | Ex RoadCar, 1989 |
|---|---|---|---|---|---|---|---|

*564/5/8 are MF150/108

| 562w | E231DTV | 564 | F236HTO | 566 | E233DTV | 567 | E234DTV | 568 | F235HTO |
|---|---|---|---|---|---|---|---|---|---|
| 563 | E232DTV | 565 | F237HTO | | | | | | |

| 601-673 | | Leyland Olympian ONLXB/1R* | Eastern Coach Works | H45/32F* | 1981-85 | *671 is DPH43/29F |
|---|---|---|---|---|---|---|

*671/3 are ONLXCT/1R

| 601 | NKU601X | 616 | SHE616Y | 631 | A631WDT | 646 | A646OCX | 660 | B660CET |
|---|---|---|---|---|---|---|---|---|---|
| 602 | NKU602X | 617 | SHE617Y | 632 | A632WDT | 647 | A647OCX | 661 | B661CET |
| 603 | NKU603X | 618 | SHE618Y | 633 | A633WDT | 648 | A648OCX | 662 | B662CET |
| 604 | OWG604X | 619 | SHE619Y | 634 | A634WDT | 649 | A649OCX | 663 | B663CET |
| 605 | OWG605X | 620 | SHE620Y | 635 | A635WDT | 650 | A650OCX | 664 | B664CET |
| 606 | OWG606X | 621 | SHE621Y | 636 | A636WDT | 651 | A651OCX | 665 | B665CET |
| 607 | OWG607X | 622 | SHE622Y | 637 | A637WDT | 652 | A652OCX | 666 | B666EWE |
| 608 | OWG608X | 623 | SHE623Y | 638 | A638WDT | 653 | A653OCX | 667 | B667EWE |
| 609 | SHE609Y | 624 | SHE624Y | 639 | A639WDT | 654 | A654OCX | 668 | B668EWE |
| 610 | SHE610Y | 625 | SHE625Y | 640 | A640WDT | 655 | A655OCX | 669 | C669GET |
| 611 | SHE611Y | 626 | SHE626Y | 641 | A641WDT | 656 | A656OCX | 670 | C670GET |
| 612 | SHE612Y | 627 | UKY627Y | 642 | A642WDT | 657 | A657OCX | 671 | C671GET |
| 613 | SHE613Y | 628 | UKY628Y | 643 | A643WDT | 658 | A658OCX | 672 | C672GET |
| 614 | SHE614Y | 629 | UKY629Y | 644 | A644WDT | 659 | B659CET | 673 | C673GET |
| 615 | SHE615Y | 630 | A630WDT | 645 | A645OCX | | | | |

| 701 | D701NWG | MCW Metrobus DR102/57 | MCW | H46/33F | 1986 |
|---|---|---|---|---|---|
| 702 | D702NWG | MCW Metrobus DR102/57 | MCW | H46/33F | 1986 |
| 703 | D703NWG | MCW Metrobus DR102/57 | MCW | H46/33F | 1986 |
| 704 | D704NWG | MCW Metrobus DR102/57 | MCW | H46/33F | 1986 |
| 705 | D705NKY | MCW Metrobus DR102/56 | MCW | H46/33F | 1986 |
| 706 | D706NKY | MCW Metrobus DR102/56 | MCW | H46/33F | 1986 |

| 707-716 | | MCW Metrobus DR102/56 | MCW | H46/33F | 1986 |
|---|---|---|---|---|---|

| 707 | D707NKY | 709 | D709NKY | 711 | D711NKY | 713 | D713NKY | 715 | D715NKY |
|---|---|---|---|---|---|---|---|---|---|
| 708 | D708NKY | 710 | D710NKY | 712 | D712NKY | 714 | D714NKY | 716 | D716NKY |

| 723w | GOG160W | MCW Metrobus DR102/18 | MCW | H43/30F | 1980 | Ex West Midlands Travel, 1990 |
|---|---|---|---|---|---|---|
| 724 | BOK24V | MCW Metrobus DR102/12 | MCW | H43/30F | 1980 | Ex West Midlands Travel, 1990 |
| 901 | E734HFW | Volvo B10M-55 | East Lancashire | CH49/31F | 1988 | Ex Lincoln, 1993 |
| 902 | E735HFW | Volvo B10M-55 | East Lancashire | CH49/31F | 1988 | Ex Lincoln, 1993 |
| 903 | E736HFW | Volvo B10M-55 | East Lancashire | CH49/31F | 1988 | Ex Lincoln, 1993 |
| 904 | E737HFW | Volvo B10M-55 | East Lancashire | CH49/31F | 1988 | Ex Lincoln, 1993 |
| 1944 | KTL27V | Bristol VRT/SL3/6LXB | Eastern Coach Works | H43/31F | 1979 | On extended loan from Roadcar |
| 1952 | LVL807V | Bristol VRT/SL3/6LXB | Eastern Coach Works | H43/31F | 1980 | On extended loan from Roadcar |
| 1957 | PFE541V | Bristol VRT/SL3/6LXB | Eastern Coach Works | H43/31F | 1980 | On extended loan from Roadcar |

**Previous Registrations:**

| | | | |
|---|---|---|---|
| 1619HE | G78MWJ | E737HFW | KIB6708 |
| 1737HE | G115VMM,MSV922 | FHE428 | G890VNA |
| 1901HE | JHE98W | HE5362 | L53NWJ |
| 1975HE | JHE99W, UHE383 | HE6762 | From new |
| 2316HE | M656VWE | HE8054 | M655VWE |
| 2408HE | G77MWJ | HE8899 | E99AAK |
| 2542HE | J293YHE | HSV389 | E353EVH |
| 3030HE | K803FWE | J416CWF | LDZ6040 |
| 3141HE | C752CWX | NHE340 | E665UNE |
| 374YTC | J241BWE | NIL5383 | D92ALX |
| 4195HE | C95KET | 0HE50 | J964YWJ |
| 5562HE | K802FWE | PHE692 | F268RJX |
| 6078HE | K801FWE | RHE194 | L54NWJ |
| 6087HE | E215RDW | RHE353 | E213RDW |
| 6290HE | J19ARK | YHE91 | E69WWF |
| 6341HE | E214RDW | YTC49 | G125MNG, MSV927 |
| E734HFW | KIB6474 | YTC838 | M957VKY |
| E735HFW | KIB6527 | YTC856 | G76MWJ |
| E736HFW | KIB6620 | YTC858 | E906TOJ |

Livery: Red, white and blue; National Express 1-4, 53-60, 71/5-8, 80-2;

# YORKSHIRE TRAVEL

Yorkshire Travel Ltd, Unit 27, Savile Business Centre, Wharf Street,
Dewsbury, West Yorkshire, WF12 2AH

| 4 | N324HUA | Volvo B6-9.9M | Alexander Dash | B40F | 1995 | |
| 5 | N325HUA | Volvo B6-9.9M | Alexander Dash | B40F | 1995 | |
| 6 | N326HUA | Volvo B6-9.9M | Alexander Dash | B40F | 1995 | |
| 7 | N787EUB | Volvo B6-9.9M | Alexander Dash | B40F | 1995 | |
| 8 | N788EUB | Volvo B6-9.9M | Alexander Dash | B40F | 1995 | |
| 9 | N789EUB | Volvo B6-9.9M | Alexander Dash | B40F | 1995 | |
| 10 | N390EUG | Volvo B6-9.9M | Alexander Dash | B40F | 1996 | |
| 11 | N391EUG | Volvo B6-9.9M | Alexander Dash | B40F | 1996 | |
| 15 | ABA15T | Leyland National 11351A/1R | | DP42F | 1979 | Ex GMS Buses, 1996 |
| 17 | ABA17T | Leyland National 11351A/1R | | B49F | 1979 | Ex GMS Buses, 1996 |
| 30 | ABA30T | Leyland National 11351A/1R | | B49F | 1979 | Ex GMS Buses, 1996 |
| 110 | TUG810R | Leyland National 11351A/1R | | B49F | 1977 | Ex Mainline, 1995 |
| | F232EWG | Renault-Dodge S56 | Northern Counties | B25F | 1989 | Ex Mainline, 1996 |
| | F235EWG | Renault-Dodge S56 | Northern Counties | B25F | 1989 | Ex Mainline, 1996 |
| | F239EWG | Renault-Dodge S56 | Northern Counties | B25F | 1989 | Ex Mainline, 1996 |

Livery: White

Yorkshire Travel enters and leaves the local bus market at periodic intervals. Having previously tried to run bus services in Wakefield, the company is now running services in the Huddersfield area. Having started with new Volvo B6 midibuses, recent expansion has been resourced with Leyland Nationals and Renault-Dodge S56 minibuses. A former Mainline Northern Counties-bodied S56 is F235EWG. *Richard Godfrey*

# Vehicle Index

| Reg | Operator | Reg | Operator | Reg | Operator | Reg | Operator |
|---|---|---|---|---|---|---|---|
| 4WA | Wallace Arnold | 6087HE | Yorkshire Traction | A114XWE | Mainline | A428YAK | Mainline |
| 32CHY | EYMS Group | 6290HE | Yorkshire Traction | A115KUM | Yorkshire Rider | A429YAK | Mainline |
| 39EYD | EYMS Group | 6341HE | Yorkshire Traction | A115XWE | Mainline | A430YAK | Mainline |
| 46EYB | EYMS Group | 6627VF | EYMS Group | A116KUM | Yorkshire Rider | A431YAK | Mainline |
| 63XMD | Pontefract Motors | 7243WA | Wallace Arnold | A116XWE | Mainline | A432YAK | Mainline |
| 80EYC | EYMS Group | 8225KH | EYMS Group | A117KUM | Yorkshire Rider | A433YAK | Mainline |
| 91RTO | Powell Bus | 8332U | Wallace Arnold | A117XWE | Mainline | A434YAK | Mainline |
| 95EYM | EYMS Group | 8665WA | Wallace Arnold | A118KUM | Yorkshire Rider | A435YAK | Mainline |
| 104CLT | Halifax Joint | 8980WA | Wallace Arnold | A118XWE | Mainline | A436YAK | Mainline |
| 128NNU | Yorkshire Terrier | 8995WY | Yorkshire Rider | A119KUM | Yorkshire Rider | A437YAK | Mainline |
| 152FRH | EYMS Group | A1EYD | EYMS Group | A119XWE | Mainline | A438YAK | Mainline |
| 165DKH | EYMS Group | A10EYD | EYMS Group | A120KUM | Yorkshire Rider | A445YWG | Gordons |
| 202YTE | EYMS Group | A11NBT | North Bank Travel | A121KUM | Yorkshire Rider | A501WGF | Sykes |
| 213ONU | Black Prince | A14ESS | Stotts | A128EPA | Barnsley & Dist | A520EVN | EYMS Group |
| 222WFM | Northern Bus | A16KDT | Keighley & Dist | A137EPA | Barnsley & Dist | A530OKH | EYMS Group |
| 223FWW | Northern Bus | A17KDT | Keighley & Dist | A139FDC | Andrews | A531OKH | EYMS Group |
| 225KUO | Leisureways | A20MCW | Wray's | A159EPA | Yorkshire Terrier | A532OKH | EYMS Group |
| 240HYU | Powell Bus | A63FNU | Ross Travel | A189RUM | Keighley & Dist | A542KUM | Yorkshire Rider |
| 260ERY | Powell Bus | A82KUM | Yorkshire Rider | A239GHN | EYMS Group | A544KUM | Yorkshire Rider |
| 271CLT | EYMS Group | A83KUM | Yorkshire Rider | A295XAK | Mainline | A545KUM | Yorkshire Rider |
| 334EYL | EYMS Group | A84KUM | Yorkshire Rider | A296XAK | Mainline | A549KUM | Yorkshire Rider |
| 374YTC | Yorkshire Traction | A85KUM | Yorkshire Rider | A297XAK | Mainline | A560KWY | Yorkshire Bus |
| 421CKH | EYMS Group | A86KUM | Yorkshire Rider | A298XAK | Mainline | A562KWY | Yorkshire Bus |
| 491JVX | EYMS Group | A87KUM | Yorkshire Rider | A299XAK | Mainline | A564KWY | Yorkshire Bus |
| 508DKH | EYMS Group | A88KUM | Yorkshire Rider | A300XAK | Mainline | A565NWX | Yorkshire Bus |
| 515VTB | EYMS Group | A89KUM | Yorkshire Rider | A301XAK | Mainline | A566NWX | Yorkshire Bus |
| 544WRA | Yorkshire Bus | A90KUM | Yorkshire Rider | A302XAK | Mainline | A567NWX | Yorkshire Bus |
| 546EYB | EYMS Group | A91KUM | Yorkshire Rider | A303XAK | Mainline | A568NWX | Yorkshire Bus |
| 551ALW | Eddie Brown | A92KUM | Yorkshire Rider | A304XAK | Mainline | A569NWX | Yorkshire Bus |
| 552UTE | EYMS Group | A92KWW | Keighley & Dist | A311XAK | Mainline | A570NWX | Yorkshire Bus |
| 583TD | EYMS Group | A93KUM | Yorkshire Rider | A312XAK | Mainline | A571NWX | Yorkshire Bus |
| 627HFM | Northern Bus | A94KUM | Yorkshire Rider | A313XAK | Mainline | A572NWX | Yorkshire Bus |
| 644LFM | Northern Bus | A95KUM | Yorkshire Rider | A314XAK | Mainline | A573NWX | Yorkshire Bus |
| 665EYL | EYMS Group | A95KWW | Keighley & Dist | A315XAK | Mainline | A573SRH | EYMS Group |
| 741DYE | EYMS Group | A96KUM | Yorkshire Rider | A316XAK | Mainline | A574HNE | Proctors |
| 774FUO | Abbotts | A96KWW | Keighley & Dist | A317XAK | Mainline | A574NWX | Yorkshire Bus |
| 7820WA | Wallace Arnold | A97KUM | Yorkshire Rider | A318XAK | Mainline | A575NWX | Yorkshire Bus |
| 782EFM | Northern Bus | A98KUM | Yorkshire Rider | A319XAK | Mainline | A576NWX | Yorkshire Bus |
| 787EYC | EYMS Group | A99KUM | Yorkshire Rider | A320XAK | Mainline | A577NWX | Yorkshire Bus |
| 794EYD | EYMS Group | A100KUM | Yorkshire Rider | A337HNX | Stotts | A578NWX | Yorkshire Bus |
| 813VPU | EYMS Group | A101KUM | Yorkshire Rider | A401YAK | Mainline | A579NWX | Yorkshire Bus |
| 834EYD | EYMS Group | A101SUU | Black Prince | A402YAK | Mainline | A580NWX | Yorkshire Bus |
| 865EYT | EYMS Group | A102KUM | Yorkshire Rider | A403YAK | Mainline | A581NWX | Yorkshire Bus |
| 902DCV | John Smith | A102SUU | Black Prince | A404YAK | Mainline | A582NWX | Yorkshire Bus |
| 926BWV | EYMS Group | A103KUM | Yorkshire Rider | A405YAK | Mainline | A583NWX | Yorkshire Bus |
| 929CVJ | Northern Bus | A103SUU | Black Prince | A406YAK | Mainline | A584NWX | Yorkshire Bus |
| 1619HE | Yorkshire Traction | A104KUM | Yorkshire Rider | A407YAK | Mainline | A585NWX | Yorkshire Bus |
| 1737HE | Yorkshire Traction | A105KUM | Yorkshire Rider | A408YAK | Mainline | A586NWX | Yorkshire Bus |
| 1901HE | Yorkshire Traction | A106KUM | Yorkshire Rider | A409YAK | Mainline | A587NWX | Yorkshire Bus |
| 1918KH | Fairway Rhodes | A106XWE | Mainline | A410YAK | Mainline | A588NWX | Yorkshire Bus |
| 1975HE | Yorkshire Traction | A107KUM | Yorkshire Rider | A411YAK | Mainline | A589NWX | Yorkshire Bus |
| 2408HE | Yorkshire Traction | A107XWE | Mainline | A412YAK | Mainline | A590NWX | Yorkshire Bus |
| 2542HE | Yorkshire Traction | A108KUM | Yorkshire Rider | A413YAK | Mainline | A599NYG | Yorkshire Rider |
| 2719DT | York Pullman | A108XWE | Mainline | A414YAK | Mainline | A600NYG | Yorkshire Rider |
| 3030HE | Yorkshire Traction | A109KUM | Yorkshire Rider | A415YAK | Mainline | A601NYG | Yorkshire Rider |
| 3141HE | Yorkshire Traction | A109XWE | Mainline | A416YAK | Mainline | A602NYG | Keighley & Dist |
| 3156WE | Mainline | A110KUM | Yorkshire Rider | A417YAK | Mainline | A603NYG | Keighley & Dist |
| 3277KH | EYMS Group | A110XWE | Mainline | A418YAK | Mainline | A604NYG | Keighley & Dist |
| 3333WA | Wallace Arnold | A111KUM | Yorkshire Rider | A419YAK | Mainline | A605NYG | Keighley & Dist |
| 3904WE | Mainline | A111XWE | Mainline | A421YAK | Mainline | A630WDT | Yorkshire Traction |
| 4030WA | Wallace Arnold | A112KUM | Yorkshire Rider | A423YAK | Mainline | A631WDT | Yorkshire Traction |
| 4195HE | Yorkshire Traction | A112XWE | Mainline | A424YAK | Mainline | A632WDT | Yorkshire Traction |
| 4395EL | Leon | A113KUM | Yorkshire Rider | A425YAK | Mainline | A633WDT | Yorkshire Traction |
| 5562HE | Yorkshire Traction | A113XWE | Mainline | A426YAK | Mainline | A634WDT | Yorkshire Traction |
| 6078HE | Yorkshire Traction | A114KUM | Yorkshire Rider | A427YAK | Mainline | A635WDT | Yorkshire Traction |

**Pictured while passing through Pontefract is Ross Travel's F33CWY, a Mercedes-Benz 811D with Optare StarRider bodwork. Optare were unusual in replacing the normal Mercedes-Benz cowl with one of their own but in so doing prompted design advantages for their own changes to the MetroRider model originally built by MCW.** *Tony Wilson*

| | | | | | | | |
|---|---|---|---|---|---|---|---|
| A636WDT | Yorkshire Traction | A750LWY | Yorkshire Rider | ANA25T | Yorkshire Rider | AYJ90T | Barnsley & Dist |
| A637WDT | Yorkshire Traction | A751LWY | Yorkshire Rider | ANA31T | Yorkshire Rider | B9TJW | T J Walsh |
| A638WDT | Yorkshire Traction | A752LWY | Yorkshire Rider | ANA34T | Yorkshire Rider | B10TJW | T J Walsh |
| A639WDT | Yorkshire Traction | A754LWY | Yorkshire Rider | ANA40T | Yorkshire Rider | B11TJW | T J Walsh |
| A640WDT | Yorkshire Traction | A756LWY | Yorkshire Rider | ANA43T | Jolly Roger | B12TJW | T J Walsh |
| A641WDT | Yorkshire Traction | A758LWY | Yorkshire Rider | ANA44T | Yorkshire Rider | B14TJW | T J Walsh |
| A642WDT | Yorkshire Traction | A760LWY | Yorkshire Rider | ANA45T | Yorkshire Rider | B15TJW | T J Walsh |
| A643WDT | Yorkshire Traction | A805RNW | Powell Bus | ANA48T | Yorkshire Rider | B17TJW | T J Walsh |
| A644WDT | Yorkshire Traction | A875THS | York Pullman | ANA49T | Leon | B20TJW | T J Walsh |
| A645OCX | Yorkshire Traction | A922LTM | York Pullman | ANA209T | Yorkshire Rider | B40UAG | York Pullman |
| A646OCX | Yorkshire Traction | AAK111T | Northern Bus | ANA234T | Jolly Roger | B90SWX | Keighley & Dist |
| A647OCX | Yorkshire Traction | AAL587A | Stephensons | ANC918T | EYMS Group | B91SWX | Keighley & Dist |
| A648OCX | Yorkshire Traction | AAL622A | Stephensons | ANH660Y | Abbotts | B92SWX | Keighley & Dist |
| A649OCX | Yorkshire Traction | ABA15T | Yorkshire Travel | ANJ311T | North Bank Travel | B109LPH | Northern Bus |
| A650OCX | Yorkshire Traction | ABA17T | Yorkshire Travel | ANJ316T | North Bank Travel | B122RWY | Yorkshire Rider |
| A651OCX | Yorkshire Traction | ABA30T | Yorkshire Travel | AOL16T | K-Line | B123RWY | Yorkshire Rider |
| A652OCX | Yorkshire Traction | ABR868S | Yorkshire Rider | APT124W | Yorkshire Terrier | B124RWY | Yorkshire Rider |
| A653OCX | Yorkshire Traction | ABR869S | Yorkshire Rider | APT125W | Yorkshire Terrier | B125RWY | Yorkshire Rider |
| A654OCX | Yorkshire Traction | ACA188S | Abbotts | ARB131T | Fairway Rhodes | B126RWY | Yorkshire Rider |
| A655OCX | Yorkshire Traction | ACC629 | Bibby's | ARB132T | Cygnet | B127RWY | Yorkshire Rider |
| A656OCX | Yorkshire Traction | ACM704X | Black Prince | ARB133T | Abbotts | B128RWY | Yorkshire Rider |
| A657OCX | Yorkshire Traction | ACM712X | Black Prince | ASA24T | Leon | B129RWY | Yorkshire Rider |
| A658OCX | Yorkshire Traction | ACW920R | Clarksons | ASA26T | Leon | B130RWY | Yorkshire Rider |
| A659KUM | Yorkshire Rider | AET183T | Northern Bus | ASD826T | Huddersfield | B131RWY | Yorkshire Rider |
| A661KUM | Yorkshire Rider | AFM105B | Northern Bus | ASD834T | Huddersfield | B132RWY | Yorkshire Rider |
| A662KUM | Yorkshire Rider | AFM113G | Northern Bus | ASD837T | Huddersfield | B133RWY | Yorkshire Rider |
| A669KUM | Yorkshire Rider | AHH202T | K-Line | AUD462R | Northern Bus | B134RWY | Yorkshire Rider |
| A671KUM | Yorkshire Rider | AHH203T | K-Line | AUP716S | EYMS Group | B135RWY | Yorkshire Rider |
| A672KUM | Yorkshire Rider | AHH205T | K-Line | AVK179V | York Pullman | B136RWY | Yorkshire Rider |
| A683MWX | Keighley & Dist | AHN397T | Northern Bus | AVS903T | Northern Bus | B137RWY | Yorkshire Rider |
| A684MWX | Keighley & Dist | AKY611T | North Bank Travel | AWE53T | York Pullman | B138RWY | Yorkshire Rider |
| A685MWX | Keighley & Dist | ALM60B | Black Prince | AWK516Y | Abbotts | B139RWY | Yorkshire Rider |
| A686MWX | Yorkshire Rider | ALM65B | EYMS Group | AWT702S | Yorkshire Terrier | B140RWY | Yorkshire Rider |
| A739PUS | Ross Travel | ALZ3260 | Thompson Travel | AYG851S | Northern Bus | B141RWY | Yorkshire Rider |

In 1995, Volvo introduced the low floor version of the B6, the B6BLE and chose the Wright Crusader body for one of its demonstrators. M918MRW has since joined the Mainline fleet as number 400 with an order for a further fifteen of the type being placed in 1996. It is seen working the Tesco park and ride service 505. *Richard Godfrey*

| | | | | | | | |
|---|---|---|---|---|---|---|---|
| B142RWY | Yorkshire Rider | B447CKW | Mainline | B592SWX | Yorkshire Bus | B922CDT | Mainline |
| B143RWY | Yorkshire Rider | B448CKW | Mainline | B592XWW | Stotts | B923CDT | Mainline |
| B145RWY | Yorkshire Rider | B449CKW | Mainline | B593SWX | Yorkshire Bus | B924CDT | Mainline |
| B161AKH | Northern Bus | B461WTC | Pontefract Motors | B594SWX | Yorkshire Bus | B926CDT | Mainline |
| B162AKH | Northern Bus | B501RWY | Yorkshire Rider | B595SWX | Yorkshire Bus | B927CDT | Mainline |
| B165XVU | Eddie Brown | B502RWY | Yorkshire Rider | B596SWX | Yorkshire Bus | B928CDT | Mainline |
| B249NVN | EYMS Group | B503RWY | Yorkshire Rider | B597SWX | Yorkshire Bus | B929CDT | Mainline |
| B250NVN | EYMS Group | B504RWY | Yorkshire Rider | B599SWX | Yorkshire Bus | B930CDT | Mainline |
| B254RAJ | EYMS Group | B505RWY | Yorkshire Rider | B601UUM | Yorkshire Bus | B931CDT | Mainline |
| B256ADM | Proctors | B506RWY | Yorkshire Rider | B602UUM | Yorkshire Bus | B932CDT | Mainline |
| B261LPH | Keighley & Dist | B514UWW | Harrogate & Dist | B603UUM | Yorkshire Bus | B933CDT | Mainline |
| B264LPH | Keighley & Dist | B515UWW | Keighley & Dist | B603UUM | Yorkshire Bus | B933NSX | Stotts |
| B265AMG | B-Line | B516UWW | Harrogate & Dist | B604UUM | Yorkshire Bus | B934CDT | Mainline |
| B265LPH | Keighley & Dist | B517UWW | Keighley & Dist | B605UUM | Yorkshire Bus | B935CDT | Mainline |
| B351CDT | Mainline | B518UWW | Yorkshire Rider | B606UUM | Yorkshire Bus | B936CDT | Mainline |
| B352CDT | Mainline | B519UWW | Yorkshire Rider | B607UUM | Yorkshire Bus | B937CDT | Mainline |
| B353CDT | Mainline | B520UWW | Yorkshire Rider | B608UUM | Yorkshire Bus | B938CDT | Mainline |
| B354CDT | Mainline | B521UWW | Keighley & Dist | B609UUM | Yorkshire Bus | B939CDT | Mainline |
| B355CDT | Mainline | B522UWW | Keighley & Dist | B610VWU | Yorkshire Rider | B940CDT | Mainline |
| B356CDT | Mainline | B523UWW | Yorkshire Rider | B659CET | Yorkshire Traction | B941FET | Mainline |
| B357CDT | Mainline | B524UWW | Keighley & Dist | B660CET | Yorkshire Traction | B942FET | Mainline |
| B358CDT | Mainline | B533WAT | EYMS Group | B661CET | Yorkshire Traction | B943FET | Mainline |
| B359CDT | Mainline | B534WAT | EYMS Group | B662CET | Yorkshire Traction | B944FET | Mainline |
| B360CDT | Mainline | B535WAT | EYMS Group | B663CET | Yorkshire Traction | B945FET | Mainline |
| B361CDT | Mainline | B561RWY | Yorkshire Rider | B664CET | Yorkshire Traction | B946FET | Mainline |
| B362CDT | Mainline | B563RWY | Yorkshire Rider | B665CET | Yorkshire Traction | BAZ7053 | Sykes |
| B363CDT | Mainline | B566RWY | Yorkshire Rider | B666EWE | Yorkshire Traction | BBT380V | Thornes |
| B375KUT | John Smith | B567RWY | Yorkshire Rider | B667EWE | Yorkshire Traction | BCB610V | Yorkshire Rider |
| B379PAJ | Jolly Roger | B570RWY | Yorkshire Rider | B668EWE | Yorkshire Traction | BCB611V | Yorkshire Rider |
| B439CKW | Mainline | B575RWY | Yorkshire Rider | B782FOG | Northern Bus | BCB612V | Yorkshire Rider |
| B441CKW | Mainline | B577RWY | Yorkshire Rider | B872FWA | Ingleby's | BCD806L | Yorkshire Terrier |
| B442CKW | Mainline | B578RWY | Yorkshire Rider | B889AJX | Bigfoot | BCP671 | Halifax Joint |
| B445CKW | Mainline | B580RWY | Yorkshire Rider | B910UPW | Gordons | BDC881T | Abbotts |
| B446CKW | Mainline | B591SWX | Yorkshire Bus | B921CDT | Mainline | BGY606T | Leon |

| Reg | Operator | Reg | Operator | Reg | Operator | Reg | Operator |
|---|---|---|---|---|---|---|---|
| BHN694N | Northern Bus | C148KBT | Yorkshire Rider | C888JWE | Mainline | CUB34Y | Yorkshire Rider |
| BIB728 | Bibby's | C149KBT | Yorkshire Rider | C889JWE | Mainline | CUB35Y | Yorkshire Rider |
| BIB3994 | Bibby's | C150KBT | Yorkshire Rider | C890JWE | Mainline | CUB36Y | Yorkshire Rider |
| BIB4843 | Bibby's | C171AWK | Leon | C920FMP | Yorkshire Bus | CUB37Y | Yorkshire Rider |
| BIB4884 | Bibby's | C318OFL | T J Walsh | C930VLB | Thornes | CUB38Y | Yorkshire Rider |
| BIB5428 | Bibby's | C343VVN | Stotts | C931VLB | Thornes | CUB39Y | Yorkshire Rider |
| BIB5491 | Bibby's | C352DND | Ingleby's | C932VLB | Thornes | CUB40Y | Yorkshire Rider |
| BIB5740 | Bibby's | C356PUJ | Proctors | C933VLB | Thornes | CUB41Y | Yorkshire Rider |
| BIB7667 | Bibby's | C405VVN | Cygnet | C935VLB | Thornes | CUB42Y | Yorkshire Rider |
| BIB7670 | Bibby's | C406VVN | EYMS Group | C936VLB | Thornes | CUB43Y | Yorkshire Rider |
| BIB9842 | Bibby's | C407VVN | EYMS Group | C938VLB | Thornes | CUB44Y | Yorkshire Rider |
| BKJ150T | Proctors | C408VVN | EYMS Group | C947HWF | Mainline | CUB45Y | Yorkshire Rider |
| BNO666T | Powell Bus | C409VVN | EYMS Group | C948HWF | Mainline | CUB46Y | Yorkshire Rider |
| BOK24V | Yorkshire Traction | C410VVN | EYMS Group | C949HWF | Mainline | CUB47Y | Yorkshire Rider |
| BPF134Y | Keighley & Dist | C411VVN | EYMS Group | C950HWF | Mainline | CUB48Y | Yorkshire Rider |
| BPJ77H | Ross Travel | C412VVN | EYMS Group | C951LWJ | Mainline | CUB51Y | Yorkshire Rider |
| BPL488T | Glenn Coaches | C413VVN | EYMS Group | C952LWJ | Mainline | CUB52Y | Yorkshire Rider |
| BPL496T | Glenn Coaches | C414VVN | EYMS Group | C953LWJ | Mainline | CUB53Y | Yorkshire Rider |
| BPT918S | EYMS Group | C415VVN | EYMS Group | C954LWJ | Mainline | CUB54Y | Yorkshire Rider |
| BPT921S | EYMS Group | C416VVN | EYMS Group | C955LWJ | Mainline | CUB55Y | Yorkshire Rider |
| BPT925S | EYMS Group | C417VVN | EYMS Group | C956LWJ | Mainline | CUB65Y | Yorkshire Rider |
| BRC135T | Abbotts | C418VVN | EYMS Group | C957LWJ | Mainline | CUB521Y | Yorkshire Rider |
| BRC136T | Abbotts | C419VVN | EYMS Group | C958LWJ | Mainline | CUB522Y | Yorkshire Rider |
| BRC137T | Fairway Rhodes | C420VVN | Cygnet | C959LWJ | Mainline | CUB523Y | Yorkshire Rider |
| BRC139T | Abbotts | C428VVN | Stotts | C960LWJ | Mainline | CUB525Y | Yorkshire Rider |
| BRF692T | EYMS Group | C430SJU | T J Walsh | CAJ168Y | Abbotts | CUB527Y | Yorkshire Rider |
| BSD860T | Huddersfield | C479YWY | Keighley & Dist | CAZ5104 | York Pullman | CUB529Y | Yorkshire Rider |
| BSD862T | Huddersfield | C480YWY | Keighley & Dist | CBV12S | Stotts | CUB530Y | Yorkshire Rider |
| BSD863T | Huddersfield | C481YWY | Harrogate & Dist | CBV307S | Thornes | CUB531Y | Yorkshire Rider |
| BSD864T | Huddersfield | C482YWY | Keighley & Dist | CBV308S | Thornes | CUB532Y | Yorkshire Rider |
| BSJ892T | Pontefract Motors | C483YWY | Yorkshire Rider | CBV309S | Thornes | CUB534Y | Yorkshire Rider |
| BTU370S | Northern Bus | C484YWY | Keighley & Dist | CBV770S | Yorkshire Terrier | CUB535Y | Yorkshire Rider |
| BUA751X | Proctors | C484YWY | Yorkshire Rider | CBV771S | Yorkshire Terrier | CUB536Y | Yorkshire Rider |
| BUF267C | Wallace Arnold | C486HAK | Ingleby's | CBV777S | Yorkshire Terrier | CUB537Y | Yorkshire Rider |
| BUF425C | Wallace Arnold | C507KBT | Yorkshire Rider | CBV778S | Yorkshire Terrier | CUV122C | Black Prince |
| BUR443T | EYMS Group | C508KBT | Yorkshire Rider | CBV788S | Yorkshire Terrier | CUV210C | EYMS Group |
| BVN371Y | Abbotts | C509KBT | Yorkshire Rider | CBV789S | Yorkshire Terrier | CWG761V | Reliance |
| BVP766V | Black Prince | C510KBT | Yorkshire Rider | CDN650V | John Smith | CWG770V | Reliance |
| BVR52T | Yorkshire Rider | C536DAT | EYMS Group | CFM345S | Northern Bus | CWR508Y | Yorkshire Bus |
| BVR53T | Yorkshire Rider | C537DAT | EYMS Group | CFM347S | Northern Bus | CWR510Y | Yorkshire Bus |
| BVR55T | Yorkshire Rider | C610ANW | Yorkshire Bus | CFM349S | Northern Bus | CWR511Y | Yorkshire Bus |
| BVR61T | Jolly Roger | C611ANW | Yorkshire Bus | CFM355S | Northern Bus | CWR512Y | Yorkshire Bus |
| BVR65T | Yorkshire Rider | C612ANW | Yorkshire Bus | CFM357S | Bigfoot | CWR513Y | Yorkshire Bus |
| BVR67T | Yorkshire Rider | C630PAU | Reliance | CGF313S | Wilfreda-Beehive | CWR514Y | Yorkshire Bus |
| BVR69T | Yorkshire Rider | C669GET | Yorkshire Traction | CGR894S | K-Line | CWR515Y | Yorkshire Bus |
| BVR70T | Yorkshire Rider | C670GET | Yorkshire Traction | CHH213T | Northern Bus | CWR516Y | Yorkshire Bus |
| BVR71T | Yorkshire Rider | C671GET | Yorkshire Traction | CIB3202 | EYMS Group | CWR517Y | Yorkshire Bus |
| BVR85T | Yorkshire Rider | C672GET | Yorkshire Traction | COF707V | Thompson Travel | CWR518Y | Yorkshire Bus |
| BVR92T | Yorkshire Rider | C673GET | Yorkshire Traction | CPT636S | Andrews | CWR519Y | Yorkshire Bus |
| BVR97T | Yorkshire Rider | C710FKE | Stephensons | CPT729S | EYMS Group | CWR520Y | Yorkshire Bus |
| C28CAJ | Proctors | C808FMC | Aston Express | CPT732S | EYMS Group | CWR521Y | Yorkshire Bus |
| C64JTU | Northern Bus | C808KBT | Ross Travel | CPT733S | EYMS Group | CWR522Y | Yorkshire Bus |
| C76XWK | Reliance | C809KBT | Leon | CPT822S | EYMS Group | CWR523Y | Yorkshire Bus |
| C82AUB | T J Walsh | C871JWE | Mainline | CPU979G | Northern Bus | CWR524Y | Yorkshire Bus |
| C101CUL | Black Prince | C872JWE | Mainline | CSU936 | Wallace Arnold | CWR527Y | Yorkshire Bus |
| C101HDT | Mainline | C873JWE | Mainline | CSU937 | Wallace Arnold | CWR528Y | Yorkshire Bus |
| C102HDT | Mainline | C874JWE | Mainline | CSU938 | Wallace Arnold | CWU136T | Yorkshire Rider |
| C103HDT | Mainline | C875JWE | Mainline | CUB21Y | Yorkshire Rider | CWU137T | Yorkshire Rider |
| C104HDT | Mainline | C876JWE | Mainline | CUB22Y | Yorkshire Rider | CWU144T | Yorkshire Rider |
| C105HDT | Mainline | C877JWE | Mainline | CUB23Y | Yorkshire Rider | CWU148T | Yorkshire Rider |
| C106HDT | Mainline | C878JWE | Mainline | CUB24Y | Yorkshire Rider | CWU149T | Yorkshire Rider |
| C107HDT | Mainline | C879JWE | Mainline | CUB25Y | Yorkshire Rider | CWU152T | Yorkshire Rider |
| C108HDT | Mainline | C880JWE | Mainline | CUB26Y | Yorkshire Rider | CWU153T | Yorkshire Rider |
| C109HDT | Mainline | C881JWE | Mainline | CUB27Y | Yorkshire Rider | CWU155T | Yorkshire Rider |
| C110HDT | Mainline | C882JWE | Mainline | CUB28Y | Yorkshire Rider | CWU156T | Yorkshire Rider |
| C111HDT | Mainline | C883JWE | Mainline | CUB29Y | Yorkshire Rider | CWX671 | Keighley & Dist |
| C112HDT | Mainline | C884JWE | Mainline | CUB30Y | Yorkshire Rider | CYC658A | EYMS Group |
| C113HDT | Mainline | C885JWE | Mainline | CUB31Y | Yorkshire Rider | D38GAJ | Abbotts |
| C146KBT | Yorkshire Rider | C886JWE | Mainline | CUB32Y | Yorkshire Rider | D39GAJ | Abbotts |
| C147KBT | Yorkshire Rider | C887JWE | Mainline | CUB33Y | Yorkshire Rider | D40GAJ | Abbotts |

| Reg | Operator | Reg | Operator | Reg | Operator | Reg | Operator |
|---|---|---|---|---|---|---|---|
| D41GAJ | Abbotts | D716NKY | Yorkshire Traction | E150LAJ | Proctors | E479UOF | Longstaff |
| D88ALX | Yorkshire Terrier | D734PWF | Leon | E170OMD | Gordons | E497HHN | Cygnet |
| D92ALX | Yorkshire Traction | D736PWF | Leon | E192XWG | Mainline | E507YSU | Ross Travel |
| D93ALX | Yorkshire Terrier | D766MUR | Pontefract Motors | E193XWG | Mainline | E515CDS | Ingleby's |
| D102UJC | Jolly Roger | D796KWR | Yorkshire Rider | E194XWG | Mainline | E532LAJ | Abbotts |
| D140RAK | B-Line | D829NRH | John Smith | E195XWG | Powell Bus | E537VKY | Yorkshire Traction |
| D204FBK | Yorkshire Bus | D869LWR | Yorkshire Rider | E196XWG | Mainline | E538VKY | Yorkshire Traction |
| D230TBW | Jolly Roger | D894EVN | Proctors | E197XWG | Mainline | E540VKY | Yorkshire Traction |
| D300OKM | Stotts | D902NUS | Abbotts | E198XWG | Mainline | E541VKY | Yorkshire Traction |
| D319NEC | Leon | D905FHN | Abbotts | E199XWG | Mainline | E542VKY | Yorkshire Traction |
| D320NEC | Leon | D905RVM | EYMS Group | E201XWG | Mainline | E543VKY | Yorkshire Traction |
| D426STT | Wallace Arnold | D912PRJ | B-Line | E202XWG | Mainline | E544VKY | Yorkshire Traction |
| D43OKH | EYMS Group | D933XMV | John Smith | E203XWG | Mainline | E545VKY | Yorkshire Traction |
| D44OKH | B-Line | DAR125T | Powell Bus | E204XWG | Mainline | E546VKY | Yorkshire Traction |
| D453KWR | Jolly Roger | DAR128T | Powell Bus | E205TUB | Yorkshire Bus | E547XWG | Yorkshire Traction |
| D459TWE | Sykes | DBZ918 | Yorkshire Terrier | E205XWG | Mainline | E548XWG | Yorkshire Traction |
| D460CKV | Cygnet | DCA531X | Northern Bus | E206XWG | Mainline | E549XWG | Yorkshire Traction |
| D471OWE | Mainline | DDZ236 | EYMS Group | E209XWG | Mainline | E551XWG | Yorkshire Traction |
| D472OWE | Mainline | DET471V | Barnsley & Dist | E210XWG | Mainline | E552YKW | Yorkshire Traction |
| D473OWE | Mainline | DET473V | Barnsley & Dist | E211XWG | Mainline | E553YKW | Yorkshire Traction |
| D474OWE | Mainline | DET474V | Andrews | E216XWG | Mainline | E554YKW | Yorkshire Traction |
| D475OWE | Mainline | DET475V | Andrews | E217XWG | Mainline | E556YKW | Yorkshire Traction |
| D476OWE | Mainline | DMS18V | Andrews | E218XWG | Mainline | E557AWF | Yorkshire Traction |
| D477OWE | Mainline | DMS23V | Andrews | E219XWG | Mainline | E558AWF | Yorkshire Traction |
| D478OWE | Mainline | DMS25V | Andrews | E231DTV | Yorkshire Traction | E558XRH | B-Line |
| D479OWE | Mainline | DNE74Y | John Smith | E232DTV | Yorkshire Traction | E559AWF | Yorkshire Traction |
| D480OWE | Mainline | DNW840T | Keighley & Dist | E233DTV | Yorkshire Traction | E560AWF | Yorkshire Traction |
| D481OWE | Mainline | DNW841T | Keighley & Dist | E234DTV | Yorkshire Traction | E561AWF | Yorkshire Traction |
| D482OWE | Mainline | DOC28V | K-Line | E254TUB | Yorkshire Bus | E603JEF | Proctors |
| D483OWE | Mainline | DOC29V | K-Line | E255TUB | Yorkshire Bus | E604JEF | Proctors |
| D484OWE | Mainline | DOC34V | North Bank Travel | E256TUB | Yorkshire Bus | E607JEF | Proctors |
| D485OWE | Mainline | DOC41V | K-Line | E257TUB | Yorkshire Bus | E639DPD | Proctors |
| D486OWE | Mainline | DOC44V | North Bank Travel | E258TUB | Yorkshire Bus | E643KYW | Aston Express |
| D487OWE | Mainline | DOC52V | K-Line | E259TUB | Yorkshire Bus | E650XWG | Yorkshire Traction |
| D488OWE | Mainline | DPH499T | Glenn Coaches | E260TUB | Yorkshire Bus | E703UEM | Barnsley & Dist |
| D489OWE | Mainline | DRB307H | EYMS Group | E261TUB | Yorkshire Bus | E704UEM | Barnsley & Dist |
| D490OWE | Mainline | DRH319L | York Pullman | E262TUB | Yorkshire Bus | E734HFW | Yorkshire Traction |
| D506GEN | Ross Travel | DRH321L | York Pullman | E263TUB | Yorkshire Bus | E735HFW | Yorkshire Traction |
| D512HUB | Yorkshire Rider | DSU708 | John Smith | E264TUB | Yorkshire Bus | E736HFW | Yorkshire Traction |
| D512HUB | Yorkshire Rider | DSV698 | Frodingham | E265WUB | Yorkshire Bus | E737HFW | Yorkshire Traction |
| D512HUB | Yorkshire Rider | DTL544T | Jaronda Travel | E266WUB | Yorkshire Bus | E770HJF | Gordons |
| D515HUB | Yorkshire Rider | DUP741S | EYMS Group | E267WUB | Yorkshire Bus | E778TPW | Fairway Rhodes |
| D516HUB | Yorkshire Rider | DUP748S | EYMS Group | E268NAJ | Abbotts | E840HAP | Aston Express |
| D522SKY | Barnsley & Dist | DUP750S | EYMS Group | E268WUB | Yorkshire Bus | E874NJD | Aston Express |
| D524SKY | Barnsley & Dist | DUP754S | EYMS Group | E269WUB | Yorkshire Bus | E905NVN | Abbotts |
| D525SKY | Barnsley & Dist | DV7890 | EYMS Group | E270WUB | Yorkshire Bus | E906NVN | Abbotts |
| D526SKY | Barnsley & Dist | DWF192V | Northern Bus | E271WUB | Yorkshire Bus | E913NEW | Powell Bus |
| D528HNW | T J Walsh | DWH684W | Andrews | E283TWW | Yorkshire Coastliner | E919HHG | Stotts |
| D528SKY | Barnsley & Dist | DWU296T | Yorkshire Rider | E286OMG | Barnsley & Dist | E961NMK | Harrogate & Dist |
| D533SKY | Yorkshire Traction | DWW926Y | Keighley & Dist | E316UUB | Gordons | E97LWP | Abbotts |
| D562RKW | York Pullman | DWW927Y | Keighley & Dist | E324SWY | Harrogate & Dist | E996NMK | Gordons |
| D564FAE | Yorkshire Rider | DWW928Y | Keighley & Dist | E325SWY | Harrogate & Dist | EAZ8409 | York Pullman |
| D567MVR | Frodingham | DWW929Y | Keighley & Dist | E401BCT | Mainline | EBW105Y | Northern Bus |
| D586MVR | Proctors | DWW930Y | Keighley & Dist | E402BCT | Mainline | EBW110Y | Northern Bus |
| D677SEM | Andrews | DWW931Y | Keighley & Dist | E403BCT | Mainline | ECS887V | Leon |
| D701NWG | Yorkshire Traction | DWW932Y | Keighley & Dist | E404BCT | Mainline | EDS221A | EYMS Group |
| D702NWG | Yorkshire Traction | DWX395T | Pontefract Motors | E405BCT | Mainline | EDT202V | Barnsley & Dist |
| D703NWG | Yorkshire Traction | E21UNE | Yorkshire Traction | E406BCT | Mainline | EDT203V | Barnsley & Dist |
| D704NWG | Yorkshire Traction | E22UNE | Yorkshire Traction | E407BCT | Mainline | EDT205V | Barnsley & Dist |
| D705NKY | Yorkshire Traction | E23UNE | Yorkshire Traction | E408BCT | Mainline | EDT206V | Barnsley & Dist |
| D706NKY | Yorkshire Traction | E24UNE | Yorkshire Traction | E409BCT | Mainline | EDT207V | Yorkshire Traction |
| D707NKY | Yorkshire Traction | E36VKP | Frodingham | E410BCT | Mainline | EDT208V | Barnsley & Dist |
| D708NKY | Yorkshire Traction | E52WAG | EYMS Group | E411BCT | Mainline | EDT209V | Yorkshire Traction |
| D709NKY | Yorkshire Traction | E74JEG | John Smith | E412BCT | Mainline | EDT210V | Andrews |
| D710NKY | Yorkshire Traction | E99OUH | Powell Bus | E412EPE | Andrews | EDT211V | Andrews |
| D711NKY | Yorkshire Traction | E101XVM | EYMS Group | E413BCT | Mainline | EDT212V | Barnsley & Dist |
| D712NKY | Yorkshire Traction | E102XVM | EYMS Group | E414BCT | Mainline | EDT213V | Yorkshire Traction |
| D713NKY | Yorkshire Traction | E109JPL | Powell Bus | E419FNB | Proctors | EDT215V | Yorkshire Traction |
| D714NKY | Yorkshire Traction | E116UTX | Yorkshire Bus | E425XKU | Mainline | EDT216V | Andrews |
| D715NKY | Yorkshire Traction | E129KYW | Aston Express | E462ANC | Proctors | EDT217V | Yorkshire Traction |

| Reg | Operator | Reg | Operator | Reg | Operator | Reg | Operator |
|---|---|---|---|---|---|---|---|
| EDT218V | Yorkshire Traction | F41ENF | Yorkshire Traction | F235HTO | Yorkshire Traction | F323FDT | Yorkshire Traction |
| EDT219V | Yorkshire Traction | F42ENF | Yorkshire Traction | F236HTO | Yorkshire Traction | F324FDT | Yorkshire Traction |
| EDT220V | Yorkshire Traction | F43ENF | Yorkshire Traction | F237EWG | Powell Bus | F325FDT | Yorkshire Traction |
| EDT221V | Yorkshire Traction | F44ENF | Yorkshire Traction | F237HTO | Yorkshire Traction | F326FDT | Yorkshire Traction |
| EDT222V | Yorkshire Traction | F53EAT | EYMS Group | F237RJX | Pride of the Road | F327FDT | Yorkshire Traction |
| EDT223V | Yorkshire Traction | F55EAT | EYMS Group | F238EWG | Mainline | F328FDT | Yorkshire Traction |
| EDT224V | Yorkshire Traction | F64SMC | Pontefract Motors | F239EWG | Yorkshire Travel | F329FDT | Yorkshire Traction |
| EDT225V | Yorkshire Traction | F78CJC | Pontefract Motors | F261RHJ | EYMS Group | F330FDT | Yorkshire Traction |
| EDT226V | Yorkshire Traction | F78TDE | Stotts | F272AWW | Yorkshire Bus | F349JAT | EYMS Group |
| EFN163L | Andrews | F89CWG | Wilfreda-Beehive | F273AWW | Yorkshire Bus | F356BWU | Pontefract Motors |
| EGB85T | K-Line | F101RTR | Leon | F274AWW | Yorkshire Bus | F369BUA | Yorkshire Traction |
| EGR571S | EYMS Group | F103RTR | Leon | F275AWW | Yorkshire Bus | F370MUT | Gordons |
| EGR708S | Stephensons | F108NRT | EYMS Group | F276AWW | Yorkshire Bus | F371CHE | Wilfreda-Beehive |
| EGV367Y | EYMS Group | F113OMJ | Black Prince | F277AWW | Yorkshire Bus | F372CHE | Wilfreda-Beehive |
| EHL335 | Black Prince | F117XTX | Yorkshire Bus | F277MGB | Ingleby's | F402XWR | Harrogate & Dist |
| EIL3018 | Fairway Rhodes | F118XTX | Yorkshire Bus | F278AWW | Yorkshire Bus | F420GAT | EYMS Group |
| EKH985T | EYMS Group | F120YVP | Aston Express | F279AWW | Yorkshire Bus | F421GAT | EYMS Group |
| EKH987T | EYMS Group | F139HNC | Ross Travel | F280AWW | Yorkshire Bus | F422GAT | EYMS Group |
| EKH990T | EYMS Group | F151XYG | Yorkshire Rider | F281AWW | Yorkshire Bus | F423GAT | EYMS Group |
| EMB363S | Northern Bus | F152XYG | Yorkshire Rider | F282AWW | Yorkshire Bus | F424GAT | EYMS Group |
| EMB365S | Northern Bus | F153XYG | Yorkshire Rider | F283AWW | Yorkshire Bus | F425GAT | EYMS Group |
| EPD504V | North Bank Travel | F154XYG | Yorkshire Rider | F284AWW | Yorkshire Bus | F426GAT | EYMS Group |
| EPD542V | Keighley & Dist | F155XYG | Yorkshire Rider | F285AWW | Yorkshire Bus | F427DUG | Thornes |
| EPH227V | Yorkshire Rider | F156GWR | Wray's | F286AWW | Yorkshire Bus | F427GAT | EYMS Group |
| EPT876S | North Bank Travel | F156XYG | Yorkshire Rider | F287AWW | Yorkshire Bus | F428GAT | EYMS Group |
| ERB534T | Cygnet | F157XYG | Yorkshire Rider | F288AWW | Yorkshire Bus | F429GAT | EYMS Group |
| EUY532W | Stephensons | F158XYG | Yorkshire Rider | F289AWW | Yorkshire Bus | F430GAT | EYMS Group |
| EWR165T | Yorkshire Rider | F159XYG | Yorkshire Rider | F290AWW | Yorkshire Bus | F431GAT | EYMS Group |
| EWT386C | Thornes | F160XYG | Yorkshire Rider | F291AWW | Yorkshire Bus | F432VUY | Abbotts |
| EWW538Y | Yorkshire Bus | F161FWY | Ross Travel | F292AWW | Yorkshire Bus | F433GAT | EYMS Group |
| EWW539Y | Yorkshire Bus | F161XYG | Yorkshire Rider | F293AWW | Yorkshire Bus | F434GAT | EYMS Group |
| EWW540Y | Yorkshire Bus | F162XYG | Yorkshire Rider | F294AWW | Yorkshire Bus | F435GAT | EYMS Group |
| EWW541Y | Yorkshire Bus | F163XYG | Yorkshire Rider | F295AWW | Yorkshire Bus | F436GAT | EYMS Group |
| EWW542Y | Yorkshire Bus | F164XYG | Yorkshire Rider | F296AWW | Yorkshire Bus | F437CJK | Aston Express |
| EWW543Y | Yorkshire Bus | F165XYG | Yorkshire Rider | F297AWW | Yorkshire Bus | F437GAT | EYMS Group |
| EWW545Y | Yorkshire Bus | F166XYG | Yorkshire Rider | F298AWW | Yorkshire Bus | F438CJK | Aston Express |
| EWW546Y | Yorkshire Bus | F167XYG | Yorkshire Rider | F299AWW | Yorkshire Bus | F438GAT | EYMS Group |
| EWW547Y | Yorkshire Bus | F168XYG | Yorkshire Rider | F300AWW | Yorkshire Bus | F439GAT | EYMS Group |
| EWW548Y | Yorkshire Bus | F169XYG | Yorkshire Rider | F301AWW | Yorkshire Bus | F440GAT | EYMS Group |
| EWW550Y | Yorkshire Bus | F170XYG | Yorkshire Rider | F302AWW | Yorkshire Bus | F441GAT | EYMS Group |
| EWW551Y | Yorkshire Bus | F171XYG | Yorkshire Rider | F302FWB | Yorkshire Traction | F442GAT | EYMS Group |
| EWW552Y | Yorkshire Bus | F172SMT | Harrogate & Dist | F303AWW | Yorkshire Bus | F443GAT | EYMS Group |
| EWX529Y | Yorkshire Bus | F172XYG | Yorkshire Rider | F303FWB | Yorkshire Traction | F443LGX | Bigfoot |
| EWX530Y | Yorkshire Bus | F173SMT | Harrogate & Dist | F304AWW | Yorkshire Bus | F444GAT | EYMS Group |
| EWX531Y | Yorkshire Bus | F173XYG | Yorkshire Rider | F304FWB | Yorkshire Traction | F445GAT | EYMS Group |
| EWX532Y | Yorkshire Bus | F174XYG | Yorkshire Rider | F305AWW | Yorkshire Bus | F462YOK | Gordons |
| EWX533Y | Yorkshire Bus | F175XYG | Yorkshire Rider | F305FWB | Yorkshire Traction | F467WFX | Thornes |
| EWX534Y | Yorkshire Bus | F220EWG | Powell Bus | F306AWW | Yorkshire Bus | F479FUA | Yorkshire Traction |
| EWX535Y | Yorkshire Bus | F221EWG | Northern Bus | F306FWB | Yorkshire Traction | F479UPB | Jolly Roger |
| EWX536Y | Yorkshire Bus | F222EWG | Mainline | F307AWW | Yorkshire Bus | F496THN | John Smith |
| EWX537Y | Yorkshire Bus | F224EWG | Powell Bus | F308AWW | Yorkshire Bus | F497THN | John Smith |
| EWY77Y | Yorkshire Rider | F226EWG | Mainline | F309AWW | Yorkshire Bus | F501EKY | Yorkshire Traction |
| EWY81Y | Yorkshire Rider | F227EWG | Mainline | F310AWW | Yorkshire Bus | F520BHD | Proctors |
| EYD1T | EYMS Group | F229EWG | Mainline | F311AWW | Yorkshire Bus | F562HPP | Aston Express |
| F26ARN | Abbotts | F229FSU | Yorkshire Rider | F312AWW | Yorkshire Bus | F563HPP | Aston Express |
| F33CWY | Ross Travel | F230EWG | Mainline | F313AWW | Yorkshire Bus | F581XWY | Yorkshire Rider |
| F37CWY | Wilfreda-Beehive | F232EWG | Yorkshire Travel | F314AWW | Yorkshire Bus | F582XWY | Yorkshire Rider |
| F39CWY | Wilfreda-Beehive | F233EWG | Mainline | F321FDT | Yorkshire Traction | F583XWY | Yorkshire Rider |
| F40CWY | Wilfreda-Beehive | F235EWG | Yorkshire Travel | F322FDT | Yorkshire Traction | F584XWY | Yorkshire Rider |

*Opposite, top*: **Selby & District 422, M422UNW is one of eight Volvo B10Ms allocated to that operation, all of which carry Alexander's Strider bodywork. Selby & District are part of the Yorkshire Bus Group which is a subsidiary of Cowie. 1998 sees the first edition of the Cowie Bus Handbook which, like the similar books for fleets on Stagecoach and FirstBus, will appear annually. At their suggestion, alloactions of vehicles to depots will also be included.** *Tony Wilson*

*Opposite, bottom*: **Two open-top Fleetlines are to be found in the Northern Bus fleet and in fine weather can be seen on local bus services. Photographed on service 206 which runs between Sheffield and Dinnington is 0375, 222WFM. Besides having a** *cherished* **mark that was originally on a Crosville bus, the Northern Counties bus also shows it's Crosville connection by carrying Happy Dragon logos and the name Beaumaris Castle.** *Terry Wightman*

| Reg | Operator | Reg | Operator | Reg | Operator | Reg | Operator |
|---|---|---|---|---|---|---|---|
| F585XWY | Yorkshire Rider | FIL7485 | Gordons | G212YDL | Wilfreda-Beehive | G343NWB | Mainline |
| F586XWY | Yorkshire Rider | FIL7486 | Gordons | G251JYG | Yorkshire Rider | G344OWE | Gordons |
| F587XWY | Yorkshire Rider | FIW738 | Stotts | G252JYG | Yorkshire Rider | G357BHN | Proctors |
| F588XWY | Yorkshire Rider | FNA927T | Powell Bus | G253JYG | Yorkshire Rider | G381MWU | Harrogate & Dist |
| F589XWY | Yorkshire Rider | FPR64V | Glenn Coaches | G254JYG | Yorkshire Rider | G382MWU | Harrogate & Dist |
| F590XWY | Yorkshire Rider | FSU359 | Pride of the Road | G255JYG | Yorkshire Rider | G383MWU | Harrogate & Dist |
| F591XWY | Yorkshire Rider | FTF702F | Black Prince | G275MWU | Harrogate & Dist | G427PWW | Yorkshire Rider |
| F592XWY | Yorkshire Rider | FTO535V | Abbotts | G293KWY | Keighley & Dist | G431MWU | Keighley & Dist |
| F593XWY | Yorkshire Rider | FTU389T | Northern Bus | G294KWY | Keighley & Dist | G432MWU | Keighley & Dist |
| F594XWY | Yorkshire Rider | FTU390T | Northern Bus | G295KWY | Keighley & Dist | G433MWU | Keighley & Dist |
| F595XWY | Yorkshire Rider | FUG324T | Keighley & Dist | G296KWY | Harrogate & Dist | G434MWU | Harrogate & Dist |
| F596XWY | Yorkshire Rider | FUG325T | Keighley & Dist | G297KWY | Harrogate & Dist | G435MWU | Keighley & Dist |
| F597XWY | Yorkshire Rider | FUM483Y | Keighley & Dist | G298KWY | Keighley & Dist | G451JYG | Yorkshire Rider |
| F598XWY | Yorkshire Rider | FUM484Y | Keighley & Dist | G299KWY | Keighley & Dist | G452JYG | Yorkshire Rider |
| F599XWY | Yorkshire Rider | FUM485Y | Keighley & Dist | G300KWY | Keighley & Dist | G453JYG | Yorkshire Rider |
| F600XWY | Yorkshire Rider | FUM486Y | Yorkshire Rider | G301NWB | Mainline | G454JYG | Yorkshire Rider |
| F601XWY | Yorkshire Rider | FUM487Y | Yorkshire Rider | G302NWB | Mainline | G455JYG | Yorkshire Rider |
| F602XWY | Yorkshire Rider | FUM488Y | Keighley & Dist | G303NWB | Mainline | G456JYG | Yorkshire Rider |
| F603XWY | Yorkshire Rider | FUM489Y | Yorkshire Rider | G303RJA | Gordons | G457JYG | Yorkshire Rider |
| F604XWY | Yorkshire Rider | FUM490Y | Keighley & Dist | G304NWB | Mainline | G458JYG | Yorkshire Rider |
| F605XWY | Yorkshire Rider | FUM491Y | Yorkshire Rider | G305NWB | Mainline | G459JYG | Yorkshire Rider |
| F615XWY | Yorkshire Rider | FUM492Y | Yorkshire Rider | G306NWB | Mainline | G460JYG | Yorkshire Rider |
| F616XWY | Yorkshire Rider | FUM493Y | Keighley & Dist | G307NWB | Mainline | G473PGE | Leon |
| F619XWY | Yorkshire Rider | FUM494Y | Yorkshire Rider | G308NWB | Mainline | G512NHH | Proctors |
| F621XWY | Yorkshire Rider | FUM495Y | Yorkshire Rider | G309NWB | Mainline | G513EFX | Gordons |
| F622XWY | Yorkshire Rider | FUM496Y | Keighley & Dist | G310NWB | Mainline | G536LWU | EYMS Group |
| F647CDT | Wilfreda-Beehive | FUM497Y | Keighley & Dist | G311NWB | Mainline | G537LWU | EYMS Group |
| F659GNL | York Pullman | FUM498Y | Yorkshire Rider | G312NWB | Mainline | G542GAC | Yorkshire Bus |
| F661GNL | York Pullman | FUM499Y | Yorkshire Rider | G313NWB | Mainline | G566SNN | Mainline |
| F694ACX | Longstaff | FUM500Y | Keighley & Dist | G314NWB | Mainline | G577WUT | Jolly Roger |
| F701CWJ | Yorkshire Traction | FUS23T | Stephensons | G315NWB | Mainline | G580TVR | Eddie Brown |
| F701ENE | Reliance | FVR261V | Abbotts | G316NWB | Mainline | G601NWA | Mainline |
| F702CWJ | Yorkshire Traction | FVR266V | Yorkshire Rider | G317NNW | Yorkshire Bus | G601OWR | Yorkshire Rider |
| F702ENE | Reliance | FVR277V | Abbotts | G317NWB | Mainline | G602NWA | Mainline |
| F702PAY | Frodingham | FWA473V | Yorkshire Rider | G318NWB | Mainline | G602OWR | Yorkshire Rider |
| F702UHD | Proctors | FWA476V | K-Line | G319NNW | Yorkshire Bus | G603NWA | Mainline |
| F703CWJ | Yorkshire Traction | FWA498V | Mainline | G319NWB | Mainline | G603OWR | Yorkshire Rider |
| F704CWJ | Yorkshire Traction | G49CVC | Yorkshire Bus | G320NWB | Mainline | G604NWA | Mainline |
| F705CWJ | Yorkshire Traction | G76RGG | Yorkshire Rider | G321NNW | Yorkshire Bus | G604OWR | Yorkshire Rider |
| F705PAY | Frodingham | G88KUB | Aston Express | G321NWB | Mainline | G605NWA | Mainline |
| F706CWJ | Yorkshire Traction | G92KUB | Aston Express | G322NNW | Yorkshire Bus | G605OWR | Yorkshire Rider |
| F706ENE | Pontefract Motors | G99CUB | Wilfreda-Beehive | G322NWB | Mainline | G606NWA | Mainline |
| F707CWJ | Yorkshire Traction | G107RNC | Stotts | G323NWB | Mainline | G606OWR | Yorkshire Rider |
| F708CWJ | Yorkshire Traction | G108OUG | Yorkshire Bus | G324NNW | Yorkshire Bus | G607NWA | Mainline |
| F709CWJ | Yorkshire Traction | G108RNC | Stotts | G324NUM | Yorkshire Bus | G607OWR | Yorkshire Rider |
| F710CWJ | Yorkshire Traction | G109OUG | Yorkshire Bus | G324NWB | Mainline | G608NWA | Mainline |
| F743LOD | Gordons | G110OUG | Yorkshire Bus | G325NWB | Mainline | G608OWR | Yorkshire Rider |
| F776GNA | EYMS Group | G111VMM | Harrogate & Dist | G326NUM | Yorkshire Bus | G609NWA | Mainline |
| F793DWT | Yorkshire Traction | G112VMM | Harrogate & Dist | G326NWB | Mainline | G609OWR | Yorkshire Rider |
| F817XUG | T J Walsh | G113VMM | Harrogate & Dist | G327NUM | Yorkshire Bus | G610NWA | Mainline |
| F846YJX | Sykes | G114VMM | Harrogate & Dist | G327NWB | Mainline | G610OWR | Yorkshire Rider |
| F873ONR | Jolly Roger | G118SNV | Stotts | G328NWB | Mainline | G611NWA | Mainline |
| F893XOE | Proctors | G123KUB | Yorkshire Traction | G329NUM | Yorkshire Bus | G611OWR | Yorkshire Rider |
| F909YWY | Ross Travel | G140GOL | Jaronda Travel | G329NWB | Mainline | G612NWA | Mainline |
| F911DRN | Bibby's | G148CHP | Yorkshire Bus | G330NUM | Yorkshire Bus | G612OWR | Yorkshire Rider |
| F992BFR | Reliance | G149CHP | Yorkshire Bus | G330NWB | Mainline | G613NWA | Mainline |
| FAZ2781 | EYMS Group | G155NJX | Abbotts | G331NUM | Yorkshire Bus | G613OWR | Yorkshire Rider |
| FAZ4478 | Northern Bus | G176JYG | Yorkshire Rider | G331NWB | Mainline | G614NWA | Mainline |
| FBV492W | Northern Bus | G177JYG | Yorkshire Rider | G332NUM | Yorkshire Bus | G614OWR | Yorkshire Rider |
| FBV500W | Northern Bus | G178JYG | Yorkshire Rider | G332NWB | Mainline | G615NWA | Mainline |
| FBV515W | Northern Bus | G179JYG | Yorkshire Rider | G333NWB | Mainline | G615OWR | Yorkshire Rider |
| FBZ2931 | EYMS Group | G180JYG | Yorkshire Rider | G334NWB | Mainline | G616NWA | Mainline |
| FBZ2932 | EYMS Group | G181JYG | Yorkshire Rider | G335NWB | Mainline | G616OWR | Yorkshire Rider |
| FBZ2933 | EYMS Group | G182JYG | Yorkshire Rider | G336NWB | Mainline | G617NWA | Mainline |
| FDC416V | Northern Bus | G183JYG | Yorkshire Rider | G337NWB | Mainline | G617OWR | Yorkshire Rider |
| FFV807Y | Bibby's | G184JYG | Yorkshire Rider | G338NWB | Mainline | G618NWA | Mainline |
| FHE428 | Yorkshire Traction | G185JYG | Yorkshire Rider | G339NWB | Mainline | G618OWR | Yorkshire Rider |
| FHE810L | York Pullman | G205YDL | Wilfreda-Beehive | G340NWB | Mainline | G619NWA | Mainline |
| FIL4145 | Leon | G207YDL | Wilfreda-Beehive | G341NWB | Mainline | G619OWR | Yorkshire Rider |
| FIL4146 | Leon | G211YDL | Wilfreda-Beehive | G342NWB | Mainline | G620NWA | Mainline |

| | | | | | | | |
|---|---|---|---|---|---|---|---|
| G620OWR | Yorkshire Rider | GHB225W | Yorkshire Terrier | H133AML | Yorkshire Traction | H364TWJ | Yorkshire Traction |
| G621NWA | Mainline | GIJ8319 | Proctors | H154BKH | EYMS Group | H364UWB | Mainline |
| G621OWR | Yorkshire Rider | GMB387T | Northern Bus | H155BKH | EYMS Group | H365TWJ | Yorkshire Traction |
| G622NWA | Mainline | GMB655T | Northern Bus | H156BKH | EYMS Group | H365UWB | Mainline |
| G622OWR | Yorkshire Rider | GMB669T | Northern Bus | H157AKH | EYMS Group | H366TWJ | Yorkshire Traction |
| G623NWA | Mainline | GNG716N | Abbotts | H157BKH | EYMS Group | H366UWB | Mainline |
| G623OWR | Yorkshire Rider | GOG154W | Yorkshire Traction | H157HAC | Gordons | H367TWJ | Yorkshire Traction |
| G624NWA | Mainline | GOG160W | Yorkshire Traction | H158BKH | EYMS Group | H367UWB | Mainline |
| G625NWA | Mainline | GOG560N | Jolly Roger | H159BKH | EYMS Group | H368TWJ | Yorkshire Traction |
| G626NWA | Mainline | GOL405N | Barnsley & Dist | H160BKH | EYMS Group | H368UWB | Mainline |
| G627NWA | Mainline | GOL433N | Andrews | H172EJF | Wray's | H369TWJ | Yorkshire Traction |
| G628NWA | Mainline | GPD295N | Powell Bus | H201FSK | Proctors | H369UWB | Mainline |
| G629NWA | Mainline | GRF694V | EYMS Group | H201TWE | Yorkshire Traction | H370TWJ | Yorkshire Traction |
| G630NWA | Mainline | GRF696V | EYMS Group | H202CRH | York Pullman | H370UWB | Mainline |
| G631NWA | Mainline | GRH2Y | EYMS Group | H202TWE | Yorkshire Traction | H371UWB | Mainline |
| G632NWA | Mainline | GRH3Y | EYMS Group | H210CVU | Clarksons | H372UWB | Mainline |
| G633NWA | Mainline | GRH4Y | EYMS Group | H270THL | Yorkshire Traction | H373UWB | Mainline |
| G634NWA | Mainline | GSD723V | Leon | H271THL | Yorkshire Traction | H374UWB | Mainline |
| G635NWA | Mainline | GSD724V | Leon | H272THL | Yorkshire Traction | H375UWB | Mainline |
| G636NWA | Mainline | GSL906N | Thornes | H273THL | Yorkshire Traction | H376UWB | Mainline |
| G637NWA | Mainline | GSU230 | Proctors | H274THL | Yorkshire Traction | H377UWB | Mainline |
| G638NWA | Mainline | GSU388 | Angl)blue | H313TWE | Yorkshire Traction | H378UWB | Mainline |
| G639NWA | Mainline | GUG128N | Andrews | H315TWE | Yorkshire Traction | H379UWB | Mainline |
| G640NWA | Mainline | GUG533N | Yorkshire Rider | H317TWE | Yorkshire Traction | H380UWB | Mainline |
| G641NWA | Mainline | GUG535N | Yorkshire Rider | H319TWE | Yorkshire Traction | H381UWB | Mainline |
| G649DKC | Pontefract Motors | GUG539N | Fairway Rhodes | H334TYG | Yorkshire Bus | H382UWB | Mainline |
| G681KNW | Barnsley & Dist | GUG542N | Yorkshire Rider | H335TYG | Yorkshire Bus | H383UWB | Mainline |
| G682KNW | Barnsley & Dist | GUG544N | Yorkshire Rider | H336TYG | Yorkshire Bus | H384UWB | Mainline |
| G690ORM | Sykes | GUG551N | Yorkshire Rider | H337TYG | Yorkshire Bus | H385UWB | Mainline |
| G799FJX | York Pullman | GUG554N | Yorkshire Rider | H338TYG | Yorkshire Bus | H386UWB | Mainline |
| G801FJX | York Pullman | GUG557N | Yorkshire Rider | H338UWT | Yorkshire Bus | H387UWB | Mainline |
| G801JYG | Yorkshire Rider | GUG558N | Fairway Rhodes | H339UWT | Yorkshire Bus | H388UWB | Mainline |
| G802JYG | Yorkshire Rider | GUG559N | Yorkshire Rider | H341UWT | Yorkshire Bus | H389UWB | Mainline |
| G803JYG | Yorkshire Rider | GUG560N | Yorkshire Rider | H342UWT | Yorkshire Bus | H390UWB | Mainline |
| G804JYG | Yorkshire Rider | GUG561N | Fairway Rhodes | H343UWT | Yorkshire Bus | H393WWY | Yorkshire Bus |
| G805JYG | Yorkshire Rider | GUG565N | Yorkshire Rider | H343UWX | Yorkshire Bus | H446YKH | EYMS Group |
| G836RDS | Ross Travel | GUG566N | Yorkshire Rider | H344EOD | EYMS Group | H447YKH | EYMS Group |
| G840VAY | Eddie Brown | GUG567N | Yorkshire Rider | H344RKU | Mainline | H449VVN | John Smith |
| G841LWR | Yorkshire Traction | GUP900N | K-Line | H344UWX | Yorkshire Bus | H460WWY | Yorkshire Bus |
| G871WML | Yorkshire Traction | GUP917N | K-Line | H345RKU | Mainline | H511SWE | Wilfreda-Beehive |
| G872WML | Yorkshire Traction | GVN914N | Abbotts | H345UWX | Yorkshire Bus | H512YCX | K-Line |
| G873WML | Yorkshire Traction | GWF571V | Leon | H346JFX | Angl.blue | H514RWX | Harrogate & Dist |
| G874WML | Yorkshire Traction | GWR176T | Yorkshire Rider | H346RKU | Mainline | H515RWX | Harrogate & Dist |
| G875WML | Yorkshire Traction | GWR177T | Yorkshire Rider | H346UWX | Yorkshire Bus | H516RWX | Harrogate & Dist |
| G876WML | Yorkshire Traction | GWR178T | Yorkshire Rider | H347JFX | Angl1blue | H517RWX | Harrogate & Dist |
| G877WML | Yorkshire Traction | GWR180T | Yorkshire Rider | H347RKU | Mainline | H519RWX | Keighley & Dist |
| G878WML | Yorkshire Traction | GWR181T | Yorkshire Rider | H347UWX | Yorkshire Bus | H547VAT | EYMS Group |
| G879WML | Yorkshire Traction | GWR182T | Yorkshire Rider | H348JFX | Anglcblue | H548VAT | EYMS Group |
| G880WML | Yorkshire Traction | GWR183T | Yorkshire Rider | H348RKU | Mainline | H549VAT | EYMS Group |
| G910UPP | Yorkshire Coastliner | GWR185T | Yorkshire Rider | H349RKU | Mainline | H550VAT | EYMS Group |
| G911UPP | Yorkshire Coastliner | GWR186T | Yorkshire Rider | H351UWB | Mainline | H551SWY | Eddie Brown |
| G912UPP | Harrogate & Dist | GWR187T | Yorkshire Rider | H352UWB | Mainline | H551VAT | EYMS Group |
| G913UPP | Harrogate & Dist | GWR188T | Yorkshire Rider | H353UWB | Mainline | H552VAT | EYMS Group |
| G914UPP | Harrogate & Dist | GWR189T | Yorkshire Rider | H354UWB | Mainline | H569SWJ | Mainline |
| G920WGS | Yorkshire Coastliner | GWR190T | Yorkshire Rider | H355UWB | Mainline | H590UUA | Bigfoot |
| G921WGS | Yorkshire Coastliner | GWR191T | Yorkshire Rider | H355WWX | Yorkshire Bus | H611VNW | Yorkshire Rider |
| G922WGS | Harrogate & Dist | GWV935V | EYMS Group | H356UWB | Mainline | H612VNW | Yorkshire Rider |
| G923WGS | Harrogate & Dist | GWY970T | Glenn Coaches | H356WWX | Yorkshire Bus | H613VNW | Yorkshire Rider |
| G997HKW | Abbotts | H12SDW | Harrogate & Dist | H357UWB | Mainline | H614VNW | Yorkshire Rider |
| GAK482N | EYMS Group | H35CNL | York Pullman | H357WWX | Yorkshire Bus | H615VNW | Yorkshire Rider |
| GAT201N | York Pullman | H83PTG | Clarksons | H358UWB | Mainline | H616VNW | Yorkshire Rider |
| GAT203N | York Pullman | H98UWA | Yorkshire Traction | H358WWY | Yorkshire Bus | H617VNW | Yorkshire Rider |
| GAT204N | York Pullman | H106RWT | Yorkshire Bus | H359UWB | Mainline | H618VNW | Yorkshire Rider |
| GDZ885 | Leon | H108RWT | Yorkshire Bus | H359WWY | Yorkshire Bus | H619VNW | Yorkshire Rider |
| GDZ9114 | Bigfoot | H109DVM | Stotts | H361TWJ | Yorkshire Traction | H620UWR | EYMS Group |
| GEF191N | Northern Bus | H114UYG | Yorkshire Rider | H361UWB | Mainline | H620VNW | Yorkshire Rider |
| GEU359N | K-Line | H126YGG | Abbotts | H362TWJ | Yorkshire Traction | H621UWR | EYMS Group |
| GGB640L | Ross Travel | H130AML | Yorkshire Traction | H362UWB | Mainline | H621VNW | Yorkshire Rider |
| GGD671T | EYMS Group | H131AML | Yorkshire Traction | H363TWJ | Yorkshire Traction | H622VNW | Yorkshire Rider |
| GGM74W | Glenn Coaches | H132AML | Yorkshire Traction | H363UWB | Mainline | H623VNW | Yorkshire Rider |

**N200VHO is numbered 136 in the Thornes fleet. Named The Spirit of Drumcondra, this Plaxton-bodied Volvo B10M was new in 1996 and has been followed in 1997 with a further example. It is seen passing through York.** *Tony Wilson*

| | | | | | | | |
|---|---|---|---|---|---|---|---|
| H624VNW | Yorkshire Rider | H646UWR | EYMS Group | H668THL | Mainline | H691THL | Mainline |
| H625VNW | Yorkshire Rider | H647RKU | Mainline | H669THL | Mainline | H701UNW | Yorkshire Bus |
| H627VNW | Yorkshire Rider | H648RKU | Mainline | H670THL | Mainline | H701YUV | Powell Bus |
| H628VNW | Yorkshire Rider | H649RKU | Mainline | H671THL | Mainline | H702UNW | Yorkshire Bus |
| H629VNW | Yorkshire Rider | H650RKU | Mainline | H672THL | Mainline | H703UNW | Yorkshire Bus |
| H630VNW | Yorkshire Rider | H651THL | Mainline | H673THL | Mainline | H703YUV | Frodingham |
| H631VNW | Yorkshire Rider | H652THL | Mainline | H674THL | Mainline | H704UNW | Yorkshire Bus |
| H632VNW | Yorkshire Rider | H653THL | Mainline | H675THL | Mainline | H705UNW | Yorkshire Bus |
| H633VNW | Yorkshire Rider | H654THL | Mainline | H676THL | Mainline | H706UNW | Yorkshire Bus |
| H634VNW | Yorkshire Rider | H655THL | Mainline | H677THL | Mainline | H706YUV | Frodingham |
| H636VNW | Yorkshire Rider | H656THL | Mainline | H678THL | Mainline | H707UNW | Yorkshire Bus |
| H637VNW | Yorkshire Rider | H656UWR | EYMS Group | H679THL | Mainline | H708UNW | Yorkshire Bus |
| H638VNW | Yorkshire Rider | H657THL | Mainline | H680THL | Mainline | H709UNW | Yorkshire Bus |
| H639VNW | Yorkshire Rider | H658THL | Mainline | H681THL | Mainline | H710UNW | Yorkshire Bus |
| H640VNW | Yorkshire Rider | H659THL | Mainline | H682THL | Mainline | H711UNW | Yorkshire Bus |
| H641VNW | Yorkshire Rider | H660AST | Gordons | H683THL | Mainline | H712UNW | Yorkshire Bus |
| H642RKU | Mainline | H660THL | Mainline | H684THL | Mainline | H713UNW | Yorkshire Bus |
| H642VNW | Yorkshire Rider | H661THL | Mainline | H685THL | Mainline | H726VNW | Yorkshire Rider |
| H643RKU | Mainline | H662THL | Mainline | H686THL | Mainline | H741WWU | Yorkshire Rider |
| H643VNW | Yorkshire Rider | H663THL | Mainline | H687THL | Mainline | H755WWW | Yorkshire Bus |
| H644RKU | Mainline | H664THL | Mainline | H688THL | Mainline | H756WWW | Yorkshire Bus |
| H645RKU | Mainline | H665THL | Mainline | H688UAK | Gordons | H757WWW | Yorkshire Bus |
| H646RKU | Mainline | H667THL | Mainline | H689UAK | Gordons | H806TWX | Yorkshire Rider |

*Opposite, top*: Embodied in the main fleet is a mono picture of the Mainline bendibus and here is one in colour. As the popularity of the double-deck reduces and the need to provide easy access for passengers grows the swap to articulated transport is likely to increase. In 1997 Mercedes-Benz will begin importing the O405N bodyshells, the O405GN Gelenken (bendi-bus) version is likely to follow. Incidentally, the interior work for the Mercedes-Benz buses is to be undertaken by UVG.
*Opposite, bottom*: Though reduced in number, the Black Prince fleet contains many interesting vehicles. The large numbers of Ailsa double-decks have been displaced, the main double-deck type now being Scania BR112s from Newport. In 1995 four Optare Vecta saloons were deliverd, each with different applications of the livery. Seen here is 74, M74WYG with its own distictive scheme.
*Tony Wilson*

| Reg | Operator | Reg | Operator | Reg | Operator | Reg | Operator |
|---|---|---|---|---|---|---|---|
| H807TWX | Yorkshire Rider | IIL2160 | EYMS Group | J565HAT | EYMS Group | JHE159W | Mainline |
| H808TWX | Yorkshire Rider | IIL2501 | Andrews | J566HAT | EYMS Group | JHE161W | Mainline |
| H809TWX | Yorkshire Rider | IIL7075 | EYMS Group | J567HAT | EYMS Group | JHE165W | Mainline |
| H810TWX | Yorkshire Rider | IIL7076 | EYMS Group | J568HAT | EYMS Group | JHE166W | Mainline |
| H841AHS | Yorkshire Rider | IIL7077 | EYMS Group | J569HAT | EYMS Group | JHE168W | Mainline |
| H854AHS | Wray's | IIL9170 | EYMS Group | J570HAT | EYMS Group | JHE174W | Mainline |
| H878LOX | Jaronda Travel | J1EXC | Gordons | J631WWK | EYMS Group | JHE176W | Mainline |
| H933DBU | Ross Travel | J43UFL | Ingleby's | J635MCU | Eddie Brown | JHE183W | Mainline |
| HAS716X | Gordons | J53GCX | Bigfoot | J685THN | Abbotts | JHE187W | Mainline |
| HBT378S | Thornes | J54GCX | Bigfoot | J686THN | Abbotts | JHJ145V | Powell Bus |
| HE5362 | Yorkshire Traction | J73VTG | EYMS Group | J689XAK | Mainline | JHP810N | Thornes |
| HE6762 | Yorkshire Traction | J120LKO | Clarksons | J690XAK | Mainline | JIL2215 | Harrogate & Dist |
| HE8054 | Yorkshire Traction | J159HAT | EYMS Group | J691AWF | Mainline | JIL2216 | Harrogate & Dist |
| HE8899 | Yorkshire Traction | J160HAT | EYMS Group | J692AWF | Mainline | JIL2426 | Pennine |
| HFB845X | Proctors | J193BNW | John Smith | J693AWF | Mainline | JIL2427 | Pennine |
| HFM594D | Northern Bus | J204JKH | EYMS Group | J694AWF | Mainline | JIL2428 | Pennine |
| HHA119L | Andrews | J205JKH | EYMS Group | J695AWF | Mainline | JIL2793 | Pennine |
| HHU636N | Pennine | J238VVN | Abbotts | J696AWF | Mainline | JIL2794 | Pennine |
| HIL5669 | Stephensons | J239VVN | Abbotts | J697AWF | Mainline | JIL2795 | Pennine |
| HIL7641 | Ross Travel | J23GCX | K-Line | J698AWF | Mainline | JIL3711 | Wilfreda-Beehive |
| HIL7642 | Ross Travel | J240VVN | Abbotts | J699AWF | Mainline | JIL3715 | Wilfreda-Beehive |
| HIL7643 | Ross Travel | J281CUL | Aston Express | J701AWF | Mainline | JIL3716 | Wilfreda-Beehive |
| HIL7644 | Ross Travel | J320AWB | Yorkshire Traction | J702AWF | Mainline | JIL4381 | John Smith |
| HIL8426 | EYMS Group | J343KTT | EYMS Group | J703AWF | Mainline | JIL4653 | Pennine |
| HIL8427 | EYMS Group | J362YWX | Yorkshire Bus | J704AWF | Mainline | JIL4698 | Pennine |
| HJI3932 | Northern Bus | J363YWX | Yorkshire Bus | J704BRM | Andrews | JIL6502 | Pennine |
| HKU361W | Leon | J364YWX | Yorkshire Bus | J705AWF | Mainline | JIL7416 | Pennine |
| HMA566T | K-Line | J365YWX | Yorkshire Bus | J714CUM | Yorkshire Bus | JIL7417 | Pennine |
| HPF316N | Powell Bus | J366YWX | Yorkshire Bus | J715CUM | Yorkshire Bus | JIL7422 | Pennine |
| HPK507N | Shoreline | J367YWX | Yorkshire Bus | J716CUM | Yorkshire Bus | JIL8353 | Pennine |
| HPY422V | Northern Bus | J368YWX | Yorkshire Bus | J717CUM | Yorkshire Bus | JJG9P | Thornes |
| HPY423V | Northern Bus | J369YWX | Yorkshire Bus | J718CUM | Yorkshire Bus | JJG884P | Andrews |
| HRN107N | Northern Bus | J370YWX | Yorkshire Bus | J719CUM | Yorkshire Bus | JJG889P | North Bank Travel |
| HRN108N | Northern Bus | J371AWT | Yorkshire Bus | J720CUM | Yorkshire Bus | JKH192V | EYMS Group |
| HSC169X | Ross Travel | J371YWX | Yorkshire Bus | J721CUM | Yorkshire Bus | JKH501V | EYMS Group |
| HSC170X | Ross Travel | J372AWT | Yorkshire Bus | J722CUM | Yorkshire Bus | JKH502V | EYMS Group |
| HSC173X | Ross Travel | J373AWT | Yorkshire Bus | J728CWT | Wallace Arnold | JKH503V | EYMS Group |
| HSV389 | Yorkshire Traction | J374AWT | Yorkshire Bus | J730CWT | Wallace Arnold | JKH505V | EYMS Group |
| HUA606Y | Yorkshire Rider | J375AWT | Yorkshire Bus | J733CWT | Wallace Arnold | JKH506V | EYMS Group |
| HUA607Y | Yorkshire Rider | J376AWT | Yorkshire Bus | J763CWT | Wallace Arnold | JKH507V | EYMS Group |
| HUI4483 | Abbotts | J377AWT | Yorkshire Bus | J764CWT | Wallace Arnold | JKH508V | EYMS Group |
| HUI9706 | John Smith | J379BWU | Yorkshire Bus | J765CWT | Wallace Arnold | JKH509V | EYMS Group |
| HUI9710 | John Smith | J380BWU | Yorkshire Bus | J766CWT | Wallace Arnold | JKH510V | EYMS Group |
| HUI9714 | John Smith | J381BWU | Yorkshire Bus | J794AWF | Mainline | JKW215W | Yorkshire Rider |
| HUP764T | EYMS Group | J382BWU | Yorkshire Bus | J798KHD | Pride of the Road | JKW216W | Yorkshire Rider |
| HWJ930W | EYMS Group | J391AWB | Yorkshire Traction | J869JNS | Eddie Brown | JLS456V | Gordons |
| HWJ931W | EYMS Group | J392AWB | Yorkshire Traction | J980AKY | Bigfoot | JNA589N | Pennine |
| HWT28N | Fairway Rhodes | J393AWB | Yorkshire Traction | J992XKU | Bigfoot | JNJ31V | Thompson Travel |
| HWT29N | Yorkshire Rider | J401XHL | Yorkshire Traction | J994GCP | Yorkshire Rider | JNO195N | Yorkshire Terrier |
| HWT30N | Yorkshire Rider | J402XHL | Yorkshire Traction | JBN947N | Barnsley & Dist | JNW73V | Yorkshire Rider |
| HWT31N | Yorkshire Rider | J403XHL | Yorkshire Traction | JBN950N | K-Line | JOX461P | Northern Bus |
| HWT33N | Yorkshire Rider | J404XHL | Yorkshire Traction | JBO82W | Black Prince | JOX510P | K-Line |
| HWT36N | Yorkshire Rider | J405XHL | Yorkshire Traction | JBO83W | Black Prince | JOX513P | K-Line |
| HWT44N | Yorkshire Rider | J406XHL | Yorkshire Traction | JBO84W | Black Prince | JOX514P | K-Line |
| HWT47N | Yorkshire Rider | J411NCP | Clarksons | JBO85W | Black Prince | JSK268 | John Smith |
| HWT50N | Yorkshire Rider | J416CWF | Yorkshire Traction | JBO86W | Black Prince | JSV476 | John Smith |
| HWT54N | Yorkshire Rider | J421NCP | Yorkshire Rider | JBO87W | Black Prince | JSV486 | EYMS Group |
| HWT59N | Yorkshire Rider | J422NCP | Yorkshire Rider | JBO88W | Black Prince | JTU578T | Northern Bus |
| HWT60N | Yorkshire Rider | J423NCP | Yorkshire Rider | JBO89W | Black Prince | JTU598T | Northern Bus |
| IAZ2326 | Abbotts | J424NCP | Yorkshire Rider | JBO90W | Black Prince | JTU599T | Northern Bus |
| IBZ5892 | Pontefract Motors | J425NCP | Yorkshire Rider | JBO91W | Black Prince | JUM78V | Yorkshire Rider |
| IBZ5893 | Pontefract Motors | J426NCP | Yorkshire Rider | JBO92W | Black Prince | JUM79V | Yorkshire Rider |
| IIL1317 | York Pullman | J447HDS | EYMS Group | JBR688T | Andrews | JUM82V | Yorkshire Rider |
| IIL1318 | York Pullman | J448HDS | EYMS Group | JBZ551 | Eddie Brown | JUM86V | Yorkshire Rider |
| IIL1319 | EYMS Group | J550RJA | Bigfoot | JCV385N | Thornes | JUM88V | Yorkshire Rider |
| IIL2155 | EYMS Group | J551BWW | Eddie Brown | JDG283V | Fairway Rhodes | JUM192V | Yorkshire Rider |
| IIL2156 | EYMS Group | J561HAT | EYMS Group | JFM234D | Northern Bus | JUM193V | Yorkshire Rider |
| IIL2157 | EYMS Group | J562HAT | EYMS Group | JHE154W | Mainline | JUM194V | Yorkshire Rider |
| IIL2158 | EYMS Group | J563HAT | EYMS Group | JHE155W | Mainline | JUM195V | Yorkshire Rider |
| IIL2159 | EYMS Group | J564HAT | EYMS Group | JHE158W | Mainline | JUM196V | Yorkshire Rider |

| Reg | Operator | Reg | Operator | Reg | Operator | Reg | Operator |
|---|---|---|---|---|---|---|---|
| JUM197V | Yorkshire Rider | K279EWA | Yorkshire Traction | K620HUG | Yorkshire Rider | KKU120W | Mainline |
| JUM198V | Yorkshire Rider | K390PJU | Gordons | K621HUG | Yorkshire Rider | KKU121W | Mainline |
| JUM199V | Yorkshire Rider | K396NGG | Proctors | K622HUG | Yorkshire Rider | KKU122W | Mainline |
| JUM200V | Yorkshire Rider | K401EDT | Mainline | K623HUG | Yorkshire Rider | KKU123W | Mainline |
| JUM201V | Yorkshire Rider | K401HWW | Yorkshire Bus | K624HUG | Yorkshire Rider | KKU124W | Mainline |
| JUM202V | Yorkshire Rider | K402HWW | Yorkshire Bus | K625HUG | Yorkshire Rider | KKU126W | Mainline |
| JUM203V | Yorkshire Rider | K403HWW | Yorkshire Bus | K626HUG | Yorkshire Rider | KKU127W | Mainline |
| JUM204V | Yorkshire Rider | K404HWW | Yorkshire Bus | K627HUG | Yorkshire Rider | KKU128W | Mainline |
| JUM205V | Yorkshire Rider | K405HWX | Yorkshire Bus | K628HUG | Yorkshire Rider | KMA404T | Bigfoot |
| JUM206V | Yorkshire Rider | K407EWA | Yorkshire Traction | K629HUG | Yorkshire Rider | KOM797P | Powell Bus |
| JUM207V | Yorkshire Rider | K408EWA | Yorkshire Traction | K630HUG | Yorkshire Rider | KON304P | Jolly Roger |
| JUM208V | Yorkshire Rider | K409EWA | Yorkshire Traction | K631HUG | Yorkshire Rider | KON327P | Shoreline |
| JUM209V | Yorkshire Rider | K410EWA | Yorkshire Traction | K632HUG | Yorkshire Rider | KPJ253W | Yorkshire Rider |
| JUM210V | Yorkshire Rider | K411EWA | Yorkshire Traction | K633HUG | Yorkshire Rider | KPJ255W | Yorkshire Rider |
| JUM211V | Yorkshire Rider | K412EWA | Yorkshire Traction | K634HUG | Yorkshire Rider | KPJ257W | Yorkshire Rider |
| JUM212V | Yorkshire Rider | K413EWA | Yorkshire Traction | K706EDT | Mainline | KPJ261W | Yorkshire Rider |
| JUM213V | Yorkshire Rider | K413GAV | Wray's | K707EDT | Mainline | KPJ263W | Yorkshire Rider |
| JUM214V | Yorkshire Rider | K414EWA | Yorkshire Traction | K708EDT | Mainline | KPJ290W | Yorkshire Rider |
| JUM215V | Yorkshire Rider | K415EWA | Yorkshire Traction | K709EDT | Mainline | KPJ291W | Yorkshire Rider |
| JUM221V | Yorkshire Rider | K417HWG | Yorkshire Traction | K710EDT | Mainline | KPJ292W | Yorkshire Rider |
| JYG433V | EYMS Group | K418HWG | Yorkshire Traction | K711EDT | Mainline | KRE276P | Yorkshire Terrier |
| K1YRL | Yorkshire Rider | K419HWG | Yorkshire Traction | K712EDT | Mainline | KRE282P | Yorkshire Terrier |
| K1YTB | Yorkshire Terrier | K420HWG | Yorkshire Traction | K713EDT | Mainline | KSA186P | EYMS Group |
| K2YCL | Keighley & Dist | K421HWG | Yorkshire Traction | K714EDT | Mainline | KSD104W | Proctors |
| K2YTB | Yorkshire Terrier | K448RRH | EYMS Group | K715EDT | Mainline | KSD105W | Proctors |
| K3YCL | Keighley & Dist | K457PNR | EYMS Group | K723HUG | Yorkshire Bus | KSU381 | EYMS Group |
| K3YTB | Yorkshire Terrier | K458PNR | EYMS Group | K724HUG | Yorkshire Bus | KSU454 | EYMS Group |
| K4YCL | Keighley & Dist | K500TMS | Thornes | K725HUG | Yorkshire Bus | KSU455 | EYMS Group |
| K5YCL | Keighley & Dist | K506RJX | Yorkshire Rider | K726HUG | Yorkshire Bus | KSU456 | EYMS Group |
| K6YCL | Keighley & Dist | K507RJX | Yorkshire Rider | K727HUG | Yorkshire Bus | KSU457 | EYMS Group |
| K7YCL | Keighley & Dist | K520RJX | Pride of the Road | K728HUG | Yorkshire Bus | KSU459 | EYMS Group |
| K9YTB | Yorkshire Terrier | K524RJX | Angloblue | K729HUG | Yorkshire Bus | KSU460 | EYMS Group |
| K23GVC | Ross Travel | K526RJX | Angloblue | K801HWW | Yorkshire Bus | KSU465 | EYMS Group |
| K101HUM | Yorkshire Rider | K527RJX | Yorkshire Rider | K802HWW | Yorkshire Bus | KTL27V | Yorkshire Traction |
| K102HUM | Yorkshire Rider | K528RJX | Yorkshire Rider | K803HWW | Yorkshire Bus | KTL28V | EYMS Group |
| K103HUM | Yorkshire Rider | K529RJX | Pride of the Road | K804HWW | Yorkshire Bus | KTL29V | EYMS Group |
| K104HUM | Yorkshire Rider | K531RJX | Angloblue | K805HWX | Yorkshire Bus | KWA22W | Mainline |
| K105HUM | Yorkshire Rider | K538RJX | Pride of the Road | K814HUM | Wray's | KWA31W | Andrews |
| K106HUM | Yorkshire Rider | K572RRH | EYMS Group | K818HUM | Wray's | KWY216V | Yorkshire Rider |
| K107HUM | Yorkshire Rider | K573RRH | EYMS Group | K945JWE | Mainline | KWY217V | Yorkshire Rider |
| K108HUM | Yorkshire Rider | K574RRH | EYMS Group | K946JWE | Mainline | KWY218V | Yorkshire Rider |
| K109HUM | Yorkshire Rider | K575RRH | EYMS Group | K947JWE | Mainline | KWY219V | Yorkshire Rider |
| K110HUM | Yorkshire Rider | K576RRH | EYMS Group | K948JWE | Mainline | KWY220V | Yorkshire Rider |
| K112HUM | Yorkshire Rider | K577RRH | EYMS Group | KAD344V | John Smith | KWY222V | Yorkshire Rider |
| K113HUM | Yorkshire Rider | K578RRH | EYMS Group | KAU327N | Northern Bus | KWY223V | Yorkshire Rider |
| K114HUM | Yorkshire Rider | K579RRH | EYMS Group | KAZ7305 | Eddie Brown | KWY224V | Yorkshire Rider |
| K115HUM | Yorkshire Rider | K580RRH | EYMS Group | KBE108P | Shoreline | KWY225V | Yorkshire Rider |
| K116HUM | Yorkshire Rider | K581RRH | EYMS Group | KDG26 | Keighley & Dist | KWY226V | Yorkshire Rider |
| K117HUM | Yorkshire Rider | K582RRH | EYMS Group | KHN85P | Abbotts | KWY227V | Yorkshire Rider |
| K118HUM | Yorkshire Rider | K583RRH | EYMS Group | KIB7257 | Proctors | KWY228V | Yorkshire Rider |
| K119HUM | Yorkshire Rider | K601HUG | Yorkshire Rider | KJW304W | Andrews | KWY229V | Yorkshire Rider |
| K120HUM | Yorkshire Rider | K601HWR | Jaronda Travel | KJW307W | Andrews | KWY230V | Yorkshire Rider |
| K123TCP | K-Line | K602HUG | Yorkshire Rider | KKU101W | Mainline | KWY231V | Yorkshire Rider |
| K124TCP | K-Line | K603HUG | Yorkshire Rider | KKU102W | Mainline | KWY232V | Yorkshire Rider |
| K136KUM | Godsons | K604HUG | Yorkshire Rider | KKU103W | Mainline | KWY233V | Yorkshire Rider |
| K161TKH | EYMS Group | K605HUG | Yorkshire Rider | KKU104W | Mainline | KWY234V | Yorkshire Rider |
| K167FYG | Black Prince | K606HUG | Yorkshire Rider | KKU105W | Mainline | KWY236V | Yorkshire Rider |
| K168FYG | Black Prince | K607HUG | Yorkshire Rider | KKU106W | Mainline | KWY237V | Yorkshire Rider |
| K211HUM | Yorkshire Rider | K608HUG | Yorkshire Rider | KKU107W | Mainline | KWY238V | Yorkshire Rider |
| K235MAP | Andrews | K609HUG | Yorkshire Rider | KKU108W | Mainline | KWY239V | Yorkshire Rider |
| K236MAP | Andrews | K610HUG | Yorkshire Rider | KKU109W | Mainline | KWY241V | Yorkshire Rider |
| K237MAP | Andrews | K611HUG | Yorkshire Rider | KKU111W | Mainline | KWY242V | Yorkshire Rider |
| K270ERM | Andrews | K612HUG | Yorkshire Rider | KKU112W | Northern Bus | KWY243V | Yorkshire Rider |
| K271ERM | Andrews | K613HUG | Yorkshire Rider | KKU113W | Mainline | KWY244V | Yorkshire Rider |
| K272ERM | Andrews | K614HUG | Yorkshire Rider | KKU114W | Northern Bus | KWY245V | Yorkshire Rider |
| K273ERM | Andrews | K615HUG | Yorkshire Rider | KKU115W | Northern Bus | KWY246V | Yorkshire Rider |
| K275EWA | Yorkshire Traction | K616HUG | Yorkshire Rider | KKU116W | Mainline | KWY247V | Yorkshire Rider |
| K276EWA | Yorkshire Traction | K617HUG | Yorkshire Rider | KKU117W | Mainline | KWY248V | Yorkshire Rider |
| K277EWA | Yorkshire Traction | K618HUG | Yorkshire Rider | KKU118W | Mainline | KWY249V | Yorkshire Rider |
| K278EWA | Yorkshire Traction | K619HUG | Yorkshire Rider | KKU119W | Mainline | KWY250V | Yorkshire Rider |

| Reg | Operator | Reg | Operator | Reg | Operator | Reg | Operator |
|---|---|---|---|---|---|---|---|
| KWY251W | Yorkshire Rider | L516EHD | Yorkshire Rider | L732MWW | Yorkshire Bus | L959NWW | Wallace Arnold |
| L4YTB | Yorkshire Terrier | L517EHD | Yorkshire Rider | L733MWW | Yorkshire Bus | L960NWW | Wallace Arnold |
| L8YCL | Yorkshire Coastliner | L518EHD | Yorkshire Rider | L734MWW | Yorkshire Bus | L961NWW | Wallace Arnold |
| L9YCL | Yorkshire Coastliner | L541XUT | Yorkshire Rider | L735PUA | Yorkshire Bus | L962NWW | Wallace Arnold |
| L22YRL | Yorkshire Rider | L542XUT | Yorkshire Rider | L736PUA | Yorkshire Bus | L963NWW | Wallace Arnold |
| L50MCW | Wray's | L543YUS | EYMS Group | L737PUA | Yorkshire Bus | L970NET | Mainline |
| L51ONW | Yorkshire Traction | L546XUT | Yorkshire Rider | L738PUA | Yorkshire Bus | L971NET | Mainline |
| L52ONW | Yorkshire Traction | L551OUM | Eddie Brown | L739PUA | Yorkshire Bus | L974OWY | Clarksons |
| L53ONW | Yorkshire Traction | L601NOS | Andrews | L740PUA | Yorkshire Bus | L975OWY | Clarksons |
| L62VAG | EYMS Group | L601PWR | Yorkshire Rider | L741PUA | Yorkshire Bus | LAK937W | EYMS Group |
| L64CKH | EYMS Group | L602NOS | Andrews | L771RWW | Yorkshire Bus | LAK938W | EYMS Group |
| L101PWR | Yorkshire Rider | L602PWR | Yorkshire Rider | L772RWW | Yorkshire Bus | LAZ2430 | Abbotts |
| L102PWR | Yorkshire Rider | L603NOS | Andrews | L773RWW | Yorkshire Bus | LAZ2431 | Abbotts |
| L103PWR | Yorkshire Rider | L603PWR | Yorkshire Rider | L774RWW | Yorkshire Bus | LAZ4376 | Abbotts |
| L104PWR | Yorkshire Rider | L604NOS | Andrews | L775RWW | Yorkshire Bus | LAZ4377 | Abbotts |
| L105PWR | Yorkshire Rider | L604PWR | Yorkshire Rider | L776RWW | Yorkshire Bus | LAZ6889 | Abbotts |
| L106PWR | Yorkshire Rider | L605NOS | Andrews | L778RWW | Yorkshire Bus | LBT380N | Thornes |
| L121PWR | Yorkshire Rider | L605PWR | Yorkshire Rider | L779RWW | Yorkshire Bus | LBZ5107 | Abbotts |
| L122PWR | Yorkshire Rider | L636PWR | Yorkshire Rider | L806NNW | Yorkshire Bus | LBZ5108 | Abbotts |
| L123PWR | Yorkshire Rider | L637PWR | Yorkshire Rider | L807NNW | Yorkshire Bus | LBZ6303 | Abbotts |
| L124PWR | Yorkshire Rider | L638PWR | Yorkshire Rider | L808NNW | Yorkshire Bus | LBZ7810 | Abbotts |
| L125PWR | Yorkshire Rider | L639PWR | Yorkshire Rider | L809NNW | Yorkshire Bus | LCW980W | Proctors |
| L126PWR | Yorkshire Rider | L640PWR | Yorkshire Rider | L810NNW | Yorkshire Bus | LDS239A | EYMS Group |
| L127PWR | Yorkshire Rider | L641PWR | Yorkshire Rider | L811NNW | Yorkshire Bus | LDS341A | Black Prince |
| L128PWR | Yorkshire Rider | L642OWY | Keighley & Dist | L812NNW | Yorkshire Bus | LDW362P | Eddie Brown |
| L129OWF | Mainline | L642PWR | Yorkshire Rider | L813NNW | Yorkshire Bus | LEO163 | Leon |
| L129PWR | Yorkshire Rider | L643OWY | Keighley & Dist | L814NNW | Yorkshire Bus | LFS288F | Viking Tours |
| L130OWF | Mainline | L643PWR | Yorkshire Rider | L815NNW | Yorkshire Bus | LGR650P | K-Line |
| L130PWR | Yorkshire Rider | L644OWY | Keighley & Dist | L816NWY | Yorkshire Bus | LHN433W | Abbotts |
| L163AVC | Andrews | L644PWR | Yorkshire Rider | L817NWY | Yorkshire Bus | LIL7960 | John Smith |
| L261AKH | EYMS Group | L645OWY | Harrogate & Dist | L818NWY | Yorkshire Bus | LIL8050 | Thompson Travel |
| L265LHE | Yorkshire Traction | L645PWR | Yorkshire Rider | L819NWY | Yorkshire Bus | LIL9412 | Glenn Coaches |
| L266LHE | Yorkshire Traction | L646OWY | Harrogate & Dist | L820NWY | Yorkshire Bus | LJX102N | Jolly Roger |
| L267LHE | Yorkshire Traction | L646PWR | Yorkshire Rider | L821NWY | Yorkshire Bus | LMA413T | Northern Bus |
| L268LHE | Yorkshire Traction | L647OWY | Harrogate & Dist | L822NWY | Yorkshire Bus | LMA414T | Northern Bus |
| L269LHE | Yorkshire Traction | L647PWR | Yorkshire Rider | L823NWY | Yorkshire Bus | LMO224L | Yorkshire Terrier |
| L301PWR | Yorkshire Rider | L648MYG | Keighley & Dist | L824NWY | Yorkshire Bus | LMS160W | Leon |
| L302PWR | Yorkshire Rider | L648OWY | Harrogate & Dist | L825NWY | Yorkshire Bus | LMS170W | Leon |
| L303PWR | Yorkshire Rider | L648PWR | Yorkshire Rider | L826NYG | Yorkshire Bus | LPB203P | North Bank Travel |
| L304PWR | Yorkshire Rider | L649MYG | Keighley & Dist | L827NYG | Yorkshire Bus | LPB213P | Bigfoot |
| L305PWR | Yorkshire Rider | L649OWY | Harrogate & Dist | L828NYG | Yorkshire Bus | LPT706T | Cygnet |
| L306PWR | Yorkshire Rider | L649PWR | Yorkshire Rider | L829NYG | Yorkshire Bus | LPY457W | Cygnet |
| L307PWR | Yorkshire Rider | L650MYG | Keighley & Dist | L830NYG | Yorkshire Bus | LPY734 | Longstaff |
| L308PWR | Yorkshire Rider | L650OWY | Harrogate & Dist | L860WVC | Yorkshire Terrier | LRA798P | Viking Tours |
| L309PWR | Yorkshire Rider | L650PWR | Yorkshire Rider | L901NWW | Wallace Arnold | LRB211W | K-Line |
| L310PWR | Yorkshire Rider | L651MYG | Keighley & Dist | L902NWW | Wallace Arnold | LUA317V | Yorkshire Rider |
| L311PWR | Yorkshire Rider | L651OWY | Harrogate & Dist | L903NWW | Wallace Arnold | LUA318V | Yorkshire Rider |
| L312PWR | Yorkshire Rider | L651PWR | Yorkshire Rider | L904NWW | Wallace Arnold | LUA319V | Yorkshire Rider |
| L313PWR | Yorkshire Rider | L652MYG | Keighley & Dist | L905NWW | Wallace Arnold | LUA321V | Yorkshire Rider |
| L314PWR | Yorkshire Rider | L652OWY | Harrogate & Dist | L915NWW | Eddie Brown | LUA323V | Yorkshire Terrier |
| L315PWR | Yorkshire Rider | L652PWR | Yorkshire Rider | L925NWW | Wallace Arnold | LUA324V | Aston Express |
| L335PWX | Wilfreda-Beehive | L653MYG | Keighley & Dist | L926NWW | Wallace Arnold | LUA329V | Yorkshire Rider |
| L401PWR | Yorkshire Rider | L653OWY | Harrogate & Dist | L927NWW | Wallace Arnold | LUF549 | Black Prince |
| L402PWR | Yorkshire Rider | L653PWR | Yorkshire Rider | L928NWW | Wallace Arnold | LUG84P | Fairway Rhodes |
| L403PWR | Yorkshire Rider | L654MYG | Keighley & Dist | L929NWW | Wallace Arnold | LUG99P | Fairway Rhodes |
| L404PWR | Yorkshire Rider | L654OWY | Harrogate & Dist | L930NWW | Wallace Arnold | LUG113P | Yorkshire Rider |
| L405PWR | Yorkshire Rider | L654PWR | Yorkshire Rider | L931UGA | Bigfoot | LUG116P | Yorkshire Rider |
| L406NUA | Yorkshire Bus | L655MYG | Keighley & Dist | L942NWW | Wallace Arnold | LUG117P | Yorkshire Rider |
| L407NUA | Yorkshire Bus | L655PWR | Yorkshire Rider | L943NWW | Wallace Arnold | LUG118P | Yorkshire Rider |
| L408NUA | Yorkshire Bus | L656MYG | Keighley & Dist | L944NWW | Wallace Arnold | LVL807V | Yorkshire Traction |
| L409NUA | Yorkshire Bus | L657MYG | Keighley & Dist | L947NWW | Wallace Arnold | LWE227W | Yorkshire Traction |
| L422LET | Yorkshire Traction | L658MYG | Keighley & Dist | L948NWW | Wallace Arnold | LWE228W | Yorkshire Traction |
| L423LET | Yorkshire Traction | L659MYG | Keighley & Dist | L951NWW | Wallace Arnold | LWE229W | Yorkshire Traction |
| L424LET | Yorkshire Traction | L660MYG | Keighley & Dist | L952NWW | Wallace Arnold | LWE230W | Yorkshire Traction |
| L425LET | Yorkshire Traction | L661MYG | Keighley & Dist | L953NWW | Wallace Arnold | LWE231W | Yorkshire Traction |
| L426LET | Yorkshire Traction | L662MYG | Keighley & Dist | L954NWW | Wallace Arnold | LWE232W | Yorkshire Traction |
| L478TDU | Andrews | L663MYG | Keighley & Dist | L955NWW | Wallace Arnold | LWE233W | Yorkshire Traction |
| L511EHD | Bigfoot | L664MYG | Keighley & Dist | L956NWW | Wallace Arnold | LWE234W | Yorkshire Traction |
| L511NYG | Yorkshire Rider | L730MWW | Yorkshire Bus | L957NWW | Wallace Arnold | LWE235W | Yorkshire Traction |
| L512EHD | K-Line | L731MWW | Yorkshire Bus | L958NWW | Wallace Arnold | LWE236W | Yorkshire Traction |

| | | | | | | | |
|---|---|---|---|---|---|---|---|
| LWE237W | Yorkshire Traction | M120UWY | Wallace Arnold | M205VWW | Yorkshire Rider | M226VWW | Yorkshire Rider |
| LWE238W | Yorkshire Traction | M121UET | Yorkshire Terrier | M206EUS | Andrews | M227VWU | Yorkshire Rider |
| LWN709L | K-Line | M121UWY | Wallace Arnold | M206VWU | Yorkshire Rider | M227VWW | Yorkshire Rider |
| M51AWW | Yorkshire Bus | M122UET | Yorkshire Terrier | M206VWW | Yorkshire Rider | M228VWU | Yorkshire Rider |
| M51WWT | Eddie Brown | M122UWY | Wallace Arnold | M207EUS | Andrews | M228VWW | Yorkshire Rider |
| M52AWW | Yorkshire Bus | M123SKY | Longstaff | M207VWW | Yorkshire Rider | M229VWU | Yorkshire Rider |
| M53AWW | Yorkshire Bus | M123UET | Yorkshire Terrier | M208EUS | Andrews | M229VWW | Yorkshire Rider |
| M54AWW | Yorkshire Bus | M123UWY | Wallace Arnold | M208VWU | Yorkshire Rider | M230VHE | Godsons |
| M55AWW | Yorkshire Bus | M124UWY | Wallace Arnold | M208VWW | Yorkshire Rider | M230VWU | Yorkshire Rider |
| M56AWW | Yorkshire Bus | M124VAK | Yorkshire Terrier | M209VWW | Yorkshire Rider | M230VWW | Yorkshire Rider |
| M67LAG | EYMS Group | M125VAK | Yorkshire Terrier | M210VWU | Yorkshire Rider | M231VWU | Yorkshire Rider |
| M68LAG | EYMS Group | M132UWY | Wallace Arnold | M210VWW | Yorkshire Rider | M231VWW | Yorkshire Rider |
| M70JJL | Longstaff | M133UWY | Wallace Arnold | M211VWW | Yorkshire Rider | M232VWU | Yorkshire Rider |
| M71WYG | Black Prince | M134UWY | Wallace Arnold | M212VWW | Yorkshire Rider | M232VWW | Yorkshire Rider |
| M73WYG | Black Prince | M135UWY | Wallace Arnold | M213VWW | Yorkshire Rider | M233VWU | Yorkshire Rider |
| M74WYG | Black Prince | M136UYG | Wallace Arnold | M214VWW | Yorkshire Rider | M233VWW | Yorkshire Rider |
| M75WYG | Black Prince | M183BFE | Proctors | M215VWW | Yorkshire Rider | M234VWW | Yorkshire Rider |
| M104UWY | Wallace Arnold | M200VHO | Thornes | M216VWU | Yorkshire Rider | M235VWU | Yorkshire Rider |
| M105UWY | Wallace Arnold | M201EUS | Andrews | M216VWW | Yorkshire Rider | M235VWW | Yorkshire Rider |
| M107RRJ | Yorkshire Rider | M201VWU | Yorkshire Rider | M217VWU | Yorkshire Rider | M236VWW | Yorkshire Rider |
| M108UWY | Wallace Arnold | M201VWW | Yorkshire Rider | M217VWW | Yorkshire Rider | M237VWW | Yorkshire Rider |
| M109UWY | Wallace Arnold | M202EUS | Andrews | M218VWW | Yorkshire Rider | M238VWW | Yorkshire Rider |
| M110UWY | Wallace Arnold | M202VWU | Yorkshire Rider | M219VWU | Yorkshire Rider | M239VWW | Yorkshire Rider |
| M112UWY | Wallace Arnold | M202VWW | Yorkshire Rider | M219VWW | Yorkshire Rider | M240VWU | Yorkshire Rider |
| M113UWY | Wallace Arnold | M203EUS | Andrews | M220VWU | Yorkshire Rider | M240VWW | Yorkshire Rider |
| M113XWB | Gordons | M203VWU | Yorkshire Rider | M220VWW | Yorkshire Rider | M241VWU | Yorkshire Rider |
| M114UWY | Wallace Arnold | M203VWW | Yorkshire Rider | M221EAF | Yorkshire Rider | M241VWW | Yorkshire Rider |
| M115UWY | Wallace Arnold | M204EUS | Andrews | M221VWU | Yorkshire Rider | M242VWU | Yorkshire Rider |
| M116UWY | Wallace Arnold | M204VWU | Yorkshire Rider | M221VWW | Yorkshire Rider | M242VWW | Yorkshire Rider |
| M117UWY | Wallace Arnold | M204VWW | Yorkshire Rider | M223VWW | Yorkshire Rider | M243VWU | Yorkshire Rider |
| M118UWY | Wallace Arnold | M205EUS | Andrews | M224VWW | Yorkshire Rider | M243VWW | Yorkshire Rider |
| M119UWY | Wallace Arnold | M205VWU | Yorkshire Rider | M225VWW | Yorkshire Rider | M244VWW | Yorkshire Rider |

**Photographed on a bright, sunny day, UNA799S shows off the double-deck livery of John Smith & Sons. This vehicle is the only double-deck in the fleet and is normally to be found working school duties. New to Greater Manchester Transport, UNA799S was latterly with Yorkshire Rider.**
*Donald Akrigg*

| Reg | Operator | Reg | Operator | Reg | Operator | Reg | Operator |
|---|---|---|---|---|---|---|---|
| M245VWW | Yorkshire Rider | M405UUB | Yorkshire Rider | M428VWW | Yorkshire Rider | M743UUA | Yorkshire Bus |
| M246VWW | Yorkshire Rider | M405VWW | Yorkshire Rider | M429UNW | Yorkshire Bus | M744UUA | Yorkshire Bus |
| M247VWW | Yorkshire Rider | M406VWW | Yorkshire Rider | M429VHE | Mainline | M745UUA | Yorkshire Bus |
| M247WWX | Yorkshire Bus | M407VWW | Yorkshire Rider | M429VWW | Yorkshire Rider | M746WWX | Yorkshire Bus |
| M248VWW | Yorkshire Rider | M408VWW | Yorkshire Rider | M430UNW | Yorkshire Bus | M748WWX | Yorkshire Bus |
| M249VWW | Yorkshire Rider | M409VWW | Yorkshire Rider | M430VHE | Mainline | M749WWR | Yorkshire Bus |
| M250VWU | Yorkshire Rider | M410UNW | Yorkshire Bus | M430VWW | Yorkshire Rider | M750WWR | Yorkshire Bus |
| M250VWW | Yorkshire Rider | M410VWW | Yorkshire Rider | M431UNW | Yorkshire Bus | M751WWR | Yorkshire Bus |
| M251VWU | Yorkshire Rider | M411UNW | Yorkshire Bus | M431VHE | Mainline | M752WWR | Yorkshire Bus |
| M251VWW | Yorkshire Rider | M411VHE | Mainline | M431VWW | Yorkshire Rider | M753WWR | Yorkshire Bus |
| M252VWU | Yorkshire Rider | M411VWW | Yorkshire Rider | M432UNW | Yorkshire Bus | M763RCP | Godsons |
| M252VWW | Yorkshire Rider | M412UNW | Yorkshire Bus | M432VHE | Mainline | M764RCP | Godsons |
| M253VWU | Yorkshire Rider | M412VHE | Mainline | M432VWW | Yorkshire Rider | M811RCP | K-Line |
| M253VWW | Yorkshire Rider | M412VWW | Yorkshire Rider | M433UNW | Yorkshire Bus | M812RCP | K-Line |
| M254VWU | Yorkshire Rider | M413UNW | Yorkshire Bus | M433VHE | Mainline | M813RCP | K-Line |
| M254VWW | Yorkshire Rider | M413VHE | Mainline | M433VWW | Yorkshire Rider | M814RCP | K-Line |
| M255VWU | Yorkshire Rider | M413VWW | Yorkshire Rider | M434VHE | Mainline | M815RCP | K-Line |
| M255VWW | Yorkshire Rider | M414UNW | Yorkshire Bus | M434VWW | Yorkshire Rider | M816RCP | K-Line |
| M256VWU | Yorkshire Rider | M414VHE | Mainline | M435VHE | Mainline | M817RCP | K-Line |
| M256VWW | Yorkshire Rider | M414VWW | Yorkshire Rider | M435VWW | Yorkshire Rider | M818RCP | K-Line |
| M257VWU | Yorkshire Rider | M415RRN | EYMS Group | M436VHE | Mainline | M819RCP | K-Line |
| M257VWW | Yorkshire Rider | M415UNW | Yorkshire Bus | M436VWW | Yorkshire Rider | M848RCP | Bigfoot |
| M258VWU | Yorkshire Rider | M415VHE | Mainline | M437VHE | Mainline | M875FVK | Wilfreda-Beehive |
| M258VWW | Yorkshire Rider | M415VWW | Yorkshire Rider | M437VWW | Yorkshire Rider | M876VWX | Harrogate & Dist |
| M259KWK | Keighley & Dist | M416RRN | EYMS Group | M438VHE | Mainline | M918MRW | Mainline |
| M259VWU | Yorkshire Rider | M416UNW | Yorkshire Bus | M438VWW | Yorkshire Rider | M922UYG | Yorkshire Coastliner |
| M259VWW | Yorkshire Rider | M416VHE | Mainline | M439VHE | Mainline | M923UYG | Yorkshire Coastliner |
| M260VWU | Yorkshire Rider | M416VWW | Yorkshire Rider | M439VWW | Yorkshire Rider | M924UYG | Yorkshire Coastliner |
| M260VWW | Yorkshire Rider | M417RRN | EYMS Group | M440VHE | Mainline | M925UYG | Yorkshire Coastliner |
| M261VWU | Yorkshire Rider | M417UNW | Yorkshire Bus | M447VWW | Yorkshire Rider | M926TYG | Leon |
| M261VWW | Yorkshire Rider | M417VHE | Mainline | M448VWW | Yorkshire Rider | M927TYG | Leon |
| M262VWU | Yorkshire Rider | M417VWW | Yorkshire Rider | M449VWW | Yorkshire Rider | M930SWX | Bigfoot |
| M262VWW | Yorkshire Rider | M418RRN | EYMS Group | M450VWW | Yorkshire Rider | M948JJU | Ingleby's |
| M263VWU | Yorkshire Rider | M418UNW | Yorkshire Bus | M551WWT | Eddie Brown | M955HRY | Godsons |
| M263VWW | Yorkshire Rider | M418VHE | Mainline | M580JBC | Wray's | M957VKY | Yorkshire Traction |
| M264VWW | Yorkshire Rider | M418VWW | Yorkshire Rider | M583DSJ | Wray's | M994CYS | Bigfoot |
| M265VWW | Yorkshire Rider | M419RRN | EYMS Group | M600TMS | Thornes | MAB160X | Bigfoot |
| M266VWW | Yorkshire Rider | M419UNW | Yorkshire Bus | M605RCP | Bigfoot | MAX261X | Proctors |
| M267VWW | Yorkshire Rider | M419VHE | Mainline | M615SBA | Yorkshire Rider | MAZ6770 | Abbotts |
| M268VWW | Yorkshire Rider | M419VWW | Yorkshire Rider | M616SBA | Yorkshire Rider | MAZ6771 | Abbotts |
| M290TWB | Yorkshire Traction | M420RRN | EYMS Group | M630NAC | Barnsley & Dist | MBO1F | Thornes |
| M291SBT | Clarksons | M420UNW | Yorkshire Bus | M636RCP | Godsons | MBO22P | Yorkshire Terrier |
| M291TWB | Yorkshire Traction | M420VHE | Mainline | M656VWE | Yorkshire Traction | MBO23P | Yorkshire Terrier |
| M292SBT | Clarksons | M420VWW | Yorkshire Rider | M700TMS | Thornes | MDM281P | Northern Bus |
| M292TWB | Yorkshire Traction | M421RRN | EYMS Group | M716VET | Mainline | MDS687P | Viking Tours |
| M293TWB | Yorkshire Traction | M421UNW | Yorkshire Bus | M717VET | Mainline | MEF821W | EYMS Group |
| M294TWB | Yorkshire Traction | M421VHE | Mainline | M718VET | Mainline | MFN119R | North Bank Travel |
| M295TWB | Yorkshire Traction | M421VWW | Yorkshire Rider | M719VET | Mainline | MFN121R | North Bank Travel |
| M296TWB | Yorkshire Traction | M422UNW | Yorkshire Bus | M720VET | Mainline | MFR306P | Cygnet |
| M297TWB | Yorkshire Traction | M422VHE | Mainline | M721VET | Mainline | MHE50P | Leon |
| M298TWB | Yorkshire Traction | M422VWW | Yorkshire Rider | M722VET | Mainline | MHE213M | Northern Bus |
| M299TWB | Yorkshire Traction | M423UNW | Yorkshire Bus | M723VET | Mainline | MHJ723V | Yorkshire Rider |
| M384VWX | Harrogate & Dist | M423VHE | Mainline | M724VET | Mainline | MHJ726V | Yorkshire Rider |
| M385VWX | Harrogate & Dist | M423VWW | Yorkshire Rider | M725VET | Mainline | MHJ729V | Yorkshire Rider |
| M386VWX | Harrogate & Dist | M424TWF | John Smith | M726VET | Mainline | MHW197Y | Proctors |
| M387VWX | Harrogate & Dist | M424UNW | Yorkshire Bus | M727VET | Mainline | MIB658 | Eddie Brown |
| M388VWX | Harrogate & Dist | M424VHE | Mainline | M728VET | Mainline | MIL1163 | John Smith |
| M389VWX | Harrogate & Dist | M424VWW | Yorkshire Rider | M729VET | Mainline | MIL7798 | Powell Bus |
| M391UWT | Godsons | M425TWF | John Smith | M730VET | Mainline | MIL7901 | Stotts |
| M391VWX | Harrogate & Dist | M425UNW | Yorkshire Bus | M731VET | Mainline | MIL7902 | Stotts |
| M392VWX | Harrogate & Dist | M425VHE | Mainline | M732VET | Mainline | MIW5839 | Wray's |
| M393VWX | Harrogate & Dist | M425VWW | Yorkshire Rider | M733VET | Mainline | MLG960P | Andrews |
| M401UUB | Yorkshire Rider | M426UNW | Yorkshire Bus | M734VET | Mainline | MLJ918P | Yorkshire Terrier |
| M401VWW | Yorkshire Rider | M426VHE | Mainline | M735VET | Mainline | MLJ921P | Yorkshire Terrier |
| M402UUB | Yorkshire Rider | M426VWW | Yorkshire Rider | M736VET | Mainline | MMB968P | K-Line |
| M402VWW | Yorkshire Rider | M427UNW | Yorkshire Bus | M737VET | Mainline | MMB975P | Bigfoot |
| M403UUB | Yorkshire Rider | M427VHE | Mainline | M738VET | Mainline | MMB977P | Northern Bus |
| M403VWW | Yorkshire Rider | M427VWW | Yorkshire Rider | M739VET | Mainline | MNC514W | Abbotts |
| M404UUB | Yorkshire Rider | M428UNW | Yorkshire Bus | M740VET | Mainline | MNU629P | Abbotts |
| M404VWW | Yorkshire Rider | M428VHE | Mainline | M742UUA | Yorkshire Bus | MNW33P | Yorkshire Rider |

| | | | | | | | |
|---|---|---|---|---|---|---|---|
| MNW130V | Yorkshire Rider | N214HWX | Wallace Arnold | N277JUG | Yorkshire Rider | N443BKY | Mainline |
| MNW132V | Yorkshire Rider | N215HWX | Wallace Arnold | N277JUM | Yorkshire Rider | N443ENW | Yorkshire Rider |
| MOD855P | Yorkshire Terrier | N216HWX | Wallace Arnold | N278JUG | Yorkshire Rider | N445BKY | Mainline |
| MOM573P | Shoreline | N217HWX | Wallace Arnold | N278JUM | Yorkshire Rider | N445ENW | Yorkshire Rider |
| MOM577P | Andrews | N218HWX | Wallace Arnold | N279JUG | Yorkshire Rider | N446BKY | Mainline |
| MPG293W | Yorkshire Rider | N219HWX | Wallace Arnold | N279JUM | Yorkshire Rider | N446ENW | Yorkshire Rider |
| MPL133W | Thompson Travel | N220HWX | Wallace Arnold | N280JUG | Yorkshire Rider | N447BKY | Mainline |
| MPL135W | Leon | N221HWX | Wallace Arnold | N281CAK | Yorkshire Traction | N448BKY | Mainline |
| MRB804P | Abbotts | N223HWX | Wallace Arnold | N281JUG | Yorkshire Rider | N449BKY | Mainline |
| MSF125P | Thompson Travel | N224HWX | Wallace Arnold | N281JUM | Yorkshire Rider | N449JUG | Yorkshire Rider |
| MSU174 | Leon | N225HWX | Wallace Arnold | N282CAK | Yorkshire Traction | N450DWJ | Mainline |
| MSU462 | Proctors | N226HWX | Wallace Arnold | N282JUG | Yorkshire Rider | N450JUG | Yorkshire Rider |
| MTD235 | Pennine | N227HWX | Wallace Arnold | N282JUM | Yorkshire Rider | N451DWJ | Mainline |
| MTJ796S | Andrews | N228HWX | Wallace Arnold | N283JUG | Yorkshire Rider | N451HWY | Yorkshire Coastliner |
| MWB849W | Mainline | N229HWX | Wallace Arnold | N283JUM | Yorkshire Rider | N451JUG | Yorkshire Rider |
| MWB851W | Mainline | N230HWX | Wallace Arnold | N284JUG | Yorkshire Rider | N452HWY | Yorkshire Coastliner |
| MWB852W | Mainline | N231HWX | Wallace Arnold | N284JUM | Yorkshire Rider | N452JUG | Yorkshire Rider |
| MWB853W | Mainline | N232HWX | Wallace Arnold | N285JUG | Yorkshire Rider | N453HWY | Yorkshire Coastliner |
| MWB854W | Mainline | N233HWX | Wallace Arnold | N285JUM | Yorkshire Rider | N453JUG | Yorkshire Rider |
| MWB855W | Mainline | N234HWX | Wallace Arnold | N286JUG | Yorkshire Rider | N454HWY | Yorkshire Coastliner |
| MWB856W | Mainline | N235HWX | Wallace Arnold | N286JUM | Yorkshire Rider | N454JUG | Yorkshire Rider |
| MWE239W | Yorkshire Traction | N236HWX | Wallace Arnold | N287JUG | Yorkshire Rider | N455HWY | Yorkshire Coastliner |
| MWE240W | Yorkshire Traction | N237HWX | Wallace Arnold | N287JUM | Yorkshire Rider | N455JUG | Yorkshire Rider |
| MWE241W | Yorkshire Traction | N238HWX | Wallace Arnold | N288JUG | Yorkshire Rider | N456JUG | Yorkshire Rider |
| MWG939X | EYMS Group | N239HWX | Wallace Arnold | N288JUM | Yorkshire Rider | N457JUG | Yorkshire Rider |
| MWG941X | EYMS Group | N240HWX | Wallace Arnold | N289DWY | Black Prince | N458JUG | Yorkshire Rider |
| N37EUG | Godsons | N241HWX | Wallace Arnold | N289JUG | Yorkshire Rider | N459JUG | Yorkshire Rider |
| N47FWU | Bibby's | N241YRJ | Bibby's | N289JUM | Yorkshire Rider | N460JUG | Yorkshire Rider |
| N51FWX | Eddie Brown | N242HWX | Wallace Arnold | N290JUG | Yorkshire Rider | N461JUG | Yorkshire Rider |
| N71EAK | Wilfreda-Beehive | N243HWX | Wallace Arnold | N290JUM | Yorkshire Rider | N462JUG | Yorkshire Rider |
| N73FWU | Godsons | N244HWX | Wallace Arnold | N291JUG | Yorkshire Rider | N463JUG | Yorkshire Rider |
| N105CET | Yorkshire Terrier | N245HWX | Wallace Arnold | N291JUM | Yorkshire Rider | N464JUG | Yorkshire Rider |
| N106CET | Yorkshire Terrier | N246HWX | Wallace Arnold | N292JUG | Yorkshire Rider | N465JUG | Yorkshire Rider |
| N107CET | Yorkshire Terrier | N247CKY | Mainline | N292JUM | Yorkshire Rider | N466JUG | Yorkshire Rider |
| N108CET | Yorkshire Terrier | N247HWX | Wallace Arnold | N293JUG | Yorkshire Rider | N467JUG | Yorkshire Rider |
| N109CET | Yorkshire Terrier | N248HWX | Wallace Arnold | N293JUM | Yorkshire Rider | N468JUG | Yorkshire Rider |
| N110CET | Yorkshire Terrier | N249HWX | Wallace Arnold | N294JUM | Yorkshire Rider | N469JUG | Yorkshire Rider |
| N112DWE | Mainline | N250HWX | Wallace Arnold | N295JUM | Yorkshire Rider | N470JUG | Yorkshire Rider |
| N113DWE | Mainline | N251HWX | Wallace Arnold | N296JUM | Yorkshire Rider | N471JUG | Yorkshire Rider |
| N114DWE | Mainline | N252HWX | Wallace Arnold | N297JUM | Yorkshire Rider | N472JUG | Yorkshire Rider |
| N115DWE | Mainline | N253HWX | Wallace Arnold | N298JUM | Yorkshire Rider | N473JUG | Yorkshire Rider |
| N116DWE | Mainline | N254HWX | Wallace Arnold | N299JUM | Yorkshire Rider | N474JUG | Yorkshire Rider |
| N117DWE | Mainline | N264JUG | Yorkshire Rider | N324HUA | Yorkshire Travel | N475JUG | Yorkshire Rider |
| N118DWE | Mainline | N265JUG | Yorkshire Rider | N325HUA | Yorkshire Travel | N476JUG | Yorkshire Rider |
| N119DWE | Mainline | N265KAG | EYMS Group | N326HUA | Yorkshire Travel | N477JUG | Yorkshire Rider |
| N120DWE | Mainline | N266JUG | Yorkshire Rider | N390EUG | Yorkshire Travel | N478JUG | Yorkshire Rider |
| N121DWE | Mainline | N266KAG | EYMS Group | N391EUG | Yorkshire Travel | N501HWY | Keighley & Dist |
| N122DWE | Mainline | N267JUG | Yorkshire Rider | N411ENW | Yorkshire Rider | N502HWY | Keighley & Dist |
| N128DDT | Godsons | N267KAG | EYMS Group | N412ENW | Yorkshire Rider | N503HWY | Keighley & Dist |
| N144BWG | Mainline | N268JUG | Yorkshire Rider | N413ENW | Yorkshire Rider | N504HWY | Keighley & Dist |
| N170AAG | EYMS Group | N268KAG | EYMS Group | N414ENW | Yorkshire Rider | N505HWY | Keighley & Dist |
| N171AAG | EYMS Group | N269JUG | Yorkshire Rider | N415ENW | Yorkshire Rider | N506HWY | Keighley & Dist |
| N172AAG | EYMS Group | N269JUM | Yorkshire Rider | N416ENW | Yorkshire Rider | N507HWY | Keighley & Dist |
| N173AAG | EYMS Group | N269KKH | EYMS Group | N417ENW | Yorkshire Rider | N508HWY | Keighley & Dist |
| N200VHO | Thornes | N270JUG | Yorkshire Rider | N418ENW | Yorkshire Rider | N509HWY | Keighley & Dist |
| N201CKY | Yorkshire Traction | N270JUM | Yorkshire Rider | N419ENW | Yorkshire Rider | N510HWY | Keighley & Dist |
| N201HWX | Wallace Arnold | N270KKH | EYMS Group | N420MWY | Yorkshire Rider | N528DWY | Leon |
| N202HWX | Wallace Arnold | N271JUG | Yorkshire Rider | N421MWY | Yorkshire Rider | N544ENW | Yorkshire Rider |
| N203HWX | Wallace Arnold | N271JUM | Yorkshire Rider | N422MWY | Yorkshire Rider | N551FWX | Eddie Brown |
| N204HWX | Wallace Arnold | N272JUG | Yorkshire Rider | N423MWY | Yorkshire Rider | N577EUG | Black Prince |
| N205HWX | Wallace Arnold | N272JUM | Yorkshire Rider | N424MWY | Yorkshire Rider | N584BRH | EYMS Group |
| N206HWX | Wallace Arnold | N273JUG | Yorkshire Rider | N425MWY | Yorkshire Rider | N585BRH | EYMS Group |
| N207HWX | Wallace Arnold | N273JUM | Yorkshire Rider | N430CHL | Yorkshire Traction | N586BRH | EYMS Group |
| N208HWX | Wallace Arnold | N274JUG | Yorkshire Rider | N431CHL | Yorkshire Traction | N587BRH | EYMS Group |
| N209HWX | Wallace Arnold | N274JUM | Yorkshire Rider | N432CHL | Yorkshire Traction | N588BRH | EYMS Group |
| N210HWX | Wallace Arnold | N275JUG | Yorkshire Rider | N440VWW | Yorkshire Rider | N589BRH | EYMS Group |
| N211HWX | Wallace Arnold | N275JUM | Yorkshire Rider | N441BKY | Mainline | N590BRH | EYMS Group |
| N212HWX | Wallace Arnold | N276JUG | Yorkshire Rider | N441ENW | Yorkshire Rider | N591BRH | EYMS Group |
| N213HWX | Wallace Arnold | N276JUM | Yorkshire Rider | N442BKY | Mainline | N592BRH | EYMS Group |
| N214ENW | Bigfoot | N277CKY | Mainline | N442ENW | Yorkshire Rider | N593BRH | EYMS Group |

In 1996, Cygnet took delivery of four coaches from the Barton operation of Trent. These entered service with little change to their livery as shown in this picture of PTV585X, now numbered 17. The route of the X5 service is detailed along the vehicle side. *Tony Wilson*

| | | | | | | | |
|---|---|---|---|---|---|---|---|
| N594BRH | EYMS Group | N757LWW | Yorkshire Bus | N787EUB | Yorkshire Travel | NIB4905 | Angloblue |
| N595BRH | EYMS Group | N758CKY | Mainline | N788EUB | Yorkshire Travel | NIB4906 | Angloblue |
| N596BRH | EYMS Group | N759CKY | Mainline | N789EUB | Yorkshire Travel | NIB4908 | Angloblue |
| N597BRH | EYMS Group | N760CKY | Mainline | N796ORY | Godsons | NIL2457 | Barnsley & Dist |
| N598BRH | EYMS Group | N761CKY | Mainline | N929CKW | Barnsley & Dist | NIL2458 | Barnsley & Dist |
| N599BRH | EYMS Group | N761HWW | Wray's | N930CKW | Barnsley & Dist | NIL2997 | Angloblue |
| N601BRH | EYMS Group | N762CKY | Mainline | N931CKW | Barnsley & Dist | NIL5383 | Yorkshire Traction |
| N602BRH | EYMS Group | N763CKY | Mainline | N935EUG | Godsons | NJA568W | Black Prince |
| N603BRH | EYMS Group | N764CKY | Mainline | N937RBC | Wray's | NJI1250 | EYMS Group |
| N621KUA | Yorkshire Bus | N765CKY | Mainline | N972EUG | Godsons | NJI1251 | EYMS Group |
| N622KUA | Yorkshire Bus | N766CKY | Mainline | N973EUG | Godsons | NJI1252 | EYMS Group |
| N623KUA | Yorkshire Bus | N767CKY | Mainline | N987FWT | Godsons | NJI1253 | EYMS Group |
| N741CKY | Mainline | N768CKY | Mainline | N993BWJ | Clarksons | NJI1254 | EYMS Group |
| N742CKY | Mainline | N769CKY | Mainline | NAH137P | Stotts | NJI1255 | EYMS Group |
| N743CKY | Mainline | N770CKY | Mainline | NAK322R | Leon | NJI5510 | Eddie Brown |
| N744CKY | Mainline | N771CKY | Mainline | NAT341M | York Pullman | NKU141X | Mainline |
| N745CKY | Mainline | N772CKY | Mainline | NAT350M | York Pullman | NKU142X | Mainline |
| N746CKY | Mainline | N773CKY | Mainline | NBD101Y | EYMS Group | NKU143X | Mainline |
| N748CKY | Mainline | N774CKY | Mainline | NBZ9148 | Sykes | NKU145X | Mainline |
| N749CKY | Mainline | N775CKY | Mainline | NCW800T | North Bank Travel | NKU146X | Mainline |
| N750CKY | Mainline | N776CKY | Mainline | NDC239W | EYMS Group | NKU147X | Mainline |
| N751CKY | Mainline | N778CKY | Mainline | NDW139X | Gordons | NKU148X | Mainline |
| N752CKY | Mainline | N779CKY | Mainline | NEL123P | Clarksons | NKU149X | Mainline |
| N753CKY | Mainline | N779EUA | Yorkshire Bus | NEV675M | Yorkshire Terrier | NKU150X | Mainline |
| N754CKY | Mainline | N780CKY | Mainline | NFB115R | Pontefract Motors | NKU151X | Mainline |
| N754LWW | Yorkshire Bus | N780EUA | Yorkshire Bus | NFM67 | Northern Bus | NKU152X | Mainline |
| N755CKY | Mainline | N781EUA | Yorkshire Bus | NFM844M | Yorkshire Terrier | NKU154X | Mainline |
| N755LWW | Yorkshire Bus | N782EUA | Yorkshire Bus | NFN78M | Barnsley & Dist | NKU155X | Mainline |
| N756CKY | Mainline | N783EUA | Yorkshire Bus | NHE340 | Yorkshire Traction | NKU156X | Mainline |
| N756LWW | Yorkshire Bus | N784EUA | Yorkshire Bus | NHN260K | Thornes | NKU157X | Mainline |
| N757CKY | Mainline | N786ORY | Godsons | NHR165M | Shoreline | NKU158X | Mainline |

One of the latest arrivals in the Leon Travel fleet is D319NEC, a Leyland Tiger with Plaxton Paramount 3200 bodywork that was previously with Blackburn where it was used in the tours fleet. It is seen shortly after receiving Leon's colours. *David Longbottom*

| | | | | | | | |
|---|---|---|---|---|---|---|---|
| NKU159X | Mainline | NKU194X | Mainline | NKU601X | Yorkshire Traction | OHL249X | Yorkshire Traction |
| NKU160X | Mainline | NKU195X | Mainline | NKU602X | Yorkshire Traction | OHL250X | Yorkshire Traction |
| NKU161X | Mainline | NKU196X | Mainline | NKU603X | Yorkshire Traction | OHL251X | Yorkshire Traction |
| NKU162X | Mainline | NKU197X | Mainline | NOC391R | Leon | OHL252X | Yorkshire Traction |
| NKU163X | Mainline | NKU198X | Mainline | NOC435R | Leon | OHL253X | Yorkshire Traction |
| NKU164X | Mainline | NKU199X | Mainline | NOC465R | Leon | OHL254X | Yorkshire Traction |
| NKU165X | Mainline | NKU200X | Mainline | NOC594R | Andrews | OHL255X | Yorkshire Traction |
| NKU166X | Mainline | NKU201X | Mainline | NOE545R | K-Line | OHL256X | Yorkshire Traction |
| NKU167X | Mainline | NKU202X | Mainline | NOE608R | K-Line | OHL257X | Yorkshire Traction |
| NKU168X | Mainline | NKU203X | Mainline | NOE609R | Bigfoot | OHL258X | Yorkshire Traction |
| NKU169X | Mainline | NKU204X | Mainline | NPD138L | Yorkshire Terrier | OHL893X | Wilfreda-Beehive |
| NKU170X | Mainline | NKU205X | Mainline | NPD168L | Yorkshire Terrier | OIW1317 | EYMS Group |
| NKU171X | Mainline | NKU206X | Mainline | NPK251R | Bigfoot | OIW1318 | EYMS Group |
| NKU172X | Mainline | NKU207X | Mainline | NRD131M | York Pullman | OIW1319 | EYMS Group |
| NKU174X | Mainline | NKU208X | Mainline | NRH801A | EYMS Group | OJD128R | Jolly Roger |
| NKU175X | Mainline | NKU209X | Mainline | NRH802A | EYMS Group | OJD175R | Jolly Roger |
| NKU176X | Mainline | NKU210X | Mainline | NRP582V | Andrews | OJD901P | North Bank Travel |
| NKU177X | Mainline | NKU211X | Mainline | NRP583V | Andrews | OJI7078 | EYMS Group |
| NKU179X | Mainline | NKU212X | Mainline | NRP584V | Andrews | OKJ507M | Yorkshire Terrier |
| NKU180X | Mainline | NKU213X | Mainline | NSU611 | Proctors | OKJ511M | Yorkshire Terrier |
| NKU181X | Mainline | NKU214X | Mainline | NTC610M | K-Line | OKJ514M | North Bank Travel |
| NKU182X | Mainline | NKU215X | Mainline | NUE594V | Stephensons | OKP980 | Thornes |
| NKU183X | Mainline | NKU216X | Mainline | NWG418R | Barnsley & Dist | OKW515R | Andrews |
| NKU184X | Mainline | NKU217X | Mainline | OAO563M | Andrews | OLS806T | K-Line |
| NKU185X | Mainline | NKU218X | Mainline | OAT822V | EYMS Group | ONN290M | Abbotts |
| NKU186X | Mainline | NKU219X | Mainline | OBT693M | EYMS Group | ONN572P | Abbotts |
| NKU187X | Mainline | NKU220X | Mainline | OCY907R | Powell Bus | ONR90R | Abbotts |
| NKU188X | Mainline | NKU242X | Yorkshire Traction | ODJ579W | Eddie Brown | ONV746 | Wilfreda-Beehive |
| NKU189X | Mainline | NKU243X | Yorkshire Traction | ODM413V | Northern Bus | OOX804R | K-Line |
| NKU190X | Mainline | NKU244X | Yorkshire Traction | OFB968R | Jaronda Travel | OOX814R | K-Line |
| NKU191X | Mainline | NKU245X | Yorkshire Traction | OFP88R | Abbotts | OOX815R | K-Line |
| NKU192X | Mainline | NKU246X | Yorkshire Traction | OHE50 | Yorkshire Traction | ORB575P | Abbotts |
| NKU193X | Mainline | NKU247X | Yorkshire Traction | OHL248X | Yorkshire Traction | ORJ356W | Yorkshire Rider |

| Reg | Operator | Reg | Operator | Reg | Operator | Reg | Operator |
|---|---|---|---|---|---|---|---|
| ORJ373W | Yorkshire Rider | P273NRH | EYMS Group | P399MDT | Frodingham | PIA2192 | Pride of the Road |
| ORJ400W | Yorkshire Rider | P274NRH | EYMS Group | P407MDT | Gordons | PIJ5017 | Wilfreda-Beehive |
| OTK802 | EYMS Group | P275NRH | EYMS Group | P408MDT | Gordons | PJI3671 | Bigfoot |
| OWE137X | Mainline | P276NRH | EYMS Group | P409MDT | Gordons | PJI4315 | Wray's |
| OWE138X | Mainline | P277NRH | EYMS Group | P426GLS | Yorkshire Rider | PJI6617 | Stotts |
| OWE139X | Mainline | P285WAT | EYMS Group | P426UUG | Yorkshire Coastliner | PJI8916 | EYMS Group |
| OWE140X | Mainline | P286WAT | EYMS Group | P427GLS | Yorkshire Rider | PJT255R | K-Line |
| OWG604X | Yorkshire Traction | P301VWR | Wallace Arnold | P427UUG | Yorkshire Coastliner | PKM117R | EYMS Group |
| OWG605X | Yorkshire Traction | P302AUM | Yorkshire Rider | P428GLS | Yorkshire Rider | PKU78X | York Pullman |
| OWG606X | Yorkshire Traction | P302VWR | Wallace Arnold | P428UUG | Yorkshire Coastliner | PNW309W | EYMS Group |
| OWG607X | Yorkshire Traction | P303AUM | Yorkshire Rider | P429GLS | Yorkshire Rider | PNW332W | EYMS Group |
| OWG608X | Yorkshire Traction | P303VWR | Wallace Arnold | P429UUG | Yorkshire Coastliner | PNW333W | Glenn Coaches |
| OWJ165X | Northern Bus | P304AUM | Yorkshire Rider | P430GLS | Yorkshire Rider | PNW598W | Yorkshire Rider |
| OWW906P | Abbotts | P304VWR | Wallace Arnold | P431GLS | Yorkshire Rider | PNW601W | Yorkshire Rider |
| OXK373 | EYMS Group | P305AUM | Yorkshire Rider | P452LWE | Mainline | PNW603W | Yorkshire Rider |
| P2BFB | Bigfoot | P305VWR | Wallace Arnold | P453LWE | Mainline | PPH461R | EYMS Group |
| P2BUS | Powell Bus | P306VWR | Wallace Arnold | P454LWE | Mainline | PPH462R | EYMS Group |
| P2JJL | Longstaff | P307VWR | Wallace Arnold | P455LWE | Mainline | PPH464R | EYMS Group |
| P6SYD | Pontefract Motors | P308VWR | Wallace Arnold | P456UUG | Yorkshire Coastliner | PPH467R | EYMS Group |
| P31XUG | Yorkshire Bus | P309VWR | Wallace Arnold | P511UUG | Keighley & Dist | PPH470R | EYMS Group |
| P58KWG | Yorkshire Traction | P310VWR | Wallace Arnold | P512UUG | Keighley & Dist | PRH244G | EYMS Group |
| P59KWG | Yorkshire Traction | P311VWR | Wallace Arnold | P513UUG | Keighley & Dist | PRH246G | EYMS Group |
| P144RWR | Leon | P312VWR | Wallace Arnold | P514UUG | Keighley & Dist | PRJ500R | Leon |
| P157XNW | Wilfreda-Beehive | P313VWR | Wallace Arnold | P515UUG | Keighley & Dist | PTD640S | Yorkshire Rider |
| P160MDT | Yorkshire Traction | P314VWR | Wallace Arnold | P542RGG | Clarksons | PTD642S | Yorkshire Rider |
| P170VUA | Yorkshire Bus | P315VWR | Wallace Arnold | P563XNW | Wilfreda-Beehive | PTD646S | Yorkshire Rider |
| P171VUA | Yorkshire Bus | P316VWR | Wallace Arnold | P564XNW | Wilfreda-Beehive | PTD649S | Yorkshire Rider |
| P172VUA | Yorkshire Bus | P317VWR | Wallace Arnold | P604SAT | EYMS Group | PTD651S | Yorkshire Rider |
| P173VUA | Yorkshire Bus | P318VWR | Wallace Arnold | P605SAT | EYMS Group | PTD658S | Yorkshire Rider |
| P174NAK | Frodingham | P319VWR | Wallace Arnold | P606SAT | EYMS Group | PTF729L | Andrews |
| P174VUA | Yorkshire Bus | P320VWR | Wallace Arnold | P607SAT | EYMS Group | PTG93Y | Black Prince |
| P175VUA | Yorkshire Bus | P321VWR | Wallace Arnold | P608SAT | EYMS Group | PTG94Y | Black Prince |
| P176VUA | Yorkshire Bus | P322VWR | Wallace Arnold | P609SAT | EYMS Group | PTG95Y | Black Prince |
| P177VUA | Yorkshire Bus | P323VWR | Wallace Arnold | P610SAT | EYMS Group | PTG96Y | Black Prince |
| P178VUA | Yorkshire Bus | P324VWR | Wallace Arnold | P611SAT | EYMS Group | PTG97Y | Black Prince |
| P179VUA | Yorkshire Bus | P325VWR | Wallace Arnold | P653VWX | Black Prince | PTG98Y | Black Prince |
| P180VUA | Yorkshire Bus | P326VWR | Wallace Arnold | P654VWX | Black Prince | PTG99Y | Black Prince |
| P181VUA | Yorkshire Bus | P327VWR | Wallace Arnold | P655VWX | Black Prince | PTG100Y | Black Prince |
| P182VUA | Yorkshire Bus | P328VWR | Wallace Arnold | P718WFR | Yorkshire Traction | PTG101Y | Black Prince |
| P183NAK | Godsons | P329VWR | Wallace Arnold | P740UNW | Pontefract Motors | PTT87R | Barnsley & Dist |
| P183VUA | Yorkshire Bus | P330VWR | Wallace Arnold | P794TGK | Pontefract Motors | PTV585X | Cygnet |
| P184NAK | Godsons | P331VWR | Wallace Arnold | P795TGK | Pontefract Motors | PTV591X | Cygnet |
| P184VUA | Yorkshire Bus | P332VWR | Wallace Arnold | P837XAG | EYMS Group | PUA252W | Yorkshire Rider |
| P185NAK | Godsons | P333VWR | Wallace Arnold | P843WUG | Clarksons | PUA253W | Yorkshire Rider |
| P185VUA | Yorkshire Bus | P334VWR | Wallace Arnold | P881PWW | Clarksons | PUA254W | Yorkshire Rider |
| P186VUA | Yorkshire Bus | P335VWR | Wallace Arnold | P885KNF | Bibby's | PUA255W | Yorkshire Rider |
| P187VUA | Yorkshire Bus | P336VWR | Wallace Arnold | P895PWW | K-Line | PUA256W | Yorkshire Rider |
| P188VUA | Yorkshire Bus | P337VWR | Wallace Arnold | P896PWW | Bibby's | PUA257W | Yorkshire Rider |
| P189VUA | Yorkshire Bus | P339VWR | Wallace Arnold | PAG511W | EYMS Group | PUA258W | Yorkshire Rider |
| P190VUA | Yorkshire Bus | P340VWR | Wallace Arnold | PAG512W | EYMS Group | PUA259W | Yorkshire Rider |
| P191VUA | Yorkshire Bus | P341VWR | Wallace Arnold | PAG513W | EYMS Group | PUA260W | Yorkshire Rider |
| P192VUA | Yorkshire Bus | P342VWR | Wallace Arnold | PAG514W | EYMS Group | PUA261W | Yorkshire Rider |
| P193VUA | Yorkshire Bus | P343VWR | Wallace Arnold | PAG515W | EYMS Group | PUA262W | Yorkshire Rider |
| P194VUA | Yorkshire Bus | P344VWR | Wallace Arnold | PAG517W | EYMS Group | PUA263W | Yorkshire Rider |
| P195VUA | Yorkshire Bus | P345VWR | Wallace Arnold | PAG518W | EYMS Group | PUA264W | Yorkshire Rider |
| P196VUA | Yorkshire Bus | P346VWR | Wallace Arnold | PAG519W | EYMS Group | PUA265W | Yorkshire Rider |
| P197VUA | Yorkshire Bus | P347VWR | Wallace Arnold | PAU208R | Jolly Roger | PUA266W | Yorkshire Rider |
| P198VUA | Yorkshire Bus | P348VWR | Wallace Arnold | PBZ3656 | Abbotts | PUA267W | Yorkshire Rider |
| P199VUA | Yorkshire Bus | P349VWR | Wallace Arnold | PBZ3657 | Abbotts | PUA268W | Yorkshire Rider |
| P201RWR | Godsons | P350VWR | Wallace Arnold | PBZ3658 | Abbotts | PUA269W | Yorkshire Rider |
| P202KKY | Yorkshire Traction | P351VWR | Wallace Arnold | PBZ8301 | Abbotts | PUA270W | Yorkshire Rider |
| P202RWR | Godsons | P352VWR | Wallace Arnold | PCK193P | Northern Bus | PUA271W | Yorkshire Rider |
| P203RWR | Godsons | P353VWR | Wallace Arnold | PDN236T | Fairway Rhodes | PUA272W | Yorkshire Rider |
| P212RWR | Jaronda Travel | P354VWR | Wallace Arnold | PEV702R | K-Line | PUA273W | Yorkshire Rider |
| P213RWR | Bibby's | P355VWR | Wallace Arnold | PEX618W | Andrews | PUA274W | Yorkshire Rider |
| P262NRH | EYMS Group | P356VWR | Wallace Arnold | PEX619W | Andrews | PUA275W | Yorkshire Rider |
| P263NRH | EYMS Group | P357VWR | Wallace Arnold | PEX622W | Andrews | PUA276W | Yorkshire Rider |
| P264NRH | EYMS Group | P366UUG | Harrogate & Dist | PFE541V | Yorkshire Traction | PUA277W | Yorkshire Rider |
| P271NRH | EYMS Group | P367UUG | Harrogate & Dist | PHE692 | Yorkshire Traction | PUA278W | Yorkshire Rider |
| P272NRH | EYMS Group | P368UUG | Harrogate & Dist | PHE814M | EYMS Group | PUA279W | Yorkshire Rider |

| | | | | | | | |
|---|---|---|---|---|---|---|---|
| PUA280W | Yorkshire Rider | R763DUB | Yorkshire Bus | SDT232Y | Mainline | SKG926S | Andrews |
| PUA282W | Yorkshire Rider | R764DUB | Yorkshire Bus | SDT233Y | Mainline | SKY32Y | Northern Bus |
| PUA283W | Yorkshire Rider | R765DUB | Yorkshire Bus | SDT234Y | Mainline | SMV24 | Thornes |
| PUA284W | Yorkshire Rider | R766DUB | Yorkshire Bus | SDT235Y | Mainline | SND301X | John Smith |
| PUA285W | Yorkshire Rider | R767DUB | Yorkshire Bus | SDT236Y | Mainline | SND352X | Reliance |
| PUA286W | Yorkshire Rider | R768DUB | Yorkshire Bus | SDT237Y | Mainline | SND415X | Yorkshire Rider |
| PUA287W | Yorkshire Rider | R769DUB | Yorkshire Bus | SDT238Y | Mainline | SPT216V | Northern Bus |
| PUA288W | Yorkshire Rider | R770DUB | Yorkshire Bus | SDT239Y | Mainline | SPT217V | Northern Bus |
| PUA289W | Yorkshire Rider | R785DUB | Yorkshire Bus | SDT240Y | Mainline | STW19W | Yorkshire Rider |
| PUA290W | Yorkshire Rider | R787DUB | Yorkshire Bus | SDT241Y | Mainline | SUA127R | Yorkshire Rider |
| PUA291W | Yorkshire Rider | R788DUB | Yorkshire Bus | SDT242Y | Mainline | SUA128R | Yorkshire Rider |
| PUA292W | Yorkshire Rider | R789DUB | Yorkshire Bus | SDT243Y | Mainline | SUA130R | Yorkshire Rider |
| PUA293W | Yorkshire Rider | R790DUB | Yorkshire Bus | SDT244Y | Mainline | SUA132R | Yorkshire Rider |
| PUA294W | Yorkshire Rider | R791DUB | Yorkshire Bus | SDT245Y | Mainline | SUA133R | Yorkshire Rider |
| PUA295W | Yorkshire Rider | R792DUB | Yorkshire Bus | SDT247Y | Mainline | SUA134R | Yorkshire Rider |
| PUA296W | Yorkshire Rider | R793DUB | Yorkshire Bus | SDT248Y | Mainline | SUA136R | Fairway Rhodes |
| PUA297W | Yorkshire Rider | R794DUB | Yorkshire Bus | SDT249Y | Mainline | SUA140R | Yorkshire Rider |
| PUA298W | Yorkshire Rider | R795DUB | Yorkshire Bus | SDT250Y | Mainline | SUA142R | Yorkshire Rider |
| PUA299W | Yorkshire Rider | R796DUB | Yorkshire Bus | SDT251Y | Mainline | SUA144R | Yorkshire Rider |
| PUA300W | Yorkshire Rider | R797DUB | Yorkshire Bus | SDT252Y | Mainline | SUA146R | Yorkshire Rider |
| PUA301W | Yorkshire Rider | R798DUB | Yorkshire Bus | SDT253Y | Mainline | SUA147R | Yorkshire Rider |
| PUA302W | Yorkshire Rider | R799DUB | Yorkshire Bus | SDT254Y | Mainline | SUA150R | Yorkshire Rider |
| PUA303W | Yorkshire Rider | R901WLG | Ingleby's | SDT255Y | Mainline | SVV585W | Andrews |
| PUA304W | Yorkshire Rider | RAH132M | Sykes | SDT256Y | Mainline | SVV587W | Andrews |
| PUA305W | Yorkshire Rider | RAU810R | EYMS Group | SDT257Y | Mainline | SWB287L | Mainline |
| PUA306W | Yorkshire Rider | RBT505T | John Smith | SDT258Y | Mainline | SWE437S | Barnsley & Dist |
| PUA307W | Yorkshire Rider | RBT506T | John Smith | SDT259Y | Mainline | SWE438S | Barnsley & Dist |
| PUA308W | Yorkshire Rider | RCC512S | Pride of the Road | SDT260Y | Mainline | SWE440S | Andrews |
| PUA309W | Yorkshire Rider | REF141R | Abbotts | SDT261Y | Mainline | SWE444S | Andrews |
| PUA310W | Yorkshire Rider | RGF231P | Sykes | SDT262Y | Mainline | SWE445S | Barnsley & Dist |
| PUA311W | Yorkshire Rider | RHE194 | Yorkshire Traction | SDT263Y | Mainline | SWE446S | Andrews |
| PUA312W | Yorkshire Rider | RHE353 | Yorkshire Traction | SDT264Y | Mainline | SWH127T | Proctors |
| PUA313W | Yorkshire Rider | RIA7809 | Proctors | SDT265Y | Mainline | SWW305R | Yorkshire Rider |
| PUA314W | Yorkshire Rider | RIB1727 | Powell Bus | SDT266Y | Mainline | SWX533W | Yorkshire Rider |
| PUA316W | Yorkshire Rider | RIB5081 | Pennine | SDT267Y | Mainline | SWX535W | Yorkshire Rider |
| PUA317W | Yorkshire Rider | RKA879T | Yorkshire Terrier | SDT268Y | Mainline | SWX536W | Andrews |
| PUA318W | Yorkshire Rider | RKA881T | Yorkshire Terrier | SDT270Y | Mainline | SWX537W | Yorkshire Rider |
| PUA319W | Yorkshire Rider | RKA885T | Yorkshire Terrier | SDT271Y | Mainline | SWX538W | Yorkshire Rider |
| PUA320W | Yorkshire Rider | RKA887T | Northern Bus | SDT272Y | Mainline | SWX539W | Barnsley & Dist |
| PUA321W | Yorkshire Rider | RKO820M | Stephensons | SDT273Y | Mainline | SWX540W | Yorkshire Rider |
| PUA321W | Yorkshire Rider | RMA434V | Northern Bus | SDT274Y | Mainline | SXU708 | Thompson Travel |
| PUA322W | Yorkshire Rider | RNG824W | Fairway Rhodes | SDZ9026 | EYMS Group | TCK200X | Reliance |
| PUA323W | Yorkshire Rider | RNV811M | Viking Tours | SEO209M | Barnsley & Dist | TCK212X | Reliance |
| PUA324W | Yorkshire Rider | ROK473M | K-Line | SFD255W | Gordons | TCY735M | Yorkshire Terrier |
| PUA325W | Yorkshire Rider | ROK475M | K-Line | SFV434P | Fairway Rhodes | TFG154 | Glenn Coaches |
| PUA326W | Yorkshire Rider | RPE556X | Glenn Coaches | SGR117R | Barnsley & Dist | THL290Y | Yorkshire Terrier |
| PUF584R | EYMS Group | RTC822 | Black Prince | SGR793V | EYMS Group | THU354G | Northern Bus |
| PUF591R | EYMS Group | RTH928S | EYMS Group | SHE609Y | Yorkshire Traction | THX166S | Barnsley & Dist |
| PUF592R | EYMS Group | RUA450W | EYMS Group | SHE610Y | Yorkshire Traction | TJI2804 | Pontefract Motors |
| PUF593R | EYMS Group | RWT534R | Yorkshire Rider | SHE611Y | Yorkshire Traction | TJI2805 | Pontefract Motors |
| PUK650R | Bigfoot | RWU54R | Yorkshire Rider | SHE612Y | Yorkshire Traction | TJI3374 | Jolly Roger |
| PUM149W | Yorkshire Rider | SBR525V | K-Line | SHE613Y | Yorkshire Traction | TJI4026 | Frodingham |
| PVB800S | Bigfoot | SDA525S | Jolly Roger | SHE614Y | Yorkshire Traction | TJI5590 | T J Walsh |
| PVO815R | Abbotts | SDA561S | Leon | SHE615Y | Yorkshire Traction | TJI9142 | T J Walsh |
| PVO821R | EYMS Group | SDA697S | Andrews | SHE616Y | Yorkshire Traction | TJI9143 | T J Walsh |
| PWY41W | Yorkshire Rider | SDA733S | Andrews | SHE617Y | Yorkshire Traction | TJI9144 | T J Walsh |
| PWY584W | Barnsley & Dist | SDA749S | Andrews | SHE618Y | Yorkshire Traction | TJI9146 | T J Walsh |
| PWY586W | Yorkshire Terrier | SDA762S | Andrews | SHE619Y | Yorkshire Traction | TJI9147 | T J Walsh |
| PWY588W | Yorkshire Rider | SDA797S | Andrews | SHE620Y | Yorkshire Traction | TJI9148 | T J Walsh |
| PXI7915 | EYMS Group | SDT221Y | Mainline | SHE621Y | Yorkshire Traction | TMU846Y | Fairway Rhodes |
| R26GNW | Reliance | SDT222Y | Mainline | SHE622Y | Yorkshire Traction | TND123X | EYMS Group |
| R278EKH | EYMS Group | SDT223Y | Mainline | SHE623Y | Yorkshire Traction | TOE477N | K-Line |
| R279EKH | EYMS Group | SDT224Y | Mainline | SHE624Y | Yorkshire Traction | TOE478N | K-Line |
| R280EKH | EYMS Group | SDT225Y | Mainline | SHE625Y | Yorkshire Traction | TOE481N | K-Line |
| R281EKH | EYMS Group | SDT226Y | Mainline | SHE626Y | Yorkshire Traction | TOE483N | K-Line |
| R758DUB | Yorkshire Bus | SDT227Y | Mainline | SIB2014 | EYMS Group | TOE501N | K-Line |
| R758DUB | Yorkshire Bus | SDT228Y | Mainline | SKF6T | Glenn Coaches | TOE506N | K-Line |
| R760DUB | Yorkshire Bus | SDT229Y | Mainline | SKF19T | Clarksons | TOE507N | K-Line |
| R761DUB | Yorkshire Bus | SDT230Y | Mainline | SKG913S | Andrews | TOE509N | K-Line |
| R762DUB | Yorkshire Bus | SDT231Y | Mainline | SKG922S | Andrews | TOE517N | K-Line |

When the last edition of this book was published K5YCL was operating in the Yorkshire Coastliner fleet. It has since moved to sister company Keighley & District. Interestingly, the Balzefield group maintain separate numbering series for each of their operations, though this does not deter interchange of vehicles from taking place. Numbered 915 in the Keighley & District fleet, the vehicle is seen in Eastgate, Leeds when heading home to Keighley. *Tony Wilson*

| | | | | | | | |
|---|---|---|---|---|---|---|---|
| TOE520N | K-Line | UHG753R | K-Line | UWJ290Y | Mainline | VLT188 | EYMS Group |
| TOF711S | K-Line | UKH973R | EYMS Group | UWJ291Y | Mainline | VOD602S | Yorkshire Terrier |
| TPC105X | Northern Bus | UKK335X | Northern Bus | UWJ292Y | Mainline | VPT598R | Barnsley & Dist |
| TPD178M | Powell Bus | UKY627Y | Yorkshire Traction | UWJ293Y | Mainline | VPT599R | Barnsley & Dist |
| TPX884 | EYMS Group | UKY628Y | Yorkshire Traction | UWJ294Y | Mainline | VPT948R | Yorkshire Terrier |
| TPY802X | Abbotts | UKY629Y | Yorkshire Traction | UWW18X | Yorkshire Rider | VRC612Y | Cygnet |
| TRN731 | Ingleby's | UKY901Y | Mainline | UWW19X | Yorkshire Rider | VRP528S | Yorkshire Terrier |
| TRN772 | Stephensons | UKY902Y | Mainline | UWW20X | Yorkshire Rider | VRP529S | Yorkshire Terrier |
| TSJ34S | Leon | UKY903Y | Mainline | UWW772R | Glenn Coaches | VRP530S | Yorkshire Terrier |
| TTC535T | Northern Bus | UKY904Y | Mainline | UWY64X | Yorkshire Terrier | VSM783V | Fairway Rhodes |
| TTC538T | North Bank Travel | UNA799S | John Smith | UWY67X | Andrews | VUP731V | Sykes |
| TUG810R | Yorkshire Travel | UNA800S | Yorkshire Rider | UWY68X | Yorkshire Rider | VWU331X | Yorkshire Rider |
| TUG813R | Yorkshire Terrier | UNA834S | Yorkshire Rider | UWY69X | Yorkshire Rider | VWU332X | Yorkshire Rider |
| TUT660S | Abbotts | UNW929R | Powell Bus | UWY71X | Yorkshire Rider | VWU529 | Bibby's |
| TVP839S | K-Line | UOI4323 | Yorkshire Rider | UWY72X | Yorkshire Rider | VWW327X | Yorkshire Rider |
| TVP840S | K-Line | UPB296S | North Bank Travel | UWY74X | Yorkshire Rider | VWW328X | Yorkshire Rider |
| TVP842S | K-Line | UPB306S | Bigfoot | UWY75X | Yorkshire Rider | VWW329X | Yorkshire Rider |
| TVP846S | K-Line | UPB319S | K-Line | UWY81X | K-Line | VWW330X | Yorkshire Rider |
| TVP868S | Andrews | UPB319S | Bigfoot | UWY81X | North Bank Travel | VWW331X | Yorkshire Rider |
| TWE259Y | Yorkshire Traction | UTU982R | Northern Bus | UWY90X | Yorkshire Rider | VWW332X | Yorkshire Rider |
| TWE260Y | Yorkshire Traction | UWA155S | Shoreline | UXI551 | Eddie Brown | VWW333X | Yorkshire Rider |
| TWE261Y | Yorkshire Traction | UWJ275Y | Mainline | VBT379V | Thornes | VWW334X | Yorkshire Rider |
| TWE262Y | Yorkshire Traction | UWJ276Y | Mainline | VDV113S | Northern Bus | VWW335X | Yorkshire Rider |
| TWE263Y | Yorkshire Traction | UWJ277Y | Mainline | VDV136S | EYMS Group | VWW336X | Yorkshire Rider |
| TWE264Y | Yorkshire Traction | UWJ278Y | Mainline | VDV138S | EYMS Group | VWW337X | Yorkshire Rider |
| TWH690T | Yorkshire Rider | UWJ279Y | Mainline | VDV139S | EYMS Group | VWW338X | Yorkshire Rider |
| TWH691T | Yorkshire Rider | UWJ280Y | Mainline | VDV140S | EYMS Group | VWW339X | Yorkshire Rider |
| TWH692T | Yorkshire Rider | UWJ281Y | Mainline | VET721Y | Gordons | VWW340X | Yorkshire Rider |
| TWH693T | Yorkshire Rider | UWJ282Y | Mainline | VFN53 | Thornes | VWW341X | Yorkshire Rider |
| TWH695T | Yorkshire Rider | UWJ283Y | Mainline | VFT189T | EYMS Group | VWW342X | Yorkshire Rider |
| TWH700T | Leon | UWJ284Y | Mainline | VFX987S | Northern Bus | VWW343X | Yorkshire Rider |
| TWY7 | Yorkshire Bus | UWJ285Y | Mainline | VHB677S | Northern Bus | VWW344X | Yorkshire Rider |
| TXY978 | EYMS Group | UWJ286Y | Mainline | VHB678S | Northern Bus | VWW345X | Yorkshire Rider |
| UDT180S | Abbotts | UWJ287Y | Mainline | VHO200 | Thornes | VWW346X | Yorkshire Rider |
| UET677S | Abbotts | UWJ288Y | Mainline | VKE564S | York Pullman | VWW347X | Yorkshire Rider |
| UHG726R | Clarksons | UWJ289Y | Mainline | VKH44 | EYMS Group | VWW348X | Yorkshire Rider |

*The Yorkshire Bus Handbook*

| | | | | | | | |
|---|---|---|---|---|---|---|---|
| VWW349X | Yorkshire Rider | WKH522X | EYMS Group | WUM121S | Yorkshire Rider | YAE515V | Jaronda Travel |
| VWW350X | Yorkshire Rider | WKH523X | EYMS Group | WUM125S | Yorkshire Rider | YBW603R | Northern Bus |
| VWW351X | Yorkshire Rider | WKH524X | EYMS Group | WUM134S | Jolly Roger | YBW604R | Northern Bus |
| VWW352X | Yorkshire Rider | WKH525X | EYMS Group | WUM134S | Jolly Roger | YCD86T | Yorkshire Terrier |
| VWW353X | Yorkshire Rider | WKH526X | EYMS Group | WWW33 | Thornes | YEV305S | Powell Bus |
| VWW354X | Yorkshire Rider | WKH527X | EYMS Group | WWY70X | Northern Bus | YFB970V | Northern Bus |
| VWW355X | Yorkshire Rider | WLT324 | Halifax Joint | WWY127S | Yorkshire Rider | YFC14R | Thompson Travel |
| VWW356X | Yorkshire Rider | WLT694 | EYMS Group | XAG207X | EYMS Group | YFM282L | Northern Bus |
| VWW357X | Yorkshire Rider | WNW151S | Fairway Rhodes | XAG208X | EYMS Group | YFR496R | Proctors |
| VWW358X | Yorkshire Rider | WNW152S | Yorkshire Rider | XAK452T | Northern Bus | YHD599V | Thornes |
| VWW359X | Yorkshire Rider | WNW156S | Yorkshire Rider | XAK458T | Barnsley & Dist | YHE91 | Yorkshire Traction |
| VWW360X | Yorkshire Rider | WNW158S | Yorkshire Rider | XAK903T | EYMS Group | YKO624S | K-Line |
| VWW361X | Yorkshire Rider | WNW159S | Yorkshire Rider | XAK906T | Northern Bus | YKR702 | Glenn Coaches |
| WA3399 | Wallace Arnold | WNW161S | Yorkshire Rider | XAK907T | EYMS Group | YNA297M | EYMS Group |
| WAE189T | Jaronda Travel | WNW162S | Yorkshire Rider | XAK908T | Northern Bus | YNJ434 | Stephensons |
| WAG975S | EYMS Group | WNW163S | Yorkshire Rider | XAK910T | EYMS Group | YOI7898 | EYMS Group |
| WAG980S | EYMS Group | WNW164S | Yorkshire Rider | XAK914T | EYMS Group | YPD103Y | Mainline |
| WBN477T | Northern Bus | WNW167S | Yorkshire Rider | XBF976 | Powell Bus | YPD126Y | Mainline |
| WBN959L | EYMS Group | WNW169S | Yorkshire Rider | XBU5S | Yorkshire Rider | YPL383T | Northern Bus |
| WCK133V | Thompson Travel | WNW171S | Yorkshire Rider | XBU9S | Yorkshire Rider | YRC126M | Northern Bus |
| WCW308R | Cygnet | WNW172S | Yorkshire Rider | XBU13S | Abbotts | YSU912 | Proctors |
| WCW310R | Pontefract Motors | WNW173S | Yorkshire Rider | XBU15S | Yorkshire Rider | YSX928W | Aston Express |
| WDR274V | Pride of the Road | WNW174S | Yorkshire Rider | XBU17S | Yorkshire Rider | YTC49 | Yorkshire Traction |
| WDR675M | Barnsley & Dist | WNW175S | Yorkshire Rider | XEU860T | North Bank Travel | YTC856 | Yorkshire Traction |
| WDX396X | Jaronda Travel | WOC721T | K-Line | XKU903T | Leon | YTC858 | Yorkshire Traction |
| WGY594S | Eddie Brown | WPD30Y | Northern Bus | XMO541H | Northern Bus | YUM517S | Abbotts |
| WHK81W | Leisureways | WRC830S | EYMS Group | XOV757T | K-Line | YUU556 | EYMS Group |
| WIB4393 | Wilfreda-Beehive | WSV410 | Yorkshire Rider | XPC15S | Glenn Coaches | YWG460T | Barnsley & Dist |
| WIB5749 | Wilfreda-Beehive | WTH962T | Viking Tours | XPD234N | Pennine | YWG461T | Barnsley & Dist |
| WIB8371 | Wilfreda-Beehive | WTU487W | EYMS Group | XRF26S | Andrews | YWG462T | Andrews |
| WIJ551 | Eddie Brown | WUH172T | Glenn Coaches | XRR176S | Northern Bus | YWG463T | Andrews |
| WJN558S | York Pullman | WUM92S | Yorkshire Rider | XVO129S | Abbotts | YWG464T | Barnsley & Dist |
| WJV980 | John Smith | WUM97S | Yorkshire Rider | XVV534S | Yorkshire Terrier | YWG467T | Andrews |
| WJY758 | Viking Tours | WUM109S | Yorkshire Rider | XWK618X | Stotts | YWX333X | Yorkshire Rider |
| WKH520X | EYMS Group | WUM120S | Yorkshire Rider | XXI8968 | Bigfoot | | |

**1997 has seen the transfer of seven Volvo B10M buses from the Finglands operation in Manchester. These vehicles carry Alexander PS bodywork and entered the Finglands operation when the original Stagecoach Manchester operation was sold to that company in 1995. Seen in full East Yorkshire livery is 216, M416RRN.** *Lee Whitehead*

ISBN 1 897990 37 5 (Third Edition)

Published by *British Bus Publishing* Ltd, The Vyne, 16 St Margarets Drive, Wellington, Telford, Shropshire, TF1 3PH